Grace, Predestination, and the Permission of Sin

Grace, Predestination, and the Permission of Sin

A THOMISTIC ANALYSIS

Taylor Patrick O'Neill

THE CATHOLIC UNIVERSITY OF AMERICA PRESS
WASHINGTON, D.C.

Design and composition by Kachergis Book Design

Library of Congress Cataloging-in-Publication Data
Names: O'Neill, Taylor Patrick, author.
Title: Grace, predestination, and the permission of sin : a Thomistic analysis /
Taylor Patrick O'Neill.
Description: Washington : The Catholic University of America Press, 2019. |
Includes bibliographical references and index. | Summary: "This book discusses
Thomistic commentary on the topics of physical premotion, grace, and the
permission of sin, especially as these relate to the mysteries of predestination
and reprobation. The author examines the fundamental tenets of the classical
Thomistic account, and on this basis critiques the 20th century revisionist
theories of Domingo Báñez, Reginald Garrigou-Lagrange, Francisco Marín-Sola,
Jacques Maritain, Bernard Lonergan, and Jean-Hervé Nicolas. In conclusion,
the implications of the traditional view are considered in light of the
spiritual life"—Provided by publisher.
Identifiers: LCCN 2019027550 | ISBN 9780813232546 (cloth) |
ISBN 9780813232553 (ebook)
Subjects: LCSH: Thomas, Aquinas, Saint, 1225?–1274. | Thomism. |
Predestination—History of doctrines. | Reprobation—History of doctrines.
Classification: LCC B765.T54 O56 2019 | DDC 234/.9—dc23
LC record available at https://lccn.loc.gov/2019027550

TO ELIZABETH

Doch alles, was uns anrührt, dich und mich,
nimmt uns zusammen wie ein Bogenstrich,
der aus zwei Saiten eine Stimme zieht.
Auf welches Instrument sind wir gespannt?
Und welcher Spieler hat uns in der Hand?
O süßes Lied!

—Rainer Maria Rilke

Contents

Acknowledgments

First and foremost, I would like to thank my wife, Elizabeth, and our children. Without your constant support and patience, this work could never have reached completion. Your perpetual encouragement is the foundation for this and all of my work.

Next, I would like to thank my parents, Patrick and Jill, who have supported and facilitated my education and career in more ways than I can even begin to count. Moreover, I would like to thank you for being my first and primary educators and for introducing me to the Christian life.

I would like to give considerable thanks to Steven Long. This work would not have been possible without your mentorship, knowledge, encouragement, and good cheer. I will be forever grateful and honored to have studied under you, and I will miss late nights on your lanai discussing all manner of Thomistica with wonder and joy. I would also like to thank Roger Nutt and Michael Waldstein for your insights on this document and your incredible impact on my formation as a scholar and a man. A special thanks to Fr. Matthew Lamb† for instruction in *sapientia* and being a theologian faithful to the heart of Jesus Christ and the Church. I would also like to thank Gregory Vall and Michael Dauphinais for your instruction, guidance, and support. To all of the above, I would like to thank you not only for teaching me the content and method of the science of theology but for demonstrating the *habitus* of the theologian and authentically Christian academic.

I would also like to thank those peers whose friendship, knowledge, and love are evidenced throughout this book. Our innumerable discussions significantly impacted and deepened my consideration of these issues. Your fellowship has been a constant source of happiness, fortitude, comfort, and grace for me. In particular, I would like to thank (in no particular order) Joshua Madden, Matthew Kuhner, Brandon Wanless, Ryan Brady, Kevin Clarke, Sean Robertson, and Daniel Lendman. I would like to extend extra thanks to Ryan Brady for his help with some of the Latin translations in this text.

I would like to thank those whose friendship has been a source of companionship and growth throughout my life, especially (also in no particular order) Nicholas Semenas, Jacob Steiner, Adam Horn, Fr. Matthew Dougherty, O. Praem., and Kevin Putzer.

I would like to thank Fr. Thomas Joseph White, OP, for his advice on this manuscript. I would also like to thank John Martino and CUA Press for their assistance and hard work in turning this manuscript into a book.

I would like to give a very special thanks to Charles Renner. Without your direction and teaching I would not have taken up this career or this topic. What is more, I owe to your instrumental action my very faith in Jesus Christ. Like St. John the Baptist, your presence in my life has always pointed toward Christ. You have been a spiritual and intellectual father to me (as well as so many others), and for that I will forever be in your debt.

Finally, I would like to thank the most holy God, Father, Son, and Holy Spirit, as well as the Queen of Heaven and Seat of Wisdom, Mary. *Domine, non sum dignus.*

June 21, 2018

CHAPTER ONE

Introduction

For nearly the last five centuries the Thomistic conversation regarding premotion, the permission of sin, providence, predestination, and reprobation has largely centered around the great debates between the Order of Preachers and the Society of Jesus, arbitrated by the Church's Congregatio de Auxiliis. At the forefront of these often intense debates was an attempted rapprochement between God's causal influence on the created will and the integrity of human freedom. "The Dominicans declared that the Jesuits conceded too much to free will, and so tended toward Pelagianism. In turn, the Jesuits complained that the Dominicans did not sufficiently safeguard human liberty, and seemed in consequence to lean towards Calvinism."[1]

The period of this great debate *de auxiliis* is often said to have begun in 1581, spanning over twenty years before effectively ending in a stalemate in 1607. During its time, the Congregatio held eighty-five conferences, which were presented before Popes Clement VIII, Leo IX, and Paul V, featuring the greatest and most preeminent minds that the sixteenth-century Dominicans and Jesuits had to offer. At the heart of the beginning of the controversy was the censure of the works of Luis de Molina and the condemnations that Molina and Spanish Dominican Domingo Báñez launched against each other. By the closing of the Congregatio in 1607, both sides had been told that they could maintain and defend their respective schemas (after a brief silence for both parties), but steps were

---

1. Antonio Astrain, "Congregatio de Auxiliis," in *The Catholic Encyclopedia*, vol. 4 (New York: Robert Appleton Company, 1908).

taken to greatly limit the vitriolic climate which had erupted between the two sides.[2]

While the debate may have softened somewhat since the Congregatio, it has largely continued, spilling over even into the early twentieth century. Up until recently, much ink had been spilled continuing the debate between the Jesuit *scientia media* and simultaneous concurrence and the Dominican physical premotion and election, which is *ante praevisa merita*. This debate had certainly continued to animate much of the theological writing in the twentieth century regarding premotion, the permission of sin, providence, predestination, and reprobation. However, with the death of many of the great figures of that twentieth-century debate, the disputation between the Dominicans and the Jesuits seems to have slowed considerably.

On the Dominican side, there arose in the mid-century (in some ways taking the place of the previous interreligious debate) an intra-Dominican disputation. With the cooling of the Dominican-Jesuit contest, some of those associated with the Dominican side of things began to turn their gaze inward, attempting to root themselves in St. Thomas and the Dominican commentatorial tradition in order to critique what they saw as unsavory or overly rigid currents that had formed within that tradition. These severe aspects were attributed usually to Domingo Báñez and adherents to so-called Báñezianism.

The architects of what we shall call the Thomistic revisionist account saw Báñezianism as positing a symmetry between the line of good and the line of evil, that is, between how God governs over the salutary acts of men and how he governs over the sinful acts of men. The strong causal role of God in relation to good acts (with which the revisionist account does not necessarily seek to take exception) was said to be mirrored in evil actions as well, rendering God as having an uncomfortable intimacy with the act of sin, bringing out uneasy questions regarding God's inno-

2. Astrain, "Congregatio de Auxiliis": "The pope's decree communicated (5 September 1607) to both Dominicans and Jesuits, allowed each party to defends its own doctrine, enjoined each from censoring or condemning the opposite opinion, and commanded them to await, as loyal sons of the Church, the final decision of the Apostolic See. That decision, however, has not been reached, and both orders, consequently, maintain their respective theories, just as any other theological opinion is held. The long controversy has aroused considerable feeling, and the pope, aiming at the restoration of peace and charity between the religious orders, forbade by a decree of the Inquisition (1 December 1611) the publication of any book concerning efficacious grace until further action by the Holy See. The prohibition remained in force during the greater part of the seventeenth century."

cence in the face of his not giving the grace whereby humans will be upheld from sin.

Although the revisionist account is not represented in any way by a formal association, in the twentieth century there certainly existed an accidental affiliation of likeminded theologians and philosophers, sharing in the common goal of distancing the Dominican Thomist tradition from the strong claims of Báñezianism. Included in this group are some of the most important Catholics minds of the twentieth century, such as Francisco Marín-Sola, OP, Cardinal Charles Journet, Jacques Maritain, Bernard Lonergan, SJ, and Jean-Hervé Nicolas, OP.[3] Their work aimed to reconcile the mystery of sin with God's governance, claiming in various ways that God's governance holds no influence, neither causal nor even as a mere condition *sine qua non*, over man's defecting from goodness and falling into sin. The central focus of this debate, then, is not so much human freedom, as it had been in the Dominican-Jesuit debate, but divine innocence and distance from sin.

Molinism

While the Molinist position is not of immediate interest to this work, which centers instead on the intra-Thomistic debate, it presents the backdrop for this debate nonetheless, constituting an important figure who continually looms in the background. As such, a few very brief words ought to be said regarding the basic and most general tenets of Molinism.

The theories of Luis de Molina, SJ (1535–1600), centered on the positing of the *scientia media*. This middle knowledge of God existed as a kind of halfway point between God's prevolitional or natural knowledge of necessary truths and his postvolitional or free knowledge of contingent truths.[4] The *scientia media* was used to explain how God could know free

---

3. We include Nicolas here with the revisionist account because this is, more or less, where he ended. However, the bulk of his work throughout his life supported the classical approach. Even in his withdrawal from the classical approach, he retained several strong objections to premises found in other theologians in the revisionist camp. For this reason, Nicolas presents an especially interesting study as one who had embraced tenets from both sides over the course of his life.

4. Thomas P. Flint, *Divine Providence: The Molinist Account* (Ithaca, N.Y.: Cornell University Press, 1998), 37–38: "Of course, we ought not to think of God performing his creative act of will in a state of total ignorance. *Fore*knowledge may not guide his action, but clearly his act of will must be based on *some* knowledge already present to him. To guide his act of will, such knowledge would have to be prior to that act—that is, it would need to be *prevolitional*. And the kind of knowledge that most

creaturely actions without their being determined by his foreknowledge. Middle knowledge has as its object contingent truths, but they were held not to be determined by the divine will as are the objects of God's post-volitional knowledge.[5]

Ultimately, this account seeks to explain how God is able to exert control over creaturely actions without those actions being directly determined by God. Such a view was seen to maintain God's governance over creaturely free actions without in any way negating the liberty of the creature. Thomas P. Flint states:

The problems of foreknowledge and sovereignty are solved on this picture due to the fact that God's foreknowledge of contingent events flows from a combination of knowledge beyond his control and decisions under his control. Because he has middle knowledge and makes free choices concerning which creatures will exist in which circumstances, God has both complete foreknowledge concerning how those creatures will act and great control over their actions, in the sense that any act they perform is either intended or permitted by him. Yet because the knowledge which generates this foresight and sovereignty is not itself a product of free divine activity, our actions remains genuinely free, not the robotic effects of divine causal determination.[6]

---

readily pops to mind here is knowledge of *necessary truths*. For it seems eminently reasonable to think of such propositions as beyond God's control. Since such propositions are true independent of any free choice on God's part, and since God is (according to orthodox Christianity) essentially omniscient, it would seem to be part of his very nature to know such truths.... Now, in knowing what is necessary, God also knows what is possible. For if something *is* possible (in the sense of metaphysical possibility at issue here), then the fact that it is possible is itself necessary. So, by his natural knowledge, God knows all possibilities. And from this it follows that natural knowledge provides God with knowledge of which worlds are possible. Hence, God can be thought of as moving from knowledge of which worlds are possible to knowledge of which world is actual, and this movement is mediated by his free creative act of will.... As Molina saw it, then, we can appropriately call God's *postvolitional* knowledge of *contingent* truths his *free knowledge*."

5. Flint, *Divine Providence*, 42: "For Molina, then, true counterfactuals of creaturely freedom, being contingent propositions not under God's control, belong neither to natural nor to free knowledge, but rather to the middle ground between these two, a middle ground which, when added to our previous display, yields the following picture.

Truths known are:

Natural knowledge	Middle Knowledge	Free knowledge
Necessary	Contingent	Contingent
Independent of God's free will	Independent of God's free will	Dependent on God's free will"

See also Alfred J. Freddoso in his introduction to Luis de Molina's *On Divine Foreknowledge: (Part IV of the Concordia)*, trans. Alfred J. Freddoso (Ithaca, N.Y.: Cornell University Press, 1988), especially p. 47, 4.2, "Divine Knowledge: Natural, Middle, and Free."

6. Flint, *Divine Providence*, 44.

To put it in another way, God may not act directly upon the creaturely will to order it to this or that choice, but what he can do, based on his foreknowledge of how an individual would act in some given circumstance, is to order the universe such that the individual in question will indeed choose as God would wish him to choose. But the creaturely choice is free due to the fact that God has no direct control over it. He has simply set up a universe such that the individual in question finds himself within circumstances that God sees will result in the free, independent choice that God intends for him. Flint illustrates this by giving the example of St. Cuthbert buying an iguana. God wishes for Cuthbert to indeed buy an iguana, and he sees (according to his knowledge of how Cuthbert will act in any given circumstance) that if he were to place Cuthbert in circumstance C that he will indeed buy the iguana. God creates a universe where Cuthbert ends up in circumstance or situation C and thus Cuthbert buys the iguana. God's will has been executed, but without tampering in any way with Cuthbert's free will, since it is Cuthbert himself who freely chooses to buy the iguana in circumstance C. This is not something that God has caused in him, but something that is uniquely from Cuthbert himself, not being moved by God in any way to act as such. He is just the sort of fellow that buys iguanas in circumstance C, something that God can foresee but cannot change.[7]

7. Flint, *Divine Providence*, 44: "For example, take Cuthbert's free action of buying the iguana in C. On the Molinist picture, God does have foreknowledge of and control over this action. Prior to creation, God first (by his natural knowledge) knew infinitely many necessary truths concerning Cuthbert —for example, that it is possible that Cuthbert buy an iguana. By middle knowledge, he knew that Cuthbert would indeed freely buy the iguana if placed in situation C. Such knowledge, of course, left God with innumerable options prior to his creative act of will. He could presumably place Cuthbert in C. He could place Cuthbert in other sets of circumstances, some of them leaving him free, others not. In some of these alternative circumstances, God might see, Cuthbert would still freely buy the iguana; in others, he might see, Cuthbert would freely eschew iguanoid purchases. Finally, God might decide not to create Cuthbert at all. Whichever of these many options he might choose with respect to Cuthbert (and other), God would know via middle knowledge exactly how the world would turn out should he adopt that option. So God will exercise immense control over Cuthbert. Whatever Cuthbert does (assuming, of course, that there is a Cuthbert to do anything in the first place) he will do only because God knowingly put him in a situation in which that very action was divinely foreseen. Weighing these many options, let us assume, God performs his creative act of will, an act which includes Cuthbert's being created and put in C. This act on God's part has, as its immediate noetic effect, God's foreknowledge that Cuthbert will buy the iguana; as its remote temporal offspring, God's act results in Cuthbert's being in C, which in turn leads to his freely buying the iguana. Middle knowledge, then, affords God both foreknowledge of and control over Cuthbert's free action. It is important to note that, on this Molinist picture, God's foreknowledge is neither the effect nor the cause of our free actions."

As such, all individual creaturely free actions are entirely divorced from divine causality (though, of course, that creatures are created with a will is an effect of the divine creation). God merely foresees how creatures will will in varying circumstances. His foreknowledge is entirely "causally impotent,"[8] which Molina affirms:

> The knowledge by which God knew *absolutely* that such-and-such things would come to be is not a cause of the things, but rather, once the order of things that we see has been posited by the free determination of the divine will, then (as Origen and the other Fathers observe) the effects will issue forth from their causes—naturally from natural causes, freely and contingently with respect to both parts from free causes—just as if God had no foreknowledge of future events. From this it clearly follows that no prejudice at all is done to freedom of choice or to the contingency of things by God's foreknowledge.[9]

God's foreknowledge may be said to be temporally prior to the free action of the creature's will, but that foreknowledge is based on an ontologically antecedent truth that exists within Cuthbert. God's foreknowledge is based on that antecedent truth, rather than that foreknowledge causing the truth to be subsequently true. As such, Flint states:

> We can indeed say with Molina that "it is not because [God] knows that something is going to be that that thing is going to be. Just the opposite, it is because the thing will come to be from its causes that He knows that it is going to be."[10]

---

8. Flint, *Divine Providence*, 45: "Even so, that foreknowledge should not be seen as in any sense the cause of that which is foreknown. God's foreknowledge and the contingent event foreknown are, in effect, two separate consequences of the creative act of will God selects. Indeed, foreknowledge is virtually epiphenomenal, in the sense that it is the causally impotent byproduct of a causally cornucopian act of divine will. As Molina saw it, recognizing this causal impotence of foreknowledge helps free us from the fear that such knowledge compromises our freedom."

9. Luis de Molina, *On Divine Foreknowledge: (Part IV of the Concordia)*, trans. Alfred J. Freddoso (Ithaca, N.Y.: Cornell University Press, 1988), q. 14, a. 13, disputation 52, section 29 (184): ". . . imo vero cum scientia, qua Deus absolute novit has vel illas res esse futuras, non sit causa rerum, quin Pontius, posito ex libera determinatione voluntatis divinae hoc ordine rerum quem cernimus, perinde a suis causis (ut Origenes et alii Patres adnotarunt) effectus eveniant, a naturalibus quidem naturaliter, a liberis libere et in utramvis partem contingenter, ac si in Deo nulla esset praescientia circa eventus futuros; fit plane ut praescientia Dei, per quam ob infinitam omnique ex parte illimitatam perfectionem et acumen sui intellectus certo penetrat quid causae liberae positae in quocunque ordine rerum sint facturae, cum re ipsa, si velint, possint contrarium efficere, nullum omnino praejudicium libertati arbitrii et contingentiae rerum afferat" (Molina, 327).

10. Molina, *On Divine Foreknowledge*, disp. 52, sect. 19 (179): "Ex his facile intelligi potest, quamvis Deus nullam scientiam sumat a rebus, sed quicquid cognoscit, id in sua essentia et in determinatione liberae suae voluntatis cognoscat et comprehendat; attamen non quia cognoscit aliquid esse futurum,

So God knows that Cuthbert will buy the iguana because Cuthbert will buy the iguana—not in the sense that Cuthbert's future action *causes* God's prior knowledge, but in the sense that God's knowledge, though flowing from that same divine act which gives rise to Cuthbert's buying the iguana, is logically posterior to that Cuthbertian action.[11]

Indeed, without placing Cuthbert in a circumstance in which he foresees that Cuthbert will buy the iguana (let us say, if he places Cuthbert in a circumstance where he foresees that Cuthbert will *not* buy the iguana), it is beyond God's capability to make it such that Cuthbert will buy the iguana. Alfred J. Freddoso says, "For instance, if He knows prevolitionally in [the galaxy represented by] *CS(w)* that Adam will sin if placed in *H*, then He cannot arrange things in such a way that Adam will be in *H* and yet not sin." Furthermore, "Over this fact God has no control."[12]

Divine aid, therefore, is not seen as actualizing or causing free choice in man. It is an aid that man renders efficacious for a salutary act by his own good use. Rather than God causing the good in man (which man accompanies in causing as a secondary or instrumental cause), God and man work together in the partnership of a simultaneous concurrence. Molina states, "The total effect, indeed, comes both from God and from secondary causes; but it comes neither from God nor from secondary causes as total but as partial causes, each at the same time requiring the concurrence and influx of the other cause, just as when two men are pulling a boat."[13] The two, God and man, must work together in order to bring about the good effect. God cannot simply cause man to will the good effect freely, for such a movement would be seen as crushing fragile human liberty. As such, while it is true that God must throw the rope of rescue to the man trapped at the bottom of the well, God cannot exert any causal influence on whether the man will accept the rope and be lifted to safety. The most that can be done by God is to organize the circumstances such that they are the ones that he foresees will result in

---

ideo illud futurum, sed e contrario, quia illud futurum est ex suis causis, ideo cognoscere illud esse futurum" (Molina, 324).

11. Flint, *Divine Providence*, 45.

12. Fredosso, *On Divine Foreknowledge*, 49.

13. Molina, *Concordia*, q. 14, a. 13, disp. 26: "totus quippe effectus et a Deo est, et a causis secundis, ut a tota causa, sed ut a parte causae, quae simul exigit concursum et influxum alterius: non secus ac cum duo trahunt navim." Translation is from Garrigou's *Predestination*.

the trapped man grabbing the rope and holding on. In relation to grace, all that God can do is to set up the circumstances in such a way that man will respond to grace. Grace in and of itself is not efficacious, but must be rendered efficacious via the good participation of the patient. A boat with one rower goes nowhere. God needs man to help row. He needs man to correspond with the grace that he offers to achieve its effect. This is why Molina states, "Given equal help, it can happen that of two persons called, one is converted and the other not."[14]

The Twentieth-Century Intra-Dominican Debate and Beyond

The Thomistic objections to the Molinist thesis are varied. To name some of the most important:

- It posits passivity in pure act, posing significant questions for the divine simplicity.
- God loses omnipotence in not being able to move free creatures freely.
- The divine governance is not complete given God's impotence in regard to free creaturely acts.
- It flirts with Pelagianism insofar as man has some good that does not come from God, and may even have more good than another even though he is given less grace.

Of course, these objections do not constitute the primary object of this work. The Molinist thesis did, however, represent one extreme regarding creaturely freedom and God's governance over human acts.

The other extreme was to be found in the rigid double predestination of Jansen and the Protestant Reformers who posited that God moved man to sin in the very same way (or at least a very similar way) as to how he moved man to good works. This view held that God's governance over both the line of the good and the line of evil was executed in the same manner, giving God the first initiative in both. Calvin explicitly rejected

---

14. Taken from the index of the *Concordia* (Paris) on p. 630, under the heading of "Liberum arbitrium, et libertas," which states, "Libertas arbitrii sufficit, ut e duobus vocatis interius aequali auxilio, unus convertatur, alius non item." This index reference points to p. 51, where Molina's position is further fleshed out.

any distinction between God's *cause* of good acts and *permission* of sinful ones. Indeed, Calvin stated:

It seems absurd that man should be blinded by the will and command of God, and yet be forthwith punished for his blindness. Hence, recourse is had to the evasion that this is done only by the permission, and not also by the will of God. He himself, however, openly declaring that he does this, repudiates the evasion.... Therefore, whatever men or Satan himself devise, God holds the helm, and makes all their efforts contribute to the execution of his Judgments. God wills that the perfidious Ahab should be deceived; the devil offers his agency for that purpose, and is sent with a definite command to be a lying spirit in the mouth of all the prophets (2 Kings 22:20). If the blinding and infatuation of Ahab is a Judgment from God, the fiction of bare permission is at an end; for it would be ridiculous for a judge only to permit, and not also to decree, what he wishes to be done at the very time that he commits the execution of it to his ministers.... Even these expressions many would confine to permissions as if, by deserting the reprobate, he allowed them to be blinded by Satan. But since the Holy Spirit distinctly says, that the blindness and infatuation are inflicted by the just Judgment of God, the solution is altogether inadmissible.... The sum of the whole is this, since the will of God is said to be the cause of all things, all the counsels and actions of men must be held to be governed by his providence; so that he not only exerts his power in the elect, who are guided by the Holy Spirit, but also forces the reprobate to do him service.[15]

Calvin continues: "We say, therefore, as the Scriptures evidently show, that God has decreed at the same time by His eternal and immutable plan those whom He willed to take to eternal salvation and those whom He willed to sacrifice to perdition."[16]

The Jansenists and Reformers stated that God could in no way be said to will the salvation of all men, and thus the performance of the good acts to which we are all called is not always possible, with the principal salutary action of final perseverance in faith and charity being impossible for the reprobate.[17] Unlike Molinism, which essentially posits that all graces

15. John Calvin, *Institution de la religion chrétienne*, trans. Henry Beveridge, bk. I, chap. 18, § 1–2. See also *Institution de la religion chrétienne*, bk. II, chap. 4.

16. Calvin, *Institution*, bk. III, chap. 21, §7 (431).

17. See the condemned proposition of Jansen in Denzinger 1092: "Some of God's precepts are impossible to the just, who wish and strive to keep them, according to the present powers which they have; the grace, by which they are made possible, is also wanting." See also Reginald Garrigou-Lagrange, *Predestination*, trans. Dom Bede Rose, O.S.B., D.D. (Charlotte, N.C.: TAN Books, 1998), 119–120: "The antilapsarians, who were disciples of Calvin, said that even before Adam's sin was

are themselves only sufficient, rendered efficacious by the acceptance and participation of the patient of the grace, Calvinism and Jansenism render grace only efficacious, robbing man of any power for further good acts. Human nature is so wounded by sin that it does not have even a power to do good unless it is actually being moved to that good here and now by the divine will. The power to act is not truly present unless the act itself is present, and thus there is no such thing as sufficient graces.

If the Dominican treatment had tackled and satisfactorily dispelled the tenets of Molinism, perhaps it had not focused enough on defending itself against the attacks of the Molinists, especially those which claimed that the traditional Dominican treatment, in positing God's exhaustive governance over every aspect of the universe (including both of the lines of good and evil), was too closely aligned with Jansenism or Calvinism. The impetus of the revisionist treatment seems to lie in this, that in the exuberance of debating the Molinists regarding the reconciliation of God's providential ordering and creaturely freedom, the traditional Dominican and Thomistic account had failed to defend God's innocence in the face of sin.

This work attempts to analyze the parameters of the twentieth-century intra-Thomistic debate regarding grace, freedom, predestination, and reprobation through the work of several of its chief figures. It will be important to look at both the line of good and the line of evil as laid out by each of these figures in order that we might compare what relation exists between them. We will begin with the Angelic Doctor himself, treating his later, more mature texts and how they deal with the matters at hand. After this, we shall move on to a brief look at Domingo Báñez, OP, to give us a glimpse of his own principles in order that we may make sense of their place within the twentieth-century debate and the criticisms of so-called Báñezianism. From there, the work will take up Fr. Reginald Garrigou-Lagrange, OP, seen by many as the last great bastion of Báñezianism. These works will be juxtaposed with three figures from the revisionist

---

foreseen, God did not will to save all mankind. On the contrary, the infralapsarians said that, as a consequence of this foreseen sin, God does not will to save all mankind. Calvin, following up the stand taken by Wyclif, added that those who come under the sentence of reprobation are purified only externally by baptism, not receiving the grace of this sacrament. In the sacrament of the Lord's supper, the predestined do not receive the body of Christ, but merely a divine power that emanates from Christ's body present in heaven. The Church is invisible, consisting of the assembly of the predestined."

account: Francisco Marín-Sola, OP, Jacques Maritain, and the later work of Jean-Hervé Nicolas, OP. Each in his own way posits a divine causality that is sometimes rendered intentionally impedible by God, thus allowing for it to be frustrated by human action. We will also consider a short treatment of Bernard Lonergan's novel interpretation of divine premotion and the efficient causality of creaturely free acts in St. Thomas, a treatment which wishes to reject Báñezianism without positing the defeated divine will of Marín-Sola and Maritain. The major tenets of these revisers will be analyzed over and against the traditional treatment.

Our aim is ultimately to consider the objections of the revisionist account as well as the ramifications of their modifications to the so-called Báñezian schema. Are the alterations helpful and justified? Do they improve on the thought of the traditional school? Most importantly, are they loyal to the thought of the Angelic Doctor himself, and are they necessary to properly safeguard the distinction between the line of good and the line of evil?

We will attempt to show that those within the revisionist camp, while raising significant questions and points of new emphasis, have wrought undue alteration to the traditional account. The classical Dominican treatment, often maligned with the epithet of "Báñezianism," was already poised and ready to defend itself against the errors of Calvin or Jansen, maintaining both God's all-encompassing providential power and his complete dissociation from sin and evil. While the rise in the objections of the revisionist account has provided a fertile opportunity to expand and nuance the traditional account, this account already properly regarded the dissymmetry between the lines of good and of evil at its core, even if this dissymmetry has unfortunately not always been a point that was given proper attention. Moreover, it is only the traditional account that sufficiently regards and holds together all of the mysteries associated with premotion, providence, and evil. Like the child collecting berries in a bucket with a hole in the bottom, the theories of Marín-Sola, Maritain, and Nicolas, while laudable in their intent, fail to safeguard the entire tradition, accidentally forsaking important elements of classical theism all along the way.

A short note on translations: I have retained the original Latin and Spanish text of Domingo Báñez, as well as the original French of Jean-Hérve Nicolas in the footnotes. In general, I have not included the original Latin for St. Thomas, the original French for Reginald Garrigou-Lagrange or Jacques Maritain, or the original Spanish for Francisco Marín-Sola. This was in order to keep the footnotes to a manageable length and because either I have used a definitive translation of the work that is already present or the original text is quite easy to come by for those who want to view it. In certain rare instances wherein advertence to the original text is deemed necessary by the author, I have given it.

CHAPTER TWO

St. Thomas Aquinas

Any consideration of the true teaching of St. Thomas on divine causality and human free acts must be rooted fundamentally within the actual texts of the Angelic Doctor. In this chapter, we shall aim to situate and anchor each of the crucial pieces of the traditional, commentatorial treatment of this issue within the thought of St. Thomas himself. We will give advertence to the entire *corpus* of St. Thomas but will chiefly consider his later, more mature works on these issues. With each piece set into its proper place, the profundity and sophistication of the entire system will reveal itself. This clear picture of St. Thomas's thought will be the touchstone by which the traditional and revisionist accounts may be compared and ultimately judged.

The Will as Moved by an Exterior Principle, Which Is God

For St. Thomas, God alone is self-subsistent being and pure act. Therefore, in order that any agent other than himself should be able to be or to act at all, it must participate in the power of God. In other words, it must be moved from potency, the ability to operate, to act, that is actually operating. St. Thomas says:

It is evident, next, that God is the cause enabling all operating agents to operate. In fact, every operating agent is a cause of being in some way, either of substantial or of accidental being. Now, nothing is a cause of being unless by virtue of its acting through the power of God, as we showed. Therefore, every operating agent acts through God's power.[1]

This pertains to all operating agents, including human beings, who are said to act in accordance with God as the secondary cause of their own effects, while God is the primary cause insofar as he is the one on whom causality primarily rests.

The fact, therefore, that a creature is the cause of some other creature does not preclude that God operate immediately in all things, insofar as His power is like an intermediary that joins the power of any secondary cause with its effect. In fact, the power of a creature cannot achieve its effect except by the power of the Creator, from whom is all power, preservation of power, and order [of cause] to effect. For this reason, as is said in the same place of the *Book of Causes*, the causality of the secondary cause is rooted in the causality of the primary cause.[2]

Thus St. Thomas speaks of God reducing some operation or power in the creature from potency to act, and this he calls a "motion."

It is certain, and evident to our senses, that in the world some things are in motion. Now whatever is in motion is put in motion by another, for nothing can be in motion except it is in potentiality to that towards which it is in motion; whereas a thing moves inasmuch as it is in act. For motion is nothing else than the reduction of something from potentiality to actuality. But nothing can be reduced from potentiality to actuality, except by something in a state of actuality. Thus that which is actually hot, as fire, makes wood, which is potentially hot, to be actually hot, and thereby moves and changes it. Now it is not possible that the same thing should be at once in actuality and potentiality in the same respect, but only in different respects. For what is actually hot cannot simultaneously be potentially hot; but it is simultaneously potentially cold. It is therefore impossible that in the same respect and in the same way a thing should be both mover and moved, i.e. that it should move itself. Therefore, whatever is in motion must be put in motion by another.[3]

The will, for St. Thomas, is an intellectual appetite,[4] a power of the intellect.[5] In the *Summa contra Gentiles*, Aquinas states that "every operation

1. ScG III, 67, 1.

2. St. Thomas Aquinas, *Scriptum super Sententiis*, bk. II, distinctio 1, q. 1, a. 4, solution; Steven E. Baldner and William E. Carroll, trans., *Aquinas on Creation: Writings on the "Sentences of Peter Lombard"* (Toronto: Pontifical Institute of Mediaeval Studies, 1997), 85–86.

3. St. Thomas Aquinas, *Summa Theologiae* (hereafter *ST*) I, q. 2, a. 3.

4. *ST* I, q. 82, a. 5.

5. *ST* I, q. 83, a. 2.

that results from a certain power is attributed causally to the thing which has given the power."[6] The power of intellect and will is, of course, given to man by God. These operations find their source in God, and without him they cannot be operated. Insofar as man is ever capable of being an intellectual or volitional agent, these operations must be attributed to the divine power working within them.

It is evident, next, that God is the cause enabling all operating agents to operate. In fact, every operating agent is a cause of being in some way, either of substantial or of accidental being. Now, nothing is a cause of being unless by virtue of its acting through the power of God, as we showed. Therefore, every operating agent acts through God's power.[7]

This seems manifestly true, since "every action which cannot continue after the influence of a certain agent has ceased results from that agent."[8] Just as the appearance of colors would cease without the illumination of the sun, so is it also the case that "if this divine influence were to cease, every operation would cease."[9] Thus, this is not a cause *per accidens*, but an essential cause that must exist here and now for the application of the power of the will. It is not simply the first voluntary movement that requires the divine causality but each and every voluntary movement. "But every application of power to operation is originally and primarily made by God."[10]

St. Thomas is explicit that this applies not just to powers generally, but specifically to the will. "Similarly, also, every movement of a will whereby powers are applied to operation is reduced to God, as a first object of appetite and a first agent of willing. Therefore, every operation should be attributed to God, as to a first and principal agent."[11]

Of course, this is not to deny the causal role of man in willing, who acts as *causae sequentes* or *secundae causae* or as an *instrumentum*.[12] St. Thomas rebuts an objection that states exactly this. "Further, the same work cannot proceed at the same time from two sources; as neither can one and the same movement belong to two movable things. Therefore if

6. ScG III, 67, 2.
7. ScG III, 67, 1.
8. ScG III, 67, 3.
9. ScG III, 67, 3.
10. ScG III, 67, 4.
11. ScG III, 67, 4.
12. ScG III, 67, 5.

the creature's operation is from God operating in the creature, it cannot at the same time proceed from the creature; and so no creature works at all."[13] In response, St. Thomas states, "One action does not proceed from two agents of the same order. But nothing hinders the same action from proceeding from a primary and a secondary agent."[14] The secondary agent depends on the primary agent for its operation, but this presupposes that the secondary agent does indeed operate. Far from denying its operating, the primary agent is what makes it to operate.

However, it must be noted that "the cause of an action is the one by whose power the action is done rather than the one who acts: the principal agent, for instance, rather than the instrument. Therefore, God is more especially the cause of every action than are the secondary agent causes."[15] While the greater part of the action comes from the principal agent, Aquinas rejects the arguments of the occasionalists[16] on multiple grounds. All illusory secondary agents would be "employed in a useless way"[17] if they were not true causes. Moreover, such a position demonstrates an affront to the divine omnipotence, since God would be incapable of sharing his perfection to lower things. "Indeed, it is part of the fullness of perfection to be able to communicate to another being the perfection which one possesses. Therefore, this position detracts from the divine power."[18] St. Thomas gives further reasons for rejecting the thesis that in ordinary action as commonly experienced in the universe God acts directly without the mediation of secondary causes throughout the chapter, but what has been stated will suffice to show that St. Thomas rejects the thesis nonetheless.

So in what way are we to understand how two efficient causes, that is, a primary and secondary or instrumental cause, come together to bring about a shared effect? St. Thomas indeed affirms that nature does not do with two effects what can be done with one. However, St. Thomas makes a distinction between the agent that acts and the power that allows it to act. "In every agent, in fact, there are two things to consider: namely, the

13. *ST* I, q. 105, a. 5, arg. 2.
14. *ST* I, q. 105, a. 5, ad 2.
15. *ScG* III, 67, 5.
16. The occasionalists hold that only God is truly an efficient cause. All lower things that appear as causes are merely occasions of God's causality.
17. *ScG* III, 69, 13.
18. *ScG* III, 69, 15.

thing itself that acts, and the power by which it acts."[19] The secondary cause, or *inferior agens*, indeed acts as an efficient cause to bring about some effect, but it does not act entirely of its own power. It requires that it be moved to act, that it be given the power whereby it may act as an efficient cause. "But the power of a lower agent depends on the power of the superior agent, according as the superior agent gives this power to the lower agent whereby it may act; or preserves it; or even applies the action, as the artisan applies an instrument to its proper effect."[20]

This subordinated causality is not redundant even though God alone has a claim on the power that produces whatever effect is produced by the primary and secondary agents. As we have seen above, God communicates his perfection to lower things out of his goodness and love for them.

It is important to note that an effect is not attributed in part to God and in part to the human agent who wills the effect, but completely to both, just as a piece of wood is whittled wholly by both the knife and the whittler. There is a relation of subordination between the principal and instrumental cause, not of coordination, such as is the case with Molina's two rowers who together are able to move a boat forward (and alone, can only spin the boat in circles). St. Thomas states:

It is also apparent that the same effect is not attributed to a natural cause and to divine power in such a way that it is partly done by God, and partly done by the natural agent; rather, it is wholly done by both, according to a different way, just as the same effect is wholly attributed to the instrument and also wholly to the principal agent.[21]

In the *Summa Theologiae*, St. Thomas asserts that we may speak of the will being moved in two ways: to act at all and to act in this or that way. "Now a power of the soul is seen to be in potentiality to different things in two ways: first, with regard to acting or not acting; secondly, with regard to this or that action. Thus the sight sometimes sees actually, and sometimes sees not: and sometimes it sees white, and sometimes black."[22]

This first sort of movement may be said to provide the potency for volition whereas the second actually reduces that will to act. In regard to the second sort of movement, a will may be said to be moved by some

19. ScG III, 70, 5.
20. ScG III, 70, 5.
21. ScG III, 70, 8.
22. ST I-II, q. 9 , a. 1; *Quaestiones disputatae de potentia*, q. 3, a. 7.

object of the will that is apprehended by the sensitive appetite as good.[23] Some good is apprehended by the intellect and the will is subsequently inclined toward it. However, what we are chiefly concerned with here is what moves the will *to act*, not that which disposes a man to this or that good, but what moves it *to will* at all. In regard to this first type of movement, St. Thomas asserts that it comes not from the object but from the subject. "It needs therefore a mover in two respects, as to the exercise or use of the act, and as to the determination of the act. The first of these is on the part of the subject, which is sometimes acting, sometimes not acting: while the other is on the part of the object, by reason of which the act is specified."[24] However, in the very next line St. Thomas continues, "The motion of the subject itself is due to some agent."[25]

So what is this agent that moves the subject to act? St. Thomas states that the subject's being moved to act must come from an exterior principle that may reduce it from potentially acting to actually acting.

I answer that, As far as the will is moved by the object, it is evident that it can be moved by something exterior. But in so far as it is moved in the exercise of its act, we must again hold it to be moved by some exterior principle. For everything that is at one time an agent actually, and at another time an agent in potentiality, needs to be moved by a mover. Now it is evident that the will begins to will something, whereas previously it did not will it. Therefore it must, of necessity, be moved by something to will it.[26]

Finally, St. Thomas asserts that this exterior principle is indeed God. To argue for this, St. Thomas makes a distinction between moving a thing and causing a natural movement within a thing. To illustrate the point, he uses a stone and a man who moves the stone. The man may move a stone from one place to another. Such a movement is given to the stone but is not a movement that the stone can have by nature, and thus the stone in no way participates in this movement other than to receive it. However, in order to move a thing according to its nature one must be the cause of that nature.

I answer that, The movement of the will is from within, as also is the movement of nature. Now although it is possible for something to move a natural thing,

23. *ST* I-II, q. 9, a. 2.
24. *ST* I-II, q. 9, a. 1.
25. *ST* I-II, q. 9, a. 1.
26. *ST* I-II, q. 9, a. 4.

without being the cause of the thing moved, yet that alone, which is in some way the cause of a thing's nature, can cause a natural movement in that thing. For a stone is moved upwards by a man, who is not the cause of the stone's nature, but this movement is not natural to the stone; but the natural movement of the stone is caused by no other than the cause of its nature.[27]

St. Thomas asserts that this exterior principle that can move a thing according to its nature must, in the case of man, be God, for God is the cause of the rational soul from which flows the power of the will. Moreover, God is that universal good to which the will is ordered. Consequently, St. Thomas states, "God moves man's will, as the Universal Mover, to the universal object of the will, which is good. And without this universal motion, man cannot will anything."[28]

It is important to note that St. Thomas is not stating simply that God gives the power of willing to man, but that each act must be reduced from potency to act by God, who does not give merely the ability to will in general, as if giving a gift at the beginning of life that afterward does not require him. In the *Summa contra Gentiles*, St. Thomas speaks quite explicitly about the will requiring God's power every time that it wills. In other words, God provides the power to will (potency) at some point early in the life of a child, but he must also act as an exterior principle upon man in order for that potency to be reduced to act in each and every actual volitional movement.

So, man cannot use the power of will that has been given him except in so far as he acts through the power of God. Now, the being through whose power the agent acts is the cause not only of the power, but also of the act. This is apparent in the case of an artist through whose power an instrument works, even though it does not get its own form from this artist, but is merely applied to action by this man. Therefore, God is for us the cause not only of our will, but also of our act of willing.[29]

This is also made abundantly clear in *Quaestiones disputatae de potentia*. There Thomas differentiates between three kinds of causation: giving the power for movement in general, upholding the power for that movement, and actually moving a thing to act as it acts. Thomas affirms that God moves all things according to all three of these forms of causation. Here

27. *ST* I-II, q. 9, a. 6.
28. *ST* I-II, q. 9, a. 6, ad 3.
29. *ScG* III, 89, 5.

he is very explicit regarding God's causality regarding each and every movement found within the created order.

A thing is said to cause another's action by moving it to act: whereby we do not mean that it causes or preserves the active power, but that it applies the power to action, even as a man causes the knife's cutting by the very fact that he applies the sharpness of the knife to cutting by moving it to cut. And since the lower nature in acting does not act except through being moved, because these lower bodies are both subject to and cause alteration: whereas the heavenly body causes alteration without being subject to it, and yet it does not cause movement unless it be itself moved, so that we must eventually trace its movement to God, it follows of necessity that God causes the action of every natural thing by moving and applying its power to action.... Therefore, God is the cause of every action, inasmuch as every action is an instrument of the divine power operating.

Moreover, he says, "Therefore, God is the cause of everything's action inasmuch as he gives everything the power to act, and preserves it in being and applies it to action."[30] Of course, God works through lower, secondary causes, but this in no way makes God to be more remote or less causal in regard to each and every action, even if it is the effect of subordinated causes. "Both God and nature operate immediately, although as already stated there is order between them of priority and posteriority."[31]

Objections

There may exist an argument according to which Aquinas would be stating that God needs only to initiate man's power to will. After the initial power of volition is given to man, he may go on willing, with each new movement of the will being caused by a movement that preceded it, removing the necessity for God to apply the power in each and every movement of the will. In this case God would be a cause *per accidens* of human willing, but not an essential cause. Indeed, St. Thomas even summarizes an argument from Aristotle[32] with the following:

There must be a cause for the fact that a person understands, deliberates, chooses, and wills, for every new event must have some cause. But, if its cause is another act of deliberation, and another act of will preceding it, then, since one cannot

---

30. Quaestiones disputatae, q. 3, a. 7: "Sic ergo Deus est causa actionis cuiuslibet in quantum dat virtutem agendi, et in quantum conservat eam, et in quantum applicat actioni."

31. Quaestiones disputatae, q. 3, a. 7, ad 4.

32. Aristotle, *Eudemian Ethics*, bk. VIII.

go on to infinity in these acts, one must reach something that is first. Now, a first of this type must be something that is better than reason. But nothing is better than intellect and reason except God. Therefore, God is the first principle of our acts of counsel and of will.[33]

One might argue that St. Thomas is stating only that God is necessary as a First Mover of the will, the hand that winds the clock or starts the engine of human willing. It is true that every act of willing requires an antecedent cause, but perhaps, after the initial cause of God, each subsequent act of the will may be caused by a previous one. If such an argument is true, then St. Thomas is not really asserting that God must apply the power of acting to the will every time that it wills, but simply the first time that it wills. However, it is clear that St. Thomas is not stating this. In just the preceding paragraph St. Thomas asserts that "God is the cause of every action and He operates in every agent. Therefore, He is the cause of the movements of the will."[34] It is not just the first action, but *every* action that is subject to God's causation.[35] This does not mean that God causes only in the remote sense of being the source of the initiation of a power, but that man can only act through God's power each and every time that he acts. As shown above, St. Thomas likens this to the painter and the paintbrush. The brush can, of course, never paint on its own, separate from the power of the painter. Similarly, "every operation should be attributed to God"[36] without whom there is never an application of the will to act. Finally, St. Thomas states, "Of course, acts of choice and movements of the will are governed immediately by God"[37] and that "God alone directly works on the choice of man."[38] Moreover, the distinction that St. Thomas makes between God moving agents contingently and necessarily (and his affirmation that God does indeed move free creatures contingently)[39] does not make any sense if the only divine

33. *ScG* III, 89, 8.

34. *ScG* III, 89, 7.

35. See Thomas Williams, "Human Freedom and Agency," in *The Oxford Handbook of Aquinas*, eds. Brian Davies and Eleonore Stump (Oxford: Oxford University Press, 2012), 199–208; "For Aquinas holds a strong doctrine of the pervasiveness of God's causal activity. It is not merely that God providentially superintends the whole of creation, but that God is immediately active in every creaturely action, whether the creature acts by nature of by will" (206).

36. *ScG* III, 67, 4.

37. *ScG* III, 91, 2.

38. *ScG* III, 92, 2.

39. *ST* I-II, q. 10, a. 4, ad 1.

motion imparted to the will is the creation and operative actuation of the will itself, the movement of which is necessary (for humans are determined toward having a will and being ordered by that will to the universal good *by their nature*). There would exist no divine motions that could be called contingent or free (*libere*), relating to particular rather than universal goods. There would be only the one divine motion that bestows the human will and inclines that will necessarily to the universal good. And yet we know that St. Thomas explicitly states that the will is moved *by God* not only necessarily (in relation to good as such) but "freely (*libere*), which is becoming with its nature."[40]

Another strong objection in regard to the will's being moved by an exterior principle is related to the question of human freedom. How can it be said that the will remains free if it can be moved externally? Does this not negate the voluntary nature of the will? In response to this objection, St. Thomas states:

> It is essential to the voluntary act that its principle be within the agent: but it is not necessary that this inward principle be the first principle unmoved by another. Wherefore though the voluntary act has an inward proximate principle, nevertheless its first principle is from without. Thus too, the first principle of the natural movement is from without, that, to wit, which moves nature.[41]

St. Thomas is asserting that the voluntary act is based on man's ability to will. That this potency should be activated from the outside does not negate that the principle that allows it to be at all is internal,[42] that is, it follows upon man's nature as a rational and, subsequently, voluntary animal.

This leads to yet another objection that claims that the will being moved by an exterior principle is inherently violent, because "the violent act is one 'the principle of which is outside the agent.'"[43]

St. Thomas replies to this objection with one of the most salient and concise descriptions of the relation between the human will and divine causality.

---

40. *ST* I-II, q. 10, a. 4, ad 1: "quam si moveretur libere, prout competit suae naturae."

41. *ST* I-II, q. 9, a. 4, ad 1.

42. *ST* I, q. 105, a. 4, ad 2: "To be moved voluntarily, is to be moved from within, that is, by an interior principle: yet this interior principle may be caused by an exterior principle; and so to be moved from within is not repugnant to being moved by another."

43. *ST* I-II, q. 9, a. 4, arg. 2.

For an act to be violent it is not enough that its principle be extrinsic, but we must add "without the concurrence of him that suffers violence." This does not happen when the will is moved by an exterior principle: for it is the will that wills, though moved by another. But this movement would be violent, if it were counter to the movement of the will: which in the present case is impossible, since then the will would will and not will the same thing.[44]

The will is moved externally from potency to act such that it may will internally. To put it more simply, the will is moved to will that which it wills.[45] In no way can this be violent because violence requires that such a movement transgress the human will, but far from transgressing the will, God animates it. When an attacker robs a man of his money, the man is compelled to do something against his will, and this is what makes the act violent. But, according to St. Thomas, God does not work as an exterior principle that acts against the will of a man, but rather he actuates that will *to will*. And this is why St. Thomas says that violence here is impossible, for God reduces man's will from potency to act such that man actually becomes an agent. This is, of course, quite different from attempting to frustrate man's will and neutering his ability to act as an agent, or forcing him to act in a way that is in discord with his own will. On the contrary, it is through the power of God that man has the ability to be volitional, and it is through the active power of God that man moves himself to *act* volitionally. God is the source of human freedom. God's movement in man

---

44. *ST* I-II, q. 9, a. 4, ad 2. See also, *ScG* III, 88.

45. Petr Dvořák argues against this in "The Concurrentism of Thomas Aquinas: Divine Causation and Human Freedom," *Philosophia* 41, no. 3 (2013): 632–633: "Thomas Aquinas sees the cooperation of the divine and human causes predominately as the human cause participating on the action of the divine agent as its instrument. What is open to interpretation is the scope of the divine causation. The question arises whether by "acting through the divine power" Aquinas means that the divine cause causally contributes to a key aspect of the effect only: namely, its existence as such, or whether it also reaches the human agent, applying it to action. Only the former reading seems to leave enough room for libertarian human freedom." But this is expressly against the teaching of St. Thomas, who holds that not simply is the creaturely willing the subject of God's governance but also the particular effects that it wills. See *ScG* III, 94, 8–10: "However, for the purpose of answering these arguments, we must repeat some of the observations put down before, so that it may be made clear that nothing escapes divine providence; also, that the order of divine providence cannot possibly be changed; and yet that it is not necessary for all things to happen of necessity simply because they come about as a result of divine providence. First, then, we must consider the fact that, since God is the cause of all existing things, giving being to all, the order of His providence must embrace all things. Indeed, on the things on which He has lavished being He must also lavish preservation and guide them toward perfection in their ultimate end.... In the act of premeditating the order, the more perfect that providence is, the more can the order of providence be extended to *the smallest details.*"

as an external principle is for the sake that man may *move himself*, that he may be a creature of free will.[46] It is impossible for man to freely choose x and to not freely choose x at the same time; thus, there can be no violence done by the actuation of the free will by God. "Therefore, we need to say that God, since he is the first source of the movement of everything, moves certain things in such a way that they also move their very selves, as in the case of those with the power of free choice."[47]

The Active Agency of the Human Will

As we have seen above, the fact that God acts within man to will something does not injure or erase man's volition or his causality in relation to his own willing. Man, acting with God, does indeed cause his will to move. Man is not simply animated by God, but moves freely in accord with Him.

St. Thomas states, "In the order of natural perfection, only the rational creature holds dominion over his acts, moving himself freely in order to perform his actions. Other creatures, in fact, are moved to their proper workings rather than being the active agents of these operations, as is clear from what has been said."[48] Consequently, we may say that man as a rational creature is indeed the active agent of his operation. That he be moved by God, since that movement is not violent but activates man's potency to will, in no way negates that man acts as an active agent. Nonliving things or nonrational living things may be moved to their proper working in an entirely passive way, but man is moved *to move*.

The intellectual creature is thus called the "master of its acts,"[49] and this is where we see that the analogy of the painter and the paintbrush is incomplete. While it is true that man must be applied to the operation of acting by God as the paintbrush must be used by the painter to paint, the paintbrush is not rational and is thus not volitional. It does not move itself to act in accord with the painter as participant, whereas man does

46. *ST* I, q. 105, a. 4, ad 1: "A thing moved by another is forced if moved against its natural inclination; but if it is moved by another giving to it the proper natural inclination, it is not forced; as when a heavy body is made to move downwards by that which produced it, then it is not forced. In like manner God, while moving the will, does not force it, because He gives the will its own natural inclination."

47. *De malo*, q. 3, a. 2.
48. *ScG* III, 111, 1.
49. *ScG* III, 112, 1.

act as an agent in accord with God. "That which is moved only by another being has the formal character of an instrument, but that which acts of itself has the essential character of a principal agent.... Therefore, intellectual creatures are so governed by God, as objects of care for their own sakes; while other creatures are subordinated, as it were, to the rational creatures."[50]

The Contingency of the Human Will in Regard to This or That Particular Good

Man's will is determined toward goodness as such, what St. Thomas calls *universale bonum*.[51] However, because man never meets directly with universal goodness in this life, he retains a real contingency of volitional choice since he meets only limited, particular goods.[52] The will is not in any way moved necessarily toward any particular good since it may be considered from a point of view in which it is seen to lack some good. Thus, any particular good may either be chosen or rejected. While the will cannot see universal good as anything other than appetible, it can see some particular good as nonappetible. St. Thomas states that man is necessarily ordered toward universal goodness as an end constitutive of man's nature, but the choice of particular goods is merely the means toward (or away from) that end, and thus choice of particular goods is free and not determined or necessary.[53] The choice of a particular good is

50. *ScG* III, 112, 1.
51. *ST* I-II, q. 2, a. 8: "I answer that, It is impossible for any created good to constitute man's happiness. For happiness is the perfect good, which lulls the appetite altogether; else it would not be the last end, if something yet remained to be desired. Now the object of the will, i.e. of man's appetite, is the universal good; just as the object of the intellect is the universal true. Hence it is evident that naught can lull man's will, save the universal good."
52. *ST* I-II, q. 10, a. 2: "Wherefore if the will be offered an object which is good universally and from every point of view, the will tends to it of necessity, if it wills anything at all; since it cannot will the opposite. If, on the other hand, the will is offered an object that is not good from every point of view, it will not tend to it of necessity. And since lack of any good whatever, is a non-good, consequently, that good alone which is perfect and lacking in nothing, is such a good that the will cannot not-will it: and this is Happiness. Whereas any other particular goods, in so far as they are lacking in some good, can be regarded as non-goods: and from this point of view, they can be set aside or approved by the will, which can tend to one and the same thing from various points of view."
53. *ST* I-II, q. 13, a. 6: "I answer that, Man does not choose of necessity. And this is because that which is possible not to be, is not of necessity. Now the reason why it is possible not to choose, or to choose, may be gathered from a twofold power in man. For man can will and not will, act and not act; again, he can will this or that, and do this or that. The reason of this is seated in the very power of

always contingent because no particular good compels the human will.[54]

It is of course true that man is moved by God as an exterior principle even when he wills some particular good. However, this does not mean that man is moved to the particular good necessarily, for this would destroy human indeterminacy to particular goods and would thus pose significant questions in regard to man's freedom in choice. Man's relation to universal good may be determinate, but his relation to any *particular* good, even one that he wills or chooses (following upon divine motion), remains contingent, according to his nature.

St. Thomas states:

Wherefore if the will be offered an object which is good universally and from every point of view, the will tends to it of necessity, if it wills anything at all; since it cannot will the opposite. If, on the other hand, the will is offered an object that is not good from every point of view, it will not tend to it of necessity. And since lack of any good whatever, is a non-good, consequently, that good alone which is perfect and lacking in nothing, is such a good that the will cannot not-will it: and this is Happiness. Whereas any other particular goods, in so far as they are lacking in some good, can be regarded as non-goods: and from this point of view, they can be set aside or approved by the will, which can tend to one and the same thing from various points of view.[55]

Thus man, "having an indifferent relation to many things," is moved in regard to particular goods in such a way that his own movement "remains contingent and not necessary."[56] And *this* is the principle that provides for

---

the reason. For the will can tend to whatever the reason can apprehend as good. Now the reason can apprehend as good, not only this, viz. 'to will' or 'to act,' but also this, viz. 'not to will' or 'not to act.' Again, in all particular goods, the reason can consider an aspect of some good, and the lack of some good, which has the aspect of evil: and in this respect, it can apprehend any single one of such goods as to be chosen or to be avoided. The perfect good alone, which is Happiness, cannot be apprehended by the reason as an evil, or as lacking in any way. Consequently man wills Happiness of necessity, nor can he will not to be happy, or to be unhappy. Now since choice is not of the end, but of the means, as stated above (Article [3]); it is not of the perfect good, which is Happiness, but of other particular goods. Therefore man chooses not of necessity, but freely."

54. *ST* I, q. 82, a. 2, ad 1: "The will can tend to nothing except under the aspect of good. But because good is of many kinds, for this reason the will is not of necessity determined to one."

ST I, q. 82, a. 2, ad 2: "But as the capacity of the will regards the universal and perfect good, its capacity is not subjected to any individual good. And therefore it is not of necessity moved by it."

55. ST I-II, q. 10, a. 2.

56. *ST* I-II, q. 10, a. 4: "I answer that, As Dionysius says (*Div. Nom.* iv) 'it belongs to Divine providence, not to destroy but to preserve the nature of things.' Wherefore it moves all things in accordance with their conditions; so that from necessary causes through the Divine motion, effects follow of necessity; but from contingent causes, effects follow contingently. Since, therefore, the will

the freedom of the will,[57] not the incompatibilist position, which claims that human freedom requires a complete lack of influence from God's causal governance.[58]

St. Thomas stresses that God moves things according to their nature, and thus he moves man such that he retains a real freedom in regard to particular goods.

> The Divine will extends not only to the doing of something by the thing which He moves, but also to its being done in a way which is fitting to the nature of that thing. And therefore it would be more repugnant to the Divine motion, for the will to be moved of necessity, which is not fitting to its nature; than for it to be moved freely, which is becoming to its nature.[59]

If the will is moved by an exterior principle, which is God, not merely in its being able to first will but in every subsequent act of the will, then, St. Thomas asserts, it is God who works within us whenever we will or accomplish some particular good. But this movement remains contingent even if its effect always follows.

---

is an active principle, not determinate to one thing, but having an indifferent relation to many things, God so moves it, that He does not determine it of necessity to one thing, but its movement remains contingent and not necessary, except in those things to which it is moved naturally."

57. Reginald Garrigou-Lagrange, OP, *Reality: A Synthesis of Thomistic Thought*, trans. Patrick Cummins, OSB (St. Louis, Mo: B. Herder and Co.), 189: "These words [from *ST* I-II, q. 10, a. 2] contain, equivalently, the Thomistic definition of free will which runs thus: Freedom is the will's dominative indifference in relation to any object which reason proposes as in any way lacking in good. Let us dwell on this definition. Reason proposes an object which, here and now, is in one way good but in some other way not good. Faced with such an object the will can choose it or refuse it. The will, as faculty, has potential indifference; as act, it has actual indifference. Even when the will actually chooses such an object, even when it is already determined to will it, it still goes freely toward it, with its dominating indifference no longer potential but actual. . . . Freedom arises from the disproportion which exists between will, specifically distinguished and necessitated by universal good, and this or that limited and particular good, good in one way, not good in another way."

58. See Brian Davies, *The Reality of God and the Problem of Evil*, (London: Continuum, 2006), 116–29. Davies argues against the relatively ubiquitous position that the source of human freedom is the lack of divine influence, i.e., that humans are free insofar as God is not involved with their free actions. This is often referred to as incompatibilism, wherein divine causation, action, or motion on the created will is incompatible with the freedom of said will. For a classic example of this line of argumentation Davies presents Alvin Plantinga, "God, Evil, and the Metaphysics of Freedom," reprinted in *The Problem of Evil*, ed. Marilyn McCord Adams and Robert Merrihew Adams (Oxford: Oxford University Press, 2002), 106: "Of course it is up to God whether to create free creatures at all; but if he aims to produce moral good, then he must create significantly free creatures upon whose cooperation he must depend. Thus is the power of an omnipotent God limited by the freedom he confers on creature."

59. *ST* I-II, q. 10, a. 4, ad 1.

What, then, separates the man who chooses well in some instance and the man who does not? It cannot be stated that they act differently according to their nature, for they share the same power to will well according to their both being rational creatures. Yet we know that one does indeed will some good and the other does not.

Indeed, this fact, that one man chooses things beneficial to him, whereas another man chooses things harmful to him, apart from their proper reasoning, cannot be understood as resulting from differences of intellectual nature, because the nature of intellect and will is one in all men.... Hence, in so far as man's intellect is enlightened for the performance of some action, or as his will is prompted by God, the man is not said to be favored by birth, but, rather, well guarded or well governed.[60]

While Aquinas states that the action of an angel or of a celestial body may have some effect on the will, this effect is not a true movement of the will. The circumstances in which man finds himself and the object of his love or hate may persuade the will or provide a disposition toward or away from something. However, "God alone directly works on the choice made by man,"[61] because he does not merely dispose or incline the will toward something, but "God's operation is like something perfecting."[62] This means that man may sometimes act in accord with the persuasion of an angel, the insistence of a friend, or even the object of his desire, but it does not necessarily follow that he will do so. This is not, however, the case with the work that God does upon the will. "Now, since a disposition which results from a quality of the body, or from an intellectual persuasion, does not bring necessity to the act of choice, a man does not always choose what his guardian angel intends, or that toward which a celestial body gives inclination. But a man *always* chooses the object in accord with God's operation within his will."[63]

Objection: Contingency and Necessity

However, does this not mean that the will is moved by necessity when it is moved by God? If the will is determined to some particular good by

60. *ScG* III, 92, 3.
61. *ScG* III, 92, 2.
62. *ScG* III, 92, 4.
63. *ScG* III, 92, 4.

God, even if we grant that man wills in accord with his being willed by God to some good, how can it be that the will is not necessitated by that movement? It may be true that God wills man to choose particular goods contingently, but is he not still locked in, as it were, toward the particular good to which he is moved by God? In what matter may the created will be said to be contingent if it is moved by God to one determined effect?

St. Thomas addresses this in both the *Summa Theologiae* and the *Summa contra Gentiles*, wherein he makes a distinction between some particular act coming about with an absolute necessity and coming about with a conditional (or suppositional) necessity. To make this more clear, St. Thomas employs the example of Socrates engaged in the act of sitting.

I answer that, There are two ways in which a thing is said to be necessary, namely, absolutely, and by supposition. We judge a thing to be absolutely necessary from the relation of the terms, as when the predicate forms part of the definition of the subject: thus it is absolutely necessary that man is an animal. It is the same when the subject forms part of the notion of the predicate; thus it is absolutely necessary that a number must be odd or even. In this way it is not necessary that Socrates sits: wherefore it is not necessary absolutely, though it may be so by supposition; for, granted that he is sitting, he must necessarily sit, as long as he is sitting.[64]

Similarly, St. Thomas states, "Thus, it is necessary that Socrates be seated from the fact that he is seen seated. But this is not absolutely necessary or, as some say, with the necessity of the consequent; it is necessary conditionally, or with the necessity of the consequence."[65]

If Socrates finds himself in the condition of sitting, then he must necessarily be sitting while he sits. However, does this mean that Socrates must sit absolutely? Of course not, for Socrates can rise at any moment and stand. There is nothing in the predicate of *sitting thing* that is part of the essence of the subject *Socrates*. Nor is there anything in the subject *Socrates* that must be present in a *sitting thing*. Socrates may sit or he may not. A sitting thing may be Socrates or it may be something else. Contrast this with the relation of the subject of *man* to the predicate *animal*. A man is, by absolute necessity, an animal, since what it means to be a man is to be an animal of a certain sort (that is, rational). But Socrates is no more or less Socrates when he stands rather than sits, or sits rather than stands.

64. *ST* I, q. 19, a. 3.
65. *ScG* I, 67, 10.

Man is no more or less man when he chooses this particular good rather than some other particular good.

Consequently, we do not say that Socrates sits with absolute necessity. And yet, when Socrates is sitting, we do say that he sits with conditional necessity. In this certain condition of Socrates sitting, he cannot possibly be simultaneously standing. Put in another way, St. Thomas states that Socrates necessarily sits in a composite sense while he is sitting. He cannot act in the contrary to how he is acting now. It is not possible to sit and to not sit at the same time, nor is it possible to stand and not stand at the same time. To claim as much would be, of course, to deny the principle of contradiction.

Similarly, standing and sitting cannot be united in Socrates at the same time, since they are contraries. They cannot exist as a composite, as characteristics of the same man in the same moment. However, in a divided sense, Socrates can certainly stand while he sits, provided that we mean that he has the power to stand in another moment. He can stand but not stand and sit together, compositely. These two contraries are both possible to him even if he can only really do one in any given moment. Thus, we may say that Socrates retains a divided contingency in regard to sitting in a certain moment, even if there is a composite or conditional necessity that he sits in a moment in which he is sitting.[66] This is essentially the same distinction between the necessity of the consequence and the necessity of the consequent. Insofar as Socrates is not standing or lying or anything else except sitting, he sits with the necessity of the consequence. But this does not mean that Socrates must sit *simpliciter*. In other words, Socrates does not sit with the necessity of the consequent. His sitting is only necessary given the contingent antecedent of his deciding to sit rather than to stand.

In a similar manner, St. Thomas addresses the question of whether

---

66. *ScG* I, 67, 10: "There is more. If each thing is known by God as seen by Him in the present, what is known by God will then have to be. Thus, it is necessary that Socrates be seated from the fact that he is seen seated. But this is not absolutely necessary or, as some say, with the necessity of the consequent; it is necessary conditionally, or with the necessity of the consequence. For this is a necessary conditional proposition: if he is seen sitting, he is sitting. Hence, although the conditional proposition may be changed to a categorical one, to read what is seen sitting must necessarily be sitting, it is clear that the proposition is true if understood of what is said, and compositely; but it is false if understood of what is meant, and dividedly. Thus, in these and all similar arguments used by those who oppose God's knowledge of contingents, the fallacy of composition and division takes place." See also *ScG* I, 85.

God could change the past. While God has the power to make it such that Socrates did not sit at a given moment, once Socrates has sat, God cannot make it such that Socrates did not sit in that moment, for this would imply that Socrates both sat and did not sit, which is a contradiction.

I answer that, As was said above, there does not fall under the scope of God's omnipotence anything that implies a contradiction. Now that the past should not have been implies a contradiction. For as it implies a contradiction to say that Socrates is sitting, and is not sitting, so does it to say that he sat, and did not sit. But to say that he did sit is to say that it happened in the past. To say that he did not sit, is to say that it did not happen. Whence, that the past should not have been, does not come under the scope of divine power.[67]

This does not mean that Socrates sat in a past moment with absolute necessity, nor that God was impotent to make it such that Socrates did not sit in that moment, for Socrates is the sort of creature that can stand, sit, lie down, walk on his hands, and more. But once it is the case that Socrates sat in a given moment, it is no longer possible that he simultaneously, or in a composite sense, also did not sit. And although Socrates did sit in that moment, it is nevertheless true that he might not have. As such, that he sat was a contingent act, even if it will never be that he did not sit in that moment.

In this way, we can make sense of how St. Thomas says that it is possible that a man could be certainly moved to a determinate good effect but be moved in a way that is contingent rather than absolutely necessary. The will's ability to choose against some good is not revoked by the fact that it does not actually do so this time (as a condition of being moved by God). In the composite sense, the will is moved according to the divine will, but it is a movement of contingency because the human will retains its potency to have done otherwise (as opposed to, for example, the lack of man's potency to be a lower good rather than the *universale bonum*).

All of this means that the movement of man toward some particular good is both contingent and yet follows infallibly, given the nature of the primary mover, which is God. As we have seen above, the created will is determined only to goodness itself. Since man meets only with particular goods in this life (which cannot completely compel his will), he is not determined to any particular good with necessity. Man chooses the par-

67. ST I, q. 25, a. 4.

ticular good contingently, even if God moves him to choose it. He retains the real power to have chosen otherwise, according to his nature, which is compelled only by the *universale bonum*. And insofar as it retains this real potency, we may say that the act is free because it was not done with absolute necessity. It could have willed to the contrary just as a fire could grill a steak, whether it actually ends up doing so or not (although, of course, a steak is not a volitional creature like man). However, this does not mean that the creaturely movement does not follow with necessity. The human will infallibly does according as it is willed by God. However, the movement derives its infallibility not in regard to the human will as such, but in regard to divine providence, insofar as the contingent human will is governed by an infallible and unchangeable providential ordering.

We must therefore say that fate, considered in regard to second causes, is changeable; but as subject to Divine Providence, it derives a certain unchangeableness, not of absolute but of conditional necessity. In this sense we say that this conditional is true and necessary: "If God foreknew that this would happen, it will happen." Wherefore Boethius, having said that the chain of fate is fickle, shortly afterwards adds—"which, since it is derived from an unchangeable Providence must also itself be unchangeable."[68]

That the Divine Will Is Always Fulfilled

While it is true that God wills contingent things contingently, this does not mean that the divine will is mutable or frustrated. On the contrary, St. Thomas states that the will of God "must needs always be fulfilled"[69] and that it is "entirely unchangeable."[70] St. Thomas is quick to point out that this does not mean that the divine will does not will a thing sometimes and against that same thing other times. "It does not follow from this argument that God has a will that changes, but that He sometimes wills that things should change."[71] Sometimes God may will that a storm forms, and other times he may not. This does not mean that God changes his mind, as it were, nor does it mean that his will is frustrated, but simply that God wills different things at different times.

68. *ST* I, q. 116, a. 3.
69. *ST* I, q. 19, a. 6.
70. *ST* I, q. 19, a. 7.
71. *ST* I, q. 19, a. 7, ad 3.

However, in regard to the same thing, God's will is always fulfilled, for God's will does not change. The will changes toward a given thing based on a change in the disposition of the willer or with the accumulation of some new knowledge that effects in the willer a reconsideration of the thing willed. While such a change is possible in those with a finite and mutable will, such a change is not possible in the divine will. God does not change his disposition toward a thing, nor does he acquire new information that may result in reevaluating the circumstances and choosing something different than was originally chosen. In short, God does not change his mind.

The will would be changed, if one should begin to will what before he had not willed; or cease to will what he had willed before. This cannot happen, unless we presuppose change either in the knowledge or in the disposition of the substance of the willer.... Now it has already been shown that both the substance of God and His knowledge are entirely unchangeable. Therefore, His will must be entirely unchangeable.[72]

An objection to this assertion brings us back to the different senses of necessity. St. Thomas provides an objection that states that because God does not will with necessity in regard to contingent things, he must be undetermined in regard to those things, thus positing some potency or mutability in the divine will.

Further, God does not will of necessity what He wills, as said before. Therefore, He can both will and not will the same thing. But whatever can incline to either of the two opposites, is changeable substantially; and that which can exist in a place or not in that place, is changeable locally. Therefore, God is changeable as regards His will.[73]

St. Thomas answers with the following: "Although God's willing a thing is not by absolute necessity, yet it is necessary by supposition, on account of the unchangeableness of the divine will, as has been said above."[74] It is not with necessity that God wills the storm, but when he does will it (following upon that condition or supposition of his willing that it be) it must be the case that the storm comes, or else we would have to posit some change or frustration within the divine will, both of which St. Thomas has explicitly denied.[75]

---

72. *ST* I, q. 19, a. 7.
73. *ST* I, q. 19, a. 7, arg. 4.
74. *ST* I, q. 19, a. 7, ad. 4.
75. It is difficult for the theologian to consider just what it means for God's creation to be entirely

That God Causes Man to Will Whatever
Good That He Wills

Now we must speak of the divine motion that moves the created agent to will good. Here again St. Thomas is explicit about the complete dependence of the created will on the divine will, not only for it to have the power to will, but for it to exercise the act of willing any given good.

Now in corporeal things we see that for movement there is required not merely the form which is the principle of the movement or action, but there is also required the motion of the first mover. Now the first mover in the order of corporeal things is the heavenly body. Hence no matter how perfectly fire has heat, it would not bring about alteration, except by the motion of the heavenly body. But it is clear that as all corporeal movements are reduced to the motion of the heavenly body as to the first corporeal mover, so all movements, both corporeal and spiritual, are reduced to the simple First Mover, Who is God. And hence no matter how perfect a corporeal or spiritual nature is supposed to be, it cannot proceed to its act unless it be moved by God; but this motion is according to the plan of His providence, and not by necessity of nature, as the motion of the heavenly body. Now not only is every motion from God as from the First Mover, but all formal perfection is from Him as from the First Act. And thus the act of the intellect or of any created being whatsoever depends upon God in two ways: first, inasmuch as it is from Him that it has the form whereby it acts; secondly, inasmuch as it is moved by Him to act.[76]

This citation properly applies to man's intellect, and St. Thomas states, "Hence we must say that for the knowledge of any truth whatsoever man needs Divine help, that the intellect may be moved by God to its act."[77] Of course, the same idea applies to the human will, which St. Thomas deals with immediately thereafter: "I answer that, Man's nature may be looked at in two ways: first, in its integrity, as it was in our first parent before sin; secondly, as it is corrupted in us after the sin of our first parent.

---

ad extra. There is a temptation to anthropomorphize God such that he is somehow different if he has not created me or if he has not governed over a universe wherein the 2010 Green Bay Packers win Super Bowl XLV. It must always remain within the gaze of the theologian that God is Pure Act. He is the principle whereby all other things exist and act, but he has no room, as it were, for potencies since he has no real relation to the created order. Since we are in the created order we cannot help but to be changed by its changes, but this is not the case with God.

76. *ST* I-II, q. 109, a. 1.

77. *ST* I-II, q. 109, a. 1.

Now in both states human nature needs the help of God as First Mover, to do or wish any good whatsoever, as stated above."[78] But what of the objection[79] that man is master of his acts and is capable of willing by the very fact that he is a voluntary creature? Of course this is true, says St. Thomas, but the voluntary movement of the created will is brought about by a subordinated causality. The intrinsic principle of the human will *to will* is brought about by the extrinsic principle of the divine will moving it to move itself.

> Man is master of his acts and of his willing or not willing, because of his deliberate reason, which can be bent to one side or another. And although he is master of his deliberating or not deliberating, yet this can only be by a previous deliberation; and since it cannot go on to infinity, we must come at length to this, that man's free-will is moved by an extrinsic principle, which is above the human mind, to wit by God, as the Philosopher proves in the chapter "On Good Fortune." Hence the mind of man still unweakened is not so much master of its act that it does not need to be moved by God; and much more the free-will of man weakened by sin, whereby it is hindered from good by the corruption of the nature.[80]

The penultimate clause here is quite striking. Even man within the state of natural integrity before the Fall is not a creature that is completely independent of all necessity in regard to divine movement; it requires this movement to be the sort of creature that it is. This is a profound point about the contingent nature of the created being. To be a man, to exist as a human creature, is to receive all that we have, including intellect and will, from God, both as a general power and indeed for the exercise of that power. For St. Thomas, it is not part of man's human nature that he be the absolute or entirely separated master of his acts in seclusion from divine movement. A liberty of indifference to divine causality is not possible. On the contrary, human nature is marked by its need for God. The contingency of the human experience runs so deep that man does not exist at all without a constant divine immediacy and intimacy holding him in being and animating him forward in his humanity. How much

---

78. *ST* I-II, q. 109, a. 2.

79. *ST* I-II, q. 109, a. 2, arg. 2: "Further, man has more power over what is according to his nature than over what is beyond his nature. Now sin is against his nature, as Damascene says (*De Fide Orth.* ii, 30); whereas deeds of virtue are according to his nature, as stated. Therefore since man can sin of himself he can wish and do good."

80. *ST* I-II, q. 109, a. 2, ad 2.

more will man weakened by sin need God's aid to return to his proper humanity? And even more, how much aid he will need to rise up to the noble height of beatitude!

However, it matters not whether we speak of man in his natural integrity or man as fallen. In any and all orders of being, man requires that he be moved by God to do some good, as St. Thomas asserts when he says, "Now in both states human nature needs the help of God as First Mover, to do or wish any good whatsoever, as stated above."[81] Man is a volitional instrument; he is dependent on God's motion to exercise the operations that belong to his nature. St. Thomas says:

> It is the nature of an instrument as instrument to move something else when moved itself.... Thus an instrument has two operations, one which belongs to it according to its own form, and another which belongs to it in so far as it is moved by the principal agent and which rises above the ability of its own form.[82]

This contingency on the divine motion does not mean that these operations do not belong to his nature, but that it is in the nature of man to require God in order to operate.

> Moreover, no instrument can achieve its ultimate perfection by the power of its own form, but only by the power of the principal agent, although by its own power it can provide a certain disposition to the ultimate perfection. Indeed, the cutting of the lumber results from the saw according to the essential character of its own form, but the form of the bench comes from the skilled mind which uses the tool. Likewise, the breaking down and consumption of food in the animal body is due to the heat of fire, but the generation of flesh, and controlled growth and similar actions, stem from the vegetative soul which uses the heat of fire as an instrument. But under God Who is the first intellect and will, all intellects and wills are subordinated, as instruments under a principal agent.[83]

Moreover, man does indeed exist within a fallen order, and this makes it even more difficult for him to exercise his humanity, much less merit eternal life and divine friendship.

Furthermore, there are many impediments presented to man in the attaining of his end. For he is hindered by the weakness of his reason, which is easily drawn into error by which he is cut off from the right way of reaching his end. He is also

81. *ST* I-II, q. 109, a. 2.
82. *De veritate*, q. 27, a. 4.
83. *ScG* III, 147, 6.

hindered by the passions of his sensory nature, and by the feelings whereby he is attracted to sensible and lower things; and the more he attaches himself to these, the farther he is removed from his ultimate end, for these things are below man, whereas man's end is above him. He is further hindered by frequent bodily illness from the carrying out of his virtuous activities whereby he may tend toward happiness. Therefore, man needs divine help.[84]

As such, man finds himself in a terrible predicament: in this order, he is being called to divine friendship, something radically above his natural end, and yet he exists in a state so weakened that he finds it impossible even to be human without healing aid. He is prone to error and vice, and as such, "in the state of corrupted nature man cannot fulfill all the Divine commandments."[85] With this we arrive at the absolute necessity of grace.

Grace as Divine Aid

Grace is that divine aid that perfects and elevates man, allowing him to do natural good in a wounded state and to do what is above his nature. St. Thomas states that this special aid given to men to act well may be called grace for two reasons. First, it is not earned by men but is given gratuitously. "Since what is given a person, without any preceding merit on his part, is said to be given to him gratis, and because the divine help that is offered to man precedes all human merit, as we showed, it follows that this help is accorded gratis to man, and as a result it quite fittingly took the name grace."[86] Man does not move himself to attain this divine aid because man cannot move himself to his own perfection.[87] St. Thomas explains that

our soul acts under God, as an instrumental agent under a principal agent. So, the soul cannot prepare itself to receive the influence of divine help except in so far as it acts from divine power. Therefore, it is preceded by divine help toward good action, rather than preceding the divine help and meriting it, as it were, or preparing itself for it.[88]

84. ScG III, 147, 7.
85. ST I-II, q. 109, a. 2.
86. ScG III, 150, 1.
87. ScG III, 149, 1: "From what has been said it is quite manifest that man cannot merit divine help in advance. For everything is related as matter to what is above it. Now, matter does not move itself to its own perfection; rather, it must be moved by something else. So, man does not move himself so as to obtain divine help which is above him; rather, he is moved by God to obtain it."
88. ScG III, 149, 2. See also De veritate, q. 24, a. 15.

St. Thomas is here putting the causal priority on divine aid for our good actions. Grace must be ontologically prior to the good act, contra the Pelagian heresy. "Now, by this we set aside the error of the Pelagians, who said that this kind of help is given us because of our merits, and that the beginning of our justification is from ourselves, though the completion of it is from God."[89]

The second reason that this divine aid is called grace is because by it man is brought into a right relationship with God, what we might call coming into his good graces. "So, this help is appropriately called grace, not only because it is given gratis, as we showed, but also because by this help man is, through a special prerogative, brought into the good graces of God."[90]

All of this has the effect of healing and perfecting man. Grace moves man both to the natural good acts of which he is incapable due to sin and also to supernaturally good acts that are beyond his nature as such. Ultimately, it moves to the love of God above all things. St. Thomas is explicit that grace is the cause of whatever supernatural good is within us.

Again, God's love is causative of the good which is in us, just as a man's love is called forth and caused by some good thing which is in the object of his love. But man is aroused to love someone in a special way because of some special good which pre-exists in the person loved. Therefore, wherever there is found a special love of God for man, there must consequently be found some special good conferred on man by God. Hence, since in accord with the preceding explanation sanctifying grace marks a special love of God for man, it must be that a special goodness and perfection is marked, as being present in man, by this term.[91]

Of course, this does not negate that man participates in his own good actions. When man does some good deed, the deed comes about because of a participated and subordinated causality, with God operating as the primary cause and man operating as the secondary cause of whatever good is in him. This means that man actually wills whatever good he wills. Divine aid does not frustrate man's will but actualizes it, allowing it *to will*. As St. Thomas says, "this help does not exclude from us the act of our will, but, rather, in a special way, produces this act in us."[92] Further:

89. *ScG* III, 149, 8.
90. *ScG* III, 150, 2.
91. *ScG* III, 150, 4.
92. *ScG* III, 148, 4.

Again, that divine help is provided man so that he may act well is to be understood in this way: it performs our works in us, as the primary cause performs the operations of secondary causes, and as a principal agent performs the action of an instrument. Hence, it is said in Isaiah (26:12–13): "You have wrought all our works for us, O Lord." Now, the first cause causes the operation of the secondary cause according to the measure of the latter. So, God also causes our works in us in accord with our measure, which means that we act voluntarily and not as forced. Therefore, no one is forced to right action by the divine help.[93]

Does this mean that we cannot speak of man meriting everlasting life? No, says St. Thomas, for man actually acts when he does good deeds. These deeds can be called the cause of glory, as we shall see later on. It is simply that man acts in conjunction with grace, which moves him to act well. "Man, by his will, does works meritorious of everlasting life; but as Augustine says, in the same book, for this it is necessary that the will of man should be prepared with grace by God."[94]

St. Thomas speaks of habitual or sanctifying grace as that grace whereby the human will is "prepared to operate rightly and to enjoy God,"[95] and certainly this habitual grace is required for man to do good. But how does man receive this habitual state of grace? Is this something that man can prepare himself for apart from the divine aid? St. Thomas denies this.

Now in order that man prepare himself to receive this gift, it is not necessary to presuppose any further habitual gift in the soul, otherwise we should go on to infinity. But we must presuppose a gratuitous gift of God, Who moves the soul inwardly or inspires the good wish.... Now to prepare oneself for grace is, as it were, to be turned to God; just as, whoever has his eyes turned away from the light of the sun, prepares himself to receive the sun's light, by turning his eyes towards the sun. Hence it is clear that man cannot prepare himself to receive the light of grace except by the gratuitous help of God moving him inwardly.[96]

In this way, man is bid to turn himself to God, since he participates in God's motion within him and wills that he turn toward God. But this is not possible apart from God working within him as an exterior principle. "It is the part of man to prepare his soul, since he does this by his free-will. And yet he does not do this without the help of God moving him, and

93. *ScG* III, 148, 3.
94. *ST* I-II, q. 109, a. 5, ad 1.
95. *ST* I-II, q. 109, a. 6.
96. *ST* I-II, q. 109, a. 6.

drawing him to Himself, as was said above."[97] To put it simply, "Man can do nothing unless moved by God, according to John 15:5: 'Without Me, you can do nothing.' Hence when a man is said to do what is in him to do, this is said to be in his power according as he is moved by God."[98]

While it is true that man requires grace in a special way to act well given his corrupted nature, it is not true to assert that, for St. Thomas, man only requires divine aid given his wounded state. Even to remain free from sin in original justice would have required divine aid and upholding from human defect.

I answer that, We may speak of man in two ways: first, in the state of perfect nature; secondly, in the state of corrupted nature. Now in the state of perfect nature, man, without habitual grace, could avoid sinning either mortally or venially; since to sin is nothing else than to stray from what is according to our nature—and in the state of perfect nature man could avoid this. *Nevertheless he could not have done it without God's help to uphold him in good*, since if this had been withdrawn, even his nature would have fallen back into nothingness.[99]

It is correct that man requires habitual grace to be preserved from his wounded state and to be perfected and elevated to his supernatural end; however, even within the state of natural integrity or within a state of habitual grace, man requires God to move him to each and every good act (although this divine aid, while absolutely necessary in these circumstances, would not be considered grace as such, since grace is that divine aid that perfects and elevates). This is to say nothing other than that man is not simply given a generic power or initiation to do good but must be reduced to act in every good that he wills, whether the act be natural or supernatural, whether the acting man be in a state of natural integrity or wounded by sin.

I answer that, As stated above, in order to live righteously a man needs a twofold help of God—first, a habitual gift whereby corrupted human nature is healed, and after being healed is lifted up so as to work deeds meritoriously of everlast-

---

97. *ST* I-II, q. 109, a. 6, ad 4.

98. *ST* I-II, q. 109, a. 6, ad 2.

99. *ST* I-II, q. 109, a. 8: "Respondeo dicendum quod de homine dupliciter loqui possumus, uno modo, secundum statum naturae integrae; alio modo, secundum statum naturae corruptae. Secundum statum quidem naturae integrae, etiam sine gratia habituali, poterat homo non peccare nec mortaliter nec venialiter, quia peccare nihil aliud est quam recedere ab eo quod est secundum naturam, quod vitare homo poterat in integritate naturae. *Non tamen hoc poterat sine auxilio Dei in bono conservantis*, quo subtracto, etiam ipsa natura in nihilum decideret." Emphasis is my own.

ing life, which exceed the capability of nature. Secondly, man needs the help of grace in order to be moved by God to act. Now with regard to the first kind of help, man does not need a further help of grace, e.g. a further infused habit. Yet he needs the help of grace in another way, i.e. in order to be moved by God to act righteously, and this for two reasons: first, for the general reason that no created thing can put forth any act, unless by virtue of the Divine motion.[100]

Finally, not only can man not prepare himself for habitual grace nor perfect himself once in the state of habitual grace without the divine aid, man cannot avoid sin without the divine aid either. "But in the state of corrupt nature man needs grace to heal his nature in order that he may entirely abstain from sin."[101] Once entering into habitual grace, man requires that God continue to uphold him in grace so that he does not fall into sin. "And hence after anyone has been justified by grace, he still needs to beseech God for the aforesaid gift of perseverance, that he may be kept from evil till the end of his life. For to many grace is given to whom perseverance in grace is not given."[102]

Sin

We move now to the mystery of iniquity and sin. It is clear that men fall into sin, and this happens inevitably without the grace to resist sin.

Consequently, the opinion of the Pelagians is evidently stupid, for they said that man in the state of sin is able to avoid sin, without grace. The contrary to this is apparent from the petition in the Psalm (70:9): "When my strength shall fail, do not forsake me." And the Lord teaches us to pray: "And lead us not into temptation, but deliver us from evil.[103]

However, if man is incapable of resisting sin without the grace of God, why is that some men fall into sin and others do not? This is an especially pressing question since, as we have already seen, divine aid is given gratuitously, not as something merited by man but as something given with complete divine liberality.

And just as He does not enlighten all the blind, or heal all who are infirm, in order that the working of His power may be evident in the case of those whom He heals,

100. *ST* I-II, q. 109, a. 9.
101. *ST* I-II, q. 109, a. 8.
102. *ST* I-II, q. 109, a. 10.
103. *ScG* III, 160, 4.

and in the case of the others the order of nature may be observed, so also, He does not assist with His help all who impede grace, so that they may be turned away from evil and toward the good, but only some, in whom He desires His mercy to appear, so that the order of justice may be manifested in the other cases.[104]

One may ask why God moves some but not others. To this St. Thomas replies:

However, while God does indeed, in regard to men who are held back by the same sins, come to the assistance of and convert some, while He suffers others or permits them to go ahead in accord with the order of things—there is no reason to ask why He converts the former and not the latter. For this depends on His will alone; just as it resulted from His simple will that, while all things were made from nothing, some were made of higher degree than others; and also, just as it depends on the simple will of the artisan that, from the same material uniformly disposed, he forms some vessels for noble uses and others for ignoble purposes. Hence, the Apostle says, in Romans (9:21): "Or does not the potter have power over the clay, of the same lump to make one vessel unto honor and another unto dishonor?"[105]

Notice the difference in language between those moved by God to the good and those who are not moved toward the good. It is not that God converts some and moves some to sin. It is said that he converts some and permits (*permittat*) others to fall away. In this way, St. Thomas speaks of man as placing an impediment to grace. Man, a voluntary creature even in his contingency on divine aid, sometimes freely chooses some evil. The contingency of the free choice of evil is due to man's freedom in regard to particular goods. Therefore, we say that man is free because he chooses freely. The contingency of the given effect is rooted in the nature of the proximate cause, not in its relation to God.[106] This is why St. Thomas posits that man may be held accountable for his evil.

104. *ScG* III, 161, 1.
105. *ScG* III, 161, 2.
106. Thomas M. Osborne Jr., "Thomist Premotion and Contemporary Philosophy of Religion," *Nova et Vetera*, English ed., 4, no. 3 (2006): 607–32, 630: "An event is contingent with respect to its proximate cause. Disputes over whether events are in themselves necessary or contingent are consequently disputes that are either over that necessity that results from a creature's nature or that necessity that results from an effect's necessarily following upon its proximate cause. If contingency is required for free choice, then human choices cannot be determined by some proximate cause. The question of whether God predetermines is irrelevant to such a dispute." Osborne states, "Thomas answers that whatever event follows from the divine will has that necessity or contingency that God wills it to have [*ST* I, q. 19, a. 8, ad 3]. Although everything that happens may be necessary when considered

To settle this difficulty, we ought to consider that, although one may neither merit in advance nor call forth divine grace by a movement of his free choice, he is able to prevent himself from receiving this grace: Indeed, it is said in Job (21:34): "Who have said to God: Depart from us, we desire not the knowledge of Your ways"; and in Job (24:13): "They have been rebellious to the light." And since this ability to impede or not to impede the reception of divine grace is within the scope of free choice, not undeservedly is responsibility for the fault imputed to him who offers an impediment to the reception of grace. In fact, as far as He is concerned, God is ready to give grace to all; "indeed He wills all men to be saved, and to come to the knowledge of the truth," as is said in 1 Timothy (2:4). But those alone are deprived of grace who offer an obstacle within themselves to grace; just as, while the sun is shining on the world, the man who keeps his eyes closed is held responsible for his fault, if as a result some evil follows, even though he could not see unless he were provided in advance with light from the sun.[107]

Does this negate the necessity of divine aid in order to resist temptation and sin? No, for without grace man can do no good, including the avoidance of evil. And yet, when man is not upheld in divine aid, he still freely chooses or intends the evil that he wills. In the composite sense, it is not possible for man to will contrary to how God simply wills him to will. Similarly, in the composite sense, it is not possible for man to not sin when he is not upheld by God, but in neither case does this negate a free motion of his will—which wills either the good or the evil act—as retaining the potency in the divided or absolute sense to have done otherwise. In short, the sinful movement remains entirely volitional and free, and thus man is culpable for his sin. "Besides, although he who is in sin does not have, of his own power, the ability entirely to avoid sin, he has it in his power at present to avoid this or that sin, as we said. Hence, whatever one he does commit, he does so voluntarily. And so, not undeservedly, he is held responsible for his fault."[108]

Does this not then make God accountable for man's sin? St. Thomas asserts that God *can* prevent even the would-be sinner's impediment to

in conjunction with God's will, not everything is necessary absolutely.... Even though contingent natural events and free actions have this secundum quid necessity, they are not necessary in an absolute sense. Contingent effects are contingent because they have contingent proximate causes. Such contingency is not just logical but founded in the proximate cause and effect. Ultimately, this contingency has its source in God's will to produce the effect contingently through secondary causes" (617–618).

107. *ScG* III, 159, 2.
108. *ScG* III, 160, 6.

grace. "At times, out of the abundance of His goodness, He offers His help in advance, even to those who put an impediment in the way of grace, turning them away from evil and toward the good."[109] How, therefore, can it be said that God is no way the cause of sin? For St. Thomas, it is important that we recognize that God merely permits that man act, of his own volition, in a sinful way. He does not in any way move man to sin as such, and therefore he cannot be called the cause of sin in any proper way. St. Thomas states, "Although God does not convert certain sinners to Himself, but leaves them in their sins according to their merits, He does not lead them into sinful action."[110]

It is not God who is the cause of sin, but man, insofar as he places an impediment to divine grace and divine grace is subsequently sometimes withheld. In this sense, St. Thomas speaks of a defect in the proximate or secondary agent. It is not God, the primary agent, who errs, but man, who presents an impediment (which God permits) to a divine motion.

Moreover, every sin stems from a defect in the proximate agent, and not from the influence of the primary agent: as the defect of limping results from the condition of the leg bone and not from the motor power, for, in fact, whatever perfection of motion is apparent in the act of limping, it is due to this power. But the proximate agent of human sin is the will. Therefore, the defect of sin comes from the will of man and not from God Who is the primary agent; from Him, however, comes whatever pertains to perfection of action in the sinful act.[111]

What exactly is this defect? St. Thomas speaks of the defect as a negation, not yet an evil action in and of itself, but one which precedes the evil act, bringing it about when man does go to act. It is a nonconsideration of reason in regard to the natural law or a nonconsideration of the law of God. It is the absence of a proper vision that results in the forsaking of a higher good for a lower one. This negation will then of course result in an evil deed when it is applied to action, as a carpenter who does not measure correctly or who decides not to measure at all will indeed make a bad cut.

And the will as a deficient good causes evil because prior to the very choice that is deficient—the choice wherein the will chooses something good in some re-

109. *ScG* III, 161, 1.
110. *ScG* III, 162, 1.
111. *ScG* III, 162, 1.

spect that is in an absolute sense evil—there is necessarily a deficient consideration. And so this is clear. For in all things of which one ought to be the rule and
measure of another, good results in what is regulated and measured from the fact
that it is regulated and conformed to the rule and measure, while evil results from
the fact that it is not ruled or measured. Therefore, suppose there is a carpenter
who ought to cut a piece of wood straight by using a ruler; if he does not cut
straight, which is to make a bad cut, the bad cutting will be due to his failure to
use the ruler or measuring bar. Likewise, pleasure and everything else in human
affairs should be measured and regulated by the rule of reason and God's law.
And so the nonuse of the rule of reason and God's law is presupposed in the will
before the will made its disordered choice.[112]

This deficiency or defect is not itself an evil for which the created will is
culpable, but it is the cause of the fact of evil in the evil act.[113] This defect
is something necessarily caused in the created will, but is simply a result
of its fallible nature. It can either consider or not consider the rule. "And
there is no need to seek a cause of this nonuse of the aforementioned
rule, since the very freedom of the will, by which it can act or not act, is
enough to explain the nonuse."[114]

Of course, this does not negate the fact that these defects do not escape divine providence. It is not as if God's will, which is radically simple,
is frustrated, nor is it that the divine will moves man indifferently, such
that it gives to man a motion that may go one way or the other. The impediment is caused by man, resulting in his culpability for the subsequent
sin. The impediment is permitted by God, however, which is clear according to certain biblical passages. St. Thomas points this out by stating:

However, some passages are found in Scripture, from which it seems that God is
the cause of sinning for certain men. Indeed, it is said in Exodus (10:1): "I have
hardened Pharaoh's heart, and the heart of his servants"; and in Isaiah (6:10):

---

112. *De malo*, q. 1, a. 3.

113. *De malo*, q. 1, a. 3: "And absolutely considered, not actually attending to such a rule is itself not
evil, neither moral nor punishment, since the soul is not held, nor is it able, always actually to attend
to such a rule. But not attending to the rule first takes on the aspect of evil because the soul proceeds
to make a moral choice without considering the rule. Just so, the carpenter errs because he proceeds
to cut the piece of wood without using the measuring bar, not because he does not always use the bar.
And likewise, the moral fault of the will consists in the fact that the will proceeds to choose without
using the rule of reason or God's law, not simply in the fact that the will does not actually attend to
the rule. And it is for this reason that Augustine says in the *City of God* [XII, 7] that the will causes
sin insofar as the will is deficient, but he compares that deficiency to silence or darkness, since the
deficiency is just a negation."

114. *De malo*, q. 1, a. 3.

"Blind the heart of this people, and make their ears heavy ... lest they see with their eyes ... and be converted, and I heal them"; and in Isaiah (63:17): "You made us err from Your ways; You have hardened our heart, lest we fear You." Again, in Romans (1:28) it is said: "God delivered them up to a reprobate sense, to do those things which are not convenient." All these texts are to be understood in this way: God does not grant to some people His help in avoiding sin, while to others He does grant it.... So, when He takes away these aids from some, according to the merit of their action, as His justice demands, He is said to harden or to blind them, or to do any of the other things mentioned.[115]

St. Thomas further elucidates how it is the case that God cannot be called the cause of sin. In no way does he cause man to sin, either directly or indirectly.[116]

Now God cannot be directly the cause of sin, either in Himself or in another, since every sin is a departure from the order which is to God as the end: whereas God inclines and turns all things to Himself as to their last end, as Dionysius states (*Div. Nom.* i): so that it is impossible that He should be either to Himself or to another the cause of departing from the order which is to Himself. Therefore, He cannot be directly the cause of sin. In like manner neither can He cause sin indirectly. For it happens that God does not give some the assistance, whereby they may avoid sin, which assistance were He to give, they would not sin. But He does all this according to the order of His wisdom and justice, since He Himself is Wisdom and Justice: so that if someone sin it is not imputable to Him as though He were the cause of that sin; even as a pilot is not said to cause the wrecking of the ship, through not steering the ship, unless he cease to steer while able and bound to steer. It is therefore evident that God is nowise a cause of sin.[117]

It must be stated, however, that insofar as man acts while sinning, and insofar as man requires a divine movement in order to act at all, God is said, according to St. Thomas, to be the cause of the act of sin, but not of its sinfulness.[118]

115. *ScG* III, 162, 7–8.
116. Michal Paluch, *La Prondeur de L'Amour Divin: Évolution de la doctrine de la prédestination dans l'oeuvre de saint Thomas d'Aquin* (Paris: Librairie Philosophique J. Vrin, 2004), 31–32: "God is not the cause, either directly or indirectly, of sin. He only decides *not* to prevent the defect of the creature in this particular situation. And it should be emphasized that God is not obliged to aid it because it is not due this good" ("Dieu n'est cause ni directe ni indirecte du péché, il décide uniquement de *ne pas* empêcher la défaillance de la créature dans une situation concréte. Et il faut souligner que Dieu n'est pas obligé de 'aider parce qu'il ne s'agit pas ici d'un bien dû"). All translations of Paluch are mine.
117. *ST* I-II, q. 79, a. 1. See also *De malo*, q. III, a. 1.
118. See Thomas M. Osborne Jr., "How Sin Escapes Premotion: The Development of Thomas Aquinas' Thought by Spanish Thomists," in *Thomism and Predestination: Principles and Disputations,*

I answer that, The act of sin is both a being and an act; and in both respects it is from God. Because every being, whatever the mode of its being, must be derived from the First Being, as Dionysius declares (*Div. Nom.* v). Again every action is caused by something existing in act, since nothing produces an action save in so far as it is in act; and every being in act is reduced to the First Act, viz. God, as to its cause, Who is act by His Essence. Therefore, God is the cause of every action, in so far as it is an action. But sin denotes a being and an action with a defect: and this defect is from the created cause, viz. the free-will, as falling away from the order of the First Agent, viz. God. Consequently this defect is not reduced to God as its cause, but to the free-will: even as the defect of limping is reduced to a crooked leg as its cause, but not to the motive power, which nevertheless causes whatever there is of movement in the limping. Accordingly God is the cause of the act of sin: and yet He is not the cause of sin, because He does not cause the act to have a defect.[119]

The sinful act becomes sinful not in its being an act, but in its being an act with a defect. God is said to cause the action, but not the defect that renders the action to be sinful, in the same way that a limp does not come from the power of movement but from the defective limb. In this way, we do not speak of the power of movement as the cause of the limp but rather the limb. The defect arises within the proximate agent, who is man.

---

ed. Steven A. Long, Roger W. Nutt, and Thomas Joseph White, OP (Ave Maria, Fla.: Sapientia Press, 2016), 192–213. See also Davies, *Reality of God and the Problem of Evil*, 177–78: "When it comes to evil suffered, therefore, we are dealing with what, though no illusion, does not, in a serious sense, exist. The evil in evil suffered is not an existent *entity*. It is no identifiable *substance* or *positive quality*. Evil suffered occurs as existing things fail to be as good as they could be. In that case, however, I imme-diately conclude that evil in evil suffered cannot be caused by God. For God, as I have argued, is the cause of the being of all that is real apart from himself, and the evil in evil suffered is not something with being, not something actual, and, therefore, not something created by him. It cannot be thought of as a creature that God creates. Considered as amounting to the gap between what is there and what should be but is not, it is neither createable nor created. Considered as such, it cannot be attributed to God as an agent-cause, whose causality primarily extends to making things to be. There are holes in walls, but holes have no independent existence. There are holes in walls only because there are walls with something missing. There are blind people. But blindness has no independent existence. There are blind people only because there are people who cannot see. In a similar way, evil suffered has no independent existence." Continuing, 184: "I have already argued that God is what makes everything to be. So I seem to be committed to the conclusion that when Fred goes in for evil done God is the cause of all that is real in Fred. And this is a conclusion which I do, indeed, accept. I do not, however, think that this conclusion commits me to the view that evil done is God's doing. In Aquinas' language, what it commits me to is the view that God causes the 'act of sin' but does not cause sin itself. . . . A slinky, grey cat prowling around a flower bed is God's doing since God is present to it as making it to be as it prowls around. Yet the evil in evil done cannot, in this sense, be God's doing."

119. *ST* I-II, q. 79, a. 2. See also *De malo*, q. 3, a. 2: "Augustine says in his work *On the Trinity* that the will of God causes every species and movement. But acts of sin are indeed movements of free choice. Therefore, the acts come from God."

Thus God makes it possible for man to act, but man sometimes places an impediment to the divine motion (which God permits, as we have already seen, otherwise man would not place the impediment) that further specifies the power to act given by God as sinful. In this way St. Thomas says that man, and not God, is the cause of sin, though God is said to be the cause of the act of sin.

Not only the act, but also the defect, is reduced to man as its cause, which defect consists in man not being subject to Whom he ought to be, although he does not intend this principally. Wherefore man is the cause of the sin: while God is the cause of the act, in such a way, that nowise is He the cause of the defect accompanying the act, so that He is not the cause of the sin.[120]

The cause of sin, then, is man, since the power imparted to him by the divine aid only becomes corrupted in him insofar as he is the secondary cause of the act and the one who introduces the defect that renders that act to be sinful.

But if something is not properly disposed or fit to receive the causal movement of the first mover, imperfect action results. And then we trace what belongs to the activity in it to the first mover as the cause. And we do not trace what is in it regarding deficiency to the first mover as the cause, since such deficiency in the activity results because the secondary cause defects from the ordination of the first mover, as I have said.[121]

Now, it must be stated that often the permission of the impediment that man places to divine aid is the result of man's previous sins. In this way, there is a manner of speaking in which we might say that God causes spiritual blindness or hardness of heart insofar as he allows these impediments to persist in a man due to his previous failings. The permitted defects act as a punishment.

I answer that, Spiritual blindness and hardness of heart imply two things. One is the movement of the human mind in cleaving to evil, and turning away from the Divine light; and as regards this, God is not the cause of spiritual blindness and hardness of heart, just as He is not the cause of sin. The other thing is the withdrawal of grace, the result of which is that the mind is not enlightened by God to see aright, and man's heart is not softened to live aright; and as regards this God is the cause of spiritual blindness and hardness of heart.[122]

120. ST I-II, q. 79, a. 2, ad 2.
121. De malo, q. 3, a. 2.
122. ST I-II, q. 79, a. 3.

This does, not, however, mean that God causes the sins which follow from this state of spiritual blindness. God permits that men remain in this state as a form of just penalty for previous sins. In this way, we may speak of God withholding grace as punishment. "Blindness and hardheartedness, as regards the withholding of grace, are punishments, and therefore, in this respect, they make man no worse. It is because he is already worsened by sin that he incurs them, even as other punishments."[123] Of course, original sin cannot be the result of previous sin, and yet it could never arise without God's permission. However, this permission must not be confused for an active cause.

An adult may give to a child a bit of money, telling him to drop by the local candy store. If the child uses the money to buy cigarettes, we do not say that the adult is the cause of the child's misbehavior, even if the adult somehow knew that the boy was planning on buying cigarettes. It is the will of the boy that misdirects the money toward an evil end, that is, the procuring of cigarettes as a minor. The adult does not wish that the boy should lie or smoke, nor does he encourage the boy to do so in any way.

The adult may allow such a deed to happen, however, that a greater good will result. Perhaps the boy will be caught and the gravity of his action will be made clear to him. However, it is true that unless there were some greater good that may come from allowing the boy to misbehave, the adult would not allow him to make his mistake.

In a similar manner, there may be said to be a twofold reason for God's withdrawal of grace as punishment. In the elect, it serves as a form of punishment that will lead to humility and conversion, whereas in the reprobate it acts as a form of justice.

I answer that, Blindness is a kind of preamble to sin. Now sin has a twofold relation—to one thing directly, viz. to the sinner's damnation—to another, by reason of God's mercy or providence, viz. that the sinner may be healed, in so far as God permits some to fall into sin, that by acknowledging their sin, they may be humbled and converted, as Augustine states (*De Nat. et Grat.* xxii). Therefore, blindness, of its very nature, is directed to the damnation of those who are blinded; for which reason it is accounted an effect of reprobation. But, through God's mercy, temporary blindness is directed medicinally to the spiritual welfare of those who are blinded. This mercy, however, is not vouchsafed to all those who are blinded, but only to the predestinated, to whom "all things work together

---

123. *ST* I-II, q. 79, a. 3, ad 1.

unto good" (Rm. 8:28). Therefore, as regards some, blindness is directed to their healing; but as regards others, to their damnation; as Augustine says (*De Quaest. Evang.* iii).[124]

Furthermore, "That God directs the blindness of some to their spiritual welfare, is due to His mercy; but that the blindness of others is directed to their loss is due to His justice."[125]

The good that results from this permission of sin is clear in the predestined. It serves to wake men up to the evil of their sin, to humble them in their pride and arrogance, acting as a tool to direct them back to love of God.

The good that results from the permission of sin in the reprobate is not as easily traced. Ultimately, it exists to bring about some good to others, even if it provides no good for the one who sins, as St. Thomas says. "Every evil that God does, or permits to be done, is directed to some good; yet not always to the good of those in whom the evil is, but sometimes to the good of others, or of the whole universe: thus He directs the sin of tyrants to the good of the martyrs, and the punishment of the lost to the glory of His justice."[126] The permission of evil itself, both generally and in each individual reprobate, is for the greater good of the entire created order.[127] With this, we move now to the mystery of predestination and reprobation.

Predestination

For St. Thomas, predestination, election, and reprobation "constitute a certain part of divine providence."[128] Men are ordered according to God's providence,[129] some to achieve their ultimate end of beatitude and friend-

---

124. *ST* I-II, q. 79, a. 4.

125. *ST* I-II, q. 79, a. 4, ad 3.

126. *ST* I-II, q. 79, a. 4, ad 1.

127. As we shall see later, it is fitting for God to bring good out of evil, but it is certainly not necessary as a means. God is not dependent on creation in any way to manifest his goodness or to create that which is good. Evil, therefore, is not necessary, but it is permitted by God as a fitting way to make known his goodness to creatures.

128. *ScG* III, 163, 2.

129. *ST* I, q. 23, a. 1: "I answer that, It is fitting that God should predestine men. For all things are subject to His providence, as was shown above. Now it belongs to providence to direct things towards their end, as was also said. The end towards which created things are directed by God is twofold; one which exceeds all proportion and faculty of created nature; and this end is life eternal, that consists

ship with God. These are called the elect. Some other men are not given the grace to achieve their ultimate end. These are called the reprobate.

So, since we have shown that some men are directed by divine working to their ultimate end as aided by grace, while others who are deprived of the same help of grace fall short of their ultimate end, and since all things that are done by God are foreseen and ordered from eternity by His wisdom, as we showed above, the aforementioned differentiation of men must be ordered by God from eternity. According, then, as He has preordained some men from eternity, so that they are directed to their ultimate end, He is said to have predestined them. Hence, the Apostle says, in Ephesians (1:5): "Who predestinated us unto the adoption of children ... according to the purpose of His will." On the other hand, those to whom He has decided from eternity not to give His grace He is said to have reprobated or to have hated, in accord with what we find in Malachi (1:2–3): "I have loved Jacob, but have hated Esau." By reason of this distinction, according to which He has reprobated some and predestined others, we take note of divine election, which is mentioned in Ephesians (1:4): "He chose us in Him, before the foundation of the world."[130]

St. Thomas treats first of the predestined, or the elect. Because predestination is a "certain part" (*quaedam pars*) of providence, St. Thomas asserts that it is not to be understood as anything active in the predestined themselves since providence exists as a form of government in the mind of the governor. The governor is the active agent in the execution of government. Since God is the divine governor of all things, he is the active agent of all providence. Man shares in this providential ordering but only as a passive participant.

I answer that, Predestination is not anything in the predestined; but only in the person who predestines. We have said above that predestination is a part of providence. Now providence is not anything in the things provided for; but

---

in seeing God which is above the nature of every creature, as shown above. The other end, however, is proportionate to created nature, to which end created being can attain according to the power of its nature. Now if a thing cannot attain to something by the power of its nature, it must be directed thereto by another; thus, an arrow is directed by the archer towards a mark. Hence, properly speaking, a rational creature, capable of eternal life, is led towards it, directed, as it were, by God. The reason of that direction pre-exists in God; as in Him is the type of the order of all things towards an end, which we proved above to be providence. Now the type in the mind of the doer of something to be done, is a kind of pre-existence in him of the thing to be done. Hence the type of the aforesaid direction of a rational creature towards the end of life eternal is called predestination. For to destine, is to direct or send. Thus it is clear that predestination, as regards its objects, is a part of providence."

130. *ScG* III, 163, 1.

is a type in the mind of the provider, as was proved above. But the execution of providence which is called government, is in a passive way in the thing governed, and in an active way in the governor. Whence it is clear that predestination is a kind of type of the ordering of some persons towards eternal salvation, existing in the divine mind. The execution, however, of this order is in a passive way in the predestined, but actively in God.[131]

The predestination of the elect is then God's active ordering of men to the attainment of their ultimate end, which is beatitude. "According, then, as He has preordained some men from eternity, so that they are directed to their ultimate end, He is said to have predestined them."[132] God orders some men to this end because of his love for them. And his love precedes predestination.

I answer that, Predestination presupposes election in the order of reason; and election presupposes love. The reason of this is that predestination, as stated above, is a part of providence. Now providence, as also prudence, is the plan existing in the intellect directing the ordering of some things towards an end; as was proved above. But nothing is directed towards an end unless the will for that end already exists. Whence the predestination of some to eternal salvation pre-supposes, in the order of reason, that God wills their salvation; and to this belong both election and love: — love, inasmuch as He wills them this particular good of eternal salvation; since to love is to wish well to anyone, as stated above: — election, inasmuch as He wills this good to some in preference to others; since He reprobates some, as stated above.[133]

This is the opposite of how men love, for men love the good that is already in a thing. However, when God loves men in predestining them, it is his love that causes in them the good that they have. Rather than the love being elicited by some good that already exists (which is how man's love is elicited), in God this love is precisely what accounts for something being made good by God's divine aid.

Election and love, however, are differently ordered in God, and in ourselves: be-cause in us the will in loving does not cause good, but we are incited to love by the good which already exists; and therefore we choose someone to love, and so election in us precedes love. In God, however, it is the reverse. For His will, by which in loving He wishes good to someone, is the cause of that good possessed

131. *ST* I, q. 23, a. 2.
132. *ScG* III, 163, 1.
133. *ST* I, q. 23, a. 4.

by some in preference to others. Thus it is clear that love precedes election in the order of reason, and election precedes predestination. Whence all the predestinate are objects of election and love.[134]

St. Thomas teaches that predestination is the cause of whatever good is in man. Thus it is not man's good actions or God's foresight into how men will act that accounts for whether they are numbered among the elect because it is predestination and election that bring about the good, especially final perseverance and beatitude. Simply, predestination is the cause of the good in the elect, not the effect of that good.

Moreover, that predestination and election do not find their cause in any human merits can be made clear, not only from the fact that God's grace which is the effect of predestination is not preceded by merits but rather precedes all human merits, as we showed, but it can also be shown from this, that the divine will and providence is the first cause of things that are done, but that there can be no cause of the divine will and providence, although, among the effects of providence.[135]

Similarly, St. Thomas states, "Therefore, divine help is not given to us by virtue of the fact that we initially move ourselves toward it by good works; instead, we make such progress by good works because we are preceded by divine help."[136] There are many reasons given for this. St. Thomas states that the human will is a particular agent dependent on the first universal agent of God and thus cannot precede it.[137] Man cannot merit the gift of predestination, a gift that brings man to his ultimate end of beatitude, because that end transcends and surpasses what man is capable of by his nature.[138] Also, knowledge comes before the movement of the will, and man cannot stretch out toward his ultimate end without

134. *ST* I, q. 23, a. 4.
135. *ScG* III, 163, 3.
136. *ScG* III, 149, 1.
137. *ScG* III, 149, 3: "Besides, no particular agent can universally precede the action of the first universal agent, because the action of a particular agent takes its origin from the universal agent, just as in things here below, all motion is preceded by celestial motion. But the human soul is subordinated to God as a particular agent under a universal one. So, it is impossible for there to be any right movement in it which divine action does not precede. Hence, the Lord says, in John (15:5): 'without Me you can do nothing.'"
138. *ScG* III, 149, 4: "Moreover, compensation is in proportion to merit, because in the repaying of compensation the equality of justice is practiced. Now, the influence of divine help which surpasses the capacity of nature is not proportionate to the acts that man performs by his natural ability. Therefore, man cannot merit the aforesaid help by acts of that kind."

knowledge of it, but this knowledge can only come to man as revealed by God and accepted in faith. However, the acceptance of revelation presupposes God's gift of revelation and the divine aid of grace.[139]

And, of course, St. Thomas states that man is simply an instrumental agent. He cannot act for his own perfection in any order whatsoever unless he acts under the power of the principal agent, which is God. As such, it is impossible that man could merit predestination by procuring for himself some goodness divorced from divine aid. As a secondary cause of his own movement toward the good, man can only act toward the good in participation with God's movement within him.

Again, an instrumental agent is not disposed to be brought to perfection by the principal agent, unless it acts by the power of the principal agent. Thus, the heat of fire no more prepares matter for the form of flesh than for any other form, except in so far as the heat acts through the power of the soul. But our soul acts under God, as an instrumental agent under a principal agent. So, the soul cannot prepare itself to receive the influence of divine help except in so far as it acts from divine power. Therefore, it is preceded by divine help toward good action, rather than preceding the divine help and meriting it, as it were, or preparing itself for it.[140]

In the *Summa Theologiae*, St. Thomas condemns three various errors regarding the cause of predestination being the foreseen merits of the predestined. 1) Some held that predestination was the effect of preexisting merits in a former life, an opinion that St. Thomas attributes to Origen. St. Thomas states that this cannot be the cause because men do nothing before they are called into existence by the Lord.[141] 2) Some held that predestination is an effect of good merits in this life, where some men prepare themselves well for grace and are thus rewarded with that grace.

---

139. *ScG* III, 149, 5: "Furthermore, knowledge precedes the movement of the will. But the knowledge of the supernatural end comes to man from God, since man could not attain it by natural reason because it exceeds his natural capacity. So, divine help must precede the movements of our will toward the ultimate end."

140. *ScG* III, 149, 2.

141. *ST* I, q. 23, a. 5: "Accordingly there were some who held that the effect of predestination was pre-ordained for some on account of pre-existing merits in a former life. This was the opinion of Origen, who thought that the souls of men were created in the beginning, and according to the diversity of their works different states were assigned to them in this world when united with the body. The Apostle, however, rebuts this opinion where he says (Rm. 9:11,12): 'For when they were not yet born, nor had done any good or evil ... not of works, but of Him that calleth, it was said of her: The elder shall serve the younger.'"

St. Thomas attributes this view to the Pelagians. He condemns this by quoting St. Paul, who says that "we are not sufficient to think anything of ourselves as of ourselves" (2 Cor 3:5).[142] 3) Finally, St. Thomas mentions those who believe that God grants predestination on account of a fore-knowledge of how men will respond to grace. Those who are foreseen as responding well will be given grace, and those who are foreseen as not re-sponding well will have the gift of predestination withheld. But St. Thom-as states that this is a confusion between that which comes from free will and that which comes from predestination. For St. Thomas there is no competition between these two realities. Predestination causes the will to act in accord with God. As such, there is no separation between how the will acts and the fact of predestination. It is not possible to divorce that a will acts in accord with God and that it be predestined precisely because predestination is the cause of the good acts of anyone numbered among the predestined.

And so others said that merits following the effect of predestination are the rea-son of predestination; giving us to understand that God gives grace to a person, and pre-ordains that He will give it, because He knows beforehand that He will make good use of that grace, as if a king were to give a horse to a soldier because he knows he will make good use of it. But these seem to have drawn a distinction between that which flows from grace, and that which flows from free will, as if the same thing cannot come from both. It is, however, manifest that what is of grace is the effect of predestination; and this cannot be considered as the reason of predestination, since it is contained in the notion of predestination. Therefore, if anything else in us be the reason of predestination, it will outside the effect of predestination. Now there is no distinction between what flows from free will, and what is of predestination; as there is not distinction between what flows from a secondary cause and from a first cause. For the providence of God produces effects through the operation of secondary causes, as was above shown (q. 22, a. 3). Wherefore, that which flows from free-will is also of predestination. We must say, therefore, that the effect of predestination may be considered in a twofold

142. *ST* I, q. 23, a. 5: "Others said that pre-existing merits in this life are the reason and cause of the effect of predestination. For the Pelagians taught that the beginning of doing well came from us; and the consummation from God: so that it came about that the effect of predestination was granted to one, and not to another, because the one made a beginning by preparing, whereas the other did not. But against this we have the saying of the Apostle (2 Cor. 3:5), that 'we are not sufficient to think anything of ourselves as of ourselves.' Now no principle of action can be imagined previous to the act of thinking. Wherefore it cannot be said that anything begun in us can be the reason of the effect of predestination."

light—in one way, in particular; and thus there is no reason why one effect of predestination should not be the reason or cause of another; a subsequent effect being the reason of a previous effect, as its final cause; and the previous effect being the reason of the subsequent as its meritorious cause, which is reduced to the disposition of the matter. Thus we might say that God pre-ordained to give glory on account of merit, and that He pre-ordained to give grace to merit glory.[143]

St. Thomas states unequivocally that there is nothing in man that is the cause of his choosing this or that man to be numbered among the elect.

In another way, the effect of predestination may be considered in general. Thus, it is impossible that the whole of the effect of predestination in general should have any cause as coming from us; because whatsoever is in man disposing him towards salvation, is all included under the effect of predestination; even the preparation for grace. For neither does this happen otherwise than by divine help, according to the prophet Jeremiah (Lam 5:21): "convert us, O Lord, to Thee, and we shall be converted." Yet predestination has in this way, in regard to its effect, the goodness of God for its reason; towards which the whole effect of predestination is directed as to an end; and from which it proceeds, as from its first moving principle.[144]

It is not man that is the cause of predestination but God. St. Thomas asserts that predestination has no cause other than the divine will. "I answer that, Since predestination includes will, as was said above, the reason of predestination must be sought for in the same way as was the reason of the will of God. Now it was shown above, that we cannot assign any cause of the divine will on the part of the act of willing."[145] The reason for predestination is unknown to us because it does not rest in us, but in the hidden inner mystery of the divine will. It is known only to God for it is his will, not our actions, that determines the predestined, otherwise God, the source of all good, would be passive to our own best actions.

It should be stated here that there is a distinction to be made between grace and glory. Grace is the effect of predestination, which man in no way merits. Grace is, in turn, the cause of good acts and holiness in men. This is, subsequently, said to be the cause of glory, and in this way, we may say that man merits glory but does not in any way merit the grace that moves him to merit in the first place. "Now, we must distinguish two

143. *ST* I, q. 23, a. 5.
144. *ST* I, q. 23, a. 5.
145. *ST* I, q. 23, a. 5.

aspects of predestination, the eternal predestination itself and its twofold temporal effect, grace and glory. Glory has human acts as its meritorious cause, but grace cannot have human acts as its meritorious cause."[146]

The question naturally arises as to why God chooses some men to be numbered among the elect and not others, but since there is no cause of predestination to be found in men, men cannot know why God chooses this one rather than another one, just as man cannot know the divine will. "Yet why He chooses some for glory, and reprobates others, has no reason, except the divine will. Whence Augustine says (Tract. xxvi in Joan.): 'Why He draws one, and another He draws not, seek not to judge, if thou dost not wish to err.'"[147]

Finally, St. Thomas asserts that predestination is certain given that divine providence is certain. In other words, predestination is infallible; it is not subject to change in any way. That which God wills is done. "I answer that, Predestination most certainly and infallibly takes effect."[148] St. Thomas is sure to point out that this does not remove the contingency of the good effects that flow from predestination, as was shown above.

I answer that, Predestination most certainly and infallibly takes effect; yet it does not impose any necessity, so that, namely, its effect should take place from necessity. For it was said above, that predestination is a part of providence. But not all things subject to providence are necessary; some things happening from contingency, according to the nature of the proximate causes, which divine providence has ordained for such effects. Yet the order of providence is infallible, as was shown above. So also the order of predestination is certain; yet free-will is not destroyed; whence the effect of predestination has its contingency. Moreover all that has been said about the divine knowledge and will must also be taken into consideration; since they do not destroy contingency in things, although they themselves are most certain and infallible.[149]

The infallibility of predestination rests in the fact that God has so willed it. This does not in any way remove the possibility that he could have willed otherwise, nor does it remove the real potency that the predestined have to reject final perseverance and the attainment of their ultimate end. In the composite or suppositional sense, predestination will

146. *De veritate*, q. 6, a. 2.
147. *ST* I, q. 23, a. 5, ad 3.
148. *ST* I, q. 23, a. 6.
149. *ST* I, q. 23, a. 6.

infallibly bring about the effect of beatitude because it has been so willed by the immutable God. However, in the divided or absolute sense, predestination places no necessity on the created will nor does it mean that God could not have chosen differently for any individual.

Since predestination includes the divine will as stated above (Article [4]): and the fact that God wills any created thing is necessary on the supposition that He so wills, on account of the immutability of the divine will, but is not necessary absolutely; so the same must be said of predestination. Wherefore one ought not to say that God is able not to predestinate one whom He has predestinated, taking it in a composite sense, thought, absolutely speaking, God can predestinate or not. But in this way the certainty of predestination is not destroyed.[150]

It follows then that "the number of the predestined is certain"[151] as well. St. Thomas is clear to assert that this is true not just formally (as if it is certain that some number of men, say 3.5 billion, will be saved) but also materially (that this or that individual will be saved).[152] This follows not from some knowledge of God, as if it is certain based on something that is foreseen in humanity. The knowledge of the predestined is known to God according to the decree of his divine will, which is the cause of predestination, not the effect of something foreseen. He knows that which he does, and he knows it because he does it.

It must, however, be observed that the number of the predestined is said to be certain to God, not by reason of His knowledge, because, that is to say, He knows how many will be saved (for in this way the number of drops of rain and the sands of the sea are certain to God); but by reason of His deliberate choice and determination.[153]

Reprobation

Just as predestination is a part of divine providence, so is reprobation. Reprobation is a permission of defect and sin that subsequently results in

150. *ST* I, q. 23, a. 6, ad 6.

151. *ST* I, q. 23, a. 7.

152. *ST* I, q. 23, a. 7: "I answer that, The number of the predestined is certain. Some have said that it was formally, but not materially certain; as if we were to say that it was certain that a hundred or a thousand would be saved; not however these or those individuals. But this destroys the certainty of predestination; of which we spoke above. Therefore we must say that to God the number of the predestined is certain, not only formally, but also materially."

153. *ST* I, q. 23, a. 7.

damnation as punishment for freely turning away from God and remaining obstinate to him even up to death. It is the allowance that some men not attain their ultimate end. The distinct difference between the providence of predestination and the providence of reprobation is to be found in the different ways in which they are willed by God. Predestination is willed positively as a good that God intends for the one who is predestined. Reprobation, on the other hand, is not an evil that is intended but one that is merely permitted. If it were not permitted it would not happen, and thus it is said to be part of the providential ordering of all things. However, the permissive will is certainly distinct from the active willing of a good. And this is precisely how St. Thomas defines reprobation.

I answer that, God does reprobate some. For it was said above that predestination is a part of providence. To providence, however, it belongs to permit certain defects in those things which are subject to providence, as was said above. Thus, as men are ordained to eternal life through the providence of God, it likewise is part of that providence to permit some to fall away from that end; this is called reprobation.[154]

As with predestination, this does not mean simply that God foresees that some men will not respond well to grace and thus he withholds it. St. Thomas asserts that reprobation implies something more or something further than that ("aliquid addit secundum rationem").

Thus, as predestination is a part of providence, in regard to those ordained to eternal salvation, so reprobation is a part of providence in regard to those who turn aside from that end. Hence reprobation implies not only foreknowledge, but also something more, as does providence, as was said above. Therefore, as predestination includes the will to confer grace and glory; so also reprobation includes the will to permit a person to fall into sin, and to impose the punishment of damnation on account of that sin.[155]

This something is not to be considered as the same kind of movement that is seen in predestination. God positively ordains the elect to beatitude. St. Thomas does not assert that the reprobate is ordained to sin and damnation, but that their sin is permitted. This requires a certain congruence or compatibility with the divine will, otherwise it would not happen, but the divine will does not will it positively or simply. Instead

154. *ST* I, q. 23, a. 3.
155. *ST* I, q. 23, a. 3.

it merely allows that reprobation take place. This distinction is a crucial one. "However, reprobation is said to belong to God's foreknowledge for this reason, that there is nothing positive on the part of His will that has any relation to sin. He does not will sin as He wills grace."[156]

Reprobation is, of course, still included under providence and as such is infallible and certain, but it in no way imposes necessity upon those who are said to be reprobated due to man's continued contingency under divine providence, as we have addressed above.

Reprobation also does not make God responsible for the sinful actions and final impenitence that follow from reprobation precisely for the reason that God does not actually cause reprobation in any way. The cause of reprobation is the failed or defective proximate cause, which, as we have already stated, is not caused by God but merely permitted.

Reprobation differs in its causality from predestination. This latter is the cause both of what is expected in the future life by the predestined—namely, glory—and of what is received in this life—namely, grace. Reprobation, however, is not the cause of what is in the present—namely, sin; but it is the cause of abandonment by God. It is the cause, however, of what is assigned in the future—namely, eternal punishment. But guilt proceeds from the free-will of the person who is reprobated and deserted by grace. In this way, the word of the prophet is true—namely, "Destruction is thy own, O Israel."[157]

St. Thomas clarifies a statement by St. Augustine ("God inclines men's wills to good and evil,") in order to further elucidate this important distinction. In regards to the good, God moves man directly and positively, but in regard to evil, God's will only permits, that is, it may only be said to act negatively. Rather than a positive movement of the will, with the sinner God merely abstains from a positive movement. As such, it is a nonact.

As to the words of the Apostle, the solution is clear from the text. For if God delivered some up to a reprobate sense, it follows that they already had a reprobate sense, so as to do what was not right. Accordingly, He is said to deliver them up to a reprobate sense, in so far as He does not hinder them from following that reprobate sense, even as we are said to expose a person to danger if we do not protect him. The saying of Augustine (*De Grat. et Lib. Arb.* xxi, whence the gloss quoted is taken) to the effect that "God inclines men's wills to good and evil," is

---

156. *De veritate*, q. 6, a. 1, answers to contrary difficulties.
157. *ST* I, q. 23, a. 3, ad 2.

to be understood as meaning that *He inclines the will directly to good*; and *to evil, in so far as He does not hinder it,* as stated above.[158]

Again, this does not place any absolute necessity upon the reprobate. It cannot be stated that it is absolutely impossible for him to obtain the grace of final perseverance and the gift of eternal life. However, insofar as reprobation is included under providence, it is certain that the reprobate will *freely choose* to impede God's grace and will be justly punished. It is necessary only suppositionally, in the composite sense, and this in no way takes away the liberty of the reprobate.

Reprobation by God does not take anything away from the power of the person reprobated. Hence, when it is said that the reprobated cannot obtain grace, this must not be understood as implying absolute impossibility: but only conditional impossibility: as was said above, that the predestined must necessarily be saved; yet a conditional necessity, which does not do away with the liberty of choice. Whence, although anyone reprobated by God cannot acquire grace, nevertheless that he falls into this or that particular sin comes from the use of his free-will. Hence it is rightly imputed to him as guilt.[159]

St. Thomas answers the objection of human culpability for permitted sin and damnation. The objection states:

Further, movement is attributed to the mover rather than to the one moved; wherefore homicide is not ascribed to the stone, but to the thrower. Therefore, if God moves the will, it follows that voluntary actions are not imputed to man for reward or blame. But this is false. Therefore God does not move the will.[160]

He responds with the following: "If the will were so moved by another as in no way to be moved from within itself, the act of the will would not be imputed for reward or blame. But since its being moved by another does not prevent its being moved from within itself, as we have stated (ad 2), it does not thereby forfeit the motive for merit or demerit."[161]

Objection

We have already seen that St. Thomas condemns the idea that man may speculate about why one man is predestined and another one is reprobat-

---

158. *ST* I-II, q. 79, a. 1, ad 1.
159. *ST* I, q. 23, a. 3, ad 3.
160. *ST* I, q. 105, a. 4, arg. 3.
161. *ST* I, q. 105, a. 4, ad 3.

ed, but this leaves the question as to why anyone should be reprobated at all. How is such a permission of reprobation just, and why is it allowed?

To the first question it must be stated that God loves all men and he wishes them all more good than they are due. But eternal life is not due to man since it is something above his nature; it is something to which he has no natural claim. As we have already seen, predestination to glory is a gratuitous gift, one that can be given or withheld freely without any injustice on behalf of the one giving.[162] As St. Thomas states, "God loves all men and all creatures, inasmuch as He wishes them all some good; but He does not wish every good to them all."[163] Insofar as predestination is a gift that is not due to man, God is not required to give it, just as a man is not required to give equal gifts of charity to those that he meets on the street. If the rich man wishes to freely give $100 to one man that he meets randomly on the street and $1,000 to another (so long as the money is not owed in any way but is entirely a gift), the rich man cannot be called out as unjust[164] but only generous to varying degrees. This is precisely

162. Paluch, *La Prondeur de L'Amour Divine*, 210: "We see, therefore, that Thomas's thoughts are led by a profound conviction, that God is perfectly merciful in all His works, and He gives to the creature all that is necessary in order that it may be saved. It is impossible that God not be sufficiently merciful. Such an accusation is unthinkable according to the metaphysical plan. Mercy is the source of the divine work. However, the doctrine of reprobation poses a point for all reflection on the cause of predestination. God does not owe grace to anyone" ("Nous voyons donc que Thomas est conduit dans sa pensée par une conviction profonde, selon laquelle Dieu est parfaitement miséricordieux en toutes ses ouevres et donne à la créature tout ce qui lui est nécessaire pour le salut: il est impossible que Dieu ne soit pas suffisamment miséricordieux. Une telle accusation est impensable au plan métaphysique: la miséricorde est la source de l'oeuvre divine. Toutefois, la doctrine sur la réprobation pose une borne pour toute réflexion sur la cause de la prédestination: Dieu n'est redevable de la grâce envers personne.").

163. *ST* I, q. 23, a. 3, ad 1.

164. Paluch, *La Prondeur de L'Amour Divine*, 257: "Distributive justice concerns only those situations where there is something due. We cannot speak of distributive justice when it comes to things that are given spontaneously or according to mercy. If someone gives alms to one of the poor that one comes across or if one who is hurt does not pardon someone who has hurt them, that one is merciful in regard to the first situation and is just in regard to the second. He is unjust to no one. All human beings are born after the sin of the first parents in a state which merits condemnation. Therefore, if God liberates someone, it is done by grace and by mercy. If He does not liberate, it is done according to justice. He is, however, unjust to no one" ("La justice distributive concerne uniquement les situations où il y a chose due. On ne peut pas parler de justice distributive lorsqu'il s'agit de choses données spontanément et par miséricorde. Si quelqu'un donne l'aumône à un des pauvres recontrés ou bien si un offensé ne pardonne qu'à un de ceux qui l'ont offensé, il est miséricordieux à l'égard de l'un d'entre eux et juste à legard de l'autre; il n'est pourtant injuste envers personne. Tous les hommes naissent aprés le péché des premiers parents dans un état qui mérite condamnation. Dés lors, si Dieu libére quelqu'un, il le fait par grâce et par miséricorde; s'il ne le libère pas, il le fait par justice: il n'est pourtant injuste envers personne").

what we see in the parable of the workers in the vineyard in the Gospel of Matthew. God already gives more than is due to all individuals, and thus is not a debtor to any man.[165]

Neither on this account can there be said to be injustice in God, if He prepares unequal lots for not unequal things. This would be altogether contrary to the notion of justice, if the effect of predestination were granted as a debt, and not gratuitously. In things which are given gratuitously, a person can give more or less, just as he pleases (provided he deprives nobody of his due), without any infringement of justice. This is what the master of the house said: "Take what is thine, and go thy way. Is it not lawful for me to do what I will?" (Mt 20:14, 15).[166]

Accordingly, St. Thomas asserts that God does not will or wish the loss of any man when considering that man antecedently, or in regard to the man himself, but he does permit that some men, defectible creatures not due to be always upheld, shall fall. "God does not take pleasure in the loss of man, as regards the loss itself, but by reason of His justice, or of the good that ensues from the loss."[167]

As to the second question, for what reason does God give out unequal lots? St. Thomas's answer is simply that it is fitting for God's goodness to be made manifest in his creation in a multitude of ways. In predestination, God shows forth his mercy; in reprobation God shows forth his justice. Of course, God need not do these things in order to be merciful or to be just. God does not depend in any way on creation, but it is fitting that he should show forth both sides, as it were, of his divinity. Creation will be a better mirror of the Creator.

All of creation is hierarchical, with some things holding a higher pride of place than others, and it is for the good of the universe as a whole that

---

165. *De veritate*, q. 6, a. 2, ad 8: "It would be contrary to the nature of distributive justice if things that were due to persons and were to be distributed to them were given out unequally to those that had equal rights. But things given out of liberality do not come under any form of justice. I may freely choose to give them to one person and not to another. Now, grace belongs to this class of things. Consequently, it is not contrary to the nature of distributive justice if God intends to give grace to one person and not to another, and does not consider their unequal merits." Also, *De veritate*, q. 6, a. 2, ad 9: "The election by which God chooses one man and reprobates another is reasonable. There is no reason why merit must be the reason for His choice, however, since the reason for this is the divine goodness. As Augustine says, moreover, a justifying reason for reprobation [in the present] is the fact of original sin in man—for reprobation in the future, the fact that mere existence gives man no claim to grace. For I can reasonably deny something to a person if it is not due to him."

166. *ST* I, q. 23, a. 5, ad 3.

167. *ST* I-II, q. 79, a. 4, ad 2.

it is ordered in this way. In this hierarchy, there is a great multiplicity and variety that gives glory to the one so fecund as to bring forth such a diversity and assortment of being. As with the stone bridge, not all bricks may be the capstone, but all bricks work together for the good of the whole, be they the lowliest supporting bricks or the most decorated and visible ones. Similarly, St. Thomas states:

The reason for the predestination of some, and reprobation of others, must be sought for in the goodness of God. Thus He is said to have made all things through His goodness, so that the divine goodness might be represented in things. Now it is necessary that God's goodness, which in itself is one and undivided, should be manifested in many ways in His creation; because creatures in themselves cannot attain to the simplicity of God. Thus it is that for the completion of the universe there are required different grades of being; some of which hold a high and some a low place in the universe. That this multiformity of grades may be preserved in things, God allows some evils, lest many good things should never happen, as was said above (Question [22], Article [2]). Let us then consider the whole of the human race, as we consider the whole universe. God wills to manifest His goodness in men; in respect to those whom He predestines, by means of His mercy, as sparing them; and in respect of others, whom he reprobates, by means of His justice, in punishing them. This is the reason why God elects some and rejects others. To this the Apostle refers, saying (Rm 9:22, 23): "What if God, willing to show His wrath [that is, the vengeance of His justice], and to make His power known, endured [that is, permitted] with much patience vessels of wrath, fitted for destruction; that He might show the riches of His glory on the vessels of mercy, which He hath prepared unto glory" and (2 Tm 2:20): "But in a great house there are not only vessels of gold and silver; but also of wood and of earth; and some, indeed, unto honor, but some unto dishonor." Yet why He chooses some for glory, and reprobates others, has no reason, except the divine will. Whence Augustine says (Tract. xxvi. in Joan.): "Why He draws one, and another He draws not, seek not to judge, if thou dost not wish to err." Thus too, in the things of nature, a reason can be assigned, since primary matter is altogether uniform, why one part of it was fashioned by God from the beginning under the form of fire, another under the form of earth, that there might be a diversity of species in things of nature. Yet why this particular part of matter is under this particular form, and that under another, depends upon the simple will of God; as from the simple will of the artificer it depends that this stone is in part of the wall, and that in another; although the plan requires that some stones should be in this place, and some in that place.[168]

168. *ST* I, q. 23, a. 5, ad 3.

To put it simply, that God predestines some and permits that some fall into defect and sin is for the sake of the common good of the created order. While it may be possible that God could save all, the divine will in fact willed things to exist otherwise. From the reality of reprobation, God brings forth a greater good.[169] As such, reprobation is not said to work toward the individual good of the reprobate but toward the common good instead.[170]

Every evil that God does, or permits to be done, is directed to some good; yet not always to the good of those in whom the evil is, but sometimes to the good of others, or of the whole universe: thus He directs the sin of tyrants to the good of the martyrs, and the punishment of the lost to the glory of His justice.[171]

Finally, it cannot be stated that this reality of predestination and reprobation means that God in no way loves all men and wishes for their greatest good, that is, the attainment of glory and beatitude. On the contrary, St. Thomas states, "God wills all men to be saved by His antecedent will, which is to will not simply but relatively; and not by His consequent will, which is to will simply."[172] In speaking of possible interpretations of 1 Tm 2:4 (as well as 2 Pt 3:9), St. Thomas puts forth as one possibility the view of St. John Damascene that God wills some men to be saved according to his antecedent will and some according to his consequent will, which implies not a mutability in the divine will but rather in the objects of that will. "Thirdly, according to Damascene (De Fide Orth. ii, 29), they are understood of the antecedent will of God; not of the consequent will. This distinction must not be taken as applying to the divine will itself, in which there is nothing antecedent nor consequent, but to the things willed."[173]

This distinction should be understood as referencing a different scope of the divine will and not as something antecedent or consequent in God. To every man, considered in and of himself, God wishes all pos-

---

169. Not as a means, but merely as an occasion. God does not require reprobation to manifest this greater good.

170. Of course, as we have already seen, this does not mean that God wishes no good to the reprobate. Indeed, he wills much more good to the reprobate than he is due.

171. *ST* I-II, q. 79, a. 4, ad 1.

172. *ST* I, q. 23, a. 4, ad 3. See also *De veritate*, q. 23, a. 2, especially ad 8: "Antecedent and consequent are not affirmed of God's will for the purpose of implying any succession (for that is repugnant to eternity), but to denote a diversity in its reference to the things willed."

173. *ST* I, q. 19, a. 6, ad 1.

sible goods precisely because God loves every man more than could be imagined. That necessarily results in his wishing to give to every man all possible goods. But each man (and everything within the created order) does not exist in a vacuum; he exists in relation to all other things within the created order. Consequently, God does not will things to each individual man as if he were all that existed. Instead, he wills things to men as they are, as parts of the whole of creation, acting upon and in relation to one another.[174] Due to this wider scope, the true order of things, God wills only some goods to each man. As such, we say that God wills that all men be saved antecedently but not consequently, for, as we have seen above, God wills that some perish for the greater good of the whole.

To understand this we must consider that everything, in so far as it is good, is willed by God. A thing taken in its primary sense, and absolutely considered, may be good or evil, and yet when some additional circumstances are taken into account, by a consequent consideration may be changed into the contrary. Thus that a man should live is good; and that a man should be killed is evil, absolutely considered. But if in a particular case we add that a man is a murderer or dangerous to society, to kill him is a good; that he live is an evil. Hence it may be said of a just judge, that antecedently he wills all men to live; but consequently wills the murderer to be hanged. In the same way God antecedently wills all men to be saved, but consequently wills some to be damned, as His justice exacts. Nor do we will simply, what we will antecedently, but rather we will it in a qualified manner; for the will is directed to things as they are in themselves, and in themselves they exist under particular qualifications. Hence we will a thing simply inasmuch as we will it when all particular circumstances are considered; and this is what is meant by willing consequently. Thus it may be said that a just judge wills simply the hanging of a murderer, but in a qualified manner he would will him to live, to wit, inasmuch as he is a man.[175]

However, we must be careful to point out that this is not part of God's will simply or absolutely, otherwise it would happen that all men are indeed saved. Instead, when speaking of the antecedent will, St. Thomas uses *velleitas*, a volitional movement that lacks that the willer move to act. It might be considered a sort of a wish or desire, something that is willed in the sense of marking an inclination in the willer, but not one strong

---

174. See Charles De Koninck, "The Primacy of the Common Good against the Personalists," in *The Writings of Charles De Koninck, Volume Two*, ed. and trans. by Ralph McInerny (Notre Dame, Ind.: University of Notre Dame Press, 2009), 74–108.

175. *ST* I, q. 19, a. 6, ad 1.

enough to produce that which is willed. In one sense, it is a movement of the will, since it is volitional, but in another sense, it is not a proper act of willing because it does not attempt to produce that which is willed. "Such a qualified will may be called a willingness rather than an absolute will. Thus it is clear that whatever God simply wills takes place; although what He wills antecedently may not take place."[176]

Thus concludes the overview of St. Thomas's mature views on the divine movement of the human will, sin, providence, predestination, and reprobation. This structure, of course, provides the basis for the varying Thomistic considerations of grace, premotion, predestination, and the permission of evil that arose in the twentieth century. We shall now be able to test each treatment against its source and exemplar.

176. *ST* I, q. 19, a. 6, ad 1.

CHAPTER THREE

Domingo Báñez

Domingo Báñez was one of the most influential Spanish Dominican theologians of the Thomistic commentatorial tradition. Born in 1528 in Old Castile, Báñez began studying philosophy at the University of Salamanca at just fifteen years old. He took the Dominican habit and professed vows in 1547. He blossomed into a gifted theologian under the tutelage of such eminent theologians as Melchior Cano. Báñez had a prolific teaching career, instructing at Salamanca, the Dominican University of Ávila, the University of Alcalá, and St. Gregory's Dominican College at Valladolid. Báñez's fellow Spaniards called him the *proeclarissimum jubar*, the "brightest light," due to his theological eminence. Báñez is also well-known for having been the spiritual director and confessor of St. Teresa of Ávila.

For the purpose of this work, however, Báñez is most important to us given his prominent role in the controversies surrounding the Congregatio de Auxiliis. In the contentious debate against Luis de Molina and the Society of Jesus, Báñez became synonomous with what would come to be seen as the classical Dominican position on these issues. In particular, he is associated with the Dominican theories of physical premotion, subordinated causality, the distinction between sufficient and efficacious grace, and predestination, which is *ante praevisa merita*. It became common for Jesuits to refer to these theories as characteristic of "Báñezianism," an epithet that certainly was utilized in order to distance these theories and those that held them from St. Thomas himself.[1] Even some closely asso-

---

1. For an example of this see Louis Rasolo, SJ, *Le dilemme du concours divin: Primat de l'essence ou*

ciated with the Dominican tradition held that this so-called Báñezianism was a corruption of the thought of the Angelic Doctor made by second scholasticism that ought to be purged, as we shall see in the cases of Francisco Márin-Sola and Jacques Maritain.

Of course, such an accusation would have certainly been rejected by Báñez himself, who is held to have said, "By not so much as a finger-nail's breadth, even in lesser things, have I departed from the teaching of St. Thomas" and "In and throughout all things, I determined to follow St. Thomas as he followed the Fathers."[2]

Insofar as Báñez and subsequent Báñezianism have played a vital role in the intra-Thomistic debate over the issues dealt with in this work, it is expedient for us to briefly consider Báñez's thought in relation to St. Thomas.[3] In no way will this be an extensive or comprehensive look at the thought of Domingo Báñez, whose voluminous work on these issues could itself be the subject of at least one, and plausibly of many other, works. We seek here simply to present the very basic outline of the thought of Báñez so as to better comprehend his relevance within the

---

primat de l'existence? Analecta Gregoriana, vol. 80 (Rome: Pontifical Gregorian University, 1956), or Bernard Lonergan, *Collected Works of Bernard Lonergan*, vol. 1, *Grace and Freedom: Operative Grace in the Thought of St Thomas Aquinas*, ed. Frederick E. Crowe and Robert M. Doran (Toronto: University of Toronto Press, 2013).

2. John Volz, "Domingo Báñez," in *The Catholic Encyclopedia*, vol. 2 (New York: Robert Appleton Company, 1907): "It has been contended that Báñez was at least virtually the founder of present-day Thomism, especially in so far as it includes the theories of physical premotion, the intrinsic efficacy of grace, and predestination irrespective of foreseen merit. To any reader of Báñez it is evident that he would have met such a declaration with a strenuous denial. Fidelity to St. Thomas was his strongest characteristic. 'By not so much as a finger-nail's breadth, even in lesser things,' he was wont to say, 'have I ever departed from the teaching of St. Thomas.' He singles out for special animadversion the views in which his professors and associates dissent even lightly from the opinions of the Angelic Doctor. 'In and throughout all things, I determined to follow St. Thomas, as he followed the Fathers,' was another of his favourite assurances."

3. It should be noted here that our concern is a speculative congruity between St. Thomas and Báñez. What is often missed about "Thomism," if we may use such a term, is that it is not merely a static reproduction of the words of St. Thomas and nothing more. If "Thomism" is anything it is a school of thought, rooted in the thought of St. Thomas and his metaphysical, philosophical, and theological *principles*. Such principles are set out by the Master and then further unpacked, developed, and applied to new questions, not unlike the Magisterium's ongoing contemplation of divine revelation. Serge-Thomas Bonino, OP, states in "Contemporary Thomism through the Prism of the Theology of Predestination," trans. Stefan Jetchick, eds. Barry David and Steven A. Long, *Thomism and Predestination: Principles and Disputations* (Ave Maria, Fla.: Sapientia Press, 2016), 38: " Far from being an atemporal system that came down from heaven, St. Thomas's Thomism is a 'work-in-progress theology,' a doctrine that evolves and whose internal balances are changing, as was shown for predestination by the seminal work of M. Paluch."

intra-Thomistic debate of the twentieth century and that of the general school of thought commonly attributed to him.

That All Things Require Divine Aid to
Be Moved from Potency to Act

As with St. Thomas, Báñez's treatment begins with the idea that all created beings exist in potency and can only ever be in act insofar as they are given this act by God. This is how the divine aid, *auxilium Dei*, ought to be understood. By creation and preservation, all created things that exist receive their being from God. And insofar as act follows from being, so too must created beings receive act from God. Báñez states that "as things depend in being upon first act, who is existence itself, so also will they depend upon first act for all their operations, because every thing that operates, operates insofar as it is in act."[4] The creature's need for the influx of act is answered by divine motion, which moves the creature from nonact to act. In this, Báñez attempts to assert only what St. Thomas has already said.

And the reason is because just as the being of God is the perpetual cause of the inflowing of being into the creature, it is necessary that whenever the creature passes from nonoperation into operation, or something moves or is moved, it follows that the influx of the divine motion would be prior in the order of causality. And this is confirmed by the doctrine of St. Thomas in q. 109, a. 6: "For since every agent acts for an end, every cause must direct its effect to its end, and hence since the order of ends is according to the order of agents or movers, man must be directed to the last end by the motion of the first mover."[5]

This divine motion in which the creature participates is also referred to simply as divine aid, because it is that help that is required by the crea-

---

4. Domingo Báñez, *Comentarios Inéditos a la Prima Secundae de Santo Tomás*, vol. 3, *De Gratia Dei*, qq. 109–144, ed. R. P. Mtro. Vicente Beltrán de Heredia, OP (Salamanca: Consejo Superior de Investigaciones Científicas, 1948), pars II, caput I, §1 (374–75): "Ac si diceret, sicut res dependet in esse a primo actu, qui est ipsum esse, ita etiam pendet in omni operatione sua, quia omne quod operatur, operatur inquantum est in actu." All translations of Báñez are my own unless indicated otherwise.

5. Báñez, *Comentarios Inéditos*, vol. 3, pars II, cap. I, §5 (378): "Et ratio est quia, sicut esse Dei est causa perpetuo influens esse in creaturis, ita necesse est ut quando creatura transit de non operante in operantem, vel quomodolibet alias movet aut movetur, ita influxus divinae motionis sit prior ordine causalitatis. Et confirmatur ex doctrinae divi Thomae q. 109, a. 6: 'Necesse est enim, cum omne agens agat propter finem, quod omnis causa convertat suos effectus ad suum finem; et ideo cum secundum ordinem agentium sive moventium, sit ordo finium, necesse est quod ad ultimum finem convertatur homo per motionem primi moventis.'"

ture to be or to do at all. "All creatures need, for their operation or motion, the aid of God, the first mover."[6]

Physical Premotion and the Movement of the Will

Since all creatures require this divine aid to be and to act, it follows that the creaturely will requires to be moved from potency to act whenever it wills.

First because all creatures, however much intellectual, have something potentially, but God alone is pure act; but all creatures have being as received and limited and are dependent on first being for their coming into existence and their being conserved, and accordingly in all of their operations: therefore, created free will owes its mode to having potentiality and passive indifference to its operation and free use.[7]

God, by the means of divine aid, moves the creaturely will to its very effects, actuating its potentiality such that it can be moved to real operation. "For when the motion of the heavens ceases, the motion of the inferior body ceases, as the Philosopher commonly held. Much more necessary is the influx of the primary cause, naturally moving causes and wills to their effects . . ."[8] And this is precisely what is meant by the term premotion, that God moves the creaturely will. Without such aid, it is not possible for it to will. "Therefore we hold that divine motion is so supereminent to all, however so perfect a corporeal or spiritual nature is, by the operative principle form it is not possible in its secondary act to proceed without actually being moved by God; this motion indeed is called premotion (*praemotio*)."[9]

6. Báñez, *Comentarios Inéditos*, vol. 3, pars II, cap. I, §2 (374): "idcirco [*ST* I-II q. 109 a. 1 c.] omnis creatura indiget ad suam operationem vel motum auxilio Dei primi moventis" (translation is R. J. Matava's).

7. Báñez, *Comentarios Inéditos*, vol. 3, pars I, cap. II, §6 (366): "Primo quia omnis creatura, quantumvis intellectualis, habet aliquid potentialitatis, cum solus Deus sit pursus actus; sed omnis creatura habet esse receptum et limitatum et dependens a primo esse in fieri et conservari, ac proinde in omni operatione sua: ergo et liberum arbitrium creatum suo modo debet habere potentialitatem et passivam indifferentiam ad suam operationem et usum libertatis."

8. Báñez, *Comentarios Inéditos*, vol. 3, pars II, cap. I, §1 (373–374): "Cessante enim motu caeli, motus inferiorum corporum cessarent, ut communis habet philosophia. Multo autem magis necessarius est influxus primae causae, movens et naturales causas et voluntarias ad suos effectus . . ."

9. Báñez, *Comentarios Inéditos*, vol. 3, quaest. CIX, art. 1, §2 (22): "Habemus igitur quod divina motion tam supereminems est omnibus, ut quantuncumque natura aliqua corporalis vel spiritualis ponatur perfecta, per principia formalia operativa non possit in suum actum secundum procedere nisi actualiter ipsa moveatur a Deo; quae quidem motio praemotio dicitur."

Now, it is important to demonstrate that, as with Thomas, Báñez is not positing a kind of occasionalism whereby it is only God who cooks the steak while the fire does not do so in any real way. It is important for Báñez that he posit that *auxilium* and *praemotio* are not properly understood as creating free acts because creation means that something is brought forth from nothing. On the contrary, the divine aid can only truly be an *auxilium* insofar as it acts upon something that is already in existence, and it gives to that being the power that *it may itself act*. As Báñez states, "Creation is truly a production from nothing; aid or help truly presupposes a thing already existing. We can therefore define aid to be the influence of an efficient cause ordered to some operation or motion of a pre-existing thing."[10] As such, that which God moves, this preexisting thing, is the secondary cause of whatever effect is produced by its being moved to move by God. Báñez states that "God produces the effect through the secondary cause."[11] Thus, the will of the creature is actuated by God in order to bring about the effect that God has moved it to cause.

However, this secondary causation is a true causation. It is true that it depends on a more remote and primary movement to act, but this movement, far from minimizing the real integrity of the created will to act as a cause, is actually that which imbues it with the power to be causal. Báñez says, "But contrary to these sentiments, they cry out that we destroy free will by that passive determination to God, as a truly efficient cause and movement from free will. We object, to the contrary, that they cast down free will itself, attributing it in the first place to the real and physical determination of itself, in which it continues to completion;"[12] Báñez asserts that creaturely free will is only properly executed when effected by

10. Báñez, *Comentarios Inéditos*, vol. 3, pars II, cap. 1, §2 (374): "Est enim creatio productio ex nihilo; auxilium vero seu adjutorium praesupponit rem jam existentem. Possumus itaque definire auxilium esse influentiam causae efficientis ad aliquam operationem vel motum rei praeexistentis ordinatam."

11. Báñez, *Comentarios Inéditos*, vol. 3, pars II, cap. I, §4 (377): "Hic tamen influxus immediate attingit causam et effectum, quoniam ut est a Deo non dependet a causa secunda, quamvis ipse effectus pendeat ab utraque. Et hac ratione dicitur Deus producere effectum mediante causa secunda, quia ipse facit effectum dependere ab illa in fieri, et aliquando in conservari, sicut in actionibus vitalibus contingit."

12. Báñez, *Comentarios Inéditos*, vol. 3, pars II, cap. I, §7 (382): "Sed contrarium sentientes clamant quod destruimus liberum arbitrium per istam passivam determinationem a Deo, ut a causa realiter efficiente et movente liberum arbitrium. Nos contra objicimus quod ipsi praecipitant liberum arbitrium, attribuentes ei principatum in determinatione reali et physica sui ipsius, in qua consistit consummatio consensus."

God. To state otherwise is to give too much to the will and, ironically, to divorce it from the source of first act. In so doing, this view does only disservice to the integrity of creaturely freedom.

This also negates God as the primary cause of the movement to act that we do have, which would reduce God merely to a moral cause of our action. Báñez cites just such an objection: "But this good use is not an actual effect from the causality of God's grace, but only a moral effect, that God at that time gives because He foreknows the free will will consent.... But truly they say that our will itself applies itself to accomplishment, and then after this God rushes in."[13] Báñez calls premotion *physical* because he wishes to argue against the reduction of God's causality in regard to crea-turely freedom, diminishing it from a true efficient cause to a more indirect moral cause. The term "physical" is therefore not meant as a theological novelty, but merely to guard against the idea that St. Thomas's divine mo-tion is simply a moral cause of our act, that is, that it entices or attracts the will but does not act directly upon it to move it simply and sweetly. As we saw in St. Thomas, "God is more especially the cause of every action than are the secondary agent causes."[14] But this could not be if God were merely the moral cause of our action. When a man requests that his wife pick up his favorite beer while she is at the market, he may be said in some way to cause that his wife buys the beer. But is he said to be the primary cause of her own standing in the checkout line? Is it not the man's wife who actually accomplishes the act, receiving no power from her husband but moving to the act of herself? It may be that she would not have bought the beer had the husband not exhorted her to do so, but it is, properly speaking, the wife who is mostly responsible for the act of the purchase of the beer. To put it in another way, she is the one doing the purchasing and it is by her power, and not the power of the husband, that the beer is purchased.

Or, to give another example, parents may influence the good act of their child by way of enticement. Parents often incentivize good action for their children. I may offer some reward to my son so that he is more inclined to whatever deed I wish from him. But when he does the good

13. Báñez, *Comentarios Inéditos*, vol. 3, pars II, cap. I, §7 (382): "ipse autem Deus sit dumtaxat moralis causa praebens quaedam auxilia supernaturalia, sufficientia quidem, si liberum arbitrium velit uti illis. Hic autem bonus usus non est effectus realis a causalitate gratiae Dei, sed dumtaxat moralis effectus, quatenus Deus eo tempore dedit quo praescivit liberum arbitrium fore consensurum.... At vero qui dicunt quod voluntas nostra se applicat ad opus, et statim etiam Deus influit."
14. *ScG* III, 67, §5.

deed, it is most properly attributed to him, not me, as he is the one who acts, and he is the cause of his own action. It is true that I exerted some influence, but I did not move him as an efficient cause to will his own good deed. Similarly, if God is not the one who moves us to act, activating our will, he is simply a moral cause, and in no way can it be the case that in such a scenario God is *more* the cause of an effect than the creature. God may request or entice or attract, but it is ultimately the human will that is primarily responsible that an act is accomplished. The final differentiation for whether the deed is done comes from the creature, not God. And yet this is contrary to the teaching of St. Thomas. As such, Báñez has added the label "physical" only to more explicitly bring out that which is already apparent in St. Thomas, that God gives a real motion to the will to move itself rather than just merely suggesting a motion or giving only an enticement to it.[15] It might be said that the use of the further specification of "physical" would be unnecessary were it not for later confusions of the theory of the Angelic Doctor, in particular those Báñez observed in Molina's insistence that God's acting on the will (apart from creating and preserving it in being) was merely moral or petitionary and truly real and causal.[16]

15. For a further consideration of how the term "physical premotion," though unused explicitly by St. Thomas, is still implicitly rooted in and affirmed by his texts, see Steven A. Long, "St. Thomas Aquinas, Divine Causality, and the Mystery of Predestination," in *Thomism and Predestination: Principles and Disputations*, ed. Steven A. Long, Roger W. Nutt, and Thomas Joseph White, OP (Ave Maria, Fla.: Sapientia Press, 2016), 51–76, especially 53–54: "Some scholars have denied that Thomas ever held a doctrine rightly characterized by the terms 'physical premotion.' (Here I think, in contemporary terms, of the observations of Brian Shanley, OP, recently approbated in a conspicuous footnote by John Wippel in an article titled 'Metaphysical Themes in De malo 1.') After all, the phrase 'physical premotion' as such was never used by St. Thomas Aquinas. This is often thought to settle the matter. Yet it is proper to distinguish the nature of a teaching from pedagogic terminology that may help in explaining it. For example, St. Thomas does not introduce the distinction between essence and existence with the phrase 'the real distinction of essence and existence,' a phrase which seems precisely as such to appear nowhere in his writing. Yet he does hold that essence and existence are real principles, principles of being, and he does hold them to be distinct in all creatures. And so we do not distort his meaning by using the phrase 'real distinction of essence and existence,' a phrase that is pedagogically helpful. Likewise, the term 'physical' in the phrase 'physical premotion' means 'real'; the 'pre' in 'premotion' refers to an ontological as distinct from temporal priority (as, e.g., the cause is prior to the effect even when they are simultaneous in time); and 'motion' refers to the actualization of potency. It is true that Thomas does not use the term 'physical premotion.' But in several distinct texts, especially in the middle and later part of his writing, St. Thomas does affirm that there is a real motion bestowed by God to every creature, a motion that is ontologically prior to any action whatsoever on the part of any creature, including volitional action: and this is what 'physical premotion' means. Those who reject the doctrine because Thomas does not use this precise formulation are exhibiting what one might call a semantic ipsissima verba-ism that obstructs their acknowledgment of Thomas's manifest and express teaching."

16. This can be seen throughout Molina's corpus. He often refers to the divine aid as acting upon

Báñez's consideration of this physical premotion can be understoond as being active in regard to the divine movement and passive in the creature's reception of that movement. God acts in the creaturely recipient in order for the recipient to himself act. In this sense, God is the active principle in physical premotion and man is passive. God acts and man receives so that he might be further determined to act himself as an agent. To put it simply, God of himself gives to man his own act whereby man might himself will and act by participation. Man does indeed act, but it requires that he first passively receive some participation in God's being, which is only self-subsistent in God.

But I confess myself not to understand what else that divine premotion would be, if passively considered, than the faculty of intellect itself, placed in complete act by the author of nature, who operates in all things according to the design of his providence. But if premotion is actively considered, according as it is in God, I understand it to be nothing else than the divine will, which is present in all things, effecting in them everything that they do, insofar as what they do has the notion of being and goodness.[17]

---

the created will in a way that makes it to be stimulated, stirred, or aroused (*excitatus*) but does not act as a real efficient cause. See, for example, *Concordia*, q. 14, a. 13, disp. 53, part 4: "Also, notice that, as we showed in Part I-II, question 10, no particular object is necessarily desired in this life, as regards the species of the act, with such a pervasive necessity that it cannot sometimes (even if rarely) be rejected through a negative volition because of some evil that is able to be conjoined to it. Therefore, despite the assistance in question, it was within the power of Paul, Magdalene, and the thief to will not to be converted—and this because of the great difficult involved in keeping themselves free from mortal sin throughout their entire lives, as they had to resolve to do in order for there to be genuine contrition, even if a mortal sin would very rarely or never occur in the face of assistance of such a quality and quantity. So it follows that even in these conversions the decree of the Council of Trent has a place (sess. 6, canon 4; Denzinger §1554), when it states that *a human being's faculty of choice, though moved and stirred by God toward justification through the assistance of His grace, is able to dissent if it so chooses*," Freddoso, 263 ("Illud etiam observa, ut Iᵃ IIᵃ q. X ostendimus, nullum objectum in particulari appeti in hac vita necessario quoad speciem actus necessitate omnimoda, ita uta ratione alicujus mali, quod habere potest adjunctum, non possit aliquando, licet raro, respui per nolitionem. Quare in potestate Pauli, Madgalenae, et latronis, nihil illo auxilio impediente, fuit nolle converti, ratione difficultatis quae erat in continendo se a lethalibus peccatis per totam vitam, ut ad veram contritionem statuere tenebatur: tametsi raro admodum, aut nunquam, cum tanto ac tali auxilio id eveniat. Quo fit ut etiam in his conversionibus locum habeat definitio illa concilii Trident. *qua statuit liberum hominis arbitrium a Deo per auxilia gratiae motum ad justificationem ac excitatum, posse dissentire si velit*"). Emphasis is mine.

17. Báñez, *Comentarios Inéditos*, vol. 3, pars II, cap. II, §2 (384): "Sed fateor me non intelligere quid aliud sit illa divina praemotio, si passive consideretur, quam ipsamet facultas intellectus posita in actu completo ab auctore naturae, qui operatur in omnibus secundum rationem suae providentiae. Si autem praemotio active consideretur, prout est in Deo, nihil aliud esse intelligo quam divinam voluntatem, quae in omnibus rebus intime adest, efficiens in illis omnia quae fiunt, prout habent rationem essendi et bonitatis" (translation is Matava's).

From this it follows that premotion must indeed be both predetermining and infallible. This is necessary insofar as the cause of premotion is, as we have just seen, the divine will itself, which is immutable, as was stated by St. Thomas.[18] Whatever God simply wills (something determinate) will certainly take place infallibly. "A certain and immutable decision of divine will or infallible predefinition of divine providence goes before our free operation; which decision or predefinition predefines every good free operation and indeed every operation inasmuch as it is good and is done with respect to the good."[19] The divine will is not subject to change based upon new information or new circumstances, as the human will is. Nor is the divine will frustratable when it simply wills a thing to be. God moves and wills all things simply and sweetly. He is the Lord of all, unmoved and unhindered by any part of creation. He is its master, and as such, he has complete power and control over it. As we have seen, it is possible to speak of an antecedent will (or *velleitas*) in God being "frustrated," but only insofar as this antecedent will is not actually willed simply, for if it were, then there could be no frustration. To state otherwise is to deny the divine omnipotence. God would no longer be Lord of all but only Lord of some things at some times.

Finally, this posits no necessity in the human will, however, because God moves the will to will contingently.[20] Báñez employs here the divided and composite senses (or the absolute and conditional senses, as they are sometimes called), which are used by St. Thomas.[21] Báñez rejects the opinion of those who "do not deny that it is impossible" (or, to clear the

18. *ST* I, q. 19, a. 7: "… the will would be changed, if one should begin to will what before he had not willed; or cease to will what he had willed before. This cannot happen, unless we presuppose change either in the knowledge or in the disposition of the substance of the willer…. Now it has already been shown that both the substance of God and His knowledge are entirely unchangeable. Therefore His will must be entirely unchangeable."

19. Báñez, *Sch. com. in ST I*, q. 19, a. 10 (255b B): "Antecedit operationem nostram liberam diuinae voluntatis certum et immutabile consilium, siue diuinae providentiae infallibilis praedefinitio, quae omnem bonam operationem liberam praedefiniuit, immo & omnem operationem, in quantum bona est & circa bonum exercitur" (translation is Matava's).

20. Osborne, "Thomist Premotion and Contemporary Philosophy of Religion," 619: "Báñez develops but does not depart from the way in which Thomas and Thomists understand contingency. Throughout his works, Thomas emphasizes that effects are contingent because they are not determined by their proximate causes, and, ultimately, because God has decide to produce them as contingent. Human actions are such undetermined effects. Even though present and past human actions cannot be changed, they are still contingent with respect to their proximate causes. The necessity of the past or present does not take away from the contingent nature of the effect."

21. See, for example, *ScG* I, 67, 10, and *ST* I, q. 19, a. 3.

double negation, those who do affirm) that freedom is impossible when it is subordinated to the immutable divine will.

For the understanding of the legitimate definition of free will, we suppose it to be necessary to treat of the division of the composite and divided sense, which some mock, when one treats of free operation. They do not deny that it is impossible for free will to consent and not consent for this would be to deny the first principle, namely to be and not to be, but because they think that freedom consists in the fact that, presupposing everything required for act comes from an extrinsic cause as from God pouring in and concurring, it would be the case that simultaneously the free will would not will to operate.... We confess such freedom to be in God only. In the rational creature, however, freedom is truly subordinated to the motion of the divine will and freedom. Far from freedom being destroyed, rather the will accepts the power for deliberating and doing freely that which God wills man to deliberate.[22]

Báñez is here arguing against those who hold that freedom is only possible given an indifference to the divine will and motion. They want man to be able to act precisely as divorced from God vis-à-vis the action, stating that man not being divided from God in regard to his own free action essentially erases the ability for him to act freely. But Báñez rejects this, stating that far from free will being destroyed when being moved by God as an extrinsic principle, it is actually this divine movement that activates the human free will, causing its freedom. Without the divine aid man would exist simply in a state of disassociation from Pure Act and would never achieve an actually free act because man would never receive from God what he needs in order to execute his power of willing. Insofar as man is a creature, and thus has being and act only from another, he can do nothing without this influx of *auxilium divinum*.

And yet, because man acts as the true secondary cause of the effects that he produces, his acts remain truly free even when he is moved to this

---

22. Báñez, *Comentarios Inéditos*, vol. 3, pars I, cap. I, §6 (358–59): "Nunc autem, ad legitimam diffinitionem liberi arbitrii intelligendam, supponimus necessariam esse illam divisionem de sensu composito et sensu diviso, quam aliqui irrident, quando de libera operatione agitur. Non quia negent impossibile esse liberum arbitrium simul consentire et non consentire, hoc enim esset negare primum principium, quodlibet est et non est, sed quia putant libertatem in hoc consistere, quod positis omnibus requisitis ad agendum provenientibus ab extrinseco, etiam ab ipso Deo influente et concurrente, stet simul liberum arbitrium non velle operari.... Nos vero tantam libertatem in solo Deo confitemur; in creatura vero rationali est libertas subordinata motioni divinae voluntatis et libertatis. Et tantum abest quod inde destruatur nostra libertas, ut poitus inde vim accipiat ad deliberandum et agendum libere id quod Deus vult hominem deliberare."

or that good act. He is a contingent being whose will is moved to particular goods contingently. As such he is free in the divided sense to do otherwise. He retains a real potency to act against the divine motion, even if we know that this will not happen given the divine movement. This is not an absolute necessity, however, but simply a suppositional one. Robert Joseph Matava in his work *Divine Causality and Human Free Choice: Domingo Báñez and the Controversy* de Auxiliis *Revisited* states:

The divine will does not impose necessity on the creaturely free will in the divided sense. Since freedom, on Báñez's account, only requires that the will be free in the divided sense, human actions determined by God remain free. Indeed, according to Báñez, everything is necessary with respect to the divine will. The contingency of contingent realities is not spoken of with respect to divine causality, but rather with respect to created causes, which are defectible in their operations.[23]

Grace

A distinction must be made between the natural and supernatural orders of divine aid and motion (though, of course, the latter builds off of the former).

And because our strongest purpose is to act by the aid of God as author of grace and of all supernatural order, a difference is noted between each order. First of all the order of grace presupposes the order of nature and its perfection. Wherefore the whole order of grace joined with the order of nature can be called the aid of God elevating and perfecting preexisting nature to the supernatural operation and extending to it to the supernatural end.[24]

---

23. R. J. Matava, *Divine Causality and Human Free Choice: Domingo Báñez, Physical Premotion and the Controversy* de Auxiliis *Revisited* (Leiden: Brill, 2016), 88. This is affirmed by St. Thomas in *ST* I-II, q. 10, resp. and ad 1: "I answer that, As Dionysius says (*Div. Nom.* iv) 'it belongs to Divine providence, not to destroy but to preserve the nature of things.' Wherefore it moves all things in accordance with their conditions, so that from necessary causes through the Divine motion, effects follow of necessity; but from contingent causes, effects follow contingently. Since, therefore, the will is an active principle, not determinate to one thing, but having an indifferent relation to many things, God so moves it, that He does not determine it of necessity to one thing, but its movement remains contingent and not necessary, except in those things to which it is moved naturally. Reply to Objection 1: The Divine will extends not only to the doing of something by the thing which He moves, but also to its being done in a way which is fitting to the nature of that thing. And therefore it would be more repugnant to the Divine motion, for the will to be moved of necessity, which is not fitting to its nature; than for it to be moved freely, which is becoming to its nature."

24. Báñez, *Comentarios Inéditos*, vol. 3, pars II, cap. I, §2 (374): "Et quia nostra potissima intention

This supernatural motion, the aid by which man is not only moved but elevated above his nature to supernatural virtue and holiness, is called grace. Of course, there are many important distinctions within grace that are made by Báñez, such as actual and habitual, prevenient, cooperative, and more. However, what is of most use to us here is the distinction between sufficient and efficacious grace as it plays a major role in the intra-Thomistic dispute that concerns us.

Báñez speaks of *sufficient grace*, which gives the power or potency for a certain salutary action, and *efficacious grace*, which actually gives the motion necessary for that act. Sufficient grace provides man with a real potency, whereas efficacious grace is, as it sounds, an efficacious movement of grace to actually accomplish the salutary act. Báñez defends the distinction according both to Scripture and also to the mind of the Angelic Doctor. He divides grace into sufficient and efficacious ("secunda gratia alia est sufficiens, alia efficax"),[25] stating that it is

found in Scripture and the holy fathers. For of sufficient grace it is said, "What more could I have done for it?" (Is 5:4), and "My grace is enough for thee" (2 Cor 12:9), and suchlike. And truly of efficacious grace it is said, "An attentive ear the Lord has given me; not mine to withstand him" (Is 50:5). And "[I will make my spirit penetrate you,] so that you will follow in the path of my law" (Ezek 36: 27).[26]

Báñez goes on to state that Cyril and Augustine approved of this distinction[27] and that this is echoed by St. Thomas in the *Summa Theologiae*.[28]

---

est agere auxiliis Dei ut auctoris gratiae et totius ordinis supernaturalis, notanda est differentia inter utrumque ordinem. In primis ordo gratiae praesupponit ordinem naturae et perficit ipsum. Quapropter totus ordo gratiae adjunctus ordini naturae potest dici auxilium Dei elevantis et perficientis naturam praeexistentem ad operationem supernaturalem et ad supernaturalem finem tendentem."

25. Báñez, *Comentarios Inéditos*, vol. 3, quaest. CXI, art. 3, §10 (214).

26. Báñez, *Comentarios Inéditos*, vol. 3, quaest. CXI, art. 3, §10 (215): "Secunda etiam divisio fundatur in scruptura et sanctis patribus. Nam de sufficiente dicitur Isaiae, 5 (v. 4): Quid ultra debui facere vineae meae et non feci?; et II Cor., 12 (v. 9): Sufficit tibi gratia mea; et alia hujusmodi. De efficaci vero dicitur Is., 50 (v. 5): Dominibus aperuit mihi aurem, et ego non contradico. Et Ezech., 36 (v. 27): Faciam ut in praeceptis meis ambuletis."

27. Báñez, *Comentarios Inéditos*, vol. 3, quaest. CXI, art. 3, §10 (215): "Approbant hanc distinctionem Cyrillus, lib. *De adoratione*, post medium, et Augustinus, lib. *De corrept. et gratia*, cap. 12, et lib. 1 *Ad Simplicianum*, q. 2, et lib. *Octogintatrium quaesti*. q. 68."

28. *ST* I-II, q. 109, a. 10, ad 3: "As Augustine says (*De Natura et Gratia* xliii) [*Cf. *De Correp. et Grat.* xii]: 'in the original state man received a gift whereby he could persevere, but to persevere was not given him. But now, by the grace of Christ, many receive both the gift of grace whereby they may persevere, and the further gift of persevering.'"

Here we see the distinction between the divine gift of grace whereby man is *able* to persevere (*perseverare posset*) and the grace whereby he may actually persevere (*perseveraret*). Báñez says of this section that St. Thomas "teaches habitual grace to be sufficient for perseverance, which also is efficacious for justification and eliciting contrition whenever it is directed by actual grace …"[29] In other words, grace may be sufficient for a certain act, but it is only efficacious insofar as it is moved or applied to act by another, actual grace.

Now, none of this is to say that there are two kinds of grace, one that merely gives a potency and another that gives the act. All graces are efficacious. God does not give inefficacious graces. However, as potencies reside only within things already in act, so do sufficient graces reside only within graces that are already efficacious for one thing. As Báñez asserts, "All the aid of the grace of God is efficacious for some effect, which is sent from the absolute pleasure of the divine will."[30] These efficacious graces then present the possibility of further salutary acts, just as penitence carries with it the potency for seeking out the sacrament of Confession. However, this further salutary act requires that the antecedent potency proximate to that act be actualized by divine motion—moved from potency to act—by a further efficacious grace, since potency is not act, and God is the primary and principle cause of the application of each and every power to act. A grace is said to be sufficient or efficacious, then, in regard to a certain salutary act and not in regard either to the grace itself (there are not two types of actual grace) or to how grace is received by man, as if man's good use of grace was what determined it to be either efficacious or sufficient. Matava states:

> To understand this point, it is necessary to first recognize that, in Báñez's view, all grace is 'efficacious' in the sense that all grace efficaciously brings about the effect God intends it to achieve. God's will, for Báñez, is not defectible and his causal influence is not determinable by creatures. Nevertheless, God does not always intend his *auxilium* to efficaciously result in a salutary act of free choice, so that not all grace is 'efficacious' for such an act. Grace that does not efficaciously issue

29. Báñez, *Comentarios Inéditos*, vol. 3, quaest. CXI, art. 3, §10 (215): "et divus Thomas supra, q. 109, a. 10 ad tertium, ubi docet etiam gratiam habitualem esse sufficientem ad perseverandum, quae etiam est efficax ad justificandum et ad eliciendam contritionem quando confertur per modum auxilii actualis."

30. Báñez, *Comentarios Inéditos*, vol. 3, pars II, cap. III, §6 (392): "Omne auxilium gratiae Dei est efficax alicujus effectus ad quem ex beneplacito divinae voluntatis absoluto mittitur."

in a salutary act of free choice is said to be by its very nature merely 'sufficient.' The important point here is that, according to Báñez, the efficacy of *auxilium* is not determined by the mode of human response to it (acceptance or rejection— as on Molina's view), but by the intrinsic quality of the *auxilium* itself. Báñez insists on this point in order to preserve the infallibility of divine governance. On Báñez's view, since God is not determined by creatures' actions, he infallibly determines them.[31]

Of course, according to the thought of Molina, man must make good use of the grace presented by God, otherwise man would not act well. This rejected the immutable nature of the divine will and thus the infallible nature of premotion and grace. It is primarily against this error that Báñez argues when speaking of the distinction between sufficient and efficacious grace in relation to the creature. Man requires to be moved to any and every salutary action by grace, which is stated explicitly by St. Thomas in numerous places, including the following:

Our soul acts under God, as an instrumental agent under a principal agent. So, the soul cannot prepare itself to receive the influence of divine help except in so far as it acts from divine power. Therefore, it is preceded by divine help toward good action, rather than preceding the divine help and meriting it, as it were, or preparing itself for it.[32]

I answer that, As stated above, in order to live righteously a man needs a twofold help of God—first, a habitual gift whereby corrupted human nature is healed, and after being healed is lifted up so as to work deeds meritoriously of everlasting life, which exceed the capability of nature. Secondly, man needs the help of grace in order to be moved by God to act.... No created thing can put forth any act, unless by virtue of the Divine motion.[33]

We are told to turn to God because we can do this, but not without divine help. We accordingly beg of Him (Lamentations 5:21): "Convert us, O Lord, to thee, and we shall be converted" ... for man can neither prepare nor will unless God brings this about in him, as has been said.[34]

---

31. Matava, *Divine Causality and Human Free Choice*, 47. This final line hits upon a point of Báñez's treatment that will be echoed by Garrigou four hundred years later: Either God determining or determined.

32. *ScG* III, 149, §2. See also *De veritate*, q. 24, a. 15.

33. *ST* I-II, q. 109, a. 9.

34. *De veritate*, q. 24, a. 15, ad 1 and ad 2.

Predestination

This leads to Báñez's treatment of predestination. It ought to be stated that much of the concern of Báñez's treatment of these issues stems from the long-standing tension between Dominican Thomism and Molinism. By comparison, concerns over creaturely freedom in the predestined are not as much at the forefront of the intra-Thomistic debate. As we shall see, the concern of Marín-Sola and Maritain lies not so much in rescuing creaturely freedom from predetermining, infallible motions toward the good, nor even of the infallible predestination to glory in the elect. Indeed, Maritain posits a predestination of at least some of the elect that mirrors Báñez in nearly every way. The concern lies rather with the dissymmetry between the line of good (premotion to meritorious acts/predestination) and evil (permission of evil acts/reprobation). Regarding predestination, it suits us simply to state that, for Báñez, as for St. Thomas, predestination is certain[35] and *ante praevisa merita*,[36] causing whatever good works in the elect that merit their glory rather than predestination being caused by them. Báñez states:

> It is an error against the Catholic faith to assert that the reason for predestination is in each particular predestined adult as chosen from the foreseeing of the use of their free will, and that predestination is dependent upon it, so that God predestines no one to eternal life by his absolute and efficacious will, but under the condition of the mutable good use of their free will.[37]

This suffices to show Báñez's view of man's motion toward salutary acts and, finally, predestination. However, what is most contentious (and the greatest object of ire for those within the Thomistic tradition who are concerned with "Báñezianism") is how these same premises apply to the permission of defect and the act of sin.

---

35. *ST* I, q. 23, a. 6.

36. *ST* I, q. 23, a. 5, ad 3: "Yet why He chooses some for glory, and reprobates others, has no reason, except the divine will."

37. Domingo Báñez, *Domingo Báñez y las Controversias sobre la Gracia*, ed. Vicente Beltrán de Heredia, OP (Salamanca: Apartado, 1968), 216: "Prima conclusio: Error est contra fidem catholica asserere rationem praedestinationis in particulari praedestinati cujuslibet adulti desumi ex praeviso liberi arbitrii usu et ab illo dependere, ita ut Deus neminem absoluta et efficaci voluntate praedestinaverit in vitam aeternam, sed sub conditione quadam mutabili boni usus liberi arbitrii."

Sin

As St. Thomas states,[38] God is the cause of the act of sin while in no way being the cause of the fact that the act is sinful. God moves man to act, but man sometimes places an obstacle to grace. Báñez affirms this,[39] as Thomas Osborne confirms that Báñez held that "God is only the natural cause of an act that is morally bad and not its moral cause."[40] Báñez here makes a distinction between an act that is contrary to justice by nature and the moral responsibility that may or may not follow from the human execution of said act.[41] Osborne further elucidates this point by stating:

For instance, it might be naturally contrary to justice for me to take fifty dollars from this man who does not owe me money. But it is morally contrary to justice only insofar as I knowingly take money that does not belong to me. By distinguishing between the two kinds of contrariety, Báñez explains how it is true both that God does not cause sin, and also that he is the total cause of every natural being that is in the act of a sin, including that which specifies it morally.... The

38. *ST* I-II, q. 79, a. 2: "Accordingly God is the cause of the act of sin: and yet He is not the cause of sin, because He does not cause the act to have a defect." Ad 2: "Not only the act, but also the defect, is reduced to man as its cause, which defect consists in man not being subject to Whom he ought to be, although he does not intend this principally. Wherefore man is the cause of the sin: while God is the cause of the act, in such a way, that nowise is He the cause of the defect accompanying the act, so that He is not the cause of the sin."

39. Domingo Báñez, *Scholastica Commentaria in Primam Partem Angelici Doctoris S. Thomae*, vol. 1 (Douai: Borremans, 1614), q. 49, art. 2, 453–54.

40. Thomas M. Osborne Jr., "How Sin Escapes Premotion: The Development of Thomas Aquinas' Thought by Spanish Thomists," in *Thomism and Predestination: Principles and Disputations*, ed. Steven A. Long, Roger W. Nutt, and Thomas Joseph White, OP (Ave Maria, Fla.: Sapientia Press, 2016), 192–213, 200. See also p. 202: "In dubium 1 of this commentary [on the *Prima Secundae Pars*, q. 79, a. 4], Báñez combines two positions that Medina rejects, namely, Cajetan's position that God causes the natural being of sin and the position that God is a natural and not a moral cause of sin. He rejects Cajetan's position that God is the cause of the moral malice and the privation of rectitude."

41. Domingo Báñez, *Comentarios Inéditos a la Prima Secundae de Santo Tomás*, vol. 2, *De Vitiis et Peccatis*, qq. 71–89, ed. R. P. Mtro. Vicente Beltrán de Heredia, OP (Salamanca: Consejo Superior de Investigaciones Cientificas, 1944), q. 79, a. 4, dub. 1, n. 24: "For, although these acts of justice and injustice have a moral quality to them and are freely exercised by man, nevertheless, free choice (*liberum arbitrium*) supplies that specification which is from the act's object, is natural to it, and is owing to the nature of the thing. Accordingly, the contrariety that is found in them is natural, because it arises from contrary objects. But that some act be a sin does not pertain to it except by relation to free choice, which was obliged not to perform an act of that species" (translation is Osborne's). ("Nam, quamvis ipsi actus justitiae et injustitiae sint morales et libere exerceantur ab homine, tamen specificationem quae est ex objecto suo est eis naturalis et ex natura rei, liberum arbitrium illam tribuit; sic etiam contrarietas quae in illis invenitur naturalis est, quia consurgit ex objectis contrariis. Quod autem alter actus sit peccatum, non convenit ei nisi respectu liber arbitrii, quod tenebatur non operari actum illius speciei.")

created agent in freely choosing sin is the moral cause of the act because of the deficiency in relation to the rule. The agent is bound to follow the rule. God only causes the natural effect, which is the positive being of the act, and his action is not bound by such a rule.[42]

Man cannot act without being moved to act by God. However, on account of man's being a defectible creature, he renders an act sinful by his own power alone. He causes his own nonconsideration of the rule as a freely chosen rejection of said rule. This renders the act morally evil. To illustrate this point, Báñez uses St. Thomas's example of walking with a limp. "God by efficacious concurrence premoves the crippled shin that it would walk according as it is able, otherwise [God's concurrence] would not be efficacious. But the crippled shin is not able to walk except by limping. Therefore, God moves to the act of limping."[43] The limp is not attributed to the power of movement but to the crippled shin, just as sin is not attributed to God and his aid whereby man may act, but to man, who renders the act sinful by defect.

And yet the defect can only arise if it be first permitted by God, for if it were not permitted then it would not be, since God's providence extends to all things. If this were not the case, then God would not be completely the Lord of all things. As such, Báñez states that sin can only arise if God does not give the grace by which it can be overcome. It follows from this that those who are not upheld from defect and sin will indeed fall into it, but this does not necessitate the created will, nor does it make God out to be the cause of sin. Matava states:

If a human person is not provided with the physical premotion (efficacious actual grace) needed to perform a salutary act, he or she will indefectibly *not* perform a salutary act. Yet, if one fails to perform a salutary act under the circumstances that require it, one sins. To sin, one must be free. However, freedom does not require one to be free in the composed sense, but only in the divided sense, and one is free in the divided sense with respect to one's acts of sin because, just as with one's other acts, one is able to do otherwise *at*, but not *in*, the moment of choice.[44]

42. Osborne, "How Sin Escapes Premotion," 203.
43. Domingo Báñez, *Comentarios Inéditos*, vol. 2, quaest. LXXIX, art. 4, §67 (242): "Deus efficaci concursu praemovet tibiam claudam ut ambulet modo quo potest, alias non esset efficax. Sed non potest ambulari nisi claudicando. Ergo movet ad claudicandum" (translation is Matava's).
44. Matava, *Divine Causality and Human Free Choice*, 89.

It is known that man will sin if not given efficacious grace only suppositionally, as an indispensable material occasion but not as a cause. Man is a defectible creature that is not in any way owed to be always upheld in perfection. Thus, insofar as God is not in any way the cause of sin, the cause is said to be man, as he freely chooses evil rather than good, as St. Thomas states.[45] In no way does this negate man's true potency or ability to do the good. Báñez says:

> To the second proof I reply that, because it is possible, given the divine predetermination to such an act [an act of sin], that that act not be chosen (because it is chosen freely), it is indeed imputable sin, and by consequence free; therefore, it holds good that, given such a predetermination, it is possible for the malice of the act not to follow, just as that act itself is able not to follow.[46]

As a condition of God's not giving efficacious grace, it is known that man will fall because he is a defectible creature, good only for defect and error without the power of God working within him. And yet nothing in this makes it such that man's sinful act is not free, for it is absolutely possible that man may not sin in the divided or consequent sense. Matava states:

> While one has the ability to do otherwise, however, on the hypothesis that God does not provide efficacious grace for the performance of a salutary act, the non-performance of a salutary act is infallibly ensured, for one cannot move oneself to act—even the act of sin—unless one's own self-determination is causally preceded by a divine determination (since, on this view, God is the first mover). Thus, for Báñez, God's not providing efficacious grace, infallibly ensures one's sinning. Nevertheless, one remains free by nature because none of the means under consideration in the act of choice has a necessary connection to the end intended. Lacking such a necessary connection, the outcome of the choice could

---

45. *ST* I-II, q. 79, a. 2, ad 3: "The effect which proceeds from the middle cause, according as it is subordinate to the first cause, is reduced to that first cause; but if it proceed from the middle cause, according as it goes outside the order of the first cause, it is not reduced to that first cause: thus if a servant do anything contrary to his master's orders, it is not ascribed to the master as though he were the cause thereof. In like manner sin, which the free-will commits against the commandment of God, is not attributed to God as being its cause."

46. Báñez, *Comentarios Inéditos* (all subsequent citations of Báñez's commentary refer to the commentary on *ST* I-II unless stated otherwise), vol. 2, quaest. LXXIX, art. 4, §65 (240): "Ad secundum probationem respondeo quod, quia possibile est, posita divina praedeterminatione ad talem actum, illum non elici, quia libere elicitur, est enim peccatum imputabile, et per consequens liberum, ideo bene stat quod, posita tali praedeterminatione, possit non sequi malitia actus, sicut ipse actus potest non sequi" (translation is Matava's).

have been otherwise despite what it de facto is. The decisive factor in whether one's choice is for this or for that is God's premotion of the will.[47]

Not only does sin not absolutely follow from the divine permission, but God truly wishes for the sinner to every time reject the sin. God never (and could never) intend or desire the sin, which Báñez clearly states. "I say therefore that absolutely speaking, it is clearly wrong to say that God has predefined or supplied or wished the sin or the act of sin in however much it is bad, and never has a Thomist theologian said such blasphemy."[48]

Thus, Báñez is left with two truths that must be reconciled: a) that God truly never wishes the sin, although b) he has the power to stop it but does not always do so. The answer to their reconciliation lies in the fact that God is not required to prevent defectible creatures from every defect. As such, God sometimes permits creatures to freely fall into defect or to place an impediment to divine aid. In this, God allows nothing more than what is implicit in human nature.

God could prevent the sin by giving the efficacious aid by which it would be prevented, but He is not required to give this efficacious grace; God allows that man sins according to the order of His wisdom and justice. All this is the doctrine that St. Thomas expresses, as is seen in the first article (*ST* I-II, q. 79, a. 1).[49]

This follows nearly exactly St. Thomas's own words in that article. "For it happens that God does not give some the assistance, whereby they may avoid sin, which assistance were He to give, they would not sin. But He does all this according to the order of His wisdom and justice, since He Himself is Wisdom and Justice."[50]

Why is defect allowed in defectible creatures? Certainly it sometimes works toward the good of the elect, for whom sin leads to greater humil-

47. Matava, *Divine Causality and Human Free Choice*, 89.

48. Báñez, *Controversias*, 444: "Digo pues que absolutamente hablando, es claro error decir que Dios ha predefinido o proveído o querido el pecado o el acto del pecado en cuanto es malo, y nunca teólogo tomista tal blasfemia dijo."

49. Báñez, *Controversias*, 445: "Porque Dios, aunque pudo impedir el pecado dando eficaz socorro con que se impidiera, pero no está obligado a darle; porque permitir que el hombre peque, hácelo según el orden de su sabiduría y justicia. Todo lo dicho es doctrina de Santo Tomás expresa, como se verá en aquel artículo primero."

50. "Contingit enim quod Deus aliquibus non praebet auxilium ad vitandum peccata, quod si praeberet, non peccarent. Sed hoc totum facit secundum ordinem suae sapientiae et iustitiae, cum ipse sit sapientia et iustitia."

ity and abandonment to God. But the permission of sin does not always work toward the good of the sinner, as St. Thomas says. "Every evil that God does, or permits to be done, is directed to some good; yet not always to the good of those in whom the evil is, but sometimes to the good of others, or of the whole universe: thus He directs the sin of tyrants to the good of the martyrs, and the punishment of the lost to the glory of His justice."[51] What, then, is the divine motive for reprobation and the permission of final impenitence?

Reprobation

Báñez speaks of reprobation as flowing from God's permission that some should fall from eternal life.[52] As has been stated above, however, this takes nothing from the free will of the reprobated individual. The unrepentant sinner still freely chooses sin and retains the absolute (if not the conditional) possibility to have not sinned. To put it in another way, while reprobation as a permission of final impenitence is a condition *sine qua non* of that final impenitence, it is not its cause, and thus man is free in the divided sense to choose or not to choose sin. Only in the conditional sense is it known suppositionally that this will not happen. And this is precisely what is stated by St. Thomas.

Reprobation by God does not take anything away from the power of the person reprobated. Hence, when it is said that the reprobated cannot obtain grace, this must not be understood as implying absolute impossibility: but only conditional

---

51. *ST* I-II, q. 79, a. 4, ad 1.

52. Domingo Báñez, *Scholastica Commentaria in Primam Partem*, q. 23, a. 3, 268: "There is no doubt among Catholics concerning the first conclusion, and it is sure according to faith, that we condemn most to be condemned in eternity because of their sins. We also confess God to have known from eternity that the future was as such for the predestined, and that He wished to permit those to withdraw from eternal life; this is what we say, that God reprobates some men, or that reprobation itself would be an act of the intellect or the will; on the one hand, it is explained by the positive act of divine providence or the will of all of the respected effects of reprobation. On the other hand, it is explained by the negation of providence or the divine will from respect of the permission of sin: for all these posits are from the arguments of the Theologian" ("De prima conclusione inter catholicos non est dubium, sed certa est secundum fidem, juxta quam confitemur plurimos esse condemnandos in aeternum, propter peccata sua. Confitemur etiam Deum ab aeterno cognovisse quid futurum erat de hujusmodi non praedestinatis, et voluisse permittere illos a fine vitae aeternae deficere; hoc autem est quod dicimus Deum aliquos homines reprobare, sive ipsa reprobatio sit actus intellectus, sive voluntatis; sive explicetur per actum positivum divinae providentiae aut voluntatis respectu omnium effectuum reprobationis, sive explicetur per negationem providentiae aut voluntatis divinae respectu permissionis peccati: haec enim omnia posita sunt in disputatione Theologorum").

impossibility: as was said above, that the predestined must necessarily be saved; yet a conditional necessity, which does not do away with the liberty of choice. Whence, although anyone reprobated by God cannot acquire grace, nevertheless that he falls into this or that particular sin comes from the use of his free-will. Hence it is rightly imputed to him as guilt.[53]

However, it is objected that if it is so simple for God to move man's will to will the good freely, how can he be anything other than at least an indirect cause of the evil that he does not prevent? Báñez himself recounts this objection.

If permission is a positive act of the divine will, it follows that God would be the cause of sin at least indirectly; but the consequent is false, therefore it is demonstrated that the following conclusion is a good one: God permits Peter to sin, therefore he will infallibly sin. But that which is the cause of the antecedent in the good consequence is also the cause of the consequent. Therefore, if God by a positive act is the cause of the permission of sin in Peter, He will also be the cause of his sin. And this is confirmed: God by a positive act withdraws efficacious aid from Peter because He is impeded by sin. Therefore, He is the indirect cause of sin. This consequence is proven because he who removes that which is holding something up is the indirect cause of the consequence of its falling. For the sake of example, whoever removes a column by which a stone is held up is the indirect cause of the falling of the stone.[54]

Báñez responds by denying the causal relationship between the antecedent of permission and the consequent of action. It is true that God's permission ontologically precedes action, but not every antecedent is causal in regard to the consequent. Some are, but all are not.

To the above proof, I say that the rule regarding the cause of the antecedent [being the cause of the consequent] is not always true. *I see Peter write, therefore Peter writes.* This consequence does follow. However, although I might in some way be the antecedent cause, I am not the cause of the consequent for it does not depend

---

53. *ST* I, q. 23, a. 3, ad 3.

54. Báñez, *Scholastica Commentaria in Primam Partem*, q. 23, a. 3, 273: "Sed instant aliqui Theologi: Si permissio est actus positivus divinae voluntatis, sequitur quod Deus sit causa peccati saltim indirecte; consequens est falsum: ergo. Sequela probatur: ista consequentia est bona, Deus permittit Petrum peccare, ergo peccabit infallibiliter. Sed id quod est causa antecedentis in bona consequentia, est causa consequentis: ergo si Deus per actum positivum est causa permissionis peccati in Petro, erit etiam causa peccati ejus. Et confirmatur: Deus per actum positivum subtrahit a Petro auxilium efficax; quo stante, impediretur ejus peccatum: ergo est indirecta causa peccati. Probatur consequentia, nam qui removet prohibens est indirecta causa effectus consequentis: v. g. qui tollit columnam, qua detinetur lapis, indirecta causa est descensus lapidis, qui consequitur ad remotionem columnae."

upon me that Peter is in the act of writing. It holds, therefore, that the above rule is true whenever the antecedent is the cause of the consequent, as it happens in *a priori* demonstration. But this rule should not be reduced to a common rule, namely that whatever is the cause of a cause is the cause of what is caused. But in the present example, that antecedent, namely that *God permits Peter to sin*, does not mean that He is the cause of that consequent, namely that *Peter sins*. To this confirmation, the consequent is denied. Of this proof it is said that when the preserving thing [as the column to the stone] is removed, the immediate and necessary effect follows, just as the movement of the stone follows from the removal of the column, the cause which removes perseverance indirectly concurs with that effect. Otherwise the effect does not immediately and necessarily follow from the removal of the thing which preserves, but from the mediation of another free will, then the cause which removes the preserving thing is not always said to concur with that effect, neither in natural being nor in the being of time, and not even indirectly. And so in our proposition it is said that from the subtraction of efficacious aid sin does not immediately and necessarily follow, but from the free will itself from which such aid is subtracted."[55]

The antecedent in the cause of reprobation is the antecedent of permission only. It does not force the will to choose evil, nor does it move it to sin (although God does move the created will insofar as it is in act, as we have seen). Conditionally, it follows from this antecedent that man will fall, but God is not required to prevent all failing in the defectible creature, nor is he the cause of the creature's free will to choose evil. Man, when left to his own devices, will not only choose evil, but his free will is so exercised that he will choose this or that evil. He will reject God in specific ways according to his own specific free movements influenced

---

55. Báñez, *Scholastica Commentaria in Primam Partem*, q. 23, a. 3, 273: "Ad probationem dico, quod illa regula quod est causa antecedentis, etc. non est usequequaque vera. Nam ista consequentia bona est, ego video Petrum scribere; ergo Petrus scribit, et tamen quamvis ego sim causa antecedentis, non tamen sum causa consequentis: non enim pendet a me Petrus in actu scribendi. Habet igitur dumtaxat verum illa regula, quando antecedens est causa consequentis, ut contingit in demonstrationibus a priori. Nam tunc illa regula reducitur ad aliam vulgatam, scilicet quidquid est causa causae, est caisa causat: in praesentia autem illud antecedens, Deus permittit Petrum peccare, non est causa illius consequentis, scilicet Petrus peccat. Ad confirmationem, negatur consequentia. Ad probationem dicitur, quod quando ex remotione prohibentis, immediate et necessario consequitur effectus, sicut motus lapidis deorsum consequitur subtractionem columnae, causa removens prohibens indirecte concurrit ad illum effectum; caeterum, quando effectus non sequitur immediate et necessario ad remotionem prohibentis, sed mediante libera voluntate alterius, tunc causa removens prohibens non semper dicitur concurrere ad illum effectum, neque in esse naturae, neque in esse moris, etiam indirecte. Et ita in nostro proposito dicendem est, quod ad subtractionem efficacis auxilii non sequitur peccatum immediate et necessario, sed mediante libera voluntate ejus, a quo tale auxilium subtrahitur."

by his own disordered appetites. All of this is, as we have seen, what is stated by St. Thomas. "Whence, although anyone reprobated by God cannot acquire grace, nevertheless that he falls into this or that particular sin comes from the use of his free-will. Hence it is rightly imputed to him as guilt."[56]

Dissymmetry between the Providential Ordering of Good and Evil

As we have stated, perhaps the largest concern with so-called Báñezianism is that it too closely links the lines of good and evil, making it such that God's providential control over evil is so tight that he ought to be chastised, as if the providential ordering to good were roughly equivalent to the providential ordering to evil. In this, it is said that Báñez and those who follow him dip their toes into the pool of Jansen or the Reformers. However, the great dissymmetry between the lines of good and evil are apparent, both in the thought of the Angelic Doctor and, consequently, in Báñez himself.

St. Thomas himself shows how the causal role of predestination and reprobation differ. "Reprobation differs in its causality from predestination. This latter is the cause both of what is expected in the future life by the predestined—namely, glory—and of what is received in this life—namely, grace. Reprobation, however, is not the cause of what is in the present—namely, sin."[57] The antecedent of predestination exerts a causal influence on the consequent of what is in the present, namely, meritorious works. And insofar as God is the giver of the efficacious grace that marks predestination, he is said to be the cause of those consequent good works. However, the antecedent of reprobation is not causally related to that which exists presently as a consequent, namely, sin. Sin comes about simply from the defect in the creature, the retardation of the act that is similar to the interference posed to the movement of walking by the crippled leg.[58] And this is reiterated by Báñez when he states that "God will

---

56. *ST I*, q. 23, a. 3, ad 3.
57. *ST I*, q. 23, a. 2, ad 2.
58. *De malo*, q. III, a. 2: "But if something is not properly disposed or fit to receive the causal movement of the first mover, imperfect action results. And then we trace what belongs to the activity in it to the first mover as the cause. And we do not trace what is in it regarding deficiency to the first

have willed the predestined to have remained in good; truly others He will have permitted to remain in sin, and to permanently remain in it."[59] The dissimilarity between causation and permission cannot be overstated. Far from reprobation being a positive motion or causation, it is entirely negative. The effects of reprobation are hated by God, and he in no way predetermines anyone to evil, but only to good. As Báñez states, "Therefore, if formal malice is in conformity with His predetermination, it pertains nevertheless to the law and providence of the will of God, not according to the reason of divine malice, but of good; and consequently God predetermines to it. He determines to the good and not to evil."[60]

This dissymmetry or asymmetry between good and evil, that which is truly necessary to preserve God's innocence and causal distance from sin, is found right within the work of Báñez, who posits as strongly as St. Thomas the great difference between predestination and reprobation. Matava states:

Báñez's way of saving divine justice is by positing an asymmetry between God's causal involvement in good acts and his causal involvement in bad. In the case of good acts, God has the initiative whereas in the case of sins, the human person has the initiative.... Báñez is able to maintain this asymmetry by distinguishing between the positive reality of an act and the privation that afflicts that act when it is a sin: while God is the first cause of everything that has positive existence in the act of sin, the sinner is the first cause of the malice of sin—that is, the evil or privation that constitutes an act as sin. In other words, God causes the act of sin as act, but not as sin; the sinner causes the act of sin as sin.[61]

The distinction between the causation of predestination and the permission of reprobation is the metaphysical distinction between act and nonact. It is true that the nonact of reprobation is a volitional nonact. If I do not notice a friend waving at me from across the road, my nonact

---

mover as the cause, since such deficiency in the activity results because the secondary cause defects from the ordination of the first mover, as I have said."

59. Báñez, *Scholastica Commentaria in Primam Partem*, q. 23, a. 3, 270: "quantum ad hoc quod Deus voluerit praedestinatos manere in bono, alios vero permiserit cadere in peccatum, et in illo permanere."

60. Báñez, *Comentarios Inéditos*, vol. 2, quaest. LXXIX, art. 4, §45 (225): "Ergo, si malitia formalis est conformis ejus praedeterminationi, quae pertinet ad aeternam legem et providentiam atque voluntatem Dei, non habit rationem mali, sed boni; et per consequens Deus praedeterminans ad illam, praedeterminabit ad bonum, non ad malum."

61. Matava, *Divine Causality and Human Free Choice*, 90.

of not waving back is nonvolitional. I did not intend to not wave back to him; I am merely aloof. If, on the other hand, I do not return a book to my friend because I wish to steal it, we might consider my leaving it on my shelf a volitional nonact. In regard to reprobation, God decides according to his infinite wisdom to not act in certain human circumstances to prevent sin. This volitional nonact is quite different from not noticing a friend wave and thus not waving back. However, in regard to the effect of sin, even if the nonact is recognized as volitionally, it cannot be posited as a cause. Causation requires act, and in relation to sin and acquiring the penalty of damnation, God exerts no act and no cause.

CHAPTER FOUR

Reginald Garrigou-Lagrange

Reginald Garrigou-Lagrange, OP, was an icon of preconciliar Thomism. He was perhaps one of the most prolific[1] and influential theologians of the first half of the twentieth century. Born Gontran Garrigou-Lagrange in Auch, France, in 1877, Garrigou belonged to a Catholic middle-class family. Garrigou's granduncle, his grandfather's brother, Maurice-Marie-Matthieu Garrigou, was a major inspiration for him. Maurice Garrigou had been a Catholic priest at a dangerous time, during the French Revolution. He established a religious congregation for women, the Institut de Notre-Dame de la Compassion, and was declared venerable by Pope Francis in 2013. It is said that Maurice had a major impact upon the young Garrigou.[2]

At first, Garrigou pursued a career in medicine, but he was profoundly changed upon reading the work of philosopher Ernest Hello. He subsequently entered the Order of Preachers in 1897 and took the religious name Reginald. He took vows in 1900 and was ordained to the priesthood in 1902. Garrigou studied at the Sorbonne, and while doing so he met and befriended Jacques Maritain.

Garrigou eventually took on teaching at the Angelicum in 1909, where he remained until 1959. In 1917 he became the first-ever chair of ascetical-mystical theology in the history of the Church, a position that had been

---

1. Richard Peddicord, OP, *The Sacred Monster of Thomism: An Introduction to the Life and Legacy of Reginald Garrigou-Lagrange, OP* (South Bend, Ind.: St. Augustine's Press, 2005), 3: "Garrigou lived a long life—just shy of eighty-seven years—and he wrote twenty-eight books and over 600 articles."

2. Peddicord, *The Sacred Monster*, 8: "M.-Rosaire Gagnebet recounts that Garrigou used to find inspiration in the writings of his illustrious grand-uncle."

made uniquely for him with the support of Pope Benedict XV.[3] Garrigou would give public lectures on Saturdays that became exceedingly popular with Catholic intellectuals.[4]

While at the Angelicum, Garrigou directed doctoral candidates of such esteem as Marie-Dominique Chenu, OP, Marie-Michel Labourdette, OP, and Karol Wojtyla, the future Pope St. John Paul II. Garrigou also had strong ties to the Holy Office and the various pontificates of the mid-twentieth century. As Garrigou's biographer, Richard Peddicord, OP, states:

> During his years at the Angelicum, Garrigou was consulted numerous times by the Holy Office on doctrinal matters. In Roman parlance, he was a "qualificator'—one who qualified as a theological authority. Garrigou served in this capacity from the pontificate of Benedict XV through that of John XXIII. In 1955 he was named a "consultor" for the Holy Office and for the Congregation for Religious. Now, rather than being an auxiliary to decision-making, Garrigou became an active participant in the work of the Roman curia.[5]

By 1960 Garrigou had grown old and weary. He retired from teaching and was unable to fulfill Pope John XXIII's request that he work for the theological commission on the preparatory schemas for the commencement of the Second Vatican Council.[6] Fr. Garrigou died in 1964. Pope Paul VI called him a "faithful servant of the Church and of the Holy See."[7]

Garrigou is held to be one of the great modern Thomistic commentators on St. Thomas's teaching on physical premotion, the permission of sin, providence, predestination, and reprobation. There is probably no other twentieth-century Dominican who was as widely read or as influential, especially on these topics. Garrigou wrote on these issues at length in his commentary on the *Summa Theologiae*, in standalone works on pre-

---

3. Peddicord, *The Sacred Monster*, 16: "In 1917 the Angelicum established—with the encouragement and support of Pope Benedict XV—the first chair of ascetical-mystical theology in the Church's history. Garrigou-Lagrange was from the beginning its intended recipient."

4. Peddicord, *The Sacred Monster*, 16: "The major work of the chair of spirituality was to give a public lecture every Saturday afternoon while the Angelicum was in session. Garrigou's lectures attracted people from all parts; they would become one of the unofficial tourist sites on the itineraries of theologically minded visitors to Rome."

5. Peddicord, *The Sacred Monster*, 21.

6. Peddicord, *The Sacred Monster*, 22.

7. Peddicord, *The Sacred Monster*, 23.

destination and providence, and in multiple articles.[8] He is seen as one of the last great proponents of the traditional Dominican treatment of these issues, and this brought him into personal contact—and disagreement— with Marín-Sola and Maritain themselves. Many from the Society of Jesus branded Garrigou as the premier "Báñezian" of his day. For example, Louis Rasolo, SJ, writes:

The Bannezians do not demonstrate very much disagreement regarding physical premotion itself. What divides them above all is the way of explaining the origin of moral evil. The view most in favor is the one which reclaims Thomas de Lemos. Two principle theses characterize this school: On the one hand, the infallibility and universal necessity of predetermination; and on the other hand, the presupposition of an inconsideration of the rule on the part of man, before the physical predetermination to material evil. It is to this tendency that R.P. Garrigou-Lagrange belongs. He has the principal merit of summing up all of the others [Bannezians]. It is therefore to his work that we ourselves are especially in debt [for writing about Bannezianism].[9]

While Garrigou's treatment of these issues is much in keeping with that of Báñez and the traditional reading of St. Thomas, there are a few peculiarities that have led some to include him in the reformist camp of Marín-Sola and Maritain. Maritain himself makes similar claims, as we shall see later on.[10] We will look first at Garrigou's general views and then move toward these controversial points, particularly those regarding reprobation, to see whether they are substantive transformations of the traditional teaching.

---

8. Serge-Thomas Bonino, OP, writes of Garrigou and his work *Predestination* in "Contemporary Thomism through the Prism of the Theology of Predestination," trans. Stefan Jetchick, trans. and ed. Barry David and Steven A. Long, in *Thomism and Predestination: Principles and Disputations* (Ave Maria, Fla.: Sapientia Press, 2016), 32: "Father Garrigou-Lagrange is a man of synthesis. Insensitive to the charms of 'rebellious diversity' that so fascinates postmoderns, he is a contemplative who tries to gather everything into the light of first principles, so as to systematically unify the data. He thus presents a "concordist" theology of predestination. According to his masterpiece, the doctrine of predestination developed itself homogeneously, sometimes by rejecting errors, sometimes by deepening the truth. Moreover, according to him there is a deep underlying continuity of St. Paul, St. Augustine, St. Thomas Aquinas, and finally classical Thomism, which updated the Thomasian doctrine during controversies between various post-Tridentine schools of thought."

9. Rasolo, *Le dilemme du concours divin*, 131. All translations of Rasolo are my own. For a contemporary criticism of Garrigou's "Bannezianism," see Joshua R. Brotherton, "Toward a Consensus in the De Auxiliis Debate," *Nova et Vetera*, English ed., 14, no. 3 (2016): 783–820.

10. See appendix.

Physical Premotion

Garrigou writes that the creature's need for divine motion can be known both from Scripture[11] and from reason.[12] Philosophically, Garrigou presents two major syllogistic arguments for the affirmation of the existence and necessity of physical premotion, both of which are similar to arguments given by St. Thomas in book III of the *Summa contra Gentiles*. The first states that since our limited being depends upon him who is Being Itself, so must our participation in action be entirely rooted him who is Pure Act.[13] The first argument runs like this.

God is the first Mover and first cause to whom are subordinated, even in their action, all secondary causes. Now, without physical premotion we cannot safeguard in God the primacy of causality or the subordination of secondary causes in their very action. Therefore physical premotion is the reason why all secondary causes are subordinated to God as first Mover and first Cause.[14]

Garrigou says of the major premise:

The major is certain both in philosophy and in theology. It would be rash to deny it. As, indeed, it is certain that God is the supreme Being, upon whom all beings as such immediately depend, it is equally certain that God is the supreme efficient cause to whom all secondary causes are subordinated even in their action. Subordination in action follows subordination in being, just as action follows being. To deny this major would be to deny the first two classical proofs for the existence of God as set forth by St. Thomas Aquinas.[15]

---

11. Reginald Garrigou-Lagrange, *Predestination*, trans. Dom Bede Rose, OSB, DD (Charlotte, N.C.: TAN Books, 1998) 240: "They answer first that the Scripture does not leave any doubt about this, since it says that 'God worketh in all. For in Him we live and move and are.' Even if it is a question of free acts, the Scripture is no less positive in affirming that He is the prime Mover, for we read: 'Lord … Thou hast wrought all our works for us. For it is God who worketh in you, both to will and to accomplish, according to His good will.' These Scriptural texts are so clear, they state so plainly that the action of the creature depends upon God's influx or upon the divine causality, that even Suarez, although opposed to the theory of physical premotion, wrote that it would be an error against the faith to deny the dependence of the creature in its actions upon the first Cause."

12. For more on this, see Steven A. Long, "Reginald Garrigou-Lagrange on Physical Premotion," in *Educational Theoria 1: Reginald Garrigou-Lagrange OP: Teacher of Thomism*, ed. Jude Chua Soon Meng and Thomas Crean, OP, 55–68 (Center for Educational Theoria / Thomistic E-nstitute, 2014), https://thomisticenstitute.wordpress.com/.

13. Garrigou, *Predestination*, 240: "Equally clear stands the case from the philosophical point of view; for just as the participated and limited being of creatures depends upon the causality of the first Being; who is the self-subsisting Being, so also does their action: for there is no reality that can be excluded from His controlling influence."

14. Garrigou, *Predestination*, 295.

15. Garrigou, *Predestination*, 295.

REGINALD GARRIGOU-LAGRANGE

And of the minor premise:

> The minor becomes evident to us, if we take note of the fact that subordination of causes in their action consists in this, that the first cause moves or applies secondary causes to act, and that secondary causes act only because they are moved by the primary cause.... Now this is the very definition of physical premotion, which has a priority not of time but of causality over the action of the created agent.[16]

Action follows being, and in both we are contingent upon God, who is Being and Act. We can only participate in being and action by passively receiving from God, which brings us to Garrigou's second syllogism.

> Every cause that is not of itself actually in act, but only in potentiality to act, needs to be physically premoved to act. Now such is the case with every created cause, even the free cause. Therefore every created cause needs to be physically premoved to act.[17]

In regard to the major premise, Garrigou states:

> The major is certain. The classical proofs from God's existence, such as St. Thomas understands them, have their foundation in this principle, and to refuse to admit this major is to say that the greater comes from the less, the more perfect from the less perfect; for actually to act is a greater perfection than being able to act. If, therefore, the faculty to act were not moved, it would always remain in a state of potency and would never act.[18]

And to prove the minor, he states:

> The minor is no less evident. If a created cause were of itself actually in act, it would always be in act and never in potentiality. Our intellect would always actually know all the intelligible things it can know, and our will would always actually will all the good things that will be willed by it. Moreover, this created cause, instead of being moved to act would be its own action; but, for that, it would have to be its very being, to exist of itself; for action follows being, and the mode of action the mode of being, as St. Thomas often says. Therefore every created cause, that it may act, needs to be physically premoved by God.[19]

---

16. Garrigou, *Predestination*, 296.
17. Garrigou, *Predestination*, 296.
18. Garrigou, *Predestination*, 296.
19. Garrigou, *Predestination*, 296–297.

Premotion: What It Is Not

Garrigou presents five major errors regarding physical premotion, that is, "what physical premotion is not," in order that certain common points of debate might be negated from the outset.

(1) It is not a motion such as to render the action of the secondary cause superfluous. This is directed against occasionalism. (2) It is not a motion that would interiorly compel our will to choose this particular thing rather than a certain other. This is directed against determinism. (3) Neither is it, at the opposite extreme of both occasionalism and determinism, simply a simultaneous concurrence. (4) Nor is it an indifferent and indeterminate motion. (5) It is not a purely extrinsic assistance given by God.[20]

Against the first error Garrigou asserts that physical premotion is not a creation of something *ex nihilo*, something of which the creature would be incapable, rendering it entirely divorced from the causality of its own actions. Instead it is a motion that is received in a passive manner by the creature. This motion is not to be confused with the action of God, which is separate from the motion in us which causes us to act.[21] Moreover, Garrigou argues similarly to St. Thomas that occasionalism makes secondary causes superfluous[22] and thus shows God to be impotent rather than omnipotent. Finally, Garrigou actually argues that occasionalism leads to pantheism, since God is really the only operating agent, and if He is the only operating agent then all other things become subsumed into God as action follows being. Since God is the only one who acts, He is the only one who truly exists.[23]

---

20. Garrigou, *Predestination*, 241.

21. Garrigou, *Predestination*, 241: "We shall see more clearly further on that physical premotion is: (1) A motion and not an *ex nihilo* creation, without which our acts, created in us *ex nihilo*, would not be the result of the vital actions of our faculties and would no longer be ours. It is a passive motion that is received in the creature and that is consequently something distinct either from the divine action which it presupposes, or from our action which follows it."

22. Garrigou, *Predestination*, 243: "The divine motion must not be understood in the sense held by the occasionalists in that God alone would act in all things, so that it is not the fire that gives heat, but God in the fire, the latter being the occasion of this. If such were the case, remarks St. Thomas, secondary causes would not be causes, and, not being able to act, their presence would be to no purpose."

23. Garrigou, *Predestination*, 243: "Moreover, occasionalism leads to pantheism. This is clear, because action follows being, and the mode of action the mode of being. If there is but one action, which is God's action, then there is but one being; creatures are absorbed in God; universal being is identical with the divine being, as ontologist realism postulates, a fond theory of Malebranche and one that is closely associated, according to his notion, with occasionalism."

Against the second error he goes on to state that physical premotion is "not necessitating but predetermining"[24] and that it "guarantees the intrinsic infallibility of the divine decrees and moves our will to determine itself to a certain determinate good act."[25] This means that the human will as a secondary cause is not robbed of its volitional nature. "The divine motion, since it does not render the action of secondary causes superfluous but gives rise to it, cannot be necessitating, in the sense that it would suppress all contingency and liberty."[26] This is possible because of God's omnipotence. God, the Creator of our nature, is able to will in different ways. When it comes to moving men to will, He is able to do it contingently, to move men in such a way that not only do they move toward the good that God wills but that they do this of their own choice as well. "St. Thomas connects even this property of divine motion with the sovereign efficacy of God's causality, who does not only what He wills but as He wills it; who brings it about not only that we will but that we freely will."[27] God does not move men as robots, but is able to move their wills to will. "The divine motion does not therefore suppress freedom of action, but actualizes it."[28]

The third error is directed primarily at Molinism. Garrigou quotes Molina in reference to human motion toward the good. Molina states, "The total effect, indeed, comes both from God and from the secondary causes; but it comes neither from God nor from secondary causes as total but as partial causes, each at the same time requiring the concurrence and influx of the other cause, just as when two men are pulling a boat."[29] This simultaneous concursus negates the subordinated causality of physical premotion.[30] Man no longer relies upon God entirely for his movement since the movement of the secondary cause merely participates with the

24. Garrigou, *Predestination*, 241.

25. Garrigou, *Predestination*, 241. It must be said, however, that this does not apply to bad actions, which Garrigou states when he says parenthetically within the same sentence that "the determination to a bad act, since it is itself bad and defective, comes on these grounds from a defective cause and not from God."

26. Garrigou, *Predestination*, 243–244.

27. Garrigou, *Predestination*, 244.

28. Garrigou, *Predestination*, 244.

29. Molina, *Concordia*, q. 14, a. 13, disp. 26. The translation is Garrigou's.

30. Garrigou, *Predestination*, 247: "If, in truth, the divine concurrence is merely simultaneous, it is no longer true to say that God moves secondary causes to act, since He does not apply them to their operations. We have in this case merely two partial and co-ordinated causes, not two total causes which, in their very causality, are subordinated the one to the other, as St. Thomas had said."

primary cause and is not directly moved by it.[31] Indeed, the language of primary and secondary causality becomes incomprehensible in such a schema.[32]

Indeed, what is most troubling for Garrigou in this error is that the human will is beyond divine contact,[33] and as such, there is some pocket of creation that lies outside of the scope and power of divine providence.[34] Moreover, how can it be that the human will can give itself the perfection of action that is only proper to God? "How could the will, which was only in the state of potency, give itself this perfection which it did not possess? This means that the greater comes from the less, and this is contrary to the principles of causality and of the universal causality of the first agent."[35]

Garrigou agrees with Molina's concern in regard to determinism. It is utterly important that the human will retain its freedom. However, the way to safeguard creaturely freedom is not to deny divine causality but rather to regard its omnipotence and transcendence. We have freedom insofar as we participate in it as a perfection of the divine life. We can only be said to be good, to be free, or to be at all insofar as we participate in the perfections of God and are moved and held in goodness, freedom, and being by him who is Goodness, Freedom, and Being itself. "Freedom is a perfection in God, and we can participate in it only analogically."[36]

31. Garrigou, *Predestination*, 245: "From this point of view, even if the total effect is produced by each of the two causes, in this sense that one without the other would produce no effect, in such a case the secondary cause is not premoved by the first. The concurrence of this latter is merely simultaneous, as when two men are pulling a boat, the first exerting no influence upon the second to cause it to act."

32. To further prove his claim, Garrigou continues to quote Molina. It is not within the scope of this work to treat the views of Molina in any formal respect, but I provide the quotation insofar as it aids in the present task of understanding that against which Garrigou argues: "God's universal concurrence does not immediately exert an influence on the secondary cause, so as to premove it to act and produce its effect, but it immediately exerts an influence on the action and the effect, along with the secondary cause" (*Concordia*, q. 14, a. 13, disp. 26). This influence, according to Garrigou, is merely a particular grace and is "not a physical premotion" but merely "attracting the will by reason of the object proposed to it" (245).

33. Garrigou, *Predestination*, 247: "it [human freedom] is so delicate that even God, they say, cannot contact it."

34. Garrigou, *Predestination*, 247: "But, if this is so, then there is something that is beyond the scope of the universal causality of the first agent;"

35. Garrigou, *Predestination*, 247.

36. Reginald Garrigou-Lagrange, *Grace: Commentary on the Summa theologica of St. Thomas, I-II, q.109–144*, trans. The Dominican Nuns of Corpus Christi Monastery, Menlo Park, Calif. (St. Louis, Mo.: B. Herder Book Co., 1952), 422.

Unlike lower agents, which cannot exert force upon us as external agents in such a way as to act interiorly on our will, God, who is the author of our nature and the source of our very being, can indeed do so. He is more intimate to us than we are to ourselves. And it is precisely this divine omnipotence and transcendence that best combats determinism. Molina's theory suits only to neuter the divine omnipotence and thus does not properly combat this error.[37]

Thus God moves our free will *suavely and firmly*. If the divine motion were to lose its force, it would at once lose its suavity; being unable to reach what is especially delicate and intimate in us, it would remain outside us, as it were, overlaid upon our created activity; and this is unworthy of creative activity which is more intimate to us than we are to ourselves.[38]

Of course, this does not remove the mystery of divine causality. It is not possible for man to comprehend with complete clarity the way in which God works interiorly as an external principle, but that this must be the case is clear if we are not to fall into determinism or various forms of Pelagianism.

There still remains the mystery which underlies all the great theological questions, the mystery of God, of the creative act, of the co-existence of the finite and the Infinite, and in this case the co-existence of uncreated action and created activity, of primary and secondary liberty. It is the very absence of mystery that would be surprising in this case. The seeming clearness of a simplest explanation is obtained only at the cost of an error. There must be a mystery in this, for our

37. Garrigou, *Predestination*, 247–48: "St. Thomas was of the opinion that to refute determinism, instead of attacking the principle of causality, we must insist on the transcendent efficacy of the first Cause, the only one capable of causing in us and with us that our acts be performed freely, since it is more intimate to us than we are to ourselves, and since this free mode of our acts is still being and for this reason depends upon Him who is the cause of all reality and good."

See also Reginald Garrigou-Lagrange, *God: His Existence and His Nature: A Thomistic Solution of Certain Agnostic Antinomies*, vol. 2, trans. Dom Bede Rose, OSB, DD (St. Louis, Mo.: B. Herder Book Co., 1955; Lonely Peaks Reproduction, 2007), 281–82: "In other words, for choice to be in our power we must be masters of what conditions our choice in the order of secondary causes. It is not necessary for us to be masters of the divine decree or of the divine motion, if this latter *causes in us and with us the free mode of our act*. Divine causality contains our own causality eminently, and God is more intimate to us than we are to ourselves. We should not conceive His motion as a *constraint* exerted externally by a created agent; it is entirely the interior causality of Him who creates and preserves us in being. The mystery in this case is not greater than that of creation, and is but the result of it. A person whom we love makes us *will freely* what he desires. Why could not God do so in a nobler, more certain, and very intimate manner that belongs to Him alone?"

38. Garrigou, *God: His Existence and His Nature*, vol. 2, 277.

knowledge of the divine causality is merely analogical, and it is only relatively and negatively (supreme cause, non-premoved cause) that we come to know what properly constitutes its. We cannot therefore see *how* God *suavely and firm-ly* moves our liberty to determine itself, but we see that if He could not move it He would cease to be the universal cause; there would be a reality produced, that of our free determination, which would not depend upon the first Being, and which would be in us an absolute beginning, which is contrary to the principle of causality.[39]

Finally, Garrigou believes that simultaneous concurrence posits passivity in him who is Pure Act. Rather than God, the source of all good and being, governing our actions via his divine providence, it is men who cause God's divine motion to become efficacious within themselves.[40] It is men who determine God's foresight into what we will do in various circumstances. It is men who move toward the good that God presents, rather than God working within us intimately.

Furthermore, the Thomists say that if the divine concurrence, far from inclining the will infallibly to determine itself to perform this particular act rather than a certain other, is itself determined by a particular influx of the free will to function in this particular way rather than in a certain other, then the tables are turned: God by reason of His foreknowledge and causality, instead of determining is determined. This means that by His *scientia media* He foresees what choice a certain person would make, if placed in certain circumstances. Instead of being the cause of this foreseen determination, He is determined and therefore perfected by this determination which, as such, in no way comes from Him. Now there is nothing more inadmissible than to posit a passivity or dependence in the pure Act, who is sovereignly independent and incapable of receiving any perfection whatsoever.[41]

As we shall see, this choice between God determining or being determined is that which incites and governs Garrigou's entire treatment of the issues of premotion, predestination, and reprobation.

39. Garrigou, *God: His Existence and His Nature*, vol. 2, 277–78.

40. This is executed, according to Molina, via a determination of circumstance wherein God creates the universe in such a way that a certain set of circumstances will exist. God, through his middle knowledge, knows the contingent truths about how each human being will act in any set of circumstances. Thus, God can bring it about that a given individual wills *x* but only because he is first determined by how that individual will act (and react to divine aid) in any given circumstance. God remains causally passive but can still implement his providential plan through his ability to manipulate the circumstances of the universe according to his middle knowledge.

41. Garrigou, *Predestination*, 248.

Garrigou's response to the fourth error follows much of the same argumentation as his response to the third. Insofar as premotion is indeterminate it leaves the source of determination to a good act to be man
rather than God. God becomes merely a passive onlooker in the determination of our most salutary acts.[42] Furthermore, Garrigou states that
there is no third option between premotion being determinative and
premotion being indeterminative, thus rendering passivity in God (this
being found in views that posit the *scientia media*). If the divine motion
is not predetermining then free creaturely acts can only be known via a
passive middle knowledge.

Father del Prado shows that there is no *via media* between the doctrine of the
predetermining decrees and the theory of the *scientia media*; for the divine
knowledge of conditionally free acts of the future presupposes indeed a divine
decree or it does not. If we reject the *scientia media* and say that it does, then the
decree is predetermining, for otherwise it could not infallibly make known the
conditionally free act of the future or the conditionate future.[43]

Here a word should be given about the divine simplicity. While Garrigou is speaking here of indeterminate premotion, fallible or impedible
premotions are subject to the same objections based on the simplicity of
the divine will insofar as both posit a passivity and thus a creaturely determination of the divine will. On such suppositions, the divine will does
not simply govern over all things. While Garrigou tends to emphasize
the infallibly efficacious nature of divine aid in order to preserve God's
omnipotence and the comprehensive nature of divine providence (as we
shall see, Jean-Hervé Nicolas's early arguments rely much more upon an
argument from divine simplicity), he does, of course, affirm the immuta-

---

42. Garrigou, *Predestination*, 249: "Something real would still be excluded from God's universal
causality. There would be a determination that is independent of the sovereign determination of pure
Act, a finite good independent of the supreme Good, a second liberty that would be acting independently of the first Liberty. That which is better in the work of salvation, would not come from the
Author of salvation.... This doctrine of indifferent premotion, like that of simultaneous concurrence,
cannot solve the dilemma: 'God determining or determined: there is no other alternative.' Willingly
or unwillingly, it leads to the positing of a passivity or dependence in Him who is pure Act, especially
in His foreknowledge (*scientia media*) as regards our free determinations, even the noblest which, as
free determinations, would not come from Him. Concerning these God would not be the cause of
them, but merely a passive onlooker."

43. Garrigou, *Predestination*, 251. See also *ST* I, q. 28, a. 2, ad 1: "nothing that exists in God can
have any relation to that wherein it exists or of whom it is spoken, except the relation of identity; and
this by reason of God's supreme simplicity."

bility of the divine will, its relation to providence, and divine simplicity. He states, "In Him no successive acts of will occur; there is but *one subsistent, unchanging act of will*, which is directed to all that He wills. Therefore divine simplicity or divine unity, is the absence of all composition and division in being, thought, and volition."[44]

And, finally, in regard to the fifth error, Garrigou states that divine motion is "formally immanent and virtually transitive." It is said to be immanent because God is eternal and infinite, unlike the effect that is produced in time. Of course, God has no real relation to creatures.

The doctrine of St. Thomas and his disciples is very clear on this point. They teach in common that even God's action *ad extra* is formally immanent and virtually transitive, and that there is no real relation on God's part toward us; there is only a relation of dependence of the creature on God, and this is not reciprocated.[45]

Unlike the formally transitive action, which sees an accident proceed from the agent to the patient (like the hot coal that warms water, transferring its heat to the water, which results in the coal cooling and the water warming), the divine motion "cannot be an accident; it is really identical with God's very essence."[46] Accordingly, Garrigou calls the divine motion to be virtually transitive, since it still produces a distinct effect but without the imperfections of a formally transitive action.[47] It is for this very reason that many object to the Thomistic system. They do not properly understand the great distinction between the uncreated agent and the created agent, the former of which is able to move our wills to move freely, while the latter cannot. Those who imagine God as another creature (though a rather large and powerful one) cannot comprehend how He may move the will without interfering with its liberty. However, this is to neglect that secondary causes are meant to act as secondary causes. The human will is not made to be indifferent to divine motion but to be

44. Reginald Garrigou-Lagrange, *Providence*, trans. Dom Bede Rose (Rockford, Ill.: TAN Books, 1998), 82.

45. Garrigou, *Predestination*, 252.

46. Garrigou, *Predestination*, 252.

47. Garrigou, *Predestination*, 252: "It is therefore formally immanent, and, though not having the imperfections of the formally transitive action, it resembles the latter in so far as it produces either a spiritual or corporeal effect that is really distinct from it. It is in this sense that it is said to be virtually transitive, for it contains eminently within itself all the perfection of a formally transitive action, without any of the imperfections that essentially belong to this latter."

animated by it,[48] and thus, far from divine and created agencies being competitive, the perfection of the agency and causality of the creature is itself an effect of the transcendent divine providential agency.

Premotion: What It Is

After stating what premotion is not, Garrigou presents a positive definition. He begins by providing a three-point understanding of physical premotion as a *motion*.

> To avoid all equivocation, just as we distinguish between active and passive creation, so we must distinguish here between two similar acceptations of the word 'motion.' We have (1) the active motion that in God, as we have said, is a formally immanent and virtually transitive action; (2) the passive motion by which the creature, though it had only the power to act, is passively moved by God to become actually in act; then there is: (3) the action itself of the creature, which in us is the vital and free act of the will. This distinction is commonly made to explain the influence of one created agent over another, of fire, for instance, over water. In this case we have: (1) the action of the fire: actual heating of water; (2) the effect of this action upon the water: it is heated; (3) the action of the heated water upon surrounding objects.[49]

Garrigou states that premotion is "a motion received in the created operative potency in order to apply it to act."[50] This means that it is not properly understood as being synonymous with either God's Pure Act or the good effect that flows from the divine aid working on the patient. As David S. Oderberg states, "[Premotion] is a motion received into the creature, applying it to act, and hence distinct both from the uncreated divine action constituted by the eternal decree that the creature shall act, and from the creaturely action causally resultant from the premotion."[51]

We can distinguish between three distinct senses of motion: 1) the active motion of God as the principle of the motion of the creature, 2) the

---

48. Garrigou, *Predestination*, 252: "From this we see that God's uncreated motion bears only an analogical resemblance to the motion of a created agent that is incapable of interiorly and infallibly moving our will to choose this or that. The greater number of the objections against the divine premotion are due to the fact that the divine action is conceived as being univocal with created action, which latter does not go so far as to cause our acts to be performed freely."

49. Garrigou, Predestination, 258.

50. Garrigou, *Predestination*, 281–82.

51. David S. Oderberg, "Divine Premotion," *International Journal for Philosophy of Religion* 794, no. 3 (2016): 207–22, 210.

passive motion of the creature in receiving, and 3) the act of the creature, whereby it moves with liberty and exerts an influence upon things around it. This is analogous to the 1) fire that heats, 2) the water's becoming heated, and 3) the influence that the heated water has upon surrounding objects.

These distinctions are crucial, for they allow for the possibility of subordinated and secondary causality.[52] It is not that God creates within us a good act from nothing. Such a creation *ex nihilo* would render the action unattributable to man *through any participation of his own powers.*[53] Only God has the power to create from nothing. Instead, it is God's motion within us that allows us to operate and thus bring forth the good act.[54] "Thus a great artist adapts his motion to the various instruments which he uses."[55]

In fact, it is this tripartite distinction that allows Garrigou to state that the created will is the *proper cause* of the salutary act (while being merely the instrumental cause of the being of its act).[56] In this way Garrigou can state that "the apple tree is the proper cause of this particular fruit, although God is the proper cause of the being of this same fruit."[57] Garrigou posits a robust integrity of the human will to act as a proper cause of its effects. He states: "My free determination insofar as it is individual, *mine*, has its proper cause in *my will*; but this same free determination, insofar as it *exists*, depends upon First Being, which is the proper cause of being."[58]

---

52. Garrigou, *Predestination*, 259: "As Zigliara points out, when persons object to physical premotion, they generally take in an active sense what Thomists take in a passive sense; they confound physical premotion either with the divine uncreated action, which we are incapable of receiving, or else with our own action that suppose premotion instead of being identical with it."

53. Garrigou, *Predestination*, 256–58.

54. Garrigou, *Predestination*, 282: "It is therefore a motion distinct both from the uncreated action that it presupposes, and from our action that follows it at the same moment. Efficacious grace is neither God nor the salutary act to which it is ordained. Thus our action remains truly our own; it is not created in us from nothing, but proceeds vitally from our faculty that is applied to its act by the divine premotion."

55. Garrigou, *Predestination*, 280.

56. Garrigou, *Predestination*, 281: "The created will is therefore the proper cause of its act in so far as it is this individual act; but it is the instrumental cause of being as regards the being of its act, vital and instrumental being, of course, as St. Thomas remarks."

57. Garrigou, *Predestination*, 281.

58. Reginald Garrigou-Lagrange, "Un nouvel examen de la Prédétermination physique," *Revue Thomiste* VII (1924): 505: "Ma détermination libre en tant qu'elle est individuelle, *mienne*, a sa cause propre dans *ma volonté*; mais cette même détermination libre, en tant qu'*être*, dépend du premier Être, cause propre de l'être."

Second, Garrigou speaks of premotion as *physical*, that is, a motion that is a real, efficient cause of its effect, not one that is merely moral.[59] A moral motion would move the will only by the way of attraction, in the way that an object proposed to the will might be said to move it. Only God can move us simply, and not just by way of attraction or inclination. "Under the influence of this motion, it moves itself."[60]

Third, Garrigou addresses why this physical motion is dubbed a *premotion*. It is a physical motion that moves according to an ontological priority (and not necessarily a priority of time).

We must get away, therefore, from imaginations which picture physical premotion as an entity which, like a small winch placed by God in our will, would precede in time our voluntary act.... We have here only a priority of causality, as in the case of the eternal decree, which transcends time, and the divine motion of this decree assures its execution. But with regard to this decree, we must say that it is measured by the unique instant of immobile eternity, which corresponds unchangeably to every successive instant of time, as the apex of a pyramid corresponds to all the points of its base and to each of its sides.[61]

Of course, according to the second sense of motion (that it is passively received by the creature), it is received by the created agent *in time*,[62] and particularly at the same time in which the free act comes forth. "From this we see that physical premotion and the free act following it instantaneously, do not depend infallibly upon what precedes them in time—that is, in the past—but only upon what precedes them in the ever unchangeable present (*nunc stans*) of eternity, which is the measure of the divine decrees."[63]

59. Osborne, "Thomist Premotion and Contemporary Philosophy of Religion," 613: "This word 'physical' is awkward because it brings to mind the causality of a physical body. But the word has a different meaning that can be best understood in context. Like the Thomists, many Catholics adhered to the Augustinian belief that God can infallibly move a free action, even though they differed from the Thomists by attributing this infallible motion to his final causality or some sort of sympathy caused in the will. For them, the motion is moral rather than physical. In contrast, Thomists used the word 'physical' to emphasize that God is not only the final cause of the will but also the first efficient cause." See also Oderberg, "Divine Premotion," 210: "It is a physical premotion—not in the sense that it is empirically measurable or subject to the laws of physics, but in contradistinction to merely moral or attractive premotion, whereby God inclines a secondary cause to move by virtue of proposing some end or object to be grasped by the patient as desirable."

60. Garrigou, *Predestination*, 282.

61. Garrigou, *Predestination*, 260–61.

62. Garrigou, *Predestination*, 261: "With regard to the motion received in the created will, it is received at the very moment of time in which the voluntary act is produced."

63. Garrigou, *Predestination*, 261.

The fourth aspect of Garrigou's definition highlights how premotion is *predetermining* and thus *infallibly efficacious*. It does not give merely a power that may be further specified to this or that act but actually moves the will to will this or that particular good. In this way, physical premotion is said to be determining, but not necessitating. It does not necessitate because it does not remove the contingency of the act. "In other words, this predetermination is non-necessitating, for it extends even to the free mode of our acts which, pertaining to being, comes under the adequate object of Omnipotence."[64] As such, it had always been determined by divine providence that Our Lord would give over his life and die for our salvation, though the predetermining decree in regard to his death is not called necessitating.[65] Our Lord could have done otherwise, which, indeed, seems essential to the meritorious nature of that most glorious act.

Thus, the predetermining divine will is the cause of God's foreknowledge of contingent events (and not something predetermining God that emanates from within man, as is posited by the Molinists). If contingent events are not determined by God then he would be able to know them only according to middle knowledge. Instead, Garrigou affirms that God's foreknowledge follows from his causality.

God foresaw from all eternity that Paul would freely be converted on his way to Damascus on a certain day and at a certain hour, because He had decided to convert him efficaciously in this manner. Without this decree, Paul's conversion would pertain only to the order of possible things and not to that of contingent futures.[66]

Of course, in no way does this limit human freedom, otherwise we would have to call into question the divine liberty, which may be said to

---

64. Garrigou, *Predestination*, 269–70.

65. Garrigou gives a number of scriptural examples here coupled with commentary by St. Thomas to prove his point. Garrigou, *Predestination*, 272: "The peculiar nature of predetermination is especially affirmed by St. Thomas when commenting on our Lord's words: 'My hour has not yet come.' 'By this is meant,' says St. Thomas, 'the hour of His passion, which is determined for Him not of necessity, but according to divine providence.' It is evidently here a question of a determining and infallible but not necessitating decree of the divine will. In like manner, commenting on the verse, 'They sought therefore to apprehend Him: and no man laid hands on Him, because His hour was not yet come,' he says: 'By this is meant His hour predetermined not from fatal necessity but by the three divine Persons.' Again, commenting on St. John's words, 'Jesus knowing that His hour had come, that He should pass out of this world to the Father,' he says: 'Neither are we to understand by this that fatal hour, as if subjected to the course and disposition of the stars, but the hour determined by the disposition of divine providence.' And concerning the words of our Lord, 'Father, the hour is come; glorify Thy Son,' he remarks: 'Neither is it the hour of fatal necessity, but of His Father's ordination and good pleasure.'"

66. Garrigou, *Predestination*, 279.

be always predetermined and necessary, according to God's unchanging nature: "for the free act already determined remains free; even the immutable act of divine liberty remains free in spite of its immutability."[67]

Finally, it should be noted that Garrigou posits three distinct ways in which physical premotion operates, or what we might call three modes of premotive operation. The first is before deliberation and is an inclination to one's end. The second is in conjunction with deliberation, a motion that moves one to act. The third is an extraordinary movement that transcends deliberation. This is a "movement of a higher order."[68] These types of movement are found within both the natural and supernatural order. Thus, he states that, in the natural order, man is 1) moved to will his happiness, 2) moved to deliberate and choose particular goods, and 3) moved in an extraordinary way, as with "the man of genius and with heroes."[69] The same three types of movement correspond to the supernatural order wherein man is 1) moved to will his supernatural end, 2) moved to deliberate such that he can act according to infused virtues, and 3) a special grace that excels deliberation.[70]

An Excursus regarding Scholastic Terminology

A word should be given about the term "premotion" itself. It has often been stated that this term does not appear in St. Thomas and thus it is alien to his treatment of the human will. However, as Garrigou points out, St. Thomas does indeed speak often of the divine motion. The prefix "pre-" is added only insofar as it is helpful for further specifying the authentic teaching of the Angelic Doctor against the Molinist error of simultaneous concurrence. It ought to be clear from the texts of St. Thomas

67. Garrigou, *Predestination*, 268.
68. Garrigou, *Predestination*, 293: "God moves our intellect and will in three ways: (1) before the act of deliberation; (2) after this act; (3) by a movement of a higher order."
69. Garrigou, *Predestination*, 293: "In the natural order God moves our will: (1) to will happiness in general (or to wish to be happy); (2) to determine itself to choose this particular good by an act of discursive deliberation; (3) He moves it by a special inspiration that excels any deliberation, such as happens with the man of genius and with heroes, as Aristotle remarked [*Nichomachean Ethics*, bk. VII, chap. 1] and also one of his disciples who argued as Plato would have done [*Eudemian Ethics*, bk. VII, chap. 14]."
70. Garrigou, *Predestination*, 293: "Likewise, in a proportionate manner, in the order of grace, God moves our will: (1) to direct itself to its supernatural end; (2) to determine itself to the use or practice of the infused virtues by means of a discursive deliberation; (3) He moves it in a manner that excels any deliberation by a special inspiration, and the gifts of the Holy Ghost render us docile to this movement."

that the divine motion has an ontological priority as primary cause over the motion of the human will as secondary cause of the good act. This is all that is meant by "*premotion.*" God's motion is antecedent to man's motion as a primary cause is antecedent to an instrumental cause, just as the hand of the painter is antecedent to the movement of the paint brush. The exact word of "premotion" may not exist within St. Thomas, but its use merely further specifies an aspect of the nature of the divine motion as taught by St. Thomas. This term is used only to speak to the theory of Molinism (which did not exist when St. Thomas was writing) or any other account that threatens to divorce the agency of the created will from the prior causal influx of divine motion. St. Thomas had no need to explicitly use this further specification at the time of his writing, though it is already in his thought implicitly.

But what is of greatest interest for us now in Molina's objection, is the way in which he avows that St. Thomas admitted that the divine motion applies secondary causes to act, which means that St. Thomas admitted not merely a simultaneous concurrence, but a premotion. This word "premotion" may seem to be a pleonasm, because every true motion has a priority, if not of time at least of causality over its effect, and in this particular case it has, for St. Thomas, a priority over the action of the secondary cause thus applied to act. The Thomists use the word "premotion" solely for the purpose of showing that the motion of which they speak is truly a motion that applies the secondary cause to act, and that it is not merely a simultaneous concurrence.[71]

The same is to be said of the term "physical," which for the commentators simply means "real." Premotion is a true efficient cause of motion in the patient (and thus is the principle of the patient's self-motion), not merely a moral cause that moves only indirectly by attraction. God actually moves the will to move. He does not merely entice it. Again, this is clearly the thought of St. Thomas and, as Garrigou asserts, the commentators would have been happy to continue speaking about divine motion and grace without the further specification that it was physical if the opinion of the Angelic Doctor had not been challenged. In other words, there was no need for St. Thomas to use the term "physical" because it was so obvious as to be assumed and presupposed. There was no question that it was indeed a real cause, as St. Thomas so often states. The commentators who

71. Garrigou, *Predestination*, 246–47.

use it, therefore, use it only in an attempt to *preserve* the thought of their master. The same is true for "predetermining," which means only that the divine motion is antecedent to the movement of the patient and that it is a determinate rather than a nondeterminate motion.

Therefore the Thomists use the expression "predetermining physical premotion" only for the purpose of excluding the theories of simultaneous concurrence and indifferent premotion. If these theories had not been proposed, as Thomas de Lemos remarked on several occasions, the Thomists would have been satisfied to speak about divine motion as St. Thomas did, for every motion as such is a premotion, and every divine motion, as divine, cannot receive a determination or perfection that is not virtually included in the divine causality.[72]

Sufficient and Efficacious Grace

In order to properly understand the mind of Garrigou on grace and the divine movement to the good, one must understand the distinction between sufficient and efficacious grace, a distinction that is of particular importance to Garrigou's treatment of this mystery.

Garrigou defines sufficient grace as "that which confers upon man the power of doing good, beyond which he requires another grace, namely, efficacious, that he may do the good."[73] It is quite clear that Garrigou is here applying the metaphysical distinction of potency and act to grace. Sufficient grace gives the power or potency to do some good, whereas efficacious grace reduces that potency to act. It truly produces the good that previously existed only in potency. "We see that this serious problem of the sufficiency of the divine help given to all men is solved by the general principle which is the dominating element in all Thomistic doctrine. It is the principle that being is divided into potency and act."[74] That

72. Garrigou, *Predestination*, 250. For objections to the usage of the term *physical premotion*,, see John F. Wippel, "Metaphysical Themes in De malo, 1," in *Aquinas's Disputed Questions on Evil: A Critical Guide*, ed. M. V. Dougherty (Cambridge: Cambridge University Press, 2016), 12–33. See also Brian Shanley, "Divine Causation and Human Freedom in Aquinas," *American Catholic Philosophical Quarterly* 72, no. 1 (1998): 99–122, and *The Thomist Tradition* (Dordrecht: Kluwer, 2002), 204. Therein Shanley argues that physical premotion is an affront to the divine transcendence, human freedom, and a true secondary causality. For a proper response to especially the first objection, see Joseph G. Trabbic, "*Praemotio Physica* and Divine Transcendence," in *Thomism and Predestination: Principles and Disputations* (Ave Maria, Fla.: Sapientia Press, 2016), 152–65.

73. Garrigou, *Grace*, 208.

74. Garrigou, *God: His Existence and His Nature*, vol. 2, 292.

which reduces a sufficient grace to a real act via efficacious grace must be God, otherwise the greatest good in us, that which spurs us forward to act well, comes not from God, the source of all good, but from man.

Otherwise, and this is the refutation of Molinism, the greatest activity of all, namely, the passage into a free supernatural act, would belong exclusively to the free will and not to God. Thus, what is greatest in the affair of salvation would not derive from the author of salvation; from God would proceed only the unstable sufficient grace which effects nothing but an indeliberate motion. God would wait upon our will for our consent.[75]

As with Báñez, Garrigou affirms that the division between sufficient and efficacious grace is in relation to a certain object or salutary action, not to the form of grace itself, which is always efficacious. Sufficient grace refers to a potency toward a further good founded upon an effacious grace to a previous good.

Garrigou does not spend significant time defending this distinction between sufficient and efficacious grace according to the work of St. Thomas because it is based on the metaphysical principle that undergirds all of reality and all of the thought of the Angelic Doctor. There are, however, numerous passages in which St. Thomas explicitly mentions the distinction.[76]

75. Garrigou, *Grace*, 208.

76. *ST* I-II, q. 106, a. 2, ad 2: "Although the grace of the New Testament helps man to avoid sin, yet it does not so confirm man in good that he cannot sin: for this belongs to the state of glory. Hence if a man sin after receiving the grace of the New Testament, he deserves greater punishment, as being ungrateful for greater benefits, and as not using the help given to him. And this is why the New Law is not said to 'work wrath': because as far as it is concerned it gives man sufficient help to avoid sin." *ST* I-II, q. 109, a. 2: "And thus in the state of perfect nature man needs a gratuitous strength superadded to natural strength for one reason, viz. in order to do and wish supernatural good; but for two reasons, in the state of corrupt nature, viz. in order to be healed, and furthermore in order to carry out works of supernatural virtue, which are meritorious. Beyond this, in both states man needs the Divine help, that he may be moved to act well." *Commentary on Ephesians*, chap. 3, lect. 2: "When he writes according to the gift of the grace of God he touches on the aid granted him to carry out the mysteries. This type of assistance was twofold. One was the capacity to put them into effect, and another was the very actions or activities themselves. God bestows the capability by infusing the virtue and grace through which a man is able and fit for action; while he confers the action itself insofar as be moves us interiorly and spurs us on to good.... inasmuch as his power causes us both to will and to act in accord with good will." *Commentary on Timothy*, chap. 1, lect. 2: "He is the propitiation for our sins, efficaciously for some, but sufficiently for all, because the price of His blood is sufficient for the salvation of all; but it has its effect only in the elect, because of the obstacle to it." *Commentary on Isaiah*, chap. 53: "Third, the salvation of the those he subjugated, for he did not subject them to himself as a tyrant, in order to abuse them, but to save them, and he has born, taken away, the sins of many efficaciously, though sufficiently for all, and has prayed for the transgressors: Father, forgive them, for they know not what they do (Lk 23:34)."

Clearly Garrigou believes that this distinction is already present in the mind of St. Thomas, and not just latently or in potency, but explicitly. Garrigou mentions the objection that this distinction was "invented by Báñez to avoid censure after the condemnation of Jansenism." He agrees with Del Prado[77] that this was "a farce invented by the Molinists" and that it was "staged by the Molinists to avoid the appearance of any opposition between Molinism and St. Thomas himself, declaring that their teaching was contrary to Báñez, not to St. Thomas."[78] Indeed, Garrigou states, regarding the entire so-called school of Báñezianism: "Treating the questions of God's foreknowledge, of predestination and of grace, many Molinists, in order to denote themselves as Thomists, refer to classic Thomism under the name of 'Bannesianism.' Informed theologians see in this practice an element of pleasantry, even of comedy."[79]

Furthermore, it should be stated that this distinction between sufficient and efficacious grace is one that naturally arises out of the distinction between the antecedent and consequent will, explicitly employed by St. Thomas. The antecedent will is the principle of sufficient grace, while the consequent will is the principle of efficacious grace.[80]

Hence we see that for St. Thomas and his school, the distinction between efficacious grace and sufficient grace has its ultimate foundation in the distinction between God's consequent will (which concerns good infallibly to be realized at the present moment) and his antecedent will (which concerns good taken in the absolute sense and not as considered in certain determined circumstances), such as, for instance, the salvation of all men in so far as it is good for all to be saved. From this antecedent or universal will to save come the sufficient graces that make it really possible for us to keep the commandments, without causing anyone, however, effectively to do so. God's consequent will in its relation to our salutary acts is the cause, on the contrary, of our effectively fulfilling our duty.[81]

The distinction is an uncomplicated one, but this does not mean that it is not controversial. As we have seen, the differing conceptions of this

---

77. Norberto Del Prado, OP, *De gratia et libero arbitrio: introductio generalis* (Fribourg: Ex Typis Consociationis Sancti Pauli, 1907), chap. 12.

78. Garrigou, *Grace*, 216.

79. Reginald Garrigou-Lagrange, *Reality: A Synthesis of Thomistic Thought*, 7th ed., trans. Patrick Cummins OSB (Ex Fontibus Company, 2012), 339.

80. Garrigou, *Predestination*, 80: "In no less clear terms than St. Augustine, St. Thomas expresses what is the foundation for the principle of predilection, in the fine distinction he draws between the antecedent will, which is the principle of sufficient grace, and the consequent will, which is the principle of efficacious grace."

81. Garrigou, *Predestination*, 238.

distinction, particularly in regard to sufficient grace, are the main point of divergence between Marín-Sola and Garrigou. It is important to speak to the various objections to Garrigou's characterization of the distinction and his replies. This will allow us to properly understand how grace and physical premotion are to be understood according to both good and bad acts in the mind of Garrigou.

Objection: That Sufficient Grace Is Insufficient
If Not Reduced to Efficacious Grace

The first and perhaps most common objection to Garrigou's definition of sufficient grace states that it is not truly sufficient. For the man who has only sufficient grace but not efficacious grace, it is not really possible to truly do good. It is argued that since man requires to be moved by God efficaciously, and since this movement is given gratuitously and not in relation to foreseen merits, the man who is not moved to do good but merely receives the potency to do so does not really have the ability to do good, and thus sufficient grace is not sufficient. Garrigou mentions this objection in his work, though he does not attribute it to anyone in particular. It is found to some extent in Marín-Sola, however, and in other modern scholars, such as Fr. William Most, Fr. Matthew Lamb, and John Hardon, SJ.[82]

---

82. William G. Most, *Predestination, and the Salvific Will of God: New Answers to Old Questions* (Front Royal, Va.: Christendom Press, 1997), 435: "But, the first reason he gives does not explain the case: for it is not enough that 'the created ability in its own category can produce such an act.' This means merely that man has the ability. But it does not explain at all how he can get also the application. He is no more capable of applying himself than a fire can apply itself to the food that is to be cooked, even though the fire too 'in its own category can produce such an act,' namely, the act of cooking. So, in spite of the first explanation, it still remains true that man, in the adequate, undistinguished sense, cannot apply himself." See also Matthew Lamb, "The Mystery of Divine Predestination: Its Intelligibility According to Bernard Lonergan," in *Thomism and Predestination: Principles and Disputations*, ed. Steven A. Long, Roger W. Nutt, and Thomas Joseph White, OP (Ave Maria, Fla.: Sapientia Press, 2016), 214–225, 219: "Neither Báñez nor Molina understood the immediacy of divine causality as Aquinas had. Physical premotion is created; it is not God. Therefore efficacious and sufficient grace is not adequate in grasping Aquinas's position. One the one hand, Báñez does not have God cause the sinner's sinning, but sufficient grace makes it impossible for the sinner to do what is right. Merely sufficient grace is not sufficient!" See also John Hardon, SJ, *History and Theology of Grace: The Catholic Teaching on Divine Grace* (Ypsilanti, Mich.: Veritas Press, 2002), 266: "In the Banezian system, before efficacious grace is received there is no real power to perform a salutary act. After its reception there is no corresponding ability to do anything but that act." Presumably Hardon means by "power" and "ability" a potency. As we have shown, it is quite erroneous to state that the only true potencies are those that are actuated. One has a potency for something even if it isn't yet actuated, and one truly

Garrigou's response is that those who make this objection are falling into the error of the Megarians, which had been condemned by Aristotle[83] and St. Thomas. Essentially, this error collapses potency and act together, rendering potency to be nothing unless it is in act.

He [Aristotle] draws his intended conclusion, saying that, if the absurdities mentioned above cannot be admitted, it is obvious that potency and actuality are distinct. But those who hold the foregoing position make potency and actuality the same insofar as they say that something has potency only when it is in a state of actuality. And from this it is evident that they wish to remove from nature something of no little importance, for they eliminate motion and generation, as has been stated (1802). Hence, since this cannot be admitted, it is obvious that something is capable of being which yet is not, and that something is capable of not being which yet is. And "it is similar in the case of the other categories," or predicaments, because it is possible from someone who is not walking to walk, and conversely it is possible from someone who is walking not to walk.[84]

To claim that man can only do good when he is doing good is to do away with potency all together. We do not say that a fire could not have cooked a steak just because it does not do so. The potency was retained even if it was never reduced to act. In this way, Garrigou states that "sufficient grace is really sufficient in its own order, since it confers the proximate power of doing good."[85] In no way does this mean that if the power is not

---

had a potency for some other choice even if they might have made this one. One might as well say that, under the Banezian system, each human being could in no way imaginable have gone to a different school, pursued a different career, married someone different, entered a different religious order, etc., but this is absurd precisely because potency is truly distinct from act. That one goes to Paris for a vacation rather than Belfast in no way means that one is not able to go to Belfast. Thus, Osborne is exactly right when he states: "It is my belief that the contemporary dismissals of physical premotion are unfounded because they neglect key distinctions that are developed by such commentators as Dominic Báñez and John of St. Thomas in the context of their reading of Thomas Aquinas" ("Thomist Premotion and Contemporary Philosophy of Religion," 609).

83. Aristotle, *Metaphysics*, bk. IX, chap. 3: "There are some, such as the members of the Megaric school, who say a thing has a potency for acting only when it is acting, and that when it is not acting it does not have this potency; for example, one who is not building does not have the power of building, but only one who is building when he is building; and it is the same in other cases. It is not difficult to see the absurd consequences of this position.... Therefore, if it is impossible to maintain this, it is evident that potency and actuality are distinct. But these views make potency and actuality the same, and for this reason it is no small thing which they seek to destroy. Hence it is possible for a thing to be capable of being and yet not be, and for a thing not to be and yet be capable of being. And it is similar in the case of the other categories; for example, a thing may be capable of walking and yet not walking, and be capable of not walking and yet walk. Moreover, a thing has a potency if there is nothing impossible in its having the actuality of that which it is said to have the potency."

84. Aquinas, *Commentary on Aristotle's Metaphysics*, bk. IX, chap. 3, para. 1803.

85. Garrigou, *Grace*, 219.

actualized that it would have been impossible for it to be actualized. This
is like saying that insofar as Socrates sits in this moment he never had the
ability to stand. In this we return once again to the distinction between divided and composite possibility. More will be said about this in chapter 9.

How Sufficient Grace Becomes Efficacious

As the fruit is offered within the flower, so is efficacious grace offered
within sufficient grace, provided that it not be impeded by man.[86] Sufficient grace will turn into efficacious grace if the reduction of this potency
to act is not interrupted by the placing of an impediment by the created
agent.[87] Garrigou states:

For sufficient grace is indeed the principle of a good work, virtually containing it,
and would in fact accomplish it (under the continuous influence of God, as the
flower under the continuous influence of the sun), did not man, by his defective
liberty, resist it. Thus a good seed, consigned to the earth, bears fruit unless it is
prevented by some deficiency in the soil.[88]

As we have stated, efficacious grace is that which produces the good act. It
reduces to act the potency that is virtually offered within sufficient grace.
"It is of faith that God grants us efficacious graces which are not only
followed by the good consent of free will, but which in a certain manner
produce it: for efficacious or effective grace makes us act."[89] Efficacious
grace is a supernatural predetermining physical premotion, and thus it
must be said to be intrinsically and infallibly efficacious.[90]

86. Garrigou, *Grace*, 221: "As the fruit is offered to us in the flower, although, if a hailstorm occurs,
the flower is destroyed and the fruit does not appear which would have developed from the flower,
under the continued influence of the sun and of the moisture in the plant, so is efficacious grace offered to us in sufficient grace, although, if resistance or sin occurs, sufficient grace is rendered sterile
and efficacious grace is not given."

87. Steven A. Long speaks similarly in "Providence, Freedom, and the Natural Law," *Nova et
Vetera*, English ed., 4, no. 3 (2006), 557–606, 559n46: "Of course, divine aid is only withheld because
of prior resistance; but this prior resistance itself traces to defect and negation, and these must be permitted if they are to be (no other answer is consistent with the omnipotence of God)." "Providence,
liberté, et loi naturelle," trans. Hyacinthe Defos du Rau, OP, and Serge-Thomas Bonino, OP, *Revue
Thomiste* 102, no. 3 (2002): 355–406; n53: "Dieu ne refuse évidemment son secours qu'en raison de la
libre résistance antérieure. Mais cette résistance antérieure elle-même a sa racine dans la défaillance et
la négation qui, elles, doivent être permises si elles doivent être (il n'y a pas d'autre réponse qui fasse
droit à la toute-puissance de Dieu)."

88. Garrigou, *Grace*, 221.

89. Garrigou, *Predestination*, 309.

90. Garrigou, *Predestination*, 311: "Now if we admit the fact of intrinsically and infallibly efficacious

While some have claimed that efficacious grace acts only as a moral cause of our good deeds, this is denied because moral causes or motions are not infallible. Moral movements are ones that entice or enchant the will. They attract it rather than working directly on it, moving it to will what it wills. As such, these kinds of movements can never be infallible. We may be able to attract the will of a friend to some good on many occasions, but there are always times when this attraction fails.

The fundamental reason that they give is that God cannot infallibly move the will by means of a moral or objective motion. Now intrinsically efficacious grace is that by which God infallibly moves the will to make the salutary choice. Therefore intrinsically efficacious grace cannot be explained by simply a moral or objective motion. The major of this premise rests upon the principle that by a moral or objective motion the will is reached only through the medium of the intellect by way of objective attraction, and is not infallibly drawn by this motion. Undoubtedly, God seen face to face would infallibly attract our will because He adequately satisfies its capacity for love. But every attraction, however exalted it may be, is unable to fully satisfy this capacity and is fallible; it leaves the will undetermined whether to consent or not, especially with a weak will, with one that is hard and indocile to the divine call, so long as it is not intrinsically changed.[91]

Furthermore, a moral cause is not an efficient cause. It helps to bring about a movement of the will in another, but it does not entirely explain it since the movement is merely the movement of attraction. It leaves the will undecided.[92] Again we return to the idea that man moves to some good without being moved entirely by God. He would be attracted by grace, but ultimately it would be up to man to assent to that attraction and to go with it, as it were. Such a thesis would leave God, rather than man, as the one who is most determined, at least in regard to free creaturely acts. The impossibility of this conclusion means that the premotion of

---

grace, how can we account for it except by saying that it is so by reason of the predetermining physical premotion in the sense just explained?"

91. Garrigou, *Predestination*, 312.

92. Garrigou, *Predestination*, 313: "The multiplicity of the graces of attraction would not give the salutary acts an infallible efficacy; for the will remains undecided whether to consent or not, although it is ardently solicited or inclined to give its salutary consent. Thus the persecutors promised all the goods of this world to the holy martyrs, at the same time attempting to frighten them by the threat of all the torments; but neither these promises nor threats of torments could infallibly influence their liberty of action. In like manner, inefficacious good movements incline the will to make the salutary choice, but they cannot infallibly cause this act; for they, too, leave our free will *undecided*. They do not effect the free choice, to say nothing of the fact that they often have to contend with great temptations and the fickleness of our free will in the performance of good."

efficacious grace must be physical. It does not pose an attraction to the intellect, soliciting the will indirectly. "It must exert its effect immediately *from within*; on the will itself, and not through the intervention of the intellect."[93] And, of course, this sort of physical premotion can only come from God, for "He alone by His unsullied contact can so move the will as not to destroy its liberty, and can reconcile His infallible motion with the free mode of our acts."[94]

As was the case with Báñez, it ought not to be said that Garrigou is positing two distinct graces for each individual act, as if God first gives a grace that is exclusively a potency that must be reduced to act by a second grace. There is some agreement here (as we shall see) between Marín-Sola and Garrigou insofar as both agree that every grace must actually do something. Graces do not give only potencies toward the good. Potencies must be rooted in things that are in act just as matter does not exist without form. According to Garrigou, each grace is efficacious for one thing. Within that efficacious grace is the potency for a further, more perfect act. Within the efficacious grace of sorrow for having been rude to a friend is the potency to apologize and amend the friendship. Of course, that further potency must be reduced to act by a further efficacious grace, but it is not as if the potency existed apart from a different efficacious grace, somehow standing alone. "Every actual grace which is efficacious of itself with regard to an imperfect salutary act such as attrition, is sufficient with regard to a more perfect salutary act such as contrition."[95] With that being said, each further good act must be reduced to act by another grace.

Sufficient grace, which renders possible the fulfillment of duty, may therefore go very far in the order of this real possibility. But however far it may go in this order of proximate power to produce a given salutary act, for, instance, contrition, it remains distinct from the efficacious grace which will cause us to produce freely, here and now, this particular act of contrition. The latter would not in fact have been produced had it not been willed eternally by the consequent will of God.[96]

---

93. Garrigou, *Predestination*, 314.
94. Garrigou, *Predestination*, 314.
95. Garrigou, *Grace*, 431–32. (Originally found in *Revue Thomiste*, May 1937.)
96. Garrigou, *Grace*, 443.

Objection: Sufficient Grace apart from the
Accompanying Grace That Renders It Efficacious
Seems to Determine Man toward Sin

The major objection to Garrigou's schema of sufficient and efficacious grace is grounded in a concern regarding God's relation to sin. This is essentially the concern that was the basis for Maritain's work on premotion. It runs, according to Garrigou, as follows:

> If the divine motion is required for man to determine himself, and if it is infallibly although freely followed by its effect, the sinner who actually does not will what is good, does not seem to have received *sufficient help* to do so, and moreover seems to be determined by God himself to will what is evil.[97]

Garrigou's response is to state that all efficacious grace is virtually present within sufficient grace and that it will be given if the reduction from potency to act is not impeded. "All Thomists agree in saying that, if a man did not resist sufficient grace, he would receive the efficacious grace required to enable him to do his duty."[98] It is crucial to give this principle of Garrigou sufficient treatment. At the outset, it may sound as if Garrigou is proposing the frustratable motion of Marín-Sola and Maritain, though a careful parsing of Garrigou will show that this is not the case. As he states, "But here again is the mystery: for to resist sufficient grace is an evil that can come only from us; whereas not to resist sufficient grace is a good that cannot solely be the result of our action, but one which must come from God who is the source of all good."[99]

---

97. Garrigou, *God: His Existence and His Nature*, vol. 2, 283.

98. Garrigou, *Predestination*, 238–239, although this is axiom permeates all of Garrigou's work on this subject. See also Garrigou, *Grace*, 441: "In sufficient grace, we cannot repeat too often, efficacious grace is offered, as the fruit in the flower, as act in potency. But if anyone resists sufficient grace, he deserves to be deprived of the efficacious help which he would have received had it not been for this resistance."

99. Garrigou, *Predestination*, 239. See also Reginald Garrigou-Lagrange, *The One God: A Commentary on the First Part of St. Thomas's Theological Summa*, trans. Dom. Bede Rose, OSB, STD (St. Louis, Mo.: B. Herder Book Co., 1943), 555: "According to this conclusion, he who does not resist the remotely sufficient grace, will receive the proximately sufficient grace. Thus the proximately sufficient help to begin to pray is remotely sufficient with regard to the more perfect salutary act. There is the mystery, inasmuch as to resist sufficient grace is an evil that comes solely from ourselves, whereas not to resist it is a good that comes from the source of all good." Furthermore, in footnote 217, he states: "In fact, that one at the very moment does not resist sufficient grace is a good efficaciously willed by God's consequent will, which alone, as we said, is directed toward good that is at the very moment to be performed. The sufficient grace, inasmuch as it is sufficient, or as it refers to the possibility of

It is clear that in sinning (or at least in placing an impediment to efficacious grace), man resists sufficient grace, that is, he impedes that sufficient grace be turned to efficacious grace. Man resists being moved to
the further good offered to him within any given grace. But as we have already seen, all good movements in man require God as the primary cause.
It is impossible, then, for man to not impede or to not resist sufficient
grace if he is not given the efficacious grace to accept and will that further
good rather than resist it. The conclusion is that man sins because he is
deprived of efficacious grace. He sins because he is given "an insufficiency
of help." Garrigou agrees with the premises of this argument but denies
the conclusion.[100] The careful consideration of how this is possible leads
us to Garrigou's treatment of God's permissive will and the reality of sin.

Sin

Garrigou states that man is the cause of sin. In no way can God be said
to be the cause of sin, which would be an impossibility. Garrigou says
that efficacious grace is withheld as a result of the previous resistance to
sufficient grace. He states:

But it is false to say that man sins because he is deprived of efficacious grace;
rather, on the contrary, it should be said that he is deprived of efficacious grace
because by sinning he resist sufficient grace. For a man to sin, his own defective
will suffices, and resistance to sufficient grace always precedes, at least by a priority of nature (on the part of the material cause, man) the divine denial of efficacious grace; in other words, God refuses efficacious grace only to one who resists
sufficient grace; otherwise there would be an injustice involved. And what on the
part of God precedes this resistance is only the divine permission of sin. But this
divine permission must not be confused with a denial of efficacious grace, which
signifies something more.[101]

---

complying with God's commands, depends on His antecedent will; but, inasmuch as it is a gift and a
good bestowed at the very moment, it depends on His consequent will, and it truly produces in us the
good thought and often the pious desire that inclines the will in its choice of the means for salvation."

100. Garrigou, *Grace*, 223: "I insist. To neglect or resist sufficient grace is not to consent to it or to
sin at least by a sin of omission. But in order that a man may not neglect or resist sufficient grace, efficacious grace is required. Therefore man sins because he is deprived of efficacious grace, in other words,
from an insufficiency of help. Reply. I grant the major, and the minor as well, but deny the conclusion."

101. Garrigou, *Grace*, 223.

The act of sin may be said to be composed of four ontological (not necessarily temporal) moments: 1) God permits a defect to arise in the creature. 2) Due to the defect, the creature resists sufficient grace. 3) Efficacious grace is withheld as a punishment for the creature's resistance. 4) The creature falls into sin. Man still requires a motion for the sinful act insofar as it is an act, but God does not cause the act to be sinful, which comes entirely from man, the cause of sin.[102]

Garrigou states that the withholding of efficacious grace is a just punishment for an antecedent sin that resists that a sufficient grace be actualized as an efficacious one. Since man resists, God justly withholds the efficacious grace that would have resulted in his not resisting and actually accomplishing the good deed that was possible given the gift of sufficient grace. "Hence the denial of efficacious grace is an act of justice, inasmuch as it is the punishment for preceding sin, at least with the priority of nature, that is, sin at least in its incipiency."[103]

However, what of the beginning of sin or the placing of a defect or impediment to divine grace? Should these always be understood as punishments as well, insofar as they could be overcome by God upholding creatures in grace such that they never place an impediment in the first place? Certainly the beginning of sin in mankind, or even the beginning of sin in the individual, is not a punishment for a preceding sin. Therefore, some object that it is unjust to allow that first sin, or even to punish based upon sins which follow or flow from that first sin.

Garrigou responds by distinguishing the withholding of efficacious grace from the permission of sin, the former of which is said to be a punishment for sin, while the latter is not. "The notion of a denial of grace, formally signifies more than a simple permission of sin, since it includes,

---

102. Garrigou, *God: His Existence and His Nature*, vol. 2, 296: "For a better understanding of this, we must call to mind that the divine motion inclines the will first of all toward its adequate object, which is universal good, and only after that toward an inadequate object, which is a certain particular good. In the first kind of good the divine motion constitutes the *free mode* of the act; it operates interiorly in the very depths of the will taken in its widest extent, and, so to say, directs it through all the degrees of good, the proffered efficacious grace included. And it is only after a *voluntary inadvertence* to our duty that our will, through its defection, is inclined toward a certain particular good which is contrary to God's law, and it is then that God moves it to the physical act of sin. This voluntary inconsideration precedes the culpable choice according to a priority of nature, if not of time. The will, which is naturally inclined to good and not to evil, does not tend and is not straightway drawn to evil; it inclines to an apparent good only after turning away from true goods. Therefore when God moves it to the physical act of sin, it has already virtually refused the grace offered to it."

103. Garrigou, *Grace*, 222.

in addition, the punishment due to sin which is at least incipient, which punishment is not implied in the concept of permission of sin, since this latter is entirely antecedent to the sin."[104] While it is true that the upholding from defect requires an efficacious grace ("if God, at that instant, were to preserve man in goodness, there would be no sin"), Garrigou here is speaking of efficacious grace only in relation to that which is given virtually in sufficient grace for a certain good act. To be upheld from defect requires a grace that is efficacious, but when Garrigou speaks specifically of efficacious grace he means to speak of only the third ontological moment of the act. In the good act, this is the giving of efficacious grace. In the bad act, this is the withholding of efficacious grace as a punishment. Garrigou rarely, if ever, uses "efficacious grace" to refer to grace that upholds a creature from defect in moment one (the lack of which is the permission of defect, which is antecedent to the impediment in the act of sin).

The denial of God's efficacious grace is not indeed a moral evil, but it is a just punishment which presupposes the guilt of sin. To be without grace is a privation of good, and is not a moral evil but a punishment. Thus this denial of grace differs from the non-maintenance by God of anyone in the performance of good, which precedes even the first sin, and which is neither moral evil nor a punishment.[105]

Thus, efficacious grace is only withheld as a punishment for the resisting of sufficient grace, while the permission of sin cannot be said to be a punishment for the resisting of sufficient grace (at least not always). Garrigou explicitly warns against the dangers of confusing these first and third moments of act.

Calvin confuses the first principle with the third, namely, God's permission of sin with His denial of grace, whereas St. Thomas plainly distinguishes between them (I Sent., d. 40, q. 4, a. 2).... Thus there is a difference between God's permission of sin, which precedes it and which is only its indispensable condition (not being at all its cause, either direct or indirect), and being abandoned by Him, which is the result of sin.[106]

Now, it must be stated that sin would not exist in the first place if it were not for this divine permission. God's will is not frustrated. As such, there is nothing that exists that somehow escapes God's will. All good things that

104. Garrigou, *Grace*, 224.
105. Garrigou, *The One God*, 687.
106. Garrigou, *The One God*, 687–88.

really exist are willed by God simply, and all bad things are also willed, but only insofar as they are intentionally *allowed* to exist. We do not say that they are willed simply, for God does not directly will any evil, but He may permit that it exists for a greater good. We say, then, that God permits the evil or sin that does occur, or that it is part of God's permissive will.

But sin itself presupposes, not indeed as a cause, but as a condition, divine permission. Therefore the divine refusal of grace thus inflicting punishment on account of sin means something more than a simple divine permission of sin or the beginning of sin; for the permission of the incipiency of the first sin has no reason of punishment with respect to any preceding sin, and this incipiency of sin could not occur without divine permission, since if God, at that instant, were to preserve a man in goodness there would be no sin.[107]

This permissive will, or the antecedent permissive decree (an ontological "moment" that is prior to the defect, or else it would never arise), is not in any way a cause of sin, but is simply a *condicio sine qua non*. It is an indispensable condition of the sin, and thus without it the sin would not exist. However, this does not make it in any way the cause of the sin. In a similar manner, if I do not give to my beerless (and thus pitiable) neighbor the last beer in my refrigerator, this does not mean that I have caused his beerlessness, although it is true that my not giving him my last beer is an indispensable condition of his not having any beer. If I had given it to him then he would not be in his sorry state of beerlessness.

As for the disorder of sin, God who condemns it, permits it without being its cause. This divine permission is only a condition *sine qua non*. The disorder proceeds solely from the defective and deficient created will and in no sense from God, who absolutely cannot produce it; for this disorder is outside the adequate object of His will and omnipotence, just as sound is beyond the range of the sense of sight, or truth outside the adequate object of the will.[108]

But why is it that God permits defects (and thus sins) at all? The reason for this is simple: man is a defectible creature. It is not owed to him that he never be subject to defect, nor is it owed to him that God always elevate him above and beyond his nature as a creature that is quite fallible, as St. Thomas says in *ST* I, q. 23, a. 5, ad 3.[109] In a similar manner, my beer

---

107. Garrigou, *Grace*, 222–23.
108. Garrigou, *Grace*, 450.
109. "Neither on this account can there be said to be injustice in God, if He prepares unequal

is not owed to my neighbor. If it were, then I would be at least partly responsible for his state of beerlessness in my not giving him my last beer.
Indeed, Garrigou states: "But God is not bound to preserve in good forever a creature in itself deficient, and if He were held to this, no sin would
ever take place."[110]

Similarly, he states:

That the will, which by its nature is defectible, is not maintained by God in the
performance of good is not yet an evil, because it is not the privation of good to
which one is entitled. God is not bound always to maintain in the performance
of good the will which by its nature is defectible; whereas, on the contrary, He
is bound always to maintain it in existence along with the immortal soul. Similarly, on the part of the creature, the will, which by its nature is defectible, is not
bound always to be maintained in the performance of good, but only in being.
If it were entitled to the former, then it would be impeccable. Hence it is not an
evil that the will, which by its nature is defectible, is not maintained by God in
the performance of good.[111]

In this we can see why the permission of sin, which is "entirely antecedent
to sin,"[112] is still just. Human beings are fallible creatures. It is not due to
us that we be perfect as God is perfect. In fact, without a constant influx
of divine aid, without God working in us and animating us, we will certainly fall into error, sin, and the relative nonexistence that is implied by
both. This is the predicament of the human condition. We are not only
totally and completely dependent on God for our existence, but also for
our goodness and beauty, whatever of it that we do have. Garrigou quotes
Ferrariensis on this, and the citation is of use to us here.

Although sin is the demeritorious cause of abandonment by God and the disposing cause of eternal punishment, the permission, which exists first in the reprobate, is not the cause of sin, for it does not invest the reprobate with anything

---

lots for not unequal things. This would be altogether contrary to the notion of justice, if the effect of
predestination were granted as a debt, and not gratuitously. In things which are given gratuitously, a
person can give more or less, just as he pleases (provided he deprives nobody of his due), without any
infringement of justice. This is what the master of the house said: 'Take what is thine, and go thy way.
Is it not lawful for me to do what I will?' (Mt. 20:14, 15)."

110. Garrigou, *Grace*, 223.

111. Garrigou, *The One God*, 686–87.

112. Garrigou, *Grace*, 224: "I deny the major, for the notion of a denial of grace, formally, signifies
more than a simple permission of sin, since it includes, in addition, the punishment due to sin which is
at least incipient, which punishment is not implied in the concept of permission of sin, *since this latter
is entirely antecedent to the sin.*" Emphasis is mine.

whereby he falls into sin, since he sins with his free will, nor does it remove anything which would withhold him from sin.[113]

It is true that without the antecedent permission of sin, man will be withheld from sin, but in no way does the permission of sin contribute anything to man's sinning. The permission of sin permits only that man not be lifted up above himself, that he not be withheld from his own fallible and defectible nature. It does not rob man of some power that he is due whereby he may act well. It does not steal from him his inheritance, nor does it positively move or force him to fall into sin. To put it quite simply, the permission is not in any way a positive movement from God at all. It is the state of a lack of movement that man is not owed in any way, as St. Thomas states.

There are some who state that if God is the cause of the goodness in us when he bestows upon us grace, then He must be the cause of sinfulness in us when He does not give the grace needed to be upheld from defect and sin. But, as Garrigou points out, this objection has already been answered by St. Thomas himself. The objection:

Augustine says in his work *On Nature and Grace* that the soul has grace as the light whereby human beings do good, and without which they cannot do good. Therefore, grace causes merit. Therefore, by contrast, the withdrawal of grace causes sin. But God is the one who withdraws grace. Therefore, God causes sin.[114]

St. Thomas replies:

God as he is in himself communicates himself to all things in proportion to their receptivity. And so if something should deficiently share in his goodness, this is because the thing has an obstacle to participating in God. Therefore, God does not cause grace not to be supplied to someone; rather, those not supplied with grace offer an obstacle to grace insofar as they turn themselves away from the light that does not turn itself away, as Dionysius says.[115]

All of this is to say nothing other than that man is the cause of the withholding of efficacious grace. This may only be possible given the permission of defect and sin, but this permission follows simply from man being man, imperfect and contingent. It is the not-giving of something that is not due. Garrigou summarizes:

113. Ferrariensis, *Commentary on* Summa contra Gentiles, bk. III, chap. 161, 4.
114. *De malo*, q. III, a. 1, arg. 8.
115. *De malo*, q. III, a. 1, ad 8.

Thus, with regard to this objection: it is granted that if efficacious grace were given to a man he would not sin, but it does not follow that he sins for this reason or cause of not being given efficacious grace. The permission of sin is only the condition of sin, not its cause. We must beware of confusing a cause which exerts a positive influence with an indispensable condition which does not exert an influence; otherwise there would be a vicious circle, as when it is said: I believe the Church to be infallible because God revealed this; and I believe God revealed it because it is affirmed by the Church. In the second proposition "because" is not taken in the same sense as in the first, for it does not signify the formal motive of faith, but only the indispensable condition of faith, that is, the infallible proposition of the object of faith. Similarly, in our present case, the permission of the first sin and not being preserved in good is an indispensable condition of this sin but not its cause, for sin as such requires only a deficient cause. But on the other hand, not sinning or being preserved in good is an effect of the preserving hand of God.[116]

The objection that "if an affirmation is the cause of an affirmation, a negation is the cause of a negation"[117] is rooted in an incorrect view of God's responsibility and causation in regard to the defectible creature. It is viewed by many as the captain of the ship in relation to the ship. The captain is responsible for the safety of the ship, and thus when he is not piloting it properly, he can be said to be the cause of whatever peril befalls the ship. But, Garrigou says, this does not follow if we are speaking of two causes, the first of which is indefectible and not bound to uphold the second from every error. The second cause is defectible by nature. According to its mode of existence, it is the sort of thing that fails, and sometimes God allows this to actually happen (though quite often He lifts the defectible creature above itself such that it is preserved from error). But insofar as the creature is not owed to be upheld all the time, the one who can uphold it is not responsible whenever it freely defects, just as one is not responsible for the beerlessness of his pitiable neighbor even though he could indeed provide him with beer. The beer is not owed to the neighbor, nor has one caused the neighbor not to have beer. The neighbor has gone beerless on his own, by his own volitional disregard for his happiness. If, however, one does indeed provide the beer, one does it out of gratuity, as God acts out of gratuity when he so often upholds us from our own frailty.

116. Garrigou, *Grace*, 226.
117. Garrigou, *Grace*, 227.

Hence the major of the preceding objection (i.e., if an affirmation is the cause of an affirmation, a negation is the cause of a negation) is valid when there is but one cause, which is bound to act, as the pilot by his presence is the cause of the ship's safety and by his absence, when he is bound to be present, the cause of its danger. But this major is not true if there are two causes of which the first is indefectible and not bound to prevent every evil and the second is deficient; for then this latter alone is the deficient cause of its own defection.[118]

As such, the Thomists cannot be called Jansenists, Calvinists, or Lutherans, who assert that God positively determines man toward evil, such that he loses his free will and all possibility of doing good. Garrigou, summarizing an argument from Gonet, states:

Although the permissive decree may thus have an infallible connection with future sin, a consequence not of causality but of logical sequence, "it does not follow, however, that the free will of man is, of itself and by nature, determined toward evil and sin; not only because by reason of sufficient help it can do good and avoid sin (against the Jansenists), but also because it is one thing for free will to be deficient of itself and by nature and not capable of preserving itself in good according to right reason, on account of God's not preserving it by special means, and another thing for it to be of itself and by nature determined toward evil (as if it were destroyed altogether and not merely weakened). In the first case is signified only the deficiency and potentiality for sinning which belong to the rational creature by the very fact that he is made from nothing and is not the rule of his own operations.[119]

The permission of sin in no way determines man toward sin as if it removed from man his potency to do good and avoid evil. It does not positively determine anything in man, but merely leaves him to his own devices, as it were. Every man is truly provided with help that is sufficient to avoid evil and to do good. When God permits that man be allowed to

---

118. Garrigou, *Grace*, 227. See also Garrigou, *Grace*, 228, where Garrigou quotes Édouard Hugon, *De Deo uno*: "The permissive decree is a sufficient, certain, infallible medium. For if God wills to permit something, it most certainly will happen, not by causal necessity, but by logical necessity, just as, if God withholds efficacious concurrence, the good effect is not produced (however, the divine permission of sin implies the nonpreservation of the defective will in good, to which preservation God is not bound; otherwise a defective will would never fall into defect). Granting the divine permission of sin, anyone can become good, since man retains his real antecedent power; and he can avoid evil, since the omission of the decree or the permissive decree itself removes none of that real antecedent power; but as a matter of fact, if God wills to permit the evil which He is not bound to prevent, that real power will never be reduced to act. Hence, knowing His permissive decree, God infallibly recognized the deficiency, although He does not cause it."

119. Garrigou, *Grace*, 229.

act in accord with his defectible nature, man will defect, and God does not stop this. But this does not mean that man was not provided with assistance sufficient to act well. The fire that does not cook a steak is not said to never have had the ability to cook a steak. But insofar as God has permitted that man will fall, it so happens that man does infallibly choose to place an impediment to grace. He resists of his own free will and does fall, though it is not determined or necessitated by God.

Hence the divine motion does not surprise the innocent man, who would find himself poised between good and evil, so as to incline him to evil. *God never determines to the material act of sin unless the creature has already determined itself to what formally constitutes sin.* He moves the wills according to their dispositions; consequently He moves to the physical act of sin only the will already badly disposed and demanding, so to speak, to be thus moved.[120]

It is also always the case that God gives to man more than he deserves. Insofar as God upholds defectible creatures from defect at all, he gives to them gratuitously. But he does not always do so in every moment because he wishes to manifest his goodness by bringing a higher goodness out of rational creatures falling into defect and sin.[121] "God often removes the obstacle, but not always. There is the mystery."[122]

Evidently it was not God who urged Judas to betray Jesus. He merely permits the crime, though condemning it. He is not bound to prevent it. It is natural that what is defectible should sometimes fail, and the crime of Judas will be the means of bringing about a good which is greater than the salvation of the traitor. Can we say the wretched man did not receive sufficient help to avoid evil? Only the day before, Christ washed the traitor's feet; Judas, through his own fault, resisted the divine prevenient graces abundantly bestowed on him; the Lord was not the first to forsake him. At the last moment, Judas could have repented, if he had not doubted the divine mercy. Neither did God urge Peter to deny Christ. St. Peter had received sufficient helps and warnings to avoid this fall. But he relied too much on his own strength; he learnt by experience that of himself alone he could do nothing but fall, and henceforth he placed all his trust in the grace of the Savior.[123]

120. Garrigou, *God: His Existence and His Nature*, vol. 2, 297–98.
121. Garrigou, *Grace*, 261: "The first cause of the defect is our will so far as it is defective and deficient. God, however, is the unfailing cause, not bound to prevent the defect of sin, whereas He can, for higher reasons, permit it on account of a greater good."
122. Garrigou, *Predestination*, 80.
123. Garrigou, *God: His Existence and His Nature*, vol. 2, 284–85.

As we shall see when we treat reprobation, the reason for the permission of sin and final impenitence is obscure to us, though St. Thomas says that it is permitted that a greater good might come about. And this is true not only in the eternal finality of the lost soul but also in the life of the predestined. Garrigou states that even the elect are permitted to sin that greater goods might be effected in their lives. When we are allowed to fall, our human frailty and utter dependence on God are made manifest to us in a conspicuous and forceful way.

It is also more probable that the permission of sin in the predestined, inasmuch as it is the means of a greater sanctification for them, is the effect of predestination. This last statement must be understood in the right sense. Indeed it is not sin but the permission of sin that is the effect of predestination, inasmuch as this permission is meant to be the occasion of leading the elect to greater humility and more fervent charity, as is seen in the life of St. Mary Magdalen, or in St. Peter's life after his repentance for having denied the Lord.[124]

Of course, we cannot completely understand the mystery of sin in this life. We should not expect to. As Garrigou states, "It will always remain obscure for us, because we have not an adequate knowledge of grace or of liberty."[125] This leads us to the mystery of predestination and reprobation.

Predestination

Garrigou defines predestination as "the divine preordination of the elect to glory and the means by which they will infallibly obtain it."[126] This is an intellectual and volitional act of God whereby He wills the elect to glory. "From this it follows that predestination, since it is the efficacious ordination of the means of salvation to the end, is an act of the divine intellect which presuppose an act of the will."[127] Predestination is nothing more than a part of the undivided[128] providence of God.

124. Garrigou, *The One God*, 681–82.
125. Garrigou, *God: His Existence and His Nature*, vol. 2, 285.
126. Garrigou, *Predestination*, 184.
127. Garrigou, *Predestination*, 185.
128. Garrigou, *The One God*, 679: "The reason why divine providence is one and undivided is because its object is one, namely, the universe, which consists of three subordinated orders, and there is one end to which all these orders are ordained, which is God's glory."

St. Thomas says at the end of the argumentative part of this article [1]: "Predesti-nation, as regards its objects, is a part of providence." This means that predestina-tion constitutes some part of the material object of providence. Thus it is that one and the same divine providence concerns the three orders of nature, grace, and the hypostatic union, there being no virtual distinction between these kinds of providence, and it is only because of the different objects that this divine provi-dence receives different names. In this respect it resembles the divine knowledge, which in itself is only of one kind, yet because of its different material objects it is called the knowledge of simple intelligence, of vision, and of approbation.[129]

Furthermore, predestination must be said to rest upon the principle of predilection. "God, indeed, ordains for Peter in preference to Judas the efficacious means of salvation, because He wills efficaciously to save him, because He loved him with a love of predilection and chose him."[130]

The principle of predilection states that no man would be better than another if he were not loved more by God.[131] In order to prove that this is the thought of the Angelic Doctor, Garrigou quotes the following text from the *Summa Theologiae*, q. 20, a. 3 and 4.

In another way on the part of the good itself that a person wills for the beloved. In this way we are said to love that one more than another, for whom we will a greater good, though our will is not more intense. In this way we must needs say that God loves some things more than others. For since God's love is the cause of goodness in things, as has been said, no one thing would be better than another, if God did not will greater good for one than for another.[132]

I answer that, It must needs be, according to what has been said before, that God loves more the better things. For it has been shown, that God's loving one thing more than another is nothing else than His willing for that thing a greater good: because God's will is the cause of goodness in things; and the reason why some things are better than others, is that God wills for them a greater good. Hence it follows that He loves more the better things.[133]

If God is the cause of goodness in creatures then it must be the case that insofar as God gives more goodness (completely gratuitously, let us not

129. Garrigou, *The One God*, 679.
130. Garrigou, *Predestination*, 185.
131. Garrigou, *Predestination*, 75: "On the other hand, as regards the consequent will, St. Thomas affirms, more clearly than anyone had before his time, the principle of predilection, which is that one would not be better than another unless one were loved more by God."
132. *ST* I, q. 20, a. 3.
133. *ST* I, q. 20, a. 4.

forget) to some creatures, it may be said that He loves them more. This is merely a corollary of the principle that God's love is the cause or source of the goodness within the creature.[134]

The principle of predilection helps us to understand the difference between human loving and divine loving. In human love, our will is elicited by the good in another person. We choose the person based on the preexisting good within him or her. We are first attracted by that good and we thus choose this other as a friend or a spouse. From there blooms love. For God, however, the order is reversed. He is not elicited by some good in us for the very reason that he is the cause of whatever goodness that we have. Therefore, God loves us first, and this love is the subsequent cause of the goodness in us and our being chosen out among others in election and predestination.

In the second syllogism it is shown that in God, though not in ourselves, love precedes election. It is proved as follows: God's will, by which He wishes good to someone, is the cause of that good possessed by some in preference to others. But God by His love wills for some the good of eternal salvation, and by His election wills this good for them in preference to others. Therefore God's love precedes election in the order of reason, just as election precedes predestination. The case is the reverse with our will which, in loving anyone, does not cause good in the person loved, but is incited to love because of the good pre-existing in the person. Hence we choose someone whom we love, and thus in us election precedes love.[135]

For Garrigou, this is what St. Thomas makes to be the "keystone of his treatise on predestination,"[136] for it "presupposes, according to St. Thomas, that the decrees of the divine will with regard to our future salutary acts, are of themselves infallibly efficacious, and not because God foresees our consent." And also, "the same must be said of actual grace, by which we freely perform these salutary acts; it is of itself efficacious."[137]

The predestining of some souls to glory is, of course, previous to the

---

134. Garrigou, *Predestination*, 76: "This principle of predilection is the corollary of the preceding one, that God's love is the cause of the goodness of created beings. It seems to follow in the philosophical order as a necessary consequence of the principle of causality, that what comes in addition to a thing in existence has an efficient and supreme cause in Him who is Being itself, the source of all being and all good."

135. Garrigou, *The One God*, 689.

136. Garrigou, *Predestination*, 78.

137. Garrigou, *Predestination*, 78.

foreseeing of merit.[138] It is predestination working within the elect that is the cause of the good in them, not the other way around. Of course, man is first predestined to glory and this causes in him good works and faith by grace, which, in the order of execution precedes his attainment of glory. However, in the order of intention, predestination to glory comes first and is the cause of the grace and good effects that follow. Garrigou, quoting from the text of *ST* I, q. 23, a. 5, states:

Thus "God preordained to give glory on account of merit" (for in the order of execution, contrary to what the Protestants say, God does not give glory gratis, but according to merit); and "He preordained to give grace (efficacious, as a result of His consequent will) to merit glory." Thus God predestines to glory before He predestines to grace, for the wise man first intends the end before the means to the end.[139]

If predestination were nothing other than God granting to men the good that he has foreseen that they would merit, then, as Garrigou states,

the result of this would be that of two men or two angels equally loved and helped by God, one would become better than another. He would become better either because of a first or final act, or of one easy or difficult to perform, without having been loved or helped more by God; and then it would follow, exclusive of God's intention, first as to conditionally free acts of the future, and then as to future acts, that of these two men equally loved and helped, and placed in the same circumstances, one of them would be more virtuous than the other.[140]

Garrigou also states that predestination is certain.[141] However, one might ask whether it is certain only due to foreknowledge or if it is certain due to causality. Since Garrigou maintains that it is God who causes in us all of the good which we have, it must be the case that God not only foresees our predestination with certainty but actually causes it within us. He quotes St. Thomas:

Hence, it seems difficult to reconcile the infallibility of predestination with freedom of choice; for we cannot say that predestination adds nothing to the certi-

138. Garrigou, *The One God*, 695: "The merits of the elect are the effect of predestination, and hence they cannot be its cause."
139. Garrigou, *The One God*, 694.
140. Garrigou, *Predestination*, 79.
141. Garrigou, *Predestination*, 213: "Predestination is absolutely certain as regards the infallible positing of its effects, which are vocation, justification, and glorification."

tude of providence except the certitude of foreknowledge, because this would be to say that God orders one who is predestined to his salvation as He orders any other person, with this difference, that, in the case of the predestined, God knows he will not fail to be saved. According to this position, one predestined would not differ in ordination from one not predestined; he would differ only with respect to [God's] foreknowledge of the outcome. Consequently, foreknowledge would be the cause of predestination, and predestination would not take place by the choice of Him who predestines. This, however, is contrary to the authority of the Scriptures and the sayings of the saints. Thus, the ordering of predestination has an infallible certitude of its own—over and above the certitude of foreknowledge. Nevertheless, the proximate cause of salvation, free choice, is related to predestination contingently, not necessarily.[142]

Garrigou quotes St. Paul: "Who confers distinction upon you? What do you possess that you have not received? But if you have received it, why are you boasting as if you did not receive it?"[143] And, "Not that of ourselves we are qualified to take credit for anything as coming from us; rather, our qualification comes from God."[144] "St. Augustine and St. Thomas saw in all these texts of St. Paul the gratuity of predestination to eternal life. In other words, they perceived the motive of this to be a special mercy."[145]

The motive for predestination, as St. Thomas says, is thus that God manifests both his divine goodness and mercy, as well as his justice. God permits that some defectible creatures fall, but he preserves some and upholds them above their defectible nature as a gratuitous gift of mercy. The motive of predestination is thus the divine will's intention to bring about some greater good in a world where sin is permitted. "The general motive for predestination is, therefore, the manifestation of God's goodness that assumes the form of mercy in pardoning; and the motive for the predestination of this particular person rather than a certain other, is God's good pleasure."[146] God wishes to share his own divine life with creatures who are radically transcended by it. These creatures have no claim on it but are gifted it out of the sheer love of God.

142. *De veritate*, q. 6, a. 3.
143. 1 Cor 4:7.
144. 2 Cor 3:5. For more Scriptural evidence of this principle, see Garrigou, *Predestination*, 195–98.
145. Garrigou, *Predestination*, 201–2.
146. Garrigou, *Predestination*, 205.

Reprobation

It ought to be stated first and foremost that, for Garrigou, reprobation is not simply predestination to evil. In this way, Garrigou properly minds the dissymmetry between good and evil. "It is of faith that there is such a thing as reprobation, which does not mean, however, predestination to evil."[147] Some men are gratuitously gifted to be preordered to eternal life, but not all are so uplifted to be withheld from their human frailty. Those who are not so upheld and are not predestined to glory are said to be reprobated. "But the rest, whom by His judgment He left in the mass of perdition, He foreknew will perish, though He did not predestine that they should perish."[148]

Those who are not upheld will fall and will remain in their impenitence, but this impenitence is freely chosen and executed. The man left to his own devices does not cease to be a man. He does not cease to choose and to will. He chooses freely to reject God. And insofar as he wills evil and places impediments to sufficient grace, he is justly punished according to his sins. "But intellectual creatures, who are destined for glory, are of their nature defectible. Therefore it belongs to God's providence to permit that some through their own fault fail to attain their end, and to inflict the penalty of damnation for their sin."[149]

Reprobation, as with predestination, is not merely a foreknowledge but is something more, something volitional on the part of God. As St. Thomas says:

Hence reprobation implies not only foreknowledge, but also something more, as does providence, as was said above. Therefore, as predestination includes the will to confer grace and glory; so also reprobation includes the will to permit a person to fall into sin, and to impose the punishment of damnation on account of that sin.[150]

Unlike predestination, however, which moves man to the good as a positive influence, reprobation exerts no such influence. It is a nonact, as opposed to divine motion and predestination, which is an act. Predestination is causal. Reprobation is not. It simply permits that man act in accord

147. Garrigou, *The One God*, 683.
148. Garrigou, *The One God*, 684.
149. Garrigou, *The One God*, 684.
150. *ST* I, q. 23, a. 3.

with his fallible nature. Now, this permission does indeed imply something volitional, and this is why St. Thomas states that "reprobation implies not only foreknowledge, but also something more." This something more "includes the will to permit" (*voluntatem permittendi*). Permission is not causation, but it *is* something more than the lack of volition, otherwise evil would fall outside of God's providence, and He would no longer be said to be truly governing all of creation. Garrigou states, "This negative reprobation is the will to permit sin which *de facto* will not be forgiven; and, as we shall see, this negative reprobation is previous to foreseen demerits that are not to be forgiven, which are not infallibly foreseen as future without this divine permission."[151]

Garrigou is justifiably sensitive to any language that may have arisen within the Thomistic commentatorial tradition, which speaks of reprobation as a positive exclusion from glory. Garrigou takes up the following objection:

What must be said of the opinion of certain Thomists who maintain that negative reprobation, which is prior to the foreseeing of demerits, consists in the positive exclusion from glory, as a gift to which they are not entitled? Such was the opinion of Alvarez, the Salmanticenses, John of St. Thomas, Gonet, and Contenson.[152]

Garrigou responds:

It is more difficult to reconcile this opinion with God's universal will to save, and there seems to be no foundation for this theory on the present article of St. Thomas, or in any other passage of his works. All that St. Thomas says in this article and elsewhere is: "Reprobation includes the will to permit a person to fall into sin," especially into the sin of final impenitence and other sins that dispose one for it. He does not speak of the positive exclusion from glory as from a gift to which one is not entitled.[153]

For some, this distinction between permission to fail (which will contribute as a condition to the infallible failing of the creature) and positive exclusion is trivial, the splitting of theological hairs in a land of great severity. However, the difference here is actually quite crucial. It is, metaphysically, the difference between positively exerting an influence and exerting no influence.

151. Garrigou, *The One God*, 684.
152. Garrigou, *The One God*, 684.
153. Garrigou, *The One God*, 685.

But to exclude them from glory as from a gift to which they are not entitled would be not only not to will, but to be unwilling; it would be an act of positive exclusion from glory. This seems, however, too harsh a view, and by this very fact, these men, before their demerits were foreseen, would be excluded not only from their ultimate supernatural end, but also from their ultimate natural end.[154]

In the reply to the second objection of the *Summa*'s article on reprobation, St. Thomas states, "Reprobation, however, is not the cause of what is in the present—namely, sin; but it is the cause of abandonment by God."[155] Garrigou states that abandonment means only *after sin*, that is, that God abandons the reprobate justly on account of the sin that follows from the evil that is freely chosen by his fallible will.[156]

This means that God does not positively exclude the reprobate from the real *possibility* of eternal life (even if we know that the reprobate will indeed not attain it). We know that the defectible creature will fall if it is not upheld, but this does not positively exclude it from the potency to act well. Far from excluding, reprobation is a permission that does nothing. It does not invest the creature with something that makes attainment of the beatific vision impossible, nor does it divest the creature of anything that makes attainment of the beatific vision possible. This is not to say that reprobation is not something volitional, for it is a volitional permission, but it exerts no positive influence upon the reprobate. It merely leaves man to be man, a defectible creature.

In reply to the third objection it is explained that the reprobate can be saved, although *de facto* he will not be saved. This point is better explained, however, if we bear in mind that before foreseen demerits such a person is not excluded from glory as from a gift to which one is not entitled. Therefore this opinion of certain Thomists seems scarcely reconcilable with God's universal will to save. For God, to the utmost extent, sincerely wills by His antecedent will that all be saved, so that it is their own fault if they are damned. But He would not will to be saved if, before having foreseen any sin on the part of the reprobate, He had decreed positively to exclude such a person from eternal salvation as from a gift to which one is not entitled.[157]

154. Garrigou, *The One God*, 685.
155. *ST* I, q. 23, a. 3, ad 2.
156. Garrigou, *The One God*, 685: "Similarly, in the reply to the second objection it is stated that 'reprobation is the cause of abandonment by God,' that is, after sin and on account of sin."
157. Garrigou, *The One God*, 685.

Garrigou states that positively excluding any man from all possibility of attaining his supernatural or natural end before sin cannot be on account of punishment, and therefore cannot be called good in any way. But God does not positively will things unless they are good. Therefore it cannot be said that reprobation is properly called a positive exclusion from grace and glory.

God wills whatever there is of good in anything. But that a person, who is ordained to an ultimate end that is both natural and supernatural, before the foreseeing of sin, be excluded from this end as from a gift to which one is not entitled, is not in itself anything good. Therefore God, before the foreseeing of sin, does not exclude a person from the ultimate natural and supernatural end as from a gift to which one is not entitled.[158]

As such, Garrigou affirms that St. Thomas teaches a negative reprobation, not one that in any way exerts a positive movement or force upon the reprobate to evil, nor that removes or takes from man anything that is due to him or by which he has the potency to do good. We know that the man who is not predestined by God (out of sheer gratuity) will not ultimately choose the good, but this is by permission and not causal exclusion.

Hence negative reprobation is simply God's will to permit one through one's own fault to fail to reach the ultimate end. Therefore Thomist theologians generally distinguish between the permission of sin and the denial of efficacious grace; for this latter is an evil that implies a penalty and it therefore presupposes sin; whereas, on the contrary, the permission of sin precedes the sin, and is not a penalty, but something that is not good; for privation is more than a simple denial. There is a great difference, indeed, between not giving something that is gratuitous and refusing to give it.[159]

In this way Garrigou speaks of the dissymmetry between the line of good and the line of evil. God intends good but never intends evil. It is true that He permits it, for if He did not, evil would never arise. But God permits it for a greater good. This is something quite different than intending the evil in and of itself, in the same way as the good is intended.

Moreover, we must not look for absolute parallelism between reprobation and predestination, because divine providence is not related to good and evil in the same way. It directly intends good things, because these are in themselves ap-

158. Garrigou, *The One God*, 685.
159. Garrigou, *The One God*, 686.

petible; but it does not indirectly intend, but only permits, evil things, because these are not in themselves appetible; and having permitted them, it orders them to some good, and it permits them only because of some good. Hence, because God first intends the general good of the universe, which demands the manifestations of His justice, He at once and directly wills simply to permit sin, and then He ordains the punishment of the sin which has been permitted and foreseen, which is a good thing; for it is just that sin should be punished, and in this we see the splendor of God's justice.[160]

Reprobation is not simply the opposite face to predestination on the coin of providence. The dissimilarity between the providential relation to predestination and reprobation must be stressed emphatically. God gives to some gratuitously, and that is it. He does not move, push away, or reject the reprobate in any positive sense. To say as much would be to deny God's antecedent will to save all men and the sufficiency of sufficient grace.

God, in predestining some, does not intend to do the opposite of this, saying: "I will the rejection of others from glory," but He says: "I will to permit that the others, through their own fault, fail to attain the glory of heaven." This act means, indeed, the exclusion of some from being efficaciously chosen for the glory of heaven, but it does not mean their positive exclusion from glory. Nevertheless the reprobates are always destined for glory, so that this glory would be attained by them unless they themselves prevented it. Hence God does not repel them from the glory of heaven, but He permits that they fail to attain the glory of heaven, and this through their own fault.[161]

Positive exclusion would seem to imply causation, but, as we have seen in the work of Báñez, God does not (and cannot) in any way cause, directly or indirectly, sin or evil of any kind. Thus, it is not that Garrigou simply thinks that this language of positive exclusion *sounds* too harsh. What he wishes to state is that it implies something that *is* too harsh, something repugnant to God's omnibenevolence. As Báñez said, God "determines to the good, not to evil."[162] Further, Garrigou states:

For it seems to follow from positive exclusion that God is the cause that some would not be saved, since He would refuse to save them. On the other hand, the

160. Garrigou, *The One God*, 686.
161. Garrigou, *The One God*, 706–7.
162. Báñez, *Comentarios Inéditos*, vol. II, quaest. LXXIX, art. 4, §45 (225): "Deus ... praedeterminabit ad bonum, non ad malum."

only effect that follows from permissive exclusion is that those not among the elect, through their own fault, fail to persevere; and God merely permits this. There is a considerable difference between these two exclusions. Just as God is not the cause of sin, which contradicts what Calvin asserted; so also He is not the cause of perdition, or of exclusion from the glory of heaven.[163]

However, a word should be given to the thought of Alvarez, the Salmanticenses, John of St. Thomas, and others. While Garrigou rejects this language as being too severe, he gives no indication that he thinks that any of these commentators actually held a Calvinistic or Jansenistic double or positive predestination. It is not within the scope of this work to consider the thought of these commentators on this issue, but we may nonetheless ask ourselves what might have been their motive for employing language of positive exclusion given that they did not hold to positive reprobation.

Certainly reprobation *does* imply exclusion in some sense. Consider again the strong words of the Angelic Doctor himself: "So far, therefore, as He does not wish this particular good—namely, eternal life—He is said to hate or reprobate them."[164] There is a real sense in which God does not will the good of eternal life to the reprobate, and this is certainly volitional, though it is not a positive act executed upon the reprobate. St. Thomas directly speaks to the volitional character of the nonact of the will in not willing something. He says:

I answer that, Voluntary is what proceeds from the will. Now one thing proceeds from another in two ways. First, directly; in which sense something proceeds from another inasmuch as this other acts; for instance, heating from heat. Secondly, indirectly; in which sense something proceeds from another through this other not acting.... Since, then, the will by willing and acting, is able, and sometimes ought, to hinder not-willing and not-acting; this not-willing and not-acting is imputed to, as though proceeding from, the will. And thus it is that we can have the voluntary without an act; sometimes without outward act, but with an interior act; for instance, when one wills not to act; and sometimes without even an interior act, as when one does not will to act.[165]

Reprobation is a volitional nonact, *voluntarium absque actu*. Certainly the volitional nonact of reprobation refuses the reprobate the election that is

163. Garrigou, *The One God*, 707.
164. *ST* I, q. 23, a. 3, ad 1.
165. *ST* I-II, q. 6, a. 3.

necessary for actually achieving the beatific vision. It does indeed exclude the reprobate from the actual attainment of the beatific vision. Moreover, since reprobation is not something that is merited (or demerited) by defect or sin, it is truly antecedent to all defect and sin, a necessary condition of final impenitence that follows from the very fact that the reprobate is not chosen among the elect. All of this is affirmed throughout the work of Garrigou.

However, what seems to be specifically denied by Garrigou is threefold, that reprobation is a) an act, b) causal, and c) a rejection of the antecedent will for universal salvation. As we have seen above, reprobation is not in any way a positive acting upon the reprobate in the same way that predestination is a positive acting upon the elect. It is a nonact and is thus not causal of the defect that follows freely from the occasion of reprobation. Since it is not causal, it does not necessitate *simpliciter* that the reprobate either lose salvation or fall into hell. Reprobation does indeed preclude the reprobate from attaining the beatific vision in the composite sense because a defectible creature will indeed fall when not upheld from the defect of sin and final impenitence. However, this does not deny the possibility for the attainment of the beatific vision *simply*. It is not absolutely impossible, though it will not indeed come about given the circumstances at play. In the divided sense, the ability to merit eternal life is given through sufficient grace and desired according to the antecedent will. Garrigou's concern seems to be that the language of positive exclusion might be taken in this more robust sense of exclusion, making God to be unwilling *in every way* in regard to the salvation of the reprobate and thus acting upon the reprobate in order to cause him to be absolutely incapable of meriting salvation.[166]

Let us employ an example. If I phone some friends to invite them to my house for a party, I am *de facto* excluding those friends that I do not call, though I have not done anything positively through a causal act to ensure their exclusion. They are excluded through a (presumably) volitional nonact. I may know with complete certainty that they will not come if they are not called, as God knows that the reprobate will fail if not elevated above failure. If it were possible that one could show up apart

---

166. Indeed, Garrigou further elucidates the distinction between "*non velle* [not to will]" and "*nolle* [to not will]" in *The Sense of Mystery: Clarity and Obscurity in the Intellectual Life*, trans. Matthew K. Minerd (Steubenville, Ohio: Emmaus Academic, 2017), 267–68.

from the phone call (though we know this to be conditionally impossible in the case of reprobation), there would be a certain willingness to allow them into the party. However, this is quite different from making absolutely certain that coming to the party is impossible. Not calling some friends is something altogether different from hiring a bodyguard to keep those same friends out or, even more, hiring snipers to execute them the night before the shindig. It is this latter, more robust sense of exclusion which Garrigou seems to condemn, one that is an acting, causal exclusion rooted in a comprehensive desire on the part of the acting agent that inclusion be utterly impossible.

We can assume that since the commentators mentioned did not hold to positive reprobation, this is not what they meant by "positive exclusion," and thus Garrigou does not denounce any of them as having done so. By "positive exclusion" they certainly meant only to affirm that reprobation does actually exclude the reprobate from achieving the beatific vision. Insofar as one is not chosen, one is left behind. Garrigou himself assents to this negative reprobation. However, what he wishes to mitigate is any possible confusion that could spring forth from the phrase that might lend itself to an overly Calvinistic interpretation. Reprobation excludes, but only as a noncausal nonact that in no way negates the (unactualized) potency for salvation nor renders salvation to be absolutely impossible or totally undesired.

We see that God does not *positively* exclude any from all *possibility* of glory, and yet it is true that he permits that some will not attain it. What is the motive for this permission? Clearly it is not the foreseeing of the demerits of the reprobate, for the permission of sin is antecedent to sin. "More briefly: since negative reprobation is the will to permit some to fall into sin and fail to attain the glory of heaven, and since the permission of sin in the reprobates precedes this sin, this sin cannot be its motive."[167]

The answer is that some greater good for the entire created order may be manifest by the permission that men may fall into sin, even the sin of final impenitence that will lead to damnation. Garrigou states that "God wills a thing only in so far as it is good. Hence it is only on account of some good to be obtained that He wills to permit some, through their own fault, to fail to attain the glory of heaven."[168]

167. Garrigou, *The One God*, 699.
168. Garrigou, *The One God*, 700.

But what good is made manifest by negative reprobation? Garrigou answers by quoting St. Thomas, who states that it makes manifest God's justice. "God wills to manifest His goodness in men; in respect to those whom He predestines, by means of His mercy, as sparing them; and in respect of others, whom he reprobates, by means of His justice, in punishing them. This is the reason why God elects some and rejects others."[169] Similarly, St. Paul says in Rm 9: 22–23, "What if God, wishing to show his wrath and make known his power, has endured with much patience the vessels of wrath made for destruction? This was to make known the riches of his glory to the vessels of mercy, which he has prepared previously for glory." As such, Garrigou states, "Therefore the reason for negative reprobation, taken absolutely, is the manifestation of God's goodness by means of His justice. God's goodness, inasmuch as it is self-diffusive, constitutes the foundation for His mercy, and inasmuch as He has an indisputable right to be loved above all things, this constitutes the foundation for His justice."[170]

It should be stated that the defectibility of the creature is not the most proper motive for reprobation; however, it does certainly make reprobation fitting. It is certainly true that man would not fall if he were not defectible. Given the defectible nature received by man, it is fitting that some proportionate measure or quantity of imperfection be permitted, following from that nature. Given that God has made man as a less than perfect creature, it is fitting that God sometimes allow for man to act imperfectly. In the moral realm, this may result in a nonconsideration of a due good. From that defect a sin may result. Thus, while it is certainly true that God does not will our nature to be defectible in order that he might reprobate some men, it is nonetheless true that man's defectibility is an indispensable condition, a *condicio sine qua non*, of reprobation. Thus, God certainly foresees that reprobation may follow from defectibility, and he thus permits reprobation insofar as he permits that defectible creatures will sometimes fail. Garrigou says:

But it must furthermore be said that, as regards the creature or as regards the material cause, the natural defectibility of the creature or its disposition to fail, is the indispensable condition for negative reprobation. For if the creature, either human or angelic, were not by its nature defectible, God, who is the source of all goodness, could not permit it to fail. But, if anything is by nature defectible,

---

169. *ST* I, q. 23, a. 5, ad 3.
170. Garrigou, *The One God*, 700.

the consequence is that it may sometimes fail. Yet this defectibility is not, strictly speaking, the motive for reprobation, for God does not permit the defect on account of the defectibility of the nature, as being the motive for reprobation, but He permits the defect on account of some good to be derived therefrom. Therefore the natural defectibility is rather the indispensable condition, or the aptitude and disposition on the part of matter.[171]

As we have already seen, God permits reprobation because it follows as a fitting possibility given defectible human nature. Still, that human defectibility is permitted to go all the way to the root of the soul and cut it off from God would seem to require a further motive. It would be thinkable that God could either uphold every defectible creature from all defect or at least permit only nondamning defect. Of course, we know that God does not always do this. Why? What is the most proper reason for God allowing for reprobation? As we have seen, it appears that God wishes to bring about some greater good from permitting human defectibility, even defectibility that goes so far as to lead to eternal loss. God, of course, does not *require* reprobation to manifest any good, but he does permit it as a fitting means to manifest his justice and mercy. Thus, strictly speaking, the motive for reprobation appears to be most properly God's free will to manifest some further goodness in an imperfect world. However, an element of that motive (even if it is "not strictly speaking" the motive itself) would certainly include God's will that it is fitting for defectible creatures to be permitted to actually defect.

While all of this may explain the motive for reprobation universally, or in regard to all mankind, the question remains as to the motivation for reprobation in the individual. To put it another way, why does God permit that one man be finally impenitent and makes it such that another is not? We know that God is said to reprobate some insofar as it is a fitting way to manifest his justice, but why is it decided that this one rather than another will be permitted to resist God to the end? Since predestination and reprobation are previous to foreseen merits or demerits, it is certainly not something in men themselves that moves God to respond by predestining or reprobating. Even Garrigou admits:

In this whole question there is no proposition more obscure than that God permits the final impenitence of some (for instance, of the bad thief rather than of

171. Garrigou, *The One God*, 700–701.

the other) as a punishment for previous sins which *de facto* will not be forgiven and for a greater good, which includes the manifestation of infinite justice. Indeed this proposition is most obscure. But that our firm assent to this proposition should be made easier for us, we may consider the fact that its contradictory cannot be upheld, or that the aforesaid proposition cannot be proved false.[172]

In other words, one must assent that God does permit some to fall, and this one rather than another one, or else one must reject the principle of predilection and say that those who are better are not better because they have been made better by God through grace and love. There is some good, and indeed the highest and most important good, in man, the good that distinguishes the saint from the impenitent sinner, which comes from man rather than God. Toward this good, God is merely passive, hoping that we do good but without effecting it within us.

If we affirm that it *is* God who works to move us to every good and that all the good that we do have comes from him as source, then it must be the case that whoever falls to damnation only does so under the condition that God has permitted that they so fall, for to not permit that would be to will against it, and what God wills simply is infallibly brought about. As Garrigou states, in the proposition that God permits some men to fail to the point of damnation "we see clearly the application of the most exalted principle of predilection, which is a corollary to the principles of causality and finality, which state that all good comes from the supreme good and is ordered to it."[173]

All of this is to say nothing other than that the question of why God predestines one man and reprobates another is a mystery to us insofar as it is a part of the divine will, of which we have no direct knowledge unless it be so revealed to us. "The answer of St. Thomas is that negative reprobation in the selective sense, has no reason except the divine will."[174] The wayfaring theologian may say no more than this.

Objections

One objection to the above states that God need not manifest his justice in the reprobate because it is already manifest in the predestined insofar

---

172. Garrigou, *The One God*, 701.
173. Garrigou, *The One God*, 701.
174. Garrigou, *The One God*, 703–4.

as all predestined (other than Our Lord and Blessed Mother) are sinners, and as such all are punished in some way for sin and experience the suffering that accompanies evil. But, Garrigou responds, while such punishments do manifest God's justice, they do not manifest it to the extent that is fitting for sin, which is so incredibly evil in its rejection of him who deserves all reverence, praise, and thanksgiving. Similarly, if men were to be permitted to the beatific vision but not eternally, this would not manifest the infinity of God's mercy in the most fitting manner. Garrigou responds to this objection as such:

> Such a procedure would be but an imperfect manifestation of God's infinite justice. For the rewarding of the just is more an illustration of God's mercy than of his justice, and, moreover, it is not at all a manifestation of His vindictive justice. This latter is to some extent made manifest in temporal punishments, but these do not make us realize what it ought to be by reason of the infinite malice of sin, which does all it can to rob God of His dignity of being the final end of creatures. Likewise, God's mercy would be very feebly manifested if He were to reward the elect with the beatific vision only for a time.[175]

There is yet another objection that states that all of this becomes uncomfortably close to Calvinism and Jansenism since it results in God's willingness to manifest his justice by way of inflicting punishment before sin, since reprobation is previous to the foreseeing of demerits. This means that God punishes in order to manifest his justice, and in so doing he punishes the innocent. Such a treatment of reprobation shares much with the positive reprobation of Calvin or Jansen.

However, this objection has been answered above. It confuses permission with punishment. Permission is ontologically prior to the sin and punishment posterior. Thus we say that God permits defect and sin in order that his justice might be made manifest, but God never intends or wills to punish previous to sin. Punishment is only in response to sin freely chosen, to utterly free resistance and offense to God. Garrigou states that this objection

> confuses God's infinite justice with His finite chastisement. For God does not will the permission of sin because of His love and intention to impose finite chastisement, for that would be repugnant to justice. But because He wills the permission of sin for the manifestation of His infinite justice, or the inalienable

175. Garrigou, The One God, 705.

right of sovereign goodness to be loved above all things, He first wills the permission of sin, and then wills to inflict the punishment for the sin in manifestation of His justice. The punishment is but a means of manifesting infinite justice, and it is a means that is not an intermediate end with reference to the permission of sin. Punishment cannot be, indeed, an intermediate end, for to punish is a good only on the previous supposition of sin. Hence God most certainly does not will the permission of sin because of His love to punish, for this would be cruelty; but He wills it from love of His infinite justice, or from love of His goodness which has a right to be loved above all things. But it is easy to depart from the orthodox teaching on this point, and a slight error in the beginning will be great in the end.[176]

Garrigou recognizes that this major distinction may easily be lost if one is not careful. As such, some are inclined to erroneously conclude that Thomism and Calvinism are essentially the same.

Here, the smallest error, the smallest confusion between the Divine permission of the first sin and the Divine subtraction of efficacious grace—the smallest error in understanding the difference between the *non-good* and the *evil*—will lead to the enormous errors of Calvin. *Parvus error in principio, magnus est in fine.* This principle—*parvus error in principio, magnus est in fine*—explains why certain summits of truth appear to many to be rather close to very grave errors. This arises from one not being attentive to the exact formulation of these lofty truths. The least deviation from this height leads to a disastrous fall, as does the smallest wrong step on the edge of a precipice at a mountain's summit.[177]

For Calvin, reprobation *ante praevisa demerita* acts almost as a punishment insofar as it is a positive exclusion from election. For St. Thomas, reprobation is simply the *not giving* of election, which nonetheless takes nothing away from the sufficiency of grace for salvation (which, of course, cannot be said of Calvin's more positive exclusion). The result for the individual soul may end up the same, and so it is easy to conclude that the doctrines of Calvin and St. Thomas are the same, but the way in which the soul arrives at damnation could not be more different. As we have mentioned, for Calvin, God "forces" the reprobate to hell and makes of him a sacrifice to perdition. In so doing, we arrive at the error of Jansen, who held that the reprobate could not really uphold the divine law, and thus salvation was truly impossible for him in every sense. For

---

176. Garrigou, *The One God*, 705.
177. Garrigou, *The Sense of Mystery*, 269.

St. Thomas, reprobation is simply a *nonact* that permits that the defectible creature freely choose between good and evil as it pleases, the results of which are knowably certain but not necessary in the divided sense (or, according to the necessity of the consequent). This allows for both the real possibility of the divine antecedent will for universal salvation and the real possibility for the reprobated soul to have chosen God rather than having rejected him (even if things ultimately do not happen this way). These two *essentially* Catholic doctrines are not possible in the Calvinist and Jansenist doctrines and yet are fundamentally present in the doctrine of St. Thomas as elucidated by Báñez, Garrigou, and others.

The Mystery of Predestination and Reprobation

Upon final analysis, it should be stated that predestination and reprobation are indeed *mysteries*. The theologian may assert certain principles, but this is not something that can be fully comprehended by the wayfarer. No theological scheme can clarify all of the obscurities present within these mysteries. Garrigou says, "This great mystery of divine predestination is of itself more an object of contemplation than of theological discussion. For it is the nature of theological investigation to enable one to acquire a certain more sublime understanding of the mysteries of faith."[178] But there are limits to our understanding of predestination that will not be done away with until we see his divine will in an unobscured fashion. Garrigou quotes the First Vatican Council here well.

And, indeed, reason illuminated by faith, when it zealously, piously, and soberly seeks, attains with the help of God some understanding of the mysteries, and that a most profitable one, not only from the analogy of those things which it knows naturally, but also from the connection of the mysteries among themselves and with the last end of man; nevertheless, it is never capable of perceiving those mysteries in the way it does the truths which constitute its own proper object. For, divine mysteries by their nature exceed the created intellect so much that, even when handed down by revelation and accepted by faith, they nevertheless remain covered by the veil of faith itself, and wrapped in a certain mist, as it were, as long as in this mortal life, "we are absent from the Lord; for we walk by faith and not by sight" (2 Cor 5:6).[179]

178. Garrigou, *The One God*, 703.
179. *Denzinger*, 1796.

These mysteries ought to lead us not to frustration as we grasp up toward their lofty heights. On the contrary, they reveal to us our dependence on God as our divine Father. In this way, these mysteries, especially insofar as they are obscure, become objects of meditation and prayer rather than theological penetration. Garrigou speaks of the good that comes with the struggle that contemplation of these mysteries may cause.

This explains, then, why interior souls who have to undergo the passive purifications of the spirit, are generally very much tempted against hope when they think of predestination. These temptations are permitted by God so as to make these souls feel the necessity of rising above human arguments by prayer, a purer faith, and a most loving confidence and abandonment. This is then infused contemplation, the fruit of the gifts of understanding and wisdom, by means of which one begins to reach in a truly higher way, in the obscurity of faith, the culminating point of the mystery which we are discussing. Then it is that we begin to foretaste of the fruits of this exalted doctrine and, to quote the words of the Vatican Council,[180] that we attain "a certain very fruitful understanding of the mystery."[181]

The principles that must be true have been laid out here. It is true that we cannot see the summit of this mystery, but it is not because the contours are not in some way visible, nor is it that nothing true can be said about predestination and reprobation. "The obscurity is great, but we see that it is not the outcome of absurdity or incoherence. Two absolutely certain principles lead us to it, the first being that 'God never commands what is impossible,' and the other that 'no one thing would be better than another, unless it were loved more by God.'"[182]

These two principles converge in a "mysterious summit," one considered so beautifully by St. Thomas. Garrigou poetically paraphrases his hero, Ernest Hello (who had been writing on Jan van Rusbrock), applying Hello's words to the two principles of this mystery and their contemplation by the Angelic Doctor:

He is aerial like a chant and rigorous like a star. The *freedom* of his movements and *their fidelity* are founded in a singular splendor. If the one diminishes, the other will be challenged. *Boldness* and *security* prevail over it upon their tranquil and triumphant wings. Boldness does not pull it along, and security does not hold it in thrall. Both of them make the same movements, departing from the

---

180. *Denzinger*, 1796.
181. Garrigou, *Predestination*, 223.
182. Garrigou, *Predestination*, 222.

same point, going to the same goal. The powers that seem divided here below make for peace upon the heights. The great contemplative is blinded by an excess of light. His lips are closed by the immensity because it rebels in the face of explanations. Ordinary things can be spoken; extraordinary things can only be stammered. These stammered expressions seem eager to die in the shadow and in the silence where they had been conceived.[183]

All things are entrusted to the divine will and God's infinite love for us as his creatures. And, indeed, there ought to be more hope in us when it is God who is in control of our finality rather than our frail, weak selves.

In this the soul finds peace, not in descending by means of reasoning below faith, but, on the contrary, by aspiring to the contemplation of God's intimate life, a contemplation which, since it is above human reasoning, proceeds from faith enlightened by the gifts of the Holy Ghost. It is fitting to recall here that the formal motive of Christian hope, like that of the other two theological virtues, must be the uncreated Being.[184]

We must not see God in too human a way, for this further obscures the great mystery of predestination and reprobation. It sees God's mercy and grace as whimsical or random. His justice is harsh, indiscriminate, and arbitrary. But this is only because these mysteries are not properly understood in light of his other perfections and can be seen only as distinct from his perfect being. In short, the summit of these mysteries can only be properly comprehended when we behold God himself and stand within his true presence. We conclude with the profound spiritual considerations of Fr. Garrigou.

If we stress too much our analogical concepts of the divine attributes, we set up an obstacle to the contemplation of the revealed mysteries. The fact that these concepts are distinct from one another, like small squares in a mosaic reproducing a human likeness, is why they harden the spiritual aspect of God for us. Wisdom, absolute liberty, mercy, and justice seem in some way to be distinct in God, and then His sovereignly free good pleasure appears in an arbitrary light, and not entirely penetrated by wisdom; mercy seems too restricted, and justice too rigid. But by faith illumined by the gifts of understanding and wisdom, we go beyond the literal meaning of the Gospel and imbibe the very spirit of God's word. We instinctively feel, without seeing it, how all the divine perfections are identified in

---

183. Garrigou, *The Sense of Mystery*, 270. Paraphrased from Ernest Hello, *Rusbrock l'admirable: oevres choisis*, x–xi.

184. Garrigou, *Predestination*, 225.

the Deity, that is superior to being, the one, the true, the intellect, and love. The Deity is superior to all perfections that are naturally susceptible of participation, these being contained in it formally and eminently without any admixture of imperfection. The Deity is not naturally susceptible of participation, either by angel or man. It is only by grace, which is essentially supernatural, that we are permitted to participate in the Deity, in God's intimate life, inasmuch as this latter is strictly divine. Thus it is that grace is instrumental in causing us mysteriously to reach, in the obscurity of faith, the summit where the divine attributes are identified. The spiritual aspect of God for us is no longer hardened. We do not see His countenance, but we instinctively feel it, and this secret instinctive feeling, in the supernatural abandonment of ourselves, gives us peace.[185]

185. Garrigou, *Predestination*, 228–29.

CHAPTER FIVE

Francisco Marín-Sola

Born in 1873 in Cárcar, Navarre in Spain, Francisco Marín-Sola began studying with the Order of Preachers at just thirteen years of age. He joined the order at fifteen and was ordained a priest in 1897. He began his academic career teaching in Manila (he had actually been a prisoner of the Tagalog uprising for some sixteen months before beginning teaching at the College of San Juan de Letran), but also held posts in Avila and at the University of Notre Dame in the United States. He was eventually asked to fill the vacant chair of dogmatic theology at the University of Fribourg after the death of the renowned Dominican theologian Noberto del Prado. Marín-Sola would teach at Fribourg until 1927, becoming well-known for his work on the evolution of dogma. Marín-Sola also turned to the issues of our concern, namely, premotion, grace, sin, predestination, and reprobation. He published several articles on these topics that we will deal with here. In so doing, he drew criticism from some of his Dominican conferes, perhaps most notably Reginald Garrigou-Lagrange, with Marín-Sola and Garrigou alternating a number of public critiques back and forth.[1] With the election of a new Master of the Order, Buenaventura Garcia de Paredes, both Marín-Sola and Garrigou were required to end their volleying. However, Marín-Sola was also now obligated to teach the traditional Dominican theses alongside his own, without any refutations or criticisms of the former. To jump over one controversy in a storied history that is filled with them, let us say simply that Marín-Sola was eventu-

---

1. Michael D. Torre, *Do Not Resist the Spirit's Call: Francisco Marín-Sola on Sufficient Grace* (Washington, D.C.: The Catholic University of America Press, 2013), xx–xxiii.

ally found by Paredes to have violated the direction of the Master of the Order. He was required to step down from his chair at Fribourg and he spent his few remaining years teaching back in Manila, where his career had begun. He died on June 5, 1932.

The Work of Marín-Sola

During the first half of the twentieth century, the various controversies and tensions surrounding the Congregatio de Auxiliis had cooled somewhat but were certainly still burning. Francisco Marín-Sola, OP, endeavored to write upon the subjects of premotion, grace, sin, predestination, and reprobation in a "relatively new" way.[2] This did not mean that Marín-Sola wished to absolute theological novelty. His project would attempt to remain true to the work of St. Thomas and the Dominican tradition but "to write with a certain aspect of innovation."[3]

Marín-Sola's work should be seen as intentionally deviating from two particular trends that had arisen in the general Dominican treatment of these issues, trends that Marín-Sola found most regretful. The first was the aggressive and combative posture toward Jesuit Molinism, something which Marín-Sola clearly thought detracted from the importance of these matters and probably proved to be scandalous to those on the sidelines of the battle.[4] Marín-Sola wanted his writing to "work for Thomism, but without fighting with anyone."[5]

2. Francisco Marín-Sola, "El sistema tomista sobre la moción divina," *La Ciencia Tomista* 32, no. 94 (July–August 1925): 5–54, 6; repr. in Torre, *Do Not Resist the Spirit's Call*, 2. For all English translations of the original Spanish, I will use the translation of Torre.

3. Marín-Sola, "El sistema," 6; Torre, *Do Not Resist the Spirit's Call*, 3.

4. Marín-Sola, "El sistema," 7; Torre, *Do Not Resist the Spirit's Call*, 3–4: "During the nineteenth century and what we have of the twentieth, the Molinist-Thomist combat has lost much of its passion and acrimony, because the interest and importance of this question has diminished before other more modern problems. Nevertheless, neither of the two adversaries has abandoned one inch of its central positions, nor have intermittent cannonades ceased to be fired between one and the other camp. It was just yesterday, as it might be said, that the hardly gentle attacks of the Molinists Stüfler and D'Alès were launched against Thomism, and that the no sweeter replies were given by the Thomists Schultes and Garrigou-Lagrange. It is possible that this fight will continue as ever, with periods of greater or less passion, to the end of time; for, once the question has been converted not only into a question of a School, but also of a Family, being personified in two powerful religious orders, it is not easy for one of them to cede its territory, nor is there hardly a great likelihood that the Church will intervene, the only judge who could bring to an end this debate of three centuries.... While Molinists and Thomists, then, from their respective camps, occupy themselves in launching cannonades against the opposite camp, we ourself will have nothing whatsoever to do with Molinists in their camp, and will dedicate ourself simply to examining the depth of the Thomist camp."

5. "El sistema," 7; Torre, *Do Not Resist the Spirit's Call*, 4.

Second (and more substantively), Marín-Sola wanted to reform the usual Thomistic treatment of sin and reprobation. In regard to the classical Dominican approach of what Marín-Sola calls the "line of good," he claimed absolutely no disagreement.

In regards to the four points of the line of good,[6] and very especially in regards to the second and third points on efficacious grace *ab intrinseco* and completely free predestination to glory, our conviction is that these points represent the authentic doctrine of Saint Augustine and of Saint Thomas.[7]

However, in regard to the "line of evil," Marín-Sola had concerns, especially that it had been too closely identified with the line of good and not understood to be a quite distinct phenomenon.

Anyone who is up to speed on these questions will have noticed that the more obscure and more difficult points of the Thomist system are the points referring to the line of evil or of sin, and that it is against this line that the adversaries of Thomism, with greater arrogance and pretension of victory, have directed their shots, to such a point that one of the most fervent defenders of the *scientia media* has just written that, if Thomists manage to explain in an *intelligible* way how the predetermination to the material of sin can be combined with the responsibility of the creature, with this alone all the difficulties of the Thomist system would disappear and there would hardly be any reason not to accept it. Well then, for very many years we have been preoccupied, as we believe any true Thomist ought to be preoccupied, with these difficulties that the Thomist system seems to present in the entire line of evil, and with seeing whether a solution could be found that, without in any way abandoning or placing in danger the fundamental positions of Thomism, could meet the objections of its adversaries with greater clarity.[8]

Marín-Sola posits that the seeds of this work to disentangle the lines of good and of evil were sowed by such venerable Thomists as the Salmanticenses, John of St. Thomas, Lemos, and Alvarez, finding particularly visible fruit in the work of Gonet, Massoulié, Reginald, and Billuart.[9]

---

6. Marín-Sola gives these as: "(a) physical premotion to the morally good act, (b) grace *ab intrinseco* efficacious, (c) *Predestination* to glory that is completely free and independent of the use of any *scientia media*, (d) the eternal decrees predefining any morally good act": "a) la premoción física al acto moralmente bueno; b) la gracia *ab intrinseco* e infaliblemente eficaz; c) la predestinación a la gloria, completamente gratuita e independiente del uso de toda ciencia media; d) los decretos eternos predeinientes de todo acto moralmente bueno" ("El sistema," 10; Torre, *Do Not Resist the Spirit's Call*, 7).

7. Marín-Sola, "El sistema," 11; Torre, *Do Not Resist the Spirit's Call*, 8.

8. Marín-Sola, "El sistema," 10–11; Torre, *Do Not Resist the Spirit's Call*, 7–8.

9. Marín-Sola, "El sistema," 12; Torre, *Do Not Resist the Spirit's Call*, 9.

Marín-Sola also makes specific reference to Cardinal Billot, a theologian that Marín-Sola characterizes as "a Thomist theologian of the first rank, of the stripe of Cardinal Cajetan."[10] And yet Marín-Sola says of Billot that even as a Jesuit who seemed to have sincere reservations regarding Molinism, he could not move himself to accept the Dominican theses.

On the very question of physical premotion, far from being a pure Molinist, he is—among all the modern theologians of the Society of Jesus—the one who has drawn closest to the Thomists. And nevertheless, far from accepting the integral Thomist system on physical predetermination and grace, not only has he rejected it as contrary to Saint Thomas, but he does not see well how certain Thomist theses can be distinguished from Calvinism.[11]

This concern to distance Thomism from Calvinism, an apprehension regarding at least some of the traditional Dominican treatments of sin and reprobation, certainly animates the work of Marín-Sola (and, in turn, Jacques Maritain, as we shall see in the next chapter). I will move now to a brief overview of Marín-Sola's major theses followed by a consideration of how these stack up, as it were, in relation to the thought of St. Thomas, Báñez, and Garrigou.

Ten Propositions

Marín-Sola's first major work on this topic was an article published in the journal *La Ciencia Tomista* in 1925 entitled "The Thomist System regarding the Divine Motion."[12] In this article, Marín-Sola sets forth ten major propositions that define his reconstruction of the traditional Dominican teaching, the first and most important of which regards the scope of divine providence.

Although all divine providence is infallible or unfrustratable as regards the realization of the *universal end*, which is the glory of God and the good of the universe, nevertheless, *general* providence, whether natural or supernatural, is fallible or frustratable in respect to a *particular end* of each individual or of each individual act.[13]

---

10. Marín-Sola, "El sistema," 13; Torre, *Do Not Resist the Spirit's Call*, 10.
11. Marín-Sola, "El sistema," 13; Torre, *Do Not Resist the Spirit's Call*, 11.
12. Marín-Sola, "El sistema," 5–54.
13. Marín-Sola, "El sistema," 16; Torre, *Do Not Resist the Spirit's Call*, 14.

For Marín-Sola, the divine motion in particular individuals and in particular acts (as opposed to the providential ordering of the universe as a whole) is not truly infallible, but may be impeded or frustrated in even the composite sense. He asserts that God can give two different sorts of motion, one that is infallible (special providence) and one that is fallible (general providence).

If, then, as much in the natural order as the supernatural, there are two kinds of providence, one general and the other special—one fallible and the other infallible—as regards the execution of a particular end, there will also be two kinds of decrees and two kinds of premotions—fallible or infallible, respectively—regarding the accomplishment of the end of these motions.[14]

This is an absolutely fundamental thesis for Marín-Sola, so much so that he states, "One who penetrates well this first proposition and draws from it all its consequences, does not have any need to read our articles," and that "many of the obscurities and difficulties of the Thomist system derive from the forgetfulness or inadequate penetration of this proposition."[15]

For his second proposition, Marín-Sola states that:

The divine motion is always of itself towards the good: but the actual defect of the human will is what converts the premotion to the good into a premotion to the material of evil. Therefore, the actual defect of the creature is *anterior in nature* to the divine motion to evil, and thus this motion, rather than a premotion or predetermination, is a *postmotion* or *post-determination*.[16]

Marín-Sola connects this with the principal of the first proposition by stating that sin would never actually take place without the fallible motions of general providence. That which is willed with special, infallible providence will surely occur, but sin is not willed as such. Therefore, sin can only enter into the picture as the frustration of a will by man toward a good.

Sin could not take place without the motions of *general* providence, natural or supernatural, motions that are fallible as regards their particular execution or effect. If there were no more than special providence, whose decrees and premotions were infallible, sin could not occur. The motions of God, then, are not divided

14. Marín-Sola, "El sistema," 17; Torre, *Do Not Resist the Spirit's Call*, 15.
15. Marín-Sola, "El sistema," 17; Torre, *Do Not Resist the Spirit's Call*, 15.
16. Marín-Sola, "El sistema," 18; Torre, *Do Not Resist the Spirit's Call*, 16.

into infallible for *good* and infallible for *evil*, but rather infallible for *good* and fallible for *good*. In these last is where sin occurs.[17]

The third proposition may be said to be a metaphysical analysis of the terms *sufficient grace* and *efficacious grace*. The prevailing understanding of this distinction was as potency and act applied to grace, but Marín-Sola adds a third term to the equation. Rather than speaking only of the potency toward an act and the reduction to act of that potency, Marín-Sola speaks of potency, imperfect act, and perfect act, with the last two being distinguished as an act that has not yet reached its end and an act that has, respectively.

The will or power, however perfect it may be, but before being placed in or entering into movement or action is one thing; another is the will or power, already placed in movement towards a term or directed actually towards it, but before reaching the term; another, finally, is reaching the end. As one thing is the arrow before being shot towards the target; another is the arrow already shot, but before reaching it; another, finally, is reaching or arriving at the target. The first is called in Thomistic philosophy pure potency or pure *posse*; the second is called a true *agere*, but an *imperfect agere*, because it is still a *posse* with respect to the term of the perfect act; the third not only is *agere*, but *perfect agere*.[18]

The *imperfect agere* corresponds to sufficient grace for Marín-Sola. As such, sufficient grace cannot be called merely a potency to act, but truly act, only act which has not yet been perfected, act which has not yet reached its end. "The traditional Thomist aphorism that sufficient grace *does not give the agere*, but only the *posse*, can be taken in two senses essentially distinct and of consequences transcendentally different, according to whether one understands only the *perfect act* or also the *imperfect act*."[19] In other words, sufficient grace is truly something that gives act, and only when we speak of its relation to a second, perfect act can we say that it is in potency. Absolutely speaking, it is an act, not a potency, that holds within itself the potency for a further perfection, in the same way that an arrow that already flies has the potency to hit the bullseye of a target. Consequently, Marín-Sola equates acts of *perfect agere* with the acts of justification, whereas the acts of *imperfect agere* are "all those acts that prepare it and are anterior to it in time."[20]

---

17. Marín-Sola, "El sistema," 19; Torre, *Do Not Resist the Spirit's Call*, 17.
18. Marín-Sola, "El sistema," 19; Torre, *Do Not Resist the Spirit's Call*, 17.
19. Marín-Sola, "El sistema," 19; Torre, *Do Not Resist the Spirit's Call*, 18.
20. Marín-Sola, "El sistema," 19; Torre, *Do Not Resist the Spirit's Call*, 18.

Sufficient grace then infallibly gives a motion to the created will, but that motion can be impeded from reaching the end of the good act. In this way, Marín-Sola says that sufficient grace, the principle of general providence, *is* infallible in the sense that it provides the application to act, but it is fallible in regard to the completion of that act, or, in other words, it is fallible in relation to the good deed toward which the human will is aimed. It will reach that target if the human will does not impede the motion, and thus its progress to the end toward which it is willed by God.

The divine motions, if they are *sufficient*—that is, if they pertain to *general* providence—are *unfrustratable* in regards to their *application* by God to the human will, and thus as regards the *actuation* of the will or the *beginning* of the effect. But they are fallible as regards to whether this same, premoved, will might place or not place an impediment to the *course* of this sufficient motion, and, thus as regards to the continuation and term of the effect, which is called the *accomplishment of the particular end* of this general providence or motion.[21]

He states that the proposition "if God premoves me to something, for example to write, I will infallibly write" does not necessarily follow. If God moves one to write according to special providence (and thus in an infallibly efficacious way), then it does indeed follow that one will infallibly write. But God may move one to write according to general providence executed via fallibly efficacious grace (what is called sufficient grace by Garrigou and Báñez). As such, one may write or one may not. It depends upon how the recipient of the grace responds. Does he maintain the course of the grace or does he impede it? As Marín-Sola puts it, "I can place an impediment to and paralyze or deviate the *course* and term of this premotion."[22] Accordingly, if Thomists assert that good acts come from "absolute divine and efficacious grace,"[23] they ought to mean only that the beginning of a good act is absolutely efficacious, that man will begin moving in the direction of the good end intended by the divine will. Whether it actually culminates in a good act is uncertain, at least in regard to "easy or imperfect things."[24] However, perfect natural acts require infallibly efficacious aid, and perfect supernatural acts require infallibly efficacious grace.

21. Marín-Sola, "El sistema," 22; Torre, *Do Not Resist the Spirit's Call*, 20.
22. Marín-Sola, "El sistema 22; Torre, *Do Not Resist the Spirit's Call*, 1.
23. As Alvarez states in *De auxiliis*, bk. 8, disp. 8, no. 2.
24. Marín-Sola, "El sistema," 23; Torre, *Do Not Resist the Spirit's Call*, 21.

For every supernatural act, whether easy or difficult, imperfect or perfect, there is need, then, of a supernatural premotion, and, therefore, of efficacious grace. But, for the easy or imperfect acts, all that is required is a grace that is fallibly or *secundum quid* efficacious, which is what is called *sufficient grace*; and for the difficult or perfect acts there is need of a grace that is infallibly efficacious or *simpliciter* efficacious or perfectly efficacious.[25]

It is important to point out that for Marín-Sola, every act of every creature does indeed require physical premotion. It could not begin to act without this.

It is indubitable that, for *every act*, whether imperfect or perfect, easy or difficult, one has need in Thomism of ordinary physical premotion or *a general* aid of God, in the natural order, and supernatural physical premotion, or *a general* supernatural aid or *sufficient grace*, in the supernatural order. This is proper to *every* creature, in whatever *state* it is found.[26]

However, only perfect natural acts and supernatural acts require that the creature be moved beyond the beginning of an action. In easy and imperfect acts, the creature does not need to be moved to the accomplishment of the easy or imperfect act but can stay the course, as it were, on his own, apart from any motion that infallibly leads him to do so.

What is the difference, then, between perfect and imperfect acts? Or, to put it another way, what is it possible for man to do without infallibly efficacious grace, and what requires that God move him immediately and infallibly to the termination of the act? Here it is best to let Marín-Sola speak for himself. "*Perfect* acts, in general, are those that, because of the *greatness* of the work or by its *difficulty*, require *all* the power of the will, and, because of this, are absolutely impossible, without the special aid of God, for a nature that is *infirm* or not integral."[27] As examples of these sorts of acts, Marín-Sola gives:

the efficacious love of God *above all things* (which, in the supernatural order, is *justification*), the accomplishment of *all* the precepts, the conquering of *all* temptations, the removal of *all* obstacles or the not placing of *any* impediment, and even doing *anything* easy or removing *any* impediment, when it concerns *a long time*, because the length of time converts an easy work into a difficult one.[28]

25. Marín-Sola, "El sistema," 23; Torre, *Do Not Resist the Spirit's Call*, 21–22.
26. Marín-Sola, "El sistema," 24; Torre, *Do Not Resist the Spirit's Call*, 23.
27. Marín-Sola, "El sistema," 23; Torre, *Do Not Resist the Spirit's Call*, 22.
28. Marín-Sola, "El sistema," 23–24; Torre, *Do Not Resist the Spirit's Call*, 22.

Continuing, "one calls *imperfect acts* those that do not require *all* the power of a healthy or integral nature, neither by virtue of the greatness of the work nor by its difficulty, but for which *some* power is enough, which one who is infirm has, while he is not dead. These are easy works and those done in a brief time."[29] Examples of this sort are:

any imperfect act of the fear of God, of hope, of attrition, etc. (that, in the supernatural order, are *a remote* preparation for justification), the accomplishment of some easy precept, the conquering of some light temptation, the not placing of *some* light impediment, etc., so long as it does not concern *a long time.*[30]

Everyone receives these sufficient graces, these beginnings to action which can account entirely for imperfect acts. To those who receive sufficient or fallibly efficacious grace and who complete imperfect acts rather than impede then, God will eventually impart more and more grace, until these individuals are given the infallibly efficacious grace of final perseverance and beatitude.[31]

We should also state that these fallibly efficacious graces are not indeterminate. The arrow is shot toward the target, and it will reach the target if the perfection of that motion toward the target is not impeded. Therefore, it is impedible but not indeterminate.[32]

Marín-Sola thus describes the "triple character" of sufficient grace.

a) It is *infallibly efficacious* for something, that is, for the *actuation* of the free will or the free "*incoaction*" of the imperfect act.

29. Marín-Sola, "El sistema," 24; Torre, *Do Not Resist the Spirit's Call,* 22.

30. Marín-Sola, "El sistema," 24; Torre, *Do Not Resist the Spirit's Call,* 22.

31. Marín-Sola, "El sistema," 24; Torre, *Do Not Resist the Spirit's Call,* 23: "In effect: if *sufficient grace,* in being a true supernatural premotion, is enough for imperfect acts, and if, as all Thomists teach, to one who *with grace* does what he can and prays for what he cannot, God concedes, by His *mercy* but *infallibly,* further graces, it follows that no one who, with the sufficient grace that God denies to no one, does the imperfect and easy acts that he can, God infallibly will concede further and further graces, up to final perseverance."

32. Marín-Sola, "El sistema," 28–29; Torre, *Do Not Resist the Spirit's Call,* 27–28: "When we say that sufficient grace is a *fallible* physical premotion, we do not mean by *fallible* a *versatile* or *indeterminate* premotion, in the Molinist style, as the motion of wind, which pushes the sails of a ship without determining the port, but we mean that it is a motion as determined and as individual as the arrow shot accurately at the target, or of fire in regards to burning or of a sacrament in respect to its proper or sacramental grace. But as such, and not withstanding its most determined motion, the arrow can be impeded from reaching the target by a cause interposed in its path, or fire can be impeded from the effect of burning by water, or the sacrament can be impeded from causing its grace by the defect of the one who receives it; so also the most determined premotion of sufficient grace can be impeded by the will. Thomistic sufficient grace, then, does not need to be *determined* by the will; it only needs *not to be impeded.*"

b) It is *fallibly efficacious* or *proximately sufficient* for something, that is for the *continuation* or perseverance of the imperfect act or (if one wishes to speak in another way) for not placing an impediment to the course of grace in easy things and for some time.

c) It is *completely inefficacious* or *remotely sufficient* by itself alone for something, that is for the *perfect act* and even for difficult or large trajectories of the imperfect act, for which one has need of another grace: perfectly efficacious grace.[33]

We can see the appeal in this proposition for distancing Thomism from Calvinism and God from any unjust or unintelligible distinction between the predestined and the reprobate. God rewards those who make good use of smaller aids and graces with greater and greater graces, culminating in the infallibly efficacious graces needed to do the perfect acts that merit glory and the beatific vision. Of course, no man can merit final perseverance on his own and must be moved infallibly to such an act, but those who are so moved are distinguished from those who are not so moved precisely by how well they use anterior aids and graces up until the time of their death.

Marín-Sola's fourth proposition is as follows:

Predestination, not only to grace but also to glory, is completely free, without having as a cause, motive, foundation or condition either merit or any other thing on the part of man: it has no other foundation or reason of being than the pure *will of God*. But *merits* are one thing and *demerits* or *sins* something very distinct. Without going in any way against Thomistic principles, one *can* sustain that predestination as much as reprobation *supposes* the foreknowledge of *sins*.[34]

Marín-Sola affirms that no real proof of the first half of this proposition is necessary since it is such an obvious and constitutive part of St. Thomas's treatment of predestination. As to the second half, Marín-Sola explains his proposition by stating that "sins pertain to general providence, and predestination and reprobation to special providence." General providence, the providence that provides frustratable motions, is antecedent to special providence, which infallibly orders some to predestination and others to reprobation.

---

33. Marín-Sola, "El sistema," 30; *Do Not Resist the Spirit's Call*, Torre, 29.
34. Marín-Sola, "El sistema," 32; *Do Not Resist the Spirit's Call*, Torre, 31.

If, as we saw in the first proposition, there are two providences—general and special—and predestination is a *special* providence, it follows that it ought to be posterior in nature to *general* providence, to which sin always pertains. And, as we saw in the second proposition, just as for God to deny grace or premove to the material of sin supposes the previous defect of the human will, so also reprobation—as much positive as negative—correlatively ought to suppose it.[35]

Thus, it is said that God foresees defect and sin before distinguishing the predestined from the reprobate. Marín-Sola does not deny that this divine separation of the predestined from the reprobate is entirely free, but he does state that it is always supposing the defect and sin of each individual man.

Our personal opinion is that reprobation necessarily supposes the foresight of the *futurition* of the *defect* and the *futurability* of *sin*, as we will see at the end of this article. God does not reprobate anyone except because his salvation is opposed to the good of the universe, and in this sense reprobation is free; but the salvation of such a man never is opposed to the good of the universe except by his culpable defect, and in this sense it always supposes the actual defect of the creature.[36]

Consequently, Marín-Sola finishes this proposition by quoting John of St. Thomas. "God wills all men to saved, *unless they shall have failed.*"[37]

The fifth proposition is as follows:

The question as to whether predestination to glory is *completely free*—a question which every Thomist ought to resolve affirmatively—is essentially distinct from the question whether of itself it is *before* or *after* the predestination to grace or to merits. So long as one affirms that merits come not from a versatile grace or a general concurrence, but from a grace that is *instrinsically* efficacious, it is of *little importance* for Thomistic doctrine whether one says that predestination to glory is *before* or *after* predestination to merits.[38]

Marín-Sola does not say much else here other than that predestination and infallibly efficacious grace should not necessarily be seen as temporally prior to merit but as ontologically prior. Infallibly efficacious grace

35. Marín-Sola, "El sistema," 33; Torre, *Do Not Resist the Spirit's Call*, 32–33.

36. Marín-Sola, "El sistema," 34; *Do Not Resist the Spirit's Call*, Torre, 33.

37. John of St. Thomas, *Cursus Theologicus, De voluntate Dei*, disp. 5, art. 7, no. 5: "*si per ipsos non steterit.*"

38. Marín-Sola, "El sistema," 34; *Do Not Resist the Spirit's Call*, Torre, 34.

is the cause of merits, which are the effect of that grace.[39] Marín-Sola posits that it is at least possible for creaturely deeds to be temporally prior to predestination without in any way being the cause of predestination.[40]

Marín-Sola moves on to the sixth and seventh propositions, which we shall take together.

As much imperfect acts, which precede justification, and which some call congruous merits, as healthy acts posterior to justification, and which are condign merits, can be considered under two aspects: a) *in themselves*, abstracting from whether or not they are persevering to the end; b) *insofar as persevering* to the end, which is alone how they lead infallibly and in fact to glory. Well then, when the Thomists defend that predestination to glory is anterior to the foresight of *merits*, it is enough to understand merits in the second sense, insofar as they are persevering to the end, or insofar as efficaciously and infallibly connected with the attainment of glory.[41]

One can, then, defend within Thomism that the *sole elicited* or proper *effects* of predestination are glory and final perseverance, and that, therefore, *all* other acts or merits are or can be proper and *elicited* effects of *general* providence, if considered *in themselves*; although they are always *imperated* by predestination, if they are considered *insofar as persevering* or united with perseverance.[42]

While the effects of general providence and fallibly efficacious grace may be said to be related to the effects of special providence and infallibly efficacious grace (insofar as the former is the commencement of the latter), they are distinct nonetheless. Marín-Sola is concerned here with not rendering meaningless the idea of sufficient grace (or, as he calls it, efficacious grace for imperfect acts or "proximately sufficient" grace). In this way, sufficient grace is not just good for some act, but truly accomplishes something. Thus, he states that any "narrow" view which posits that all supernatural acts (imperfect or perfect) require an infallible efficacious grace "*would reduce* general supernatural providence, and the sufficient grace that pertains to it, to terms *empty of meaning*."[43]

---

39. Marín-Sola, "El sistema," 36; Torre, *Do Not Resist the Spirit's Call*, 35–36: "This is, in our judgment, the reason that Saint Thomas, in order to express that predestination is completely free, has never used the phrase *before* or *after* merits, but phrases that indicate *causality*, saying that predestination is the *cause*, and that grace and merits are the *effect*."

40. Marín-Sola, "El sistema," 36; Torre, *Do Not Resist the Spirit's Call*, 36: "Saint Thomas himself has indicated already clearly enough that there could be acts of man, for example sins, whose foresight by God *precedes* the predestination to glory, without their being the *cause* of this predestination."

41. Marín-Sola, "El sistema," 36–37; Torre, *Do Not Resist the Spirit's Call*, 36–37.

42. Marín-Sola, "El sistema," 37; Torre, *Do Not Resist the Spirit's Call*, 37.

43. Marín-Sola, "El sistema," 38; Torre, *Do Not Resist the Spirit's Call*, 38.

The eighth and ninth propositions draw upon the previous ones in order to make two differing conclusions in regard to predestination and reprobation. The eighth states, "With this alone, then, that one admits truly that final *perseverance* is completely *free*, the Thomistic thesis of the complete *gratuity* of *predestination* to glory remains saved."[44] In relation to reprobation, however, Marín-Sola states the following as his ninth proposition.

As thus, according to what we saw in the second proposition [that the divine motion is always toward the good with evil motions resulting from the defects' impeding of the divine motion to some good], one can say in Thomism that the divine motion to the material of sin is posterior in nature to the actual defect of the human will, so one *can* also say that the eternal predefining or predetermining *decrees* of this motion are posterior in nature to the *foresight* of this defect of the will, and that, therefore, one can call these decrees *postdefining* or *postdetermining*.[45]

In this way, Marín-Sola wishes to state that God wills first to save all men. This antecedent will pertains to general providence and inefficacious grace. Following upon this is God's foresight as to future defects and sins in the individual. Following upon this are the infallibly efficacious graces of special providence, which are not frustrated, given to those who God foresees will make good use of grace.[46] This leads to his tenth and final proposition, which is as follows:

Although, in God, will is solely one and He wills everything in one most simple act, nevertheless, in our human manner of understanding and on the part only of the objects willed, the *antecedent* will of God and the decrees and motions corresponding to this will are *by nature prior* to the *consequent* will and its corresponding decrees and motions. This antecedent will, with its corresponding decrees and motions, is *antecedent*, or conditioned, or inefficacious, or impedible, or fallible as regards the execution of a particular *end*; but it is *consequent*, or absolute, or *simpliciter* efficacious, or unimpedible, or infallible as regards the application of the *means* sufficient for the execution of this end.[47]

One major point that Marín-Sola now presents is that both the antecedent and the consequent will require some decree or motion, otherwise they could not truly be called properly volitional. On this point

44. Marín-Sola, "El sistema," 38; Torre, *Do Not Resist the Spirit's Call*, 38.

45. Marín-Sola, "El sistema," 40–41; Torre, *Do Not Resist the Spirit's Call*, 41.

46. Marín-Sola, "El sistema," 41; Torre, *Do Not Resist the Spirit's Call*, 42: "From this derives the need to place the foresight of sins or impediments between the antecedent will to save all men, which pertains to general providence, and predestination and reprobation, which are special providences."

47. Marín-Sola, "El sistema," 42; Torre, *Do Not Resist the Spirit's Call*, 43.

rests his thesis that there are two sorts of providence, one that is fallible and gives frustratable motions, and one that is infallible and gives unfrustratable motions. "And as there are neither will nor providence without decrees or motions, so also one must distinguish two classes of divine decrees or motions: some fallible or frustratable by the defect of the creature as regards the execution of the end, and others infallible or unfrustratable."[48] At this point Marín-Sola reminds his reader that sufficient grace (again, what he tends to call efficacious grace for imperfect acts or "proximately sufficient" grace) is meant to be merely sufficient (or frustratable) in regard to the *end* of an act. Sufficient grace, however, does infallibly give the application of the *means*.[49] Thus Marín-Sola is able to say, "From the fact, then, that a grace is a true premotion, one cannot deduce that it infallibly executes its *end*; nor from the fact that a grace is frustrated does it follow that it is not a premotion."[50] In other words, physical premotion is indeed frustratable. To put it quite simply, he finishes by stating:

Sufficient grace, as the *general* providence to which it pertains, infallibly involves the concept of premotion, but it is a *fallible premotion* as regards its result, because it moves the will, but it does not prevent it from placing, if it wishes, an impediment to the *course* of this motion. *Efficacious* grace, as the *special* providence to which it pertains, also infallibly involves premotion, but an *infallible premotion* as regards the result, because it not only moves the will, but makes it infallibly not place an impediment to the course of the motion, and it reaches its term, which is the perfect act.[51]

In conclusion, Marín-Sola points again to his intention to properly distinguish the lines of good and the lines of evil.[52] Propositions two, three, four, and nine deal with the line of evil, whereas propositions five,

48. Marín-Sola, "El sistema," 43; Torre, *Do Not Resist the Spirit's Call*, 44.

49. Marín-Sola, "El sistema," 43–44; Torre, *Do Not Resist the Spirit's Call*, 44: "Note also these two characters of the antecedent will, and thus of its decrees and premotions: a) to be conditioned or impedible as regards the *end*, because only in this sense are they called *antecedent*; b) to be absolute or unimpedible as regards the application of the *means*, because as regards the application of the *means*, the so-called antecedent will is absolute or *consequent*."

50. Marín-Sola, "El sistema" 44; Torre, *Do Not Resist the Spirit's Call*, 44.

51. Marín-Sola, "El sistena," 44; Torre, *Do Not Resist the Spirit's Call*, 44–45.

52. Marín-Sola, "El sistema," 44; Torre, *Do Not Resist the Spirit's Call*, 45: "The four [propositions] referring to the line of good, and that are the ones that probably will most shock many Thomists, could have been omitted, because we do not consider them to be *absolutely* necessary for the end that we propose, that is, to clarify, simplify, and harmonize the Thomistic concepts over the material taken principally from the side of liberty, sin, and reprobation, making the principal difficulties that its adversaries oppose to it disappear."

six, seven, and eight deal with the line of good. "Two of them, the first and the tenth, the alpha and the omega, are the two keys that in the order of *execution* (motion or general governance) and in the order of *intention* (antecedent will of God), are *common* to both *lines*, and are like the clasps that close them or join them together."[53]

Marín-Sola is sure to point out that none of this divine vision of defects and sin relies in anyway upon the Molinist *scientia media* for, "The *scientia media* is a knowledge not of futures, but of *futuribles*, and those futuribles are not of infallible connection, but of fallible or contingent connection."[54] Marín-Sola denies the contingency of human acts foreseen via the *scientia media* by arguing for decrees of special providence that move men to perfect acts infallibly, not as possibles but as certainties.

It should also be noted that Marín-Sola makes a clear distinction between the defect and the sin. The former is an error of the intellect, the latter a failure of the will,[55] both foreseen as that which occurs when God does not give the grace necessary to overcome the impediment placed to fallibly efficacious grace, which renders it to fall short of achieving the perfection of the act.

Clearly what Marín-Sola most wants to stress is that, in the line of evil, "God sees that the human will has already placed in fact a defect; and He also sees, and in consequence, that it would infallibly place sin, if He does not remove this defect by means of a special motion."[56] Marín-Sola states, finally, that whatever changes or innovations he has made to the Thomistic system are "in nothing substantial, but only in accidental matters."[57]

Analysis

Sufficient and Efficacious Grace

Following upon the release of these ten propositions in 1925, Marín-Sola released a second article just a few months later in 1926. This article also

53. Marín-Sola, "El sistema," 44; Torre, *Do Not Resist the Spirit's Call*, 45.

54. Marín-Sola, "El sistema," 48; Torre, *Do Not Resist the Spirit's Call*, 50.

55. Marín-Sola, "El sistema," 52; Torre, *Do Not Resist the Spirit's Call*, 54: "The distinction between an actual and voluntary *defect* of the intellect, and formal *sin* of the will. The first takes place in the practical judgment or termination of *consilium*, and the second in the consent or election."

56. Marín-Sola, "El sistema," *Do Not Resist the Spirit's Call*, 48.

57. Marín-Sola, "El sistema," 45; Torre, *Do Not Resist the Spirit's Call*, 46.

appeared in *La Ciencia Tomista* and was entitled "A Reply to Some Objections concerning the Thomist System regarding the Divine Motion."[58] As the title implies, Marín-Sola had received objections from at least one "Thomistic theologian,"[59] and he sought to answer those objections here. As I hope to show, however, there are some major speculative lacunae in Marín-Sola's revision of the traditional Thomistic doctrine that are not properly answered even in this defense.

The very first objection that Marín-Sola cites in this second article regards his definition of sufficient grace, particularly that it is a grace that does not give merely a potency but the act of an imperfect action. Insofar as it imparts true act it must be called a divine motion since, as we have seen, no creature can be moved from potency to act in any deed if it is not moved by God as a primary cause. The objection runs thus:

> Father Marín-Sola proposes a *new* interpretation of the doctrine of St. Thomas on grace, according to the way of González, Bancel, Massoulié, and Reginald, according to which *sufficient* grace gives not only the *potency* to the act but also the active *impulsion* to second act; more precisely, this impulsive sufficient grace is a true physical premotion or even predetermination, but *fallible*, because it does not infallibly overcome obstacles or resistance, as does *infallibly efficacious grace*.[60]

In response, Marín-Sola affirms that sufficient grace is a real premotion.[61] "This first point, which is the only one that interests us and that

58. Originally published as "Respuesta a algunas objeciones acerca del sistema tomista sobre la moción divina," *La Ciencia Tomista* 33, no. 97 (January–February 1926): 5–74.

59. Marín-Sola, "Respuesta," 5; Torre, *Do Not Resist the Spirit's Call*, 56.

60. Marín-Sola, "Respuesta," 5–6; Torre, *Do Not Resist the Spirit's Call*, 56.

61. It should be stated here that Marín-Sola spends considerable time defending his positions by arguing from the authority of other commentators. Marín-Sola's responses to these objections are often twofold. The first response is to consistently claim (and to provide quotations as evidence) that his propositions are the most common among the Thomistic commentators. There is a real tension here with Marín-Sola's numerous assertions in his first article that he is innovating upon the common treatment. Be that as it may, it is not within the scope of this work to treat the entire commentatorial tradition in order to determine whose opinions are the most common (nor is this the most formal character of the true Thomist, which is, rather, genuine faithfulness to the thought of St. Thomas). I shall treat only Marín-Sola's second line of response, which is theological treatment of the content of his propositions and an analysis of whether they truly align with the thought of St. Thomas. While the common thought of the entire tradition cannot be addressed here, the adherence and conformity of the treatments of Báñez and Garrigou to the Angelic Doctor, as well as the myriad of quotations from other commentators and St. Augustine in the work of Garrigou, will hopefully suffice at least to show that their work is far from innovative or uncommon within the Dominican and larger Thomistic tradition.

we are now treating, affirms that sufficient grace is a true *physical premotion*."[62] He states that sufficient grace must be a real premotion because the mere potency to an act is not really sufficient to act, and thus the creature can have no responsibility to act upon mere potency. "The proximate *sufficiency* and the *responsibility* of the creature begin where physical *premotion* begins. With pure potentiality, there is not nor will there ever be in the creature, however perfect one supposes it to be, any responsibility or sufficiency."[63]

All of this is, however, only to collapse potency and act together. The metaphysical distinction between potency and act loses all meaning if it is stated that potency cannot be sufficient for an act without it being reduced to act.

In lesson 3 of his *Metaphysics*, Aristotle tackles the objections of those who hold that "a thing has a potency for acting only when it is acting, and that when it is not acting it does not have this potency."[64] Aristotle highlights the absurdity of this position by using the example of a builder who is not presently building. How is it that he shall ever be able to build if there is no true distinction between potency and act? How shall he ever move from potentially building to actually building if the only thing that is sufficient for building must already be in the act of building? If there is no distinction, how is it that he should ever fall out of the act of building and into rest? St. Thomas, expounding upon Aristotle's example, states:

If a man does not have an art except when he is exercising it, then when he begins to exercise it he has it anew. Therefore he must either have learned it or acquired it in some other way. And similarly when he ceases to exercise an art it follows that he lacks that art, and thus he loses the art which he previously had either through forgetfulness or through some change or through the passage of time. But both of these are clearly false; and therefore it is not true that someone has a potency only when he is acting.[65]

And Aristotle draws this same conclusion, that to claim that a potency does not exist unless it is reduced to act is to destroy the distinction

62. Marín-Sola, "Respuesta," 8: "Ese punto primero, que es el único que ahora nos interesa y de que ahora tratamos, afrima que la gracia suficiente es una verdadera *premoción física*." Torre, *Do Not Resist the Spirit's Call*, 59. Torre's translation lacks the word "physical."
63. Marín-Sola, "Respuesta," 9; Torre, *Do Not Resist the Spirit's Call*, 60.
64. Aristotle, *Metaphysics*, bk. IX, chap. 3, lesson 4.
65. Aquinas, *Commentary on Aristotle's Metaphysics*, 1799.

altogether. "Therefore, if it is impossible to maintain this, it is evident that potency and actuality are distinct. But these views make potency and actuality the same."[66] As St. Thomas states, with this collapsing of potency into act, we lose not just act and potency but also motion and generation.

But those who hold the foregoing position make potency and actuality the same insofar as they say that something has potency only when it is in a state of actuality. And from this it is evident that they wish to remove from nature something of no little importance, for they eliminate motion and generation, as has been stated. Hence, since this cannot be admitted, it is obvious that something is capable of being which yet is not, and that something is capable of not being which yet is. And "it is similar in the case of the other categories," or predicaments, because it is possible from someone who is not walking to walk, and conversely it is possible from someone who is walking to not walk.[67]

We see then that to argue that sufficient grace (as it is understood by Báñez and Garrigou) is not sufficient is to argue against the distinction between potentiality and actuality. The potency to do good with sufficient grace is said to not exist (or at least to be irrelevant) unless it is actualized efficaciously. Shall we say of the man who sits but does not stand that he cannot stand simply because he does not do so? Is this not quite distinct from a man who does not have such a potency due to a disability? It may be true that neither stands in this given moment, but unless we are to reject potency altogether, we must admit a real distinction between having a potency and not having one, between not standing and not being able to stand. We must admit a real and relevant distinction between the two sitting men, one who can stand and one who cannot. It is quite different to sit because one is sitting and to sit because one is unable to stand. And thus it is quite different to say that a man has a potency toward a good act (even if it is never reduced to act) and to say that the same good act is utterly impossible. This is the same as saying that because a man conditionally sits, he necessarily sits, or that because a man cannot sit and stand compositely, he cannot sit and stand in the divided sense. All of this is, of course, quite absurd and clearly at odds not only with the classical Dominican tradition but St. Thomas himself.

The parent chastises the child who plays with a weapon and does not

---

66. Aristotle, *Metaphysics*, bk. IX, chap. 4, lesson 3.
67. Aquinas, *Commentary on Metaphysics*, 1803.

chastise the child who plays with a toy weapon, even if in both cases no one was injured. Why? Because, even though the result was the same in both scenarios, that is, no one was hurt, in the former scenario someone *might* very well have been hurt, a reality that must be made visible to the child. None would be so foolish as to state that a fire never had the capacity to cook a steak merely because it was not brought into proximity of a fine porterhouse. The same must be said of the man who has the potency for good even if he is not always moved to act well. When the moment for a salutary act has passed unfulfilled, there is still quite a distinct difference between not having done what was possible and not having done what was impossible.

This distinction seems to make all of the difference when it comes to man's responsibility to act well. Again, Marín-Sola states, "With pure potentiality, there is not nor will there ever be in the creature, however perfect one supposes it to be, any responsibility ..." because without act, in this case true premotion, man cannot be held responsible for what he does not have. And while it is true to say that he does not necessarily have the act in the conditional sense, he does have the power for it absolutely, as St. Thomas says,[68] and thus it cannot be said that man, of absolute necessity, is not able to act with the classical definition of sufficient grace. And if it cannot be said that it is absolutely impossible for man to act via sufficient grace then it cannot be said that man has no culpability or responsibility in regard to grace that is sufficient. All of this is shown especially to be true since, as we have seen in Báñez and Garrigou, God does not deny efficacious grace unless man first freely rejects sufficient

---

68. *ST* I, q. 19, a. 3: "I answer that, There are two ways in which a thing is said to be necessary, namely, absolutely, and by supposition. We judge a thing to be absolutely necessary from the relation of the terms, as when the predicate forms part of the definition of the subject: thus it is absolutely necessary that man is an animal. It is the same when the subject forms part of the notion of the predicate; thus it is absolutely necessary that a number must be odd or even. In this way it is not necessary that Socrates sits: wherefore it is not necessary absolutely, though it may be so by supposition; for, granted that he is sitting, he must necessarily sit, as long as he is sitting." *ScG* I, 67, 10: "There is more. If each thing is known by God as seen by Him in the present, what is known by God will then have to be. Thus, it is necessary that Socrates be seated from the fact that he is seen seated. But this is not absolutely necessary or, as some say, with the necessity of the consequent; it is necessary conditionally, or with the necessity of the consequence. For this is a necessary conditional proposition: if he is seen sitting, he is sitting. Hence, although the conditional proposition may be changed to a categorical one, to read what is seen sitting must necessarily be sitting, it is clear that the proposition is true if understood of what is said, and compositely; but it is false if understood of what is meant, and dividedly. Thus, in these and all similar arguments used by those who oppose God's knowledge of contingents, the fallacy of composition and division takes place." See also *ScG* I, 85.

grace, turning himself in some way away from God. This is certainly a movement for which man is culpable. Man did not act toward the good, and he was not lacking in the power to have done so.

With that being said, there may be some considerable overlap with Marín-Sola and the traditional Thomistic account of "Báñezianism" even in the face of dissimilar language. When Marín-Sola asserts that sufficient grace is a real premotion, he states that it is only said to be in potency in relation to perfect act. On the one hand, Marín-Sola seems to be animated here by the need for grace to actually be something. Grace is not something that only gives potential. As both Báñez and Garrigou state, every grace is efficacious for something.[69] Grace is only said to be sufficient in relation to a further end. Garrigou even employs the same usage of imperfect and perfect acts. "Every actual grace which is efficacious of itself with regard to an imperfect salutary act such as attrition, is sufficient with regard to a more perfect salutary act such as contrition."[70]

In many ways, there are agreements here. Both affirm that even for imperfect acts, real premotion is necessary. While Marín-Sola calls imperfect acts the product of sufficient grace that involves real premotion, classical Thomism[71] would call them a product of efficacious grace (also

69. Báñez, *Comentarios Inéditos*, vol. 3, pars II, cap. III, §6 (392): "All of the aid of the grace of God is efficacious for some effect, which is sent from the absolute pleasure of the divine will" ("Omne auxilium gratiae Dei est efficax alicujus effectus ad quem ex beneplacito divinae voluntatis absoluto mittitur").

70. Garrigou, *Grace*, 431–32 (originally found in *Revue Thomiste*, May 1937).

71. It should be noted that some, including Marín-Sola, hold that Báñez is somehow not included under the umbrella of the Thomism that was exonerated by Pope Benedict XIV and the Congregatio. Indeed, Marín-Sola states, "Whoever admits of the first two hypotheses [that defect arises either from a) the creature stopping the movement of premotion in him or b) God stopping it *after* the defect is placed] is with Thomists, but also with us. One who admits the third [that God, before the *defect*, does not give the motion required to be upheld from the defect, i.e. the antecedent permissive decree] is against us but also against Thomists, at least against those before Báñez and after Gonet. In addition, we *do not see* how, in admitting this third hypothesis, one can avoid falling into the theory of a completely corrupted nature, and of being accused of not being sufficiently distanced from Jansenism and Calvinism" (Torre, 67). Further, Torre himself states, "It is sometimes remarked that both Clement XII (in 1730) and Benedict XIV (in 1748) affirmed that the condemnation of Jansenism was not meant to include a condemnation of 'Thomism' (see *Denzinger* #2509 and #2564), since 'Thomists' were able to distinguish their position from Jansenism. However, 'Thomists' here cannot be supposed to include all that Thomists held since (as Thomists themselves admitted) they held contradictory positions on some of the key points at issue. . . . The magisterial teaching, of course, was certainly not aimed at Báñez who had been dead for over fifty years! Nevertheless, if the Thomist position on actual, impedible, grace affirmed against Jansenism is to be rejected, it then becomes uncertain how stating that all actual grace is unimpedible and irresistible can appropriate the solemn teaching of the Magisterium in *Unigenitus* (or at least not without having to respond carefully to real and obvious

involving real premotion). However, since both speak of the premotion necessary for these imperfect acts as real premotion, both agree that for having even imperfect acts, an initiative must be made on the part of God to move man toward said act. Both agree that grace is never merely a potency but is always a real movement toward the good, also having a potency toward a greater or more perfect good. When Marín-Sola says that sufficient grace is only in potency in regard to something beyond the proximate motion he is really saying that all premotion (insofar as, for Marín-Sola, sufficient grace is a true premotion) is efficacious for one thing and in potency only for a further end. And this is exactly what is stated by Garrigou above.

---

difficulties)" (328–29). Báñez is seemingly implicated by Marín-Sola (and perhaps by Torre) as falling under the condemnations of Jansenism, or at least not being acquitted by Benedict XIV. However, a closer look at the words of Benedict indicate that this is certainly not the case. See Steven Long's "God Alone Suffices: An Answer to Marín-Sola & Michael Torre," 7–10: "'Thomist' is an ecclesial term of art whose provenance derives largely from its use at the *Congregatio de Auxiliis*. It would be odd for the Church—without any sufficient criteria being given nor any indication provided that a change in its use had been introduced—suddenly to use the term derived from the Dominican argument from the *Congregatio de Auxiliis* to designate a radically divergent school. But were Marín-Sola correct in his view, then his *true* 'Thomists' newly designated by the Pope would indeed be a radically divergent school from that of the Dominican Thomists of the *Congregatio de Auxiliis*, the latter (according to Marín-Sola) being preponderantly prone to what would later be identified as the Jansenist heresy. *This last is a spurious claim*, but the composite evidence must suffice to address it. As for the work of interpreting the authors taken up by Marín-Sola as alone the true Thomists intended by Benedict XIV, this would require another full essay. But even were it ceded that all the authors cited by Marín-Sola are to be interpreted precisely as he suggests, this would not imply that the Holy See referred exclusively to those authors whom Marín-Sola identified. One must point out that the term 'Thomist' is derived from the *Congregatio* and Benedict XIV states that the Thomist position 'has never been condemned by the Apostolic See'. This 'never' in and of itself indicates that *prior account* is what the Holy See has in mind by the term *Thomist*, since 'never' clearly includes a period far more extensive than that which according to Marín-Sola witnessed the emergence of those who—in his view, and to the exclusion of Báñez & confreres—supposedly alone merit the approbation of the Holy See. The term 'never' rather clearly includes the period antecedent to Jansenism: i.e., it includes the Holy See *never* condemning the Thomist position of the *Congregatio* (the term, again, is *never*). Surely had Benedict XIV thought that the Thomism that the Holy See had *never* condemned—that from which the ecclesial designation was *derived*—was such as to fall under the condemnation of the Jansenists he would have indicated this. Yet this is the text that Torre, alongside Marín-Sola, supposes indicates *disapprobation* of the earlier Thomism and approbation of just those Thomist respondents to Jansenism whom Marín-Sola prefers under just that interpretation he provides? While the rest are to be understood as implicitly falling under the condemnation of Jansenism? I have actually heard some argue that the teaching of Báñez falls under the condemnations of Jansenism and the approbation of Thomism offered by the Holy See does not extend to it. Scholars are free to hold the first part of this view if they so wish, and to argue for it; but as to the second, it is a material distortion of the teaching of the Holy See, which clearly extended its approbation precisely to the Thomism from the *Congregatio* in saying that that doctrine (the ecclesial term is denominated from the *Congregatio de Auxiliis*) has *never* been condemned by the Apostolic See."

The major difference between these two sides at first seems to be only semantic and accidental. Whereas Garrigou begins with a potency rooted in an antecedent grace, moving on to either the completion or impeding of that potency, Marín-Sola begins with an efficacious premotion, an act that has already been begun, and he calls it "sufficient," looking forward to the potency found within this imperfect act to its completion. To put it in another way, let us consider the imperfect act of being moved to sorrow over one's sins. This imperfect act virtually contains within it a potency for a more perfect act of rushing off to confession. Garrigou tends to speak of this whole series as a sufficient grace for attending confession, a potency rooted in a previous act. It may or may not be reduced to act, but if it is, this is due to efficacious grace. Marín-Sola, on the other hand, begins with that previous imperfect act. He speaks of sorrow being the effect of premotion, carrying with it the potency for a perfect act like going to confession. If one attends confession this is because one has received an efficacious grace. The only difference here is that Marín-Sola calls the premotion necessary for the imperfect act sufficient, rather than efficacious. And semantically, this does not make much sense, for as Marín-Sola himself asserts, even for the imperfect act, true premotion is necessary. This is all that the classical Thomist means by "efficacious"; it is not merely possible premotion or grace, but real premotion or grace.

It would seem that Marín-Sola has simply given two names ("sufficient" and "efficacious") for the one reality of grace that brings about its effect. Some of those effects are imperfect and some are perfect, but insofar as both are true graces that really bring about their effect, Garrigou would call them both efficacious. There is *agere* that produces imperfect things and *agere* that produces perfect things, but both are *agere*. The classical treatment divides grace here according to its mode of giving, not according to the perfection of its effects. It is either *agere* or *posse*, giving this thing or capable of giving a further thing. There is no imperfect *agere* and perfect *agere*, but only *agere* that sometimes gives imperfect acts and sometimes gives perfect acts. This is why Garrigou speaks of efficacious grace for imperfect acts and efficacious grace for perfect acts. Both require a grace that is efficacious, something that gives the act.

Within Marín-Sola's sufficient grace there is a further potency for a further end, and this is all Garrigou and Báñez mean by sufficient grace. Again, rather than dividing grace according to ends, they are dividing according to the metaphysical principle of act and potency in order to maintain the reality of both in relation to grace. Within the tradition, the distinction was never about imperfect or perfect acts but about how grace both gives a good and also presents the possibility of a further good.

Of course, Marín-Sola's rejection of the sufficiency of potency itself is certainly problematic, as we have stated. But in terms of the division between act and potency and the relation of that division to grace, Marín-Sola has seemed up until this point largely consistent *in substance* with the traditional approach, if not in language. The language is needlessly innovative and less precise. It seems that Marín-Sola felt this permutation was necessary in order to maintain that grace always does something and is never itself pure potency. However, this was already staunchly declared by the tradition. Marín-Sola's definitions of sufficient and efficacious grace thus use novelty in such a way as to muddy what was already clear for Thomists: all grace is efficacious for some thing. All acts, imperfect or perfect, require efficacious grace (true premotion) in order to be moved to act.

This is why Marín-Sola says that sufficient grace alone is enough for the *agere* of some acts. He does not mean to say that *potency* provides the act because for him sufficient grace *is agere*, at least for the beginning of the imperfect act. "All perfectly efficacious grace is a supernatural premotion, but not all supernatural premotion is a perfectly efficacious grace, because it is able to be imperfectly efficacious or *sufficient*."[72] Of course, if Marín-Sola were to grant the classical definition of efficacious grace as any supernatural premotion that gives *agere* then he would presumably agree that all supernatural premotion is properly called efficacious grace. And thus, in order to avoid confusion, I will henceforth use the classical distinction of sufficient and efficacious grace with a further division between efficacious grace for the beginning of imperfect acts (Marín-Sola's "sufficient grace") and efficacious grace for the completion of perfect acts (Marín-Sola's "efficacious grace").

However, and this cannot be overstressed, all of the above apparently applies only to the *beginning* of the imperfect act and not to its *continuation* and *accomplishment*. Thus, while it would appear that there is consid-

---

72. Marín-Sola, "Respuesta," 14: "Toda gracia perfectamente eficaz es premoción sobrenatural, pero no toda premoción sobrenatural es gracia perfectamente eficaz, pues puede ser imperfectamente eficaz o *suficiente*." Torre, *Do Not Resist the Spirit's Call*, 66.

erable overlap between Marín-Sola and the traditional school in regard to sufficient and efficacious grace, this is only true insofar as Marín-Sola is speaking about the *beginning* of imperfect acts. The addition of this wrinkle to Marín-Sola's account, a division between *beginning* and *continuation*, creates real distance between him and the traditional treatment, rendering Marín-Sola's account truly problematic.

Marín-Sola states that an imperfect act is not only fallible in regard to a more perfect act, but that it is fallible even with regard to perseverance in the very same imperfect act. He says:

In sum, the truly *sufficient* Thomistic grace joins together these four characteristics:

a) It is *infallibly efficacious* for the *beginning* of the imperfect act, and this is "*to have the act*," dealing with *transient* or imperfect acts.
b) It is *fallibly efficacious* for the *course* or continuation of the imperfect act, that is not to place an impediment to this course in easy things and for a little time.
c) It is, *by itself, infallibly inefficacious* to have the *perfect act*, and to continue the imperfect act in difficult stretches or for much time.
d) It is, by itself, *infallibly efficacious*, if one does not place an impediment, to *impetrate* from the mercy of God the infallibly efficacious grace that is necessary to have any *perfect* act, and that is also necessary to persevere, without placing an impediment, in the imperfect act, in difficult stretches or for much time.[73]

Note that Marín-Sola is not only stating that an efficacious grace for an imperfect act is fallible in regard to a more perfect act. With this Garrigou and Báñez could agree insofar as efficacious grace is only sufficient for a further act. It is not necessarily accompanied by the further grace to achieve the more perfect act because man often rejects it. However, Marín-Sola is here going much further in claiming that efficacious grace for imperfect acts is fallible with regard to the continuation of those *very same acts*. So this grace is infallible in regard to the beginning of this single imperfect act but fallible in regard to its continuation.

To put it simply, this distinction is metaphysically puzzling. It would seem that one either has the act for sorrow or one does not. In what sense can it be that man infallibly has sorrow in its beginning but does not infallibly have continuation such that sorrow actually comes about? Marín-Sola says:

---

73. Marín-Sola, "Respuesta," 17; Torre, *Do Not Resist the Spirit's Call*, 69.

If one has sufficient grace or premotion to pray, one *will begin*, infallibly, the *motus ad orandum*, which begins in *cogitatio orandi*, follows in the *volitio orandi*, continues in the *judicium de orando*, follows in *consilum orando*, etc. But as, in this trajectory or *course* of *sufficient* grace, man can place an impediment, it follows that anyone who has the sufficient grace to pray will have some *motus ad orandum*, but it does not necessarily follow that he *will pray*, because he can place an impediment.[74]

One wonders what it means to have a *motus ad orandum* that is infallibly efficacious in regard to the beginning of prayer but is fallible in regard to the patient actually praying. In what sense is this infallible? In what sense is there a real beginning to prayer if prayer is never begun? Marín-Sola continues, stating that

by means of *sufficient* grace, God concedes to *all*, at a minimum, the *grace to pray*; that is, the *motus ad orandum* with which man, if he does not place an impediment, will pray and will continue to receive sufficient graces, and ulterior efficacious graces, for the remainder of the trajectory that finishes by leading to justification and, from this, to final perseverance.[75]

But what is a grace that does not necessarily give the act? Is it not merely a movement that potentially gives the act? And is this anything else than what is usually meant by sufficient grace? A premotion is something real, active in the agent and passive in the patient, that brings about some real effect. However, for Marín-Sola, efficacious grace for imperfect acts does not necessarily bring about anything real.[76] There is no true effect in the patient. It provides a potential push toward a true effect but does not always bring it about. In this sense, Marín-Sola's "sufficient grace" seems to be closer to providing an inclination than to being an actual efficient cause of an act. Marín-Sola states:

---

74. Marín-Sola, "Respuesta," 18; Torre, *Do Not Resist the Spirit's Call*, 71.

75. Marín-Sola, "Respuesta," 18; Torre, *Do Not Resist the Spirit's Call*, 71.

76. Steven Long has argued well that this is due to the inability of Marín-Sola to see the difference between an efficacious grace (which is only suppositionally necessary and allows the creature to retain a potency to have refused it in the divided sense) and an irresistible grace (which provides no such potency for refusal in any way). "St. Thomas Aquinas," 66: "Marín-Sola also accused the classical Thomistic reading of St. Thomas's teaching undertaken by Báñez, Cajetan, John of St. Thomas, and others, of being closer to that of Calvin or Jansenius than to Aquinas. He confused efficacious grace—which can be but with hypothetic necessity is not resisted—with the Jansenist irresistible grace, which simply cannot be resisted. This is a remarkable error. Marín-Sola's admirers to this day evince failure to understand why his superiors might have thought that accusing the classical Thomistic tradition of Calvinism or Jansenism indicated a lapse of judgment. I incline to the view that this teaching of Marín-Sola's is contrary to the teaching of Aquinas and doctrinally ill founded."

This part of the route, gone through *in one stroke* by the effect of the initial or operating grace, is what is called the *beginning of the act*, and which, at a minimum, by being a truly *sufficient* grace, ought to include not only the "*cogitatio supernaturalis*," but also the "*simplex volitio* supernaturalis," because, without it, there would be no supernatural motion of the will *ex parte subjecti*, nor could this begin to move by itself *supernaturally*. This "cogitatio" or "volitio," is not yet either faith, nor attrition, nor prayer, nor anything *complete*, but it is a "*motus ad* fidem," "*motus ad* orandum."[77]

We see that Marín-Sola's sufficient grace does not actually give any *agere* but is only a motion toward *agere*. He is not stating that a complete imperfect act is in some way an as-yet unfulfilled motion or potency toward another more perfect act, as Báñez and Garrigou state. Marín-Sola states clearly that his sufficient grace does not really give anything complete. It is simply a frustratable motion, "efficacious" only insofar as it really and truly gives man an inclination, tendency, or predisposition toward some good. It is important to note here that Marín-Sola is not speaking of sufficient grace as a *motus ad* some perfect good, for he states that attrition is indeed an imperfect act. "These are easy works and those done in a brief time, such as any imperfect act of the fear of God, of hope, of attrition, etc."[78] And thus this sufficient grace only infallibly gives a *motus ad* an imperfect act. But that this imperfect good act is actually brought about (what Marín-Sola calls "continuation") seems to rest entirely upon man's good use of the *motus ad*.

First, it is unclear how one could receive a divine motion that does not result in the patient being moved. What is being imparted by the motion that is frustrated? If it is frustrated, how has a motion been given? One might be tempted to say that Marín-Sola is only using the new language to describe the traditional account of sufficient grace. Perhaps a *motus ad* is really just a *potency for*. However, as we've already seen, Marín-Sola rejects the traditional distinction and states that a potency is itself insufficient for accomplishment. Thus, his fallibly efficacious grace gives the beginning of *agere* but not its completion.

Second, the continuation of the imperfect act, its being reduced from a mere "beginning" to the perseverance of the act in reality, rests upon man not placing an impediment. And this state of being free from im-

77. Marín-Sola, "Respuesta," 25; Torre, *Do Not Resist the Spirit's Call*, 78–79.
78. Marín-Sola, "El sistema," 24; Torre, *Do Not Resist the Spirit's Call*, 22.

pediment, man's perseverance in the imperfect act, even if attributed to another grace in some way, follows from man not placing an impediment rather than God causing man to not place an impediment. Thus man either responds well to grace or he does not. That which distinguishes between these two possibilities (that is, man responding well and achieving the imperfect act or not) is not God but man himself. It is not the divine motion that renders the motion toward an imperfect good to be completed, but it is man who takes the *motus ad* and, in receiving it well (not placing an impediment, but by his own power rather than the power of an infallible grace) makes it to be true *agere*.

That Efficacious Grace for Imperfect Acts Is Fallible

Marín-Sola further explains this distinction between the beginning of the imperfect act and its continuation, stating that "sufficient grace" is used to describe both the grace that begins the imperfect act and the grace that continues the act on its course, or the grace of continuation.

Sufficient grace alone is enough *not to place* impediments to the new grace that is necessary to *do* imperfect acts. In reality, this *new* grace or *greater* grace that is needed to *continue* the beginning of the imperfect act, is also *sufficient grace*, because it is an *infallible* grace for another beginning (the imperfect act being, in its entire course, nothing more than a continual conjunction of *fieris* or *beginnings*) and *fallible* for its *continuation*, and so successively, while the *course* of the imperfect act endures. The entire course of the *imperfect* act, then, is accomplished with *sufficient grace*, because this is what Thomists mean by sufficient grace; that is, it is a grace that is *infallible* for the beginning, or, that is, *to have the act*, and *fallible* for the *course* of the imperfect act, or, that is, *to continue the act*.[79]

All of this is to state nothing other than that Marín-Sola's sufficient grace certainly gives the beginning of the imperfect act, but that this act continues is fallible, contingent upon man's reaction to the grace that infallibly gives the beginning of the act. This calls into question whether Marín-Sola truly believes that man can do good without an infallibly efficacious grace. In other words, can it be that man does some good, or responds well to some grace, without infallibly being moved by grace to do so? Marín-Sola responds:

---

79. Marín-Sola, "Respuesta," 19; Torre, *Do Not Resist the Spirit's Call*, 71–72.

The phrase, then, that "nothing, neither the perfect nor the *imperfect*, is done without *infallibly efficacious grace*" is true, when understood of the first grace. That is, it is true that "nothing, neither the perfect nor the imperfect, is done without a grace that is *infallibly efficacious as regards the beginning* of the act"; which is to say no more than that nothing happens without sufficient or *imperfectly efficacious grace*, which is also an *infallibly efficacious grace* as regards this [the beginning]. But it is not to say that nothing is had without a grace that is *infallibly efficacious as regards everything*.[80]

So indeed Marín-Sola holds that infallibly efficacious grace is not needed to have and persevere in the imperfect act. Man may impede the continuation of the imperfect act at any time, but he does not require a grace that infallibly upholds him in order to not do so, a grace that infallibly keeps man from placing an impediment or defect.

For Marín-Sola, sufficient grace may or may not actually give the *agere* of an imperfect act. It certainly gives a possibility, the beginning or inclination toward that act, but man may frustrate or impede the motion insofar as this motion that God gives is fallible regarding the actual imperfect act. Certainly Marín-Sola does not call this beginning of the imperfect act a mere potency. He claims that it is certainly a kind of *agere*, but it is unclear what this grace actually gives if it does not actually give the imperfect act. For this reason, it seems to be a kind inclination, as we have said.

Marín-Sola states that the entire motion from the beginning of the imperfect act to the completion of the perfect act is a continuous one, moving from beginning to end unless man impedes the motion.

If this shocks some theologians, it is because they conceive *the imperfect act*, and therefore *sufficient grace*, as a conjunction of unconnected or *discontinuous strokes*, in which the *action* stops and must stop, *because God does not give another stroke* of grace. This is not the true concept of St. Thomas. The course of the *imperfect* act is a *continuous current of premotion*. By the imperfect premotion or *beginning of the act*, God impresses on the will a *movement toward the perfect act*; and God never stops this movement or continuous current of grace, while man does not stop it, that is, while man does not place an impediment to the course of the movement *begun* by God, and, thus, to the course of grace.[81]

However, the Thomist does not claim that God starts and stops the continual motion from imperfect act to perfect act. What he does claim,

80. Marín-Sola, "Respuesta," 20; Torre, *Do Not Resist the Spirit's Call*, 72–73.
81. Marín-Sola, "Respuesta," 19; Torre, *Do Not Resist the Spirit's Call*, 72.

however, is that man can do no good unless God moves and preserves him in good, just as it is not sufficient that God give existence to man at some time. He must continue to preserve him in existence. Indeed, God is not merely a *per accidens* cause of man's existence and good activity, but God is a *per se* cause. As such, it is not enough to state that God infallibly begins to move man toward some good. If man is to be preserved from defect he requires that God give the grace necessary to be upheld from defect throughout the entire motion of the act, from beginning to end, from the incipiency of the imperfect act to the completion of the perfect act. God cannot simply kick-start the process, hoping that man will not impede the grace. If man does not impede the grace it must be because God infallibly upheld him from doing so, throughout its ontological and temporal continuation. If this is not the case, then either of the following conclusions must be true: a) man has some good (that is, the good of preservation) that comes more from himself than from God and thus God's will is frustrated whenever men fail to persevere in the good, or b) man has some good that comes more from himself than from God, and God simply gives generic motions, suitable for good but not in any way the product of God actually willing a specific good in the man. In this case, God's will is not frustrated (since he intends no specific act with the given motion), but the determination of that motion is made by man. However, both of these conclusions are clearly against the mind of St. Thomas since they posit man having some good that comes more from himself than from God.

Marín-Sola's intention is certainly to distance Thomism from the classical treatment, which gives God a providentially antecedent role in whatever man does. This treatment states that God does not give fallible motions. It is true that potencies reside within motions for further ends, but these potencies are not themselves motions toward that further end. God's will is not frustrated, and man does no good without being moved by God. This means that all efficacious grace, all premotions, are infallible. God's simple will is always accomplished. When man does not persevere in even an imperfect act, this can only be under the condition that (though not "because of," in the causal sense) God did not give the grace whereby he would persevere. But for Marín-Sola this is tantamount to the thought of Jansen or Calvin.

It is also true that *nothing* happens without *infallible premotion* or *infallibly effica-cious grace*, but it is not a premotion or grace that is *infallible as regards everything*, because then the *general* or *sufficient* motions or graces would disappear, and there would remain only *special* motions or graces, the *perfectly efficacious*; all of which would make it difficult for a truly sufficient grace to exist and would also make man's responsibility for sin difficult to explain, and would end by giving a pretext to the accusations of having an affinity with Jansenism and Calvinism.[82]

Marín-Sola wants for there to be efficacious graces that are not the special sort that infallibly give the act toward which they are ordered, but this necessitates that God wills fallibly or indeterminately, not actually causing all of the good within man, including the good of preservation in a good act. God only begins things, and it is up to man to not mess them up, as it were, under his own power. Man must cooperate with grace *apart from grace*. But, as we have seen, none of this is needed to rescue the Thomist position from Jansenism and Calvinism. The classical Thomistic position claims only that man requires infallibly efficacious grace in order that he not fall into defect, for man can do no good that does not come from God. For Marín-Sola this seems to be equivalent to stating that God stops the motion of grace in the man who places an impediment to it, but this is incorrect, as we shall see in the next section.

That So-Called Báñezianism Makes God the Cause of Defect

As we have seen, Marín-Sola believes that efficacious grace for imperfect acts is infallibly efficacious in regard to its beginning but that it is fallible both in regard to the continuation of that act and for the movement from imperfect act to perfect act. Marín-Sola posits three possible causes for the frustration of this single movement from imperfect act to perfect act:

a) The *creature* stops it with his actual defect.
b) God stops it, but *after* the defect is placed.
c) God stops it, *before* the defect is placed.[83]

He admits that the first two possibilities are true but denies the third, stat-ing that this is the error of Jansen and Calvin. He also seemingly attributes this view to Báñez.

---

82. Marín-Sola, "Respuesta," 20; Torre, *Do Not Resist the Spirit's Call*, 73.
83. Marín-Sola, "Respuesta," 15; Torre, *Do Not Resist the Spirit's Call*, 67.

Whoever admits whichever of the first two hypotheses is with Thomists, but also with us. One who admits the third is against us, but also against Thomists, at least against those before Báñez and after Gonet. In addition, we *do not see* how, in admitting this third hypothesis, one can avoid falling into the theory of a completely corrupted nature, and of being accused of not being sufficiently distanced from Jansenism and Calvinism.[84]

First, a word must be given as to whether Báñez and his followers truly follow this third hypothesis. Nowhere within the work of Báñez or Garrigou is it stated that God positively stops or impedes the movement from an imperfect act to a perfect one. Within the thought of both Thomists it is clear that man is the one responsible in every way for his own defect and the sin that follows. All that is claimed is that efficacious grace is withheld as punishment for a prior sin or defect, but this is to say nothing other than what is stated in the second hypothesis, which Marín-Sola himself affirms. It is true that God does not always uphold the creature from defect, but as St. Thomas states, God is not responsible to always and everywhere elevate a defectible creature to a state of perfection.[85]

Marín-Sola presents two questions to the Thomist (especially, presumably, the one associated with so-called Báñezianism): "Does the *motion* of sufficient grace [efficacious grace necessary for imperfect acts] tend or not tend by its nature to efficacious grace?" and "From whom comes the *initiative* that paralyzes the course of this motion?"[86] In response to the first question, those who follow Báñez would certainly state that the

84. Marín-Sola, "Respuesta," 15; Torre, *Do Not Resist the Spirit's Call*, 67.

85. *ST* I, q. 23, a. 5, ad 3: "Neither on this account can there be said to be injustice in God, if He prepares unequal lots for not unequal things. This would be altogether contrary to the notion of justice, if the effect of predestination were granted as a debt, and not gratuitously. In things which are given gratuitously, a person can give more or less, just as he pleases (provided he deprives nobody of his due), without any infringement of justice. This is what the master of the house said: 'Take what is thine, and go thy way. Is it not lawful for me to do what I will?' (Mt. 20:14, 15)." *De veritate*, q. 6, a. 2, ad 8: "It would be contrary to the nature of distributive justice if things that were due to persons and were to be distributed to them were given out unequally to those that had equal rights. But things given out of liberality do not come under any form of justice. I may freely choose to give them to one person and not to another. Now, grace belongs to this class of things. Consequently, it is not contrary to the nature of distributive justice if God intends to give grace to one person and not to another, and does not consider their unequal merits." *De veritate*, q. 6, a. 2, ad 9: "The election by which God chooses one man and reprobates another is reasonable. There is no reason why merit must be the reason for His choice, however, since the reason for this is the divine goodness. As Augustine says, moreover, a justifying reason for reprobation [in the present] is the fact of original sin in man—for reprobation in the future, the fact that mere existence gives man no claim to grace. For I can reasonably deny something to a person if it is not due to him."

86. Marín-Sola, "Respuesta," 15; *Do Not Resist the Spirit's Call*, Torre, 67.

imperfect act tends toward the perfect act insofar as efficacious grace pre-
disposes man for a further grace that God at least antecedently wills for a
man. This movement from the imperfect to the more perfect will follow if
not impeded by man, and in this sense we can agree with Marín-Sola when
he states that the imperfect act tends "by its nature" to the perfect act.
However, that man should not impede the movement must be attributed
primarily to God insofar as it is a good, a preservation or upholding from
the hypothetically inevitable but naturally contingent falling of the creature that will certainly follow if God is not working within it.

In relation to the second question, it is equally clear that all Thomists
reject the idea that God in any way takes a causal initiative in the paralyzation of the movement from imperfect act to perfect act. However, it *is*
stated that the paralyzation could not exist without a prior permission of
defect, or what is called an antecedent permissive decree. If this permission did not exist then the defect would never arise. In this sense, God's
providential ordering is always antecedent to every act of man, good or
bad. However, taking an initiative implies a positive act, a step taken to
bring about paralyzation, and indeed this does not come from God in any
way, as Báñez stated. "I say therefore that absolutely speaking, it is clearly
wrong to say that God has predefined or supplied or wished the sin or the
act of sin in however much it is bad, and never has a Thomist theologian
said such blasphemy."[87]

As such, it does not follow that anyone who states that responding
well to the beginning of grace itself requires grace is close to falling into
the errors of Jansen or Calvin. Man requires God to do well, but God
is not obliged always and everywhere to uphold man from every defect.
When God does not do so, man retains the ability in the divided sense
still to persevere, and that he does not is attributed only to his own free
choosing. He turns from God and he freely chooses this or that particular
evil. God is not causally or positively involved in any way. This is clearly
the opposite of God's positive initiative in relation to sin and reprobation
according to Jansen and Calvin. God only takes a positive initiative in
bringing about that man does well. When man sins, it comes from his
own failure alone.

---

87. Báñez, *Controversias*, 444: "Digo pues que absolutamente hablando, es claro error decir que
Dios ha predefinido o proveído o querido el pecado o el acto del pecado en cuanto es malo, y nunca
teólogo tomista tal blasfemia dijo."

God's Omnipotence and Inefficacious Motions

Many of the objections to Marín-Sola thus far have been based upon the fact that God's will is simple and thus, insofar as God is omnipotent, whatever he wills will surely come to pass. But Marín-Sola rejects this, stating that God can indeed will things in different ways, sometimes fully efficaciously, sometimes with no more efficacy than the motion of a feeble creature, a motion that is, consequently, quite fallible.

Some Thomists pay much attention to the fundamental principle of Saint Thomas that the will of God, by being *omnipotent*, is *most efficacious*, and do not pay as much attention to the other principle, no less fundamental, that God, in being *free*, does not always move according to *all* the efficacy of His power, but more or less efficaciously, as it pleases Him. In the same manner as the divine *being*, by being infinite, is equal to *all* beings, and can create, as it pleases Him, greater or lesser beings, incorruptibles and corruptibles; just so His action, by being infinite, is equal to *all* action, and He can work with an action more or less efficacious, with an action irresistible or resistible. God can throw a stone with a force and an efficacy such that no creature nor force can deter it in its course. But He could also, if He wished, throw it with a force and with conditions *exactly equal* to those by which a man throws it.[88]

This means, of course, that such a motion is fallible, meaning that man can impede the divine will not just in the divided sense, but absolutely:

and therefore this stone could be stopped *in sensu diviso, in sensu composito* and in all the senses, *exactly equal* as though it were thrown by a man. The motions of *general providence* are of this class; they are motions exactly *accommodated* to the exigencies and conditions of the creature, and for this reason precisely are called *general* and not special.[89]

---

88. Marín-Sola, "Respuestas," 23; *Do Not Resist the Spirit's Call,* Torre, 76. For a similar account of divine self-limiting in regard to omnipotence, see Bruce R. Reichenbach, *Divine Providence: God's Love and Human Freedom* (Eugene, Ore.: Cascade Books, 2016). On pp. 129 and 130 Reichenbach states, "If we adopt a view of God as a personal being or agent, the claim that God can impose limits on his own actions becomes intelligible, for personal agents are just the sorts of beings that can voluntarily put limits on what they do. When I arm-wrestled with my son, I put limits on my power or strength, giving him the opportunity to win so as to encourage his competitive spirit. Such self-limitation did not negate my power; I still retained it, only I chose not to use it for a good reason. I could have exercised my power, but that would have negated the very purpose of stimulating competitiveness for which I limited it. Similarly, it is within God's power to limit his employment of his power."

89. Marín-Sola, "Respuesta," 23; Torre, *Do Not Resist the Spirit's Call,* 76.

Marín-Sola speaks of divine motion as respecting both the mode of liberty and the mode of defectibility in man. Whenever God moves man, he does so in such a way that man freely wills that which God wills in him.[90] He also wills in such a way that man may freely fall into defect and resist the motion, at least according to Marín-Sola's account of God's "general providence."

When one says that divine motion accommodates itself to the nature of the moved thing, or, as Saint Thomas says, that God moves each thing "secundum *modus ejus*," this phrase can be taken in two senses. In the intellectual creature, there are two properties or modes: a) its *liberty*; b) its *defectibility*.... But, respecting the second mode, that is, its defectibility, which is an imperfection, God does not always accommodate Himself to it, but with frequency, by His liberality and mercy, acts against it and above it, as occurs in all *special* providence.[91]

He continues, further explaining that man's defectibility is overcome and man is upheld from defect according to special providence, but that he is left to his own defectibility according to general providence.

But, respecting the actual or *de facto defectibility, general* providence, with its decrees and premotions, leaves it as it is, and thus these are *de facto* resistible or defectible. By contrast, *special* providence, with its decrees and premotions called *special* or *efficacious*, works in a *praeter*-natural or *super*-natural way, moving the defectible creature in an *indefectible* way; that is, without removing its natural defectibility, it makes it *de facto* never resist.... Because, in *general* providence, natural or supernatural, God moves in a less efficacious way, that is, in an imperfect way accommodated to the *defectibility* of the creature, for this such a motion is defectible or impedible by the creature, and this is what is called a motion or grace that is *imperfectly efficacious* or *fallibly efficacious* or simply *sufficient*.[92]

In the case of special providence, it would seem that there is congruity between Marín-Sola and the traditional Thomistic treatment. Man is moved according to an infallible and efficacious motion without which he could not accomplish the perfect act. However, in regard to imperfect acts (which are according to general providence), man may do good without

---

90. Marín-Sola, "Respuesta," 24; Torre, *Do Not Resist the Spirit's Call*, 77: "When God moves the rational creature, He always preserves the first mode, moving it *freely*, because this is a perfection, and the divine motion does not destroy or diminish, but rather conserves and augments, all that there is of perfection in the creature.... Every *providence*, then, and every *decree*, and every *motion*, whether special or general, accommodates itself to, conserves, and augments the *liberty* of the creature."

91. Marín-Sola, "Respuesta," 23–24; Torre, *Do Not Resist the Spirit's Call*, 77.

92. Marín-Sola, "Respuesta," 24; Torre, *Do Not Resist the Spirit's Call*, 77.

an infallibly efficacious motion. To put it simply, this seems like a form of simultaneous concurrence. It may be true that God gives forth the beginning of the act. He inclines the will. He opens the door. He lowers the rope down the well. Whichever way one wants to put it, Marín-Sola certainly affirms this. However, that man responds well to grace comes entirely from him. It is not God who moves man to accept and move with grace, but it is man. God's motion in this case is frustratable. It is up to man to receive it well or not. Whenever he does receive it well, though the beginning of the act belongs to God, that the act continues and the imperfect act is accomplished belongs more to man than to God. While Marín-Sola wants to attribute this entirely to the sufficient grace that provides the beginning of the good act, the fact is that its continuation and perseverance rests upon man's good cooperation *apart from any further grace that makes man to cooperate.* As such, man acts well apart from the power of God, but this is so often argued against by St. Thomas himself, who states, "Now, nothing is a cause of being unless by virtue of its acting through the power of God, as we showed. Therefore, every operating agent acts through God's power,"[93] and that "if this divine influence were to cease, every operation would cease."[94] Furthermore, "it is also apparent that the same effect is not attributed to a natural cause and to divine power in such a way that it is partly done by God, and partly done by the natural agent; rather, it is wholly done by both, according to a different way, just as the same effect is wholly attributed to the instrument and also wholly to the principal agent."[95] This means that the whole act must be attributed primarily to the primary cause, through which both the secondary causation and the effect are produced. And thus, that which distinguishes man is not something in man, but it is the motion itself which distinguishes him, as St. Thomas states.

Indeed, this fact, that one man chooses things beneficial to him, whereas another man chooses things harmful to him, apart from their proper reasoning, cannot be understood as resulting from differences of intellectual nature, because the nature of intellect and will is one in all men.... Hence, in so far as man's intellect is enlightened for the performance of some action, or as his will is prompted by God, the man is not said to be favored by birth, but, rather, well guarded or well governed.[96]

---

93. *ScG* III, 67, 1.
94. *ScG* III, 67, 3.
95. *ScG* III, 70, 8.
96. *ScG* III, 92, 3.

Marín-Sola compares the difference between general providence and supernatural providence with the difference between the ascetical and mystical life. In the former, God "moves in an ordinary or *human* way,"[97] just as Marín-Sola has stated that God can throw the stone "with a force and with conditions *exactly equal* to those by which a man throws it"[98] and therefore "such a motion is defectible or impedible by the creature."[99]

But St. Thomas states quite the opposite. It is of course true that one created being acting upon another in a way that lacks full efficient causality and infallibility (necessity of consequence) does not necessarily result in a given effect in either the composite or divided sense. As such, man is not always moved according to the motion exerted on him by other creatures or lesser agents. However, St. Thomas states unequivocally that this is not the case with God and his omnipotent motion in man's will.

Now, since a disposition which results from a quality of the body, or from an intellectual persuasion, does not bring necessity to the act of choice, a man does not always choose what his guardian angel intends, or that toward which a celestial body gives inclination. *But a man always [semper] chooses the object in accord with God's operation within his will.*[100]

Similarly, St. Thomas asserts that God's will is always affirmed. "The will of God is necessarily always [semper] fulfilled."[101] It is entirely unclear in what way these uses of *semper* might be reconciled with Marín-Sola's fallible motions. In fact, St. Thomas presents an objection to the perfect efficacy of the divine will that seems quite close to that which is presented by Marín-Sola in regard to general providence. It states:

Further, since the will of God is the first cause, it does not exclude intermediate causes. But the effect of a first cause may be hindered by a defect of a secondary cause; as the effect of the motive power may be hindered by the weakness of the limb. Therefore the effect of the divine will may be hindered by a defect of the secondary causes. The will of God, therefore, is not always fulfilled.[102]

St. Thomas responds by asserting the omnipotence and infrustratability of the divine will.

97. Marín-Sola, "Respuesta," 24; Torre, *Do Not Resist the Spirit's Call*, 77.
98. Marín-Sola, "Respuesta," 23; Torre, *Do Not Resist the Spirit's Call*, 76.
99. Marín-Sola, "Respuesta," 24; Torre, *Do Not Resist the Spirit's Call*, 77.
100. *ScG* III, 92, 4.
101. *ST* I, q. 19, a. 6.
102. *ST* I, q. 19, a. 6, arg. 3.

A first cause can be hindered in its effect by deficiency in the secondary cause, when it is not the universal first cause, including within itself all causes; for then the effect could in no way escape its order. And thus it is with the will of God, as said above.[103]

And so, in summary, man requires infallibly efficacious grace for perfect acts, or those acts that are difficult or take place over a long period of time. Man also requires infallibly efficacious grace for the beginning, or the *motus ad* an imperfect act. However, for what Marín-Sola calls the "continuation," the preservation of the initial motion such that it actually results in real act, all that is necessary is a fallible motion, to which man either responds well or he does not.

In this *beginning*, by being from God alone, there can be no impediment, just as Adam could not place an impediment that God instill in him the breath of life. In the *continuation* of this life, there can be an impediment, just as Adam could commit suicide after being created. In order not to place an impediment to the continuation of this life, *general* providence is enough for an integral nature, natural or supernatural, respectively; but in a fallen or weak nature, there is need of special providence and special motion, if it concerns difficult things or for much time.[104]

And yet, for "easy works and those done in a brief time," it suffices that God give merely a *motus ad* that man carries through to completion. Yes, God provides the beginning for this act, but that it be carried through depends on man not impeding the motion, and this is apart from God giving the grace that makes man not impede it.

That One Man Might Be Better Than Another Though Both Men Receive Equal Grace

The logical conclusion of the above is that two men who receive an equal grace, say for the *motus ad* attrition, may yet respond differently to it, such that we could say that of two men with equal grace, one acts better than another by his own power. This is precisely an objection that Marín-Sola's interlocutor poses to him.

Would not Fr. Marín-Sola judge that, of two sinners equally tempted and equally aided by God through the impulse of sufficient grace, it happened that one freely

---

103. *ST* I, q. 19, a. 6, ad 3.
104. Marín-Sola, "Respuesta," 26. Torre, *Do Not Resist the Spirit's Call*, 79.

chose the act of prayer and the other not or that one placed an impediment to this and the other did not? But then this is opposed to the doctrine of D. Thomas in Matt. XXV, 15: "Whoever endeavors more receives more grace, *but that one endeavors more requires a greater cause.*" Also in the Epistle to the Ephesians IV, 7: "For who discerns you? *What do you have that you have no received* (I Cor. IV, 7)?"[105]

Marín-Sola responds with stating what we have already said, namely that

with equal grace—and, as a result, with an equal beginning of the act—one freely places an impediment and the other does not place an impediment to the course of the act, which is the same as saying to the course of the grace. Well then: as the one who places an impediment paralyzes the course of the grace and does not receive further grace, and the one who does not place an impediment continues receiving greater grace, it always results that—as the Thomists say—the act of prayer or any other easy supernatural act whatsoever, in the one who places it, is placed with greater grace than that received by the one who does not place it.[106]

Marín-Sola continues by citing the distinction between operating and cooperating grace, the former of which begins the act while the latter aids in its continuation.

If, to this, one adds that the grace by which one *begins* the act is commonly called *prevenient* or operating, and the grace with which one *continues* the course of the act is called *aiding* or cooperating, we will hold that the *act of prayer* supposes *greater aiding* or cooperating *grace*, even though no greater initial or *prevenient* grace, in the one who prays than in the one who does not pray.[107]

The issue with all of this, however, is that there does not appear to be any greater grace given that this man does not impede the operating or prevenient grace. It may be true that greater grace is given to the one who responds well, and that in some way this greater grace is said to aid in the continuation of the act, but what accounts for the fact that the man who acts well is upheld from defect? What accounts for the fact that he has distinguished himself from the man who is not upheld from defect? If an antecedent grace is not the cause of man's responding well to grace, then man responds well under his own power, quite separate from God working within him as the source of all good. In this way, some men really have something worthwhile that they have not received. Some men are

105. Marín-Sola, "Respuesta," 52; Torre, *Do Not Resist the Spirit's Call,* 109.
106. Marín-Sola, "Respuesta," 52; Torre, *Do Not Resist the Spirit's Call,* 109–10.
107. Marín-Sola, "Respuesta," 52; Torre, *Do Not Resist the Spirit's Call,* 110.

better than others insofar as they cooperate with God's grace better than others, and yet this is not the result of any work of God. If anything, it might be said that the giving of cooperating grace is the result of man not placing an impediment. And thus at least in the continuation of imperfect or easy acts, God is passive and determined according to man's good use of God's prevenient grace.

That one man may have more than another with equal grace is actually affirmed by Marín-Sola.

> It can occur, then, with *the same* grace—that is, with this same sufficient grace that is infallibly efficacious for the beginning of the act, or to have the imperfect *motus*, but that is fallibly efficacious as regards the placing or not placing of one or more impediments, in easy things and for a little time—that one places an impediment and another does not. In this sense, *and only in this sense*, one can say that, with the same grace, one can *have more* than another; that is, one can have less impediments than the other or have *none*, when it concerns short and easy stretches, as Saint Thomas says.[108]

But, to the contrary, to say *in any sense* that one man may have more than another, that he can work well with grace, upholding himself from impediment, but that this is in no way the effect of being given more by God, is to deny that all the good that man has comes first from God. When St. Paul asks "Who distinguishes you?" it is the case that, at least in terms of easy things and for a little time, it is man who distinguishes himself from his neighbor *without the aid of grace*. It may be true that greater aiding grace follows, but it follows because man chooses well with an equal prevenient grace in the first place. It is the result and not the cause of man's working well with grace, otherwise there could be no sense in which it might be said that man receives equal grace and yet may use it better or worse.

> To one who does not place an impediment to the prevenient or operating or sufficient grace already received, God gives greater aiding or cooperating grace, because God never interrupts the *course* of the same grace, if man does not interrupt it, and, with this *greater grace*, one has a *greater continuation of the act* than the other.[109]

It is with this cooperating grace that man can be said to have more than another, not because of it. And a man only receives this greater cooper-

108. Marín-Sola, "Respuesta," 54; Torre, *Do Not Resist the Spirit's Call*, 111.
109. Marín-Sola, "Respuesta," 54; Torre, *Do Not Resist the Spirit's Call*, 111.

ating grace as a consequent of not impeding it. Moreover, even though this applies only to imperfect acts, Marín-Sola appears to state that reprobation presupposes foreknowledge of sins. Therefore, God seems to withhold the special graces that relate to great acts like final impenitence to those who do not respond well to the fallible graces of general providence. As such, those who *do* respond well to general motions without any further aid from God may be said to play some role in distinguishing themselves even in regard to predestination and glory, since God does not foresee sin in them and thus does not suppose that sin when deciding upon some to be reprobated. While it is true that Marín-Sola claims that there is nothing antecedent in the creature that moves God to elect him, to claim that, on the other hand, there can be something antecedent in man (seen by God via foreknowledge) that affects his reprobation is impossible without also presupposing that God elects supposing foreknowledge. It is unclear how God could foreknow and suppose those who will not respond well to grace for imperfect acts without also recognizing who will respond well.

Marín-Sola states, "God never interrupts the *course* of the same grace, if man does not interrupt it." Compare this to the words of Garrigou, who affirms that man is the cause of impediment, but that *whenever man does not place an impediment* (since not placing an impediment is itself a good, a cooperating with grace and being upheld above his own defectibility) *this must come from God.* "For to resist sufficient grace is an evil that can come only from us; whereas not to resist sufficient grace is a good that cannot solely be the result of our action, but one which must come from God who is the source of all good."[110]

Marín-Sola attempts to argue around this by returning to the words of St. Thomas: "*Qui plus conatur, plus habet de gratia; sed quod plus conetur, indiget altiori causa.*" Marín-Sola states that we ought to make a strict distinction between, on the one hand, endeavoring, attempting, or putting effort toward grace (*conari*) and, on the other hand, not placing an impediment to it.

In the first place, the greater or lesser effort ("conato") toward grace is one thing and the greater or less *impediment* to it is another. The proof that these two things are radically distinct, and that it is most dangerous to confuse them, is that, with

---

110. Garrigou, *Predestination*, 239.

nature alone, there is *no effort at all* toward grace, and to say the opposite would be semi-Pelagian; on the other hand, with nature alone (and, therefore, with much more reason with nature premoved by *sufficient* grace), one can place or not place *some impediments* to grace, and even place *no impediment*, in easy things and for a little time, even when dealing with fallen nature. This is the current doctrine of Thomism. When Saint Thomas with frequency says that "*non ponere impedimentum ex gratia procedit*," the phrase "non ponere" means to say "*nullum ponere*" or "*numquam*" to place; that is, to avoid *all* of them and avoid them *always*.... So, then, the text of Saint Thomas cited in the objection with which we are dealing speaks of the *conato* for grace, and our doctrine speaks of the *impediment* or non-impediment to grace.[111]

First, it is unclear what exact citations from St. Thomas Marín-Sola has in mind because he does not mention them. Moreover, it is unclear as to why he would take *non ponere* to mean *nullum ponere* or *nunquam ponere*. Simply put, this is not what St. Thomas says. The quotation as such states that not placing, literally "not to place," an impediment proceeds from grace. And this is precisely what Marín-Sola has denied. In fact, even *nullum ponere* seems to be denied by Marín-Sola insofar as he has stated that "one can have less impediments than the other or have *none*," as we saw above.

Second, St. Thomas indeed affirms that man cannot not place an impediment unless he is upheld by a divine motion or grace. "However, although those who are in sin cannot avoid by their own power putting an impediment in the way of grace, as we showed, *unless they be helped in advance by grace*."[112] Furthermore, while St. Thomas does seem to posit that it may be possible for a person in the state of natural integrity before the fall to be able to not offer an impediment without the aid of grace (though not without the aid of natural divine motion as such, since all good or co-operation with the good, insofar as it is an act, requires to be moved from potency to act by God), this is not the case with man as fallen.

Now, this statement of ours, that it is within the power of free choice not to offer an impediment to grace, is applicable to those persons in whom natural potency is integrally present. But if, through a preceding disorder, one swerves toward evil, it will not at all be within his power to offer no impediment to grace.[113]

---

111. Marín-Sola, "Repuesta," 54–55; Torre, *Do Not Resist the Spirit's Call*, 112.

112. *ScG* III, q. 160, 5: "Quamvis autem illi qui in peccato sunt, vitare non possint per propriam potestatem quin impedimentum gratiae ponant, ut ostensum est, *nisi auxilio gratiae praeveniantur*." Emphasis is my own.

113. *ScG* III, q. 160, 1.

It is clear that man will place an impediment when not upheld from doing so, both because he is a defectible creature but also and especially when he is already fallen, with disordered appetites, emotions, and inclinations. As such, man requires supernatural aid not to impede grace, but this Marín-Sola denies.

Third, to say that *conari ad gratiae* and *ponere impedimentum* are anything but contradictories in the composite sense seems metaphysically and logically unfounded. Marín-Sola affirms that "with nature alone, there is *no effort at all* toward grace, and to say the opposite would be semi-Pelagian."[114] With this we certainly agree, and it is *for this very reason* that it is so important to state *non ponere impedimentum ex gratia procedit.* Not placing an impediment, *non ponere impedimentum,* is the contradictory of placing an impediment, *ponere impedimentum.* To not place an impediment cannot be anything other than cooperating with grace, striving out towards it, accepting it, making the positive *effort* to act in accord with it. The precise way that one does not act in effort toward it, does not cooperate with it, is to work against it, to hinder it, to impede it. To not have this effort toward, this cooperation with, necessarily means that one places an impediment. As such, not to do so is the same as making an effort toward, which cannot be without grace, as even Marín-Sola confirms.

Marín-Sola continues stating that his affirmation of unequal good acts resulting from equal graces means only that some can respond more poorly than another, placing an impediment while another does not.

From this, one deduces the essential difference between these two propositions: first—"With an *equal* grace, two (or one of them) can have a *greater effort than the degree of grace received*"; second—"With an *equal* grace received by two, one of them can have a *lesser effort than that had by the other.*" The first is false, because it would suppose a degree of *effort greater than the grade of grace.* The second is true, because it only supposes a degree of *effort less than the grade of grace.*[115]

However, the original objection (which is the same as our own) to which Marín-Sola is replying is not that one of these two should have a good that transcends the prevenient grace given to them both. What is objected to is that with the same prevenient grace one should continue on through this grace, persevering in it, not placing an impediment, and that

114. Marín-Sola, "Respuesta," 54; Torre, *Do Not Resist the Spirit's Call,* 112.
115. Marín-Sola, "Respuesta," 55–56; Torre, *Do Not Resist the Spirit's Call,* 113.

none of this comes in any way from God upholding the creature to do so. If it upheld the creature to do so, then it could never be said to be a fallible motion, one that is sometimes received well and sometimes not. To put it in another way, we should expect that man on his own, receiving no goodness from God other than an impedible *motum ad* some good, is, especially in his fallen state, incapable of persevering in anything, incapable of not hindering or ruining goodness if God is not directly involved with his being upheld. If both men are given a *beginning* to a good act but not the good act itself, and the *continuation* is completely fallible, we should expect both men to fall precisely because and insofar as God is not working with them. What good can we do that is not brought about by God working within us? What good can be had that does not come from the source of all good? We do not at all deny that man alone suffices to impede a *motum ad* some good, but only God suffices that man *not* impede a *motum ad* some good, otherwise man is his own source of perseverance in easy and imperfect acts for a short time. This seems much too close to the errors of the semi-Pelagians.

Finally, in response to St. Paul's question in Ephesians ("For who distinguishes you? What do you have that you have not received?"), Marín-Sola states first that he has so far only been speaking about imperfect acts and not perfect ones.

Before all, do not forget that, when we speak of the case of *equal* graces, we are speaking specifically of equal *sufficient* graces and not *infallibly efficacious graces*. Therefore, we are not speaking of the ineffable grace of *final perseverance*, which is an infallibly efficacious grace.... Neither are we dealing with the grace of *justification*, which is also an infallibly efficacious grace.... Neither, finally, is it a question now of any other infallibly efficacious grace, as is required in fallen nature for all perfect or *difficult* acts.... In the three given cases, of *final perseverance, conversion*, and *difficult acts*, the impossibility of having either more or less derives from its requiring infallibly efficacious grace: from which, it is not possible that one place *in fact* any impediment to grace, and, no *impediment* being possible, it is not possible to have *less* than that to which God moves.[116]

With all of this the classical Thomist will certainly agree, but the objection remains as regards imperfect or easy acts. Marín-Sola attempts a final answer to this charge of St. Paul in relation to imperfect acts by

116. Marín-Sola, "Respuesta," 58–59; Torre, *Do Not Resist the Spirit's Call*, 116–17.

stating that St. Paul is speaking here only of goods acts, and not the non-existence of bad acts or impediments.

The discernment of which Saint Paul speaks consists in having something *not received of God*. "Quid te discernit? Quid *habes quod non accepisti?*" And since one cannot receive anything from God except the *good*, the discernment of which Saint Paul speaks is the discernment in *good*, and consists in admitting in the creature some *good not received from God* or *more good than he received from God*. Saint Paul does not speak, therefore, of the discernment in evil; that is, the discernment of the other for having some *evil* that the other does not have, [which evil] does not proceed from God, but from the one who has it. Well then: and this is the fundamental principle that no Thomist should ever forget, man can never be the cause of *good*. He cannot be, therefore, the cause of any *good* without being premoved, nor *have more good* than that to which God premoves him. He cannot, in consequence, discern himself from the other *in good*. But he can be and is (and this is frequently forgotten) the first cause of *evil*.[117]

We do not deny that man is the first (and only) cause of sin, nor do we deny that man can never be the cause of good or have more good than another without being premoved (infallibly) to it. However, we return here to the same objection that we have made above: in this case, to not do that which is ultimately evil is to do something that is good. To not place an impediment, to not hinder God's grace, to not turn one's face away from him, *is to do something good*. An impediment may be a lack, a nonthing, but in a real subject[118] the lack of a lack, the lack of a nonthing is to really have something positively. This is always the case with contradictories if the principle of contradiction is not to be denied. To not not-eat is to eat. To not impede is to cooperate. To impede and to not impede

117. Marín-Sola, "Respuesta," 59; Torre, *Do Not Resist the Spirit's Call*, 117–18.

118. It is important that we specify that the negation of a negation is something positive in a subject that is itself in existence. This is all that is meant by 'real subject.' For example, if I were to say, "A little merry gnome does not not-sing old sea shanties in my study," it would not mean that a little merry gnome does indeed sing old sea shanties in my study, for no such little gnome exists (at least as far as I know). If I were, however, to say "I do not not-sing old sea shanties in my study," then, because I exist, I will certainly be singing old sea shanties in my study. See *De veritate*, q. 28, a. 6: "There are other opposites of which only one of the two terms is a natural being, and the other is only its removal or negation. This appears, for instance, in opposites based upon affirmation and negation or upon privation and possession. In such cases the negation of an opposite which posits a natural being is real, because it is the negation of a real being; but the negation of the other opposite is not real, because it is not the negation of any real being. It is the negation of a negation. Consequently, this negation of a negation, which is the negation of the second opposite, in no way differs in reality from the positing of the other. In reality, then, the coming to be of white and the destruction of not-white are the same."

are not merely contraries, but contradictions. There is no third possibility. One must do one or the other, and if one does one then one is necessarily not doing the other.

If St. Paul is exhorting us to remember that we can have nothing good that does not come from God, then it must be true that not placing an impediment, which is the exact same thing as to cooperate with grace, requires that God move us to this, and in an infallible way, otherwise we arrive at all of the same problems.

In the end, this is too close to a Molinist simultaneous concurrence, where that man acts well is attributed to a nonsubordinated, egalitarian cooperative causality. At least in regard to imperfect acts, the Thomistic concept of subordinated causality is certainly impossible given Marín-Sola's premises. God throws the rope, as it were, with prevenient grace, and it is ultimately up to man whether he grabs onto the rope or not. It may then be God who pulls the man out of the well, but this one decisive moment that affects the entirety of the act, the grabbing of the rope and the holding on, comes primarily from man, and God is passive to it, divorced from the good power by which some men indeed grab the rope.

Marín-Sola argues that his scheme for imperfect acts is not a simultaneous concurrence, stating, "Were one to deal with a simultaneous concurrence, indifferent for acting or not acting, for doing good or evil, one would have *much more* than that to which God moved one. In this case, one would have *something not received from God* and would discern oneself in good."[119] But it is not only in the case in which man can transcend prevenient grace and achieve something higher than that for which God gave the beginning. It would suffice for man to "have something not received from God" that he receive only the *motum ad* some good act that he can accept, or respond well to, transcending his own defectible nature, without God being involved in that transcendence. What distinguishes a *motum ad* attrition from either failing or actually becoming true attrition is man rising above his inclination to place an impediment, his susceptibility to defect, and cooperating with God. This is enough to posit a kind of simultaneous concurrence because it erases the subordinated causality of the divine and human agencies in man performing imperfect acts. If the divine motion to some good does not bring about man's self-willing

119. Marín-Sola, "Respuesta," 60; Torre, *Do Not Resist the Spirit's Call*, 118.

of that good as a secondary cause then we are left not with the classical Thomistic account of subordinated causality, but with something closer to the congruist[120] coordinate causality. Man may depend upon the *motus ad* in some way, but the divine motion must be met by the separate agency of man in order to actually achieve the good intended by the divine will. Man acts in some way outside of the order of God's motion to coordinate in bringing about the imperfect act. God may throw the rope down the well, but that man grabs it and climbs it to safety is somehow independent of God's motion in the patient. However, we know that according to St. Thomas, every single good act, big or small, perfect or imperfect, momentary or lengthy, depends primarily on him who is the source of all good and of all true act.

Moreover, it is not enough to state that these problems affect only imperfect acts, for insofar as the not-impeding of imperfect acts leads to the reward of receiving the infallibly efficacious grace for supernatural and perfect acts, Marín-Sola's analysis cuts all the way to the heart of the mystery of election and final perseverance.

That Some Providence Should Be Said to Be Fallible

We finally return to that first proposition of Marín-Sola, which, as he states, undergirds the whole, since "one who penetrates well this first proposition and draws from it all its consequences, does not have any need to read our articles," and also "many of the obscurities and difficulties of the Thomist system derive from the forgetfulness or inadequate penetration of this proposition."[121] This first proposition states that while divine providence is infallible with regard to the universal end of the whole universe, which is the glorification of God, there is such a thing as *general* providence that is fallible or frustratable, applying only to particular ends.[122] From this first principle also follows his last, regarding the antecedent and consequent will of God, the former of which is fallible as pertaining to general providence, and the latter is infallible as pertaining

---

120. See chapter 9 for a more complete discussion of congruism.

121. Marín-Sola, "El sistema," 17; Torre, *Do Not Resist the Spirit's Call*, 15.

122. Marín-Sola, "El sistema," 16; Torre, *Do Not Resist the Spirit's Call*, 14: "Although all divine providence is infallible or unfrustratable as regards the realization of the *universal end*, which is the glory of God and the good of the universe, nevertheless, *general* providence, whether natural or supernatural, is fallible or frustratable in respect to a *particular* end of each individual or of each individual act."

to special providence.[123] All of this is the basis upon which Marín-Sola has posited everything that we have seen above about fallible graces for imperfect acts and infallible ones for perfect acts.

Note the parallelism of this proposition with the first. The root of everything in the Thomistic system is the efficacy of the divine will. But, as we distinguish in God two divine wills, one antecedent and conditioned respecting the end, the other consequent or absolute, so we also distinguish two classes of efficacy or two providences: one general, conditioned, or fallible respecting the execution of the end, and the other special, absolute, and infallible respecting the execution of the end. And as there are neither will nor providence without the decrees or motions, so also one must distinguish two classes of divine decrees or motions: some fallible or frustratable by defect of the creature as regards the execution of the end, and other infallible or unfrustratable.[124]

In conclusion then, we ought to treat not just the question of fallible decrees, motions, and graces but trace all of these back to their source in a fallible divine will, ordering the universe according to a fallible general providence. We ought to ask whether it is even possible for God, who is radically simple and wholly transcendent, to will fallibly.

On this point, St. Thomas appears to be quite unambiguous. God is absolutely simple in every way,[125] having no potency and not being contingent upon anything. As such, God's will is radically simple as well, and this means that it cannot admit of any of the changeability or mutability that is required by fallible providence and fallible willing in regard to a particular end. St. Thomas states unequivocally:

The will of God is entirely unchangeable. On this point we must consider that to change the will is one thing; to will that certain things should be changed is another. It is possible to will a thing to be done now, and its contrary afterwards; and yet for the will to remain permanently the same: whereas the will would be changed, if one should begin to will what before he had not willed; or cease

123. Marín-Sola, "El sistema," 42; Torre, Do Not Resist the Spirit's Call, 43: "Although, in God, will is solely one and He wills everything in one most simple act, nevertheless, in our human manner of understanding and on the part only of the objects willed, the antecedent will of God and the decrees and motions corresponding to this will are by nature prior to the consequent will and its corresponding decrees and motions. This antecedent will, with its corresponding decrees and motions, is antecedent, or conditioned, or inefficacious, or impedible, or fallible as regards the execution of a particular end; but it is consequent, or absolute, or simpliciter efficacious, or umimpedible, or infallible as regards the application of the means sufficient for the execution of this end."

124. Marín-Sola, "El sistema," 43; Torre, Do Not Resist the Spirit's Call, 44

125. ST I, q. 3, a. 7.

to will what he had willed before. This cannot happen, unless we presuppose change either in the knowledge or in the disposition of the substance of the will-er. For since the will regards good, a man may in two ways begin to will a thing. In one way when that thing begins to be good for him, and this does not take place without a change in him. Thus when the cold weather begins, it becomes good to sit by the fire; though it was not so before. In another way when he knows for the first time that a thing is good for him, though he did not know it before; hence we take counsel in order to know what is good for us. Now it has already been shown that both the substance of God and His knowledge are entirely unchangeable. Therefore His will must be entirely unchangeable.[126]

Marín-Sola would presumably reply that he certainly agrees that God does not grow in knowledge, nor do the circumstances change for him, nor does he change his mind. He does not work in the way that a voli-tional creature set in time does. However, Marín-Sola would appear to ask why it is not possible that God can simply will something in a frus-tratable way. Why can he not sometimes will to throw the stone such that it cannot be impeded while at other times will to throw the stone similarly to how it is thrown by a man, as a motion which is impedible? Isn't he, even in the case of his general, fallible providence, still governing over either contingent outcome since he has, in a way, willed either via a fallible motion?

St. Thomas states that God's providence rules over all things. "We must say, however, that all things are subject to divine providence, not only in general, but even in their own individual selves."[127] This gover-nance is not just a generic one, ordering the whole of creation toward its end, but it truly applies to every last detail of the drama of existence, including each particular or singular good.

Again, the will of God is related to other things in so far as they participate in goodness in virtue of their order to the divine goodness, which is for God the reason of His willing. But not only the totality of goods, but even each one of them derives its goodness from the divine goodness, as well as its being. There-fore, the will of God extends to singular goods.[128]

---

126. *ST* I, q. 19, a. 7.
127. *ST* I, q. 22, a. 2.
128. *ScG* I, 78. Furthermore, he continues: "Again, the understood good, as such, is what is willed. But God understands even particular goods, as was proved above. He therefore wills even particular goods. This is confirmed by the authority of Scripture, which, in the first chapter of Genesis (1:4, 31), shows the pleasure of the divine will with each single work, in the words: 'God saw the light that it

However, while it might be stated that, according to Marín-Sola, man *beginning* an imperfect act is governed by providence, whether the act is *accomplished* according to man's cooperation is not. To put it another way, that a man finds himself *capable* of, say, attrition falls under divine providence, but *whether* he achieves attrition is not. Insofar as this general providence is fallible, it does not totally govern over those things that may render it fallible or not. The divine providence is passive in relation to those things. It is not God who governs them *exactly* as they truly turn out to be. St. Thomas similarly says, "It pertains to a king's dignity to have ministers who execute his providence. But the fact that he has not the plan of those things that are done by them arises from a deficiency in himself. For every operative science is the more perfect, the more it considers the particular things with which its action is concerned."[129]

It is precisely because man's motions are impedible and fallible that man finds himself contingent upon so many things around him. He cannot always order things according to his liking because he is not knowledgeable and powerful enough to exert himself infallibly on the circumstances around him. When man throws a stone it may often happen that the movement of the stone is impeded by some other thing, and insofar as this happens, man does not have total control over what happens to the

---

was good,' and similarly of His other works, and then of all the works together: 'And God saw all the things that He had made, and they were very good.'" See also, *ST* I, q. 22, a. 3: "Two things belong to providence—namely, the type of the order of things foreordained towards an end; and the execution of this order, which is called government. As regards the first of these, God has immediate providence over everything, because He has in His intellect the types of everything, even the smallest; and whatsoever causes He assigns to certain effects, He gives them the power to produce those effects. Whence it must be that He has beforehand the type of those effects in His mind. As to the second, there are certain intermediaries of God's providence; for He governs things inferior by superior, not on account of any defect in His power, but by reason of the abundance of His goodness; so that the dignity of causality is imparted even to creatures."

129. *ST* I, q. 22, a. 3. See also Garrigou, *God: His Existence and His Nature*, vol. 2, 120–21 : "In the second place, in the transition to act independently of God, how can the secondary cause determine the divine concurrence both as to its functioning and as to its specification? To determine it in this manner is to perfect it, which would be a reversal of the role assigned to each. God cannot wait for the human being to arouse himself from a state of indifference and perfect his own concurrence. God would thus be under the influence of created causes and would be submitting to their direction. It would be the same as if we were to admit an *indifferent promotion*, by which God would determine us merely to an indeliberate act, in such a manner that the free will would determine itself and the divine motion to produce this or that particular act. Something real would escape God's universal causality. There would be a determination independent of God's supreme determination, which is that of pure Act. A secondary liberty would be found acting independently of the primary liberty. *The main thing in the work of salvation, the determining of our salutary act, would not come from the Author of salvation.*"

stone. And so it is with God exercising providential order over imperfect acts in Marín-Sola's account. It is not enough to state that God intends to order these things fallibly. Anything ordered fallibly is governed fallibly. To say that God governs some things fallibly is really to say that He does not properly govern these things at all, and this destroys the divine omnipotence.[130] There is also more to be said here regarding the divine simplicity, but this is taken up at greater length in the earlier work of Nicolas, which we shall treat later.

130. Reichenbach's theory of the self-limiting God explicitly admits this. Reichenbach, *Divine Providence*, 256: "Since God gives us freedom with respect to his desires and purposes, it is possible, and Scripture indicates that it is the case, that God's will is often not done." Reichenbach does not in any way employ the distinction between *antecedent* and *consequent* will. Reichenbach means here that the simple will of God is often not done!

CHAPTER SIX

Jacques Maritain

Jacques Maritain was perhaps the greatest Thomistic philosopher of the twentieth century. Born in France in 1882, Maritain was raised a Protestant but became agnostic early in life. Maritain met his wife Raissa while studying at the Sorbonne, and the two began an intellectual and spiritual journey together. Jacques and Raissa had even made a suicide pact that they would fulfill if they did not discover meaning in life within a year of making the pact. Influenced by such eminent scholars as Charles Péguy and Henri Bergson, the two fell in love with St. Thomas and Aristotle. Maritain's career saw teaching posts at Collége Stanislas, the Institut Catholique de Paris, Columbia University, the University of Chicago, the University of Notre Dame, and Princeton University. Maritain also served as the French ambassador to the Vatican and played a role in the UN's Universal Declaration of Human Rights. Maritain was a world-renowned philosopher during his life, writing with special interest on metaphysics and political life.

Maritain had met Fr. Garrigou-Lagrange while studying at the Sorbonne. Garrigou and Maritain became friends, and Garrigou was a staple of Maritain's Thomist study circles, oftentimes preaching at their annual retreats. Their relationship took a rocky turn around the time of World War II, mostly over political differences, but their respect for one another's work certainly remained throughout their lives. Indeed, while criticizing the traditional Thomistic school (for which Garrigou was a bulwark) on the permission of sin and reprobation, Maritain commends Garrigou as an important figure for the progress of Thomism on these issues.[1]

---

1. See Taylor Patrick O'Neill, "Jacques Maritain and Reginald Garrigou-Lagrange on the Permission of Evil," *The Heythrop Journal* 60, no. 5 (2019): 699–710.

Maritain also had significant exposure and indirect correspondence with Fr. Marín-Sola regarding his views on grace, sin, predestination, and more.[2] Throughout 1925 and into 1926, Maritain corresponded with Marín-Sola regarding the topics of our present work, particularly regarding the line of evil. This correspondence took place through Charles Journet, who acted as a kind of conduit between the two. While it cannot be said that Maritain and Marín-Sola held exactly the same views, the letters between the two men showed a great affinity for each other's projects. They were certainly united in a concern over the traditional permissive decree for sin. Michael Torre states, "Yet it is clear that already Maritain wants to find a way to give the first initiative in sin to the creature, and not to God's permission."[3] As we shall see, there is considerable overlap between Maritain and Marín-Sola, especially regarding fallible motions. Maritain's "shatterable motions," while less theologically nuanced, are quite similar in many ways to Marín-Sola's fallible "sufficient grace." As such, both posit a frustratable or impedible antecedent will, which Maritain calls the "naked" or "uncircumstanced" will. For Marín-Sola, this antecedent will is the principle of his "general" providence. Both posit, however, that what distinguishes the antecedent from the consequent will is that the divine will is conditioned[4] or circumstanced.

Maritain's Views in *Existence and the Existent*

In *Existence and the Existent*, Maritain laid out the main propositions of his views on premotion, sin, predestination, and reprobation. Maritain would go on to consider these things at greater length in *God and the Permission of Evil*.

Maritain begins by asserting the classical Thomistic proposition of the contingency of the created being in relation to the influx of divine power to act.

2. For more on this, see Michael Torre, "Francisco Marín-Sola, OP, and the Origin of Jacques Maritain's Doctrine on God's Permission of Evil," *Nova et Vetera*, English ed., 4, no. 1 (2006): 55–94.

3. Torre, "Francisco Marín-Sola, OP, and the Origin of Jacques Maritain's Doctrine on God's Permission of Evil," 59.

4. Jacques Maritain, *Existence and the Existent*, trans. Lewis Galantiere and Gerald B. Phelan (New York: Paulist Press, 2015), 82; Torre, *Do Not Resist the Spirit's Call*, 43: "This antecedent will, with its corresponding decrees and motions, is antecedent, or conditioned, or inefficacious, or impedible, or fallible as regards the execution of a particular end."

If it is true, as has been said in a preceding section, that no created cause acts unless by virtue of the super-causality of the *Ipsum esse per se subsistens*, if it is also true that freedom of choice consists in the active and dominating indetermination of the will which itself renders efficacious the motive which determines it, then it is clear that the liberty of the created existent can be exercised only if it is activated or moved, penetrated to its depths and in the integrity of its determinations, by the influx of transcendent causality by which creative Liberty moves each created existent to act according to its own mode.[5]

Accordingly, God wills necessary things necessarily and contingent things contingently.[6]

Regarding the human will, Maritain asserts the subordinated causality of St. Thomas, where man is the second cause of whatever good is in him or which comes forth from him, while God is the first cause of this good.

Consequently, in the existential subordination of causes, the created existent possesses *the whole* initiative of good, but this initiative is *second*; creative Liberty possesses the *whole* initiative of good and its initiative is *first*. There is not in the world a shadow of beauty, a trace of actuality, a spark of being of which the subsistent Being itself is not the author. The more so where it is a question of that singular nobility and ultimate flowering of being which is the morally good act of the free will.[7]

What Maritain wants to stress more than anything, however, is the dissymmetry between the line of good and the line of evil. This dissymmetry is grounded in the fact that goodness always refers to being, while evil always refers to nonbeing. "This dissymmetry consists in the fact that whatever concerns the line of good is presented in terms of being, whereas ... whatever concerns the line of *evil as such* is presented in terms of *non-being*, of nothingness or nihilation."[8] While it is true that evil action requires being insofar as it is an action,[9] evil itself, "*evil as such*," can only be understood as a lack of being. Of course, that which separates

5. Maritain, *Existence*, 75.

6. Maritain, *Existence*, 75: "That is to say, it activates to act necessarily, those which are subject to necessary determinations, contingently those which are subject to contingent determinations, and freely those whose act is subject to no sort of determination at all, unless it be that which it bestows upon itself."

7. Maritain, *Existence*, 75–76.

8. Maritain, *Existence*, 76.

9. Maritain, *Existence*, 76: "I do not say, of evil action, for every action, insofar as it comports act or being, contains good."

the nothingness of evil from other sorts of nothingness (for example, the lack of the existence of leprechauns, which is not an evil) is that evil is the lack of a good that is due. Its nonexistence, therefore, in some way offends justice.

For evil as such is a *privation*, that is to say, not only a mere absence of good, a mere lacuna, or any sort of nothingness, but the absence of a *due* good, the nothingness of a form of being *requisite* to a given being; and the evil of the free act is the privation of a due ruling and form. This is what vitiates and wounds with nothingness, the use of liberty in the free act.[10]

This calls, then, for a completely different treatment in the line of evil than what is given to the line of the good. As Maritain states it, "The perspective has to be reversed; we have to think in terms of *nihil* instead of thinking in terms of *esse*."[11]

An evil action is, therefore, an act that is tainted in some way by nothingness.[12] It comes about as the result of an antecedent defect (antecedent ontologically, if not necessarily temporally), a nonconsideration of a moral norm or rule in regard to the act that is about to come forth. This renders the act that follows "wounded or corroded" rather than good.

In one of his most difficult and most original theses [*De malo*, q. 1, a. 3], Thomas Aquinas explains on this point that the emergence of a free and evil act resolves in two moments—distinct, not according to the priority of time, but according to an ontological priority. At a first moment there is in the will, by the fact of its very liberty, an absence or a nihilation which is not yet a *privation* or an evil, but a mere lacuna: the existence *does not* consider the norm of the *thou shouldst* upon which the ruling of the act depends. At a second moment the will produces its free act affected by the privation of its due ruling and wounded with the nothingness which results from this lack of consideration.[13]

The creature is then the first and only cause of the defect,[14] and this helps to highlight the dissymmetry between good and evil. Whereas for good

10. Maritain, *Existence*, 76.

11. Maritain, *Existence*, 76.

12. Maritain, *Existence*, 76–77: "What is the metaphysical root or precondition of evil in the free act? If that act is evil, that is to say wounded or corroded by nothingness, the reason is that before producing it, the will from which it emanates has already in some fashion withdrawn from being. It has done this freely, but without having as yet acted, or acted evilly."

13. Maritain, *Existence*, 77.

14. Maritain, *Existence*, 78: "The first cause (which is not an acting or efficient cause, but is dis-acting and de-efficient), the first cause of the non-consideration of the rule, and consequently

acts man always depends upon God, for evil acts man is working entirely alone, and this fully suffices to explain how evil acts emerge.

It follows from this that whereas the created existent is never alone when it exercises its liberty in the line of good, and has need of the first cause for all that it produces in the way of being and of good, contrariwise it has no need of God, it is truly alone, for the purpose of freely nihilating, of taking the free first initiative of this absence (or "nothingness") of consideration, which is the matrix of the evil in the free act—I mean to say, the matrix of the *privation* itself by which the free act (in which there is metaphysical good insofar as there is being) is morally deformed or purely and simply evil. "For without me, you can do nothing"; which is to say, "Without Me you can make that thing which is nothing."[15]

All of this up to this point seems quite consistent with St. Thomas and with the classical Thomistic tradition. However, Maritain then posits what he calls "shatterable motions." There are "divine activations" or premotions that move creatures to good acts. "These influxes tend in each existent to bear it forward to the fullness of its being."[16] However, God also sends shatterable motions that may be impeded by the creature.

Therefore, if, in the world, we find moral evil and free evil acts, the reason is that there are shatterable divine activations. In other words, the reason is that the First Cause sends down into free existents activations or motions which contain within themselves, in advance, the permission or possibility of being rendered sterile *if* the free existent which receives them takes the first initiative of evading them, or not-acting and not-considering, or nihilating under their touch.[17]

The reason for this is due to God's moving contingent creatures contingently, which for Maritain means that God sends motions to fallible creatures that move them only fallibly.[18]

---

of the evil of the free act that will come forth from it, is purely and simply the liberty of the created existent. The latter possesses the free initiative of an absence (or "nothingness") of consideration, of a vacuum introduced into the warp and woof of being, of a *nihil*; and this time this free initiative is a *first* initiative because it does not consist in acting freely or allowing being to pass, but in freely not-acting and not-willing, in freely frustrating the passage of being."

15. Maritain, *Existence*, 78–79.

16. Maritain, *Existence*, 79.

17. Maritain, *Existence*, 79.

18. As we shall see, this is an incorrect formulation by Maritain right from the start because "to cause contingently" does not mean "to cause fallibly." The necessity or contingency of a motion is based in the nature of the proximate cause of that motion. However, that this contingent motion follows in a determinate or infallible manner is rooted in the fact that the motion proceeds from the infallible divine will as its remote and primary cause. See Steven A. Long, "God, Freedom, and the

And if it is true that every created liberty is by nature a fallible liberty (since it is not its own rule), if it is true that God activates all things, each according to its own mode, if it is true that creative Liberty, therefore, activates created liberties according to the fallible mode proper to them, then we can understand that, in accordance with the natural order of things, before the *unshatterable* divine activation, by which the will to good of creative Liberty infallibly produces its effect in the created will, the divine activations received by the free existent must first be *shatterable* activations.[19]

And thus Maritain does indeed also posit unshatterable motions, but these are ordinarily given on the condition that the created will does not impede the fallible motions first.

It depends solely upon ourselves to shatter them by making, upon our own deficient initiative, that thing called nothing (or by nihilating). But if we have not budged, if we have done nothing, that is to say, if we have introduced no nothingness and no *non*; if we allow free passage to these influxes of being, then (and by virtue of the first design of God) the shatterable divine activations fructify by themselves into the unshatterable divine activation.[20]

These unshatterable motions are perfectly efficacious and infallible. By them man is moved to will that which God wills him to will, bringing about some salutary act. "This unshatterable divine activation is none other than the decisive *fiat*, received in us. By Its *fiat* the transcendent Cause makes that to happen which It wills. By virtue of that unshatterable divine activation, our will, this time, unfailingly exercises its liberty in the line of good, produces the good act."[21]

As such, Maritain makes a distinction between the antecedent and consequent will, though he calls them the "naked" and "circumstanced" will. As can be seen, however, this distinction is quite different than the distinction of the classical Thomist.

Permission of Evil," in *Aquinas & Maritain on Evil: Mystery and Metaphysics*, ed. James G. Hanink (Washington, D.C.: American Maritain Association Publications, 2013), 130–54; 137: "*Insofar as God moves the will, then, the will is moved, but the will is said to be a contingent cause, or to be free, because the* proximate cause *of its own willing* it is not merely ordained to one effect or one narrow range of effects, and because no finite or terrestrial object can compel it. It is expressly not denominated as free owing to its relation to God, for in relation to God, all creatures and created operations, whether contingent or necessary, are effects of the First Cause."

19. Maritain, *Existence*, 80.
20. Maritain, *Existence*, 80.
21. Maritain, *Existence*, 80.

We shall give the name of primordial or original will to the will of God considered without regard to particular conditions or circumstances—what we may also call His "naked" will. This will is not a velleity, it is a true and active will which projects into the universality of existents the being and goodness that penetrate them and the influx of incitations, motions, and activations that make them tend towards the fulfillment and towards the common good of creation. By this primordial will, the creative Love wills that all free existents attain to their supra-temporal end .... But it wills it according to the mode of their own fallible freedom, that is to say, according to shatterable motions or activations.[22]

Of the "circumstanced" will, Maritain states:

And if the will that we shall call "circumstanced," and which is the will of God considered as taking account of particular conditions and circumstances (we may also call it His "definitive" will), allows free existents to miss their supra-temporal end, what can be the circumstance of which the creative Love then takes account, unless it be that of the nihilating by which, in the course of their existence, and especially at the last instant of their existence, their freedom evades His influx and renders the divine activation sterile? Suppose that this influx of nihilation does not take place on the part of the free existent; then, as concerns that free existent, the circumstanced will purely and simply confirms, in unconditionally and unfailingly efficacious fashion, the primordial will which, in willing the final good of all, itself ordained it (conditionally) to this good.[23]

These brief thoughts are expounded upon in *God and the Permission of Evil*. The name of the work gives the reader an obvious clue at the very outset about what is most troubling to Maritain in the doctrine of the classical Thomist school. For Maritain, it is the innocence of God itself that is at stake, and this is threatened by a lack of consideration or emphasis on the dissymmetry between the line of good and the line of evil. In a chapter entitled *The Embarrassments of the "Traditional" School*, Maritain states:

The misfortune is that in the beginning it [the traditional school] insisted with so much vigor on the two principles concerning the line of good [God is the universal first cause and he knows all things through his causality of them][24] that it

22. Maritain, *Existence*, 82.
23. Maritain, *Existence*, 82–83.
24. Jacques Maritain, *God and the Permission of Evil*, trans. Joseph W. Evans (Milwaukee: The Bruce Publishing Company, 1966), 13: "I call the 'traditional' school the one which holds firmly to the two primordial truths concerning the line of good. Stated anew, these are: 1° God is the absolutely universal first cause, on the motion of whom depends the action of the creature down to the least

seemed to leave more or less in the shadows the other two primordial principles
which concern the line of evil: 1° Of evil as such God is nowise the cause even
indirectly—it is the creature who is the first cause of evil; 2° Evil is known by
God without being in any way caused by Him. In other words, the "traditional"
school envisaged everything, it endeavored to explain everything, even evil, in
the perspective of being or of good. God thus seemed—one tried everything to
avoid this, but finally God seemed—the initiator of the evil which He punished,
as well as of the good which He rewarded.[25]

Maritain goes on to call the perpetrators of this symmetrical view between good and evil "Cyclopean Thomists" because "they had their eyes
fixed solely on the perspective of being, or of good, even when they spoke
of evil." Maritain names Báñez, John of Saint Thomas, and the Carmelites
of Salamanca as examples of these "rigid" or Cyclopean Thomists.[26] As
such, Maritain labels this school "neo-Báñezianism."[27]

What is most important to Maritain is that two particular points regarding the line of evil be reformed: the antecedent permissive decree
and negative reprobation. The antecedent permissive decree is that first
ontological "moment" in the evil act. It precedes the defect, allowing a
defectible creature to not consider the rule (as seen in *De malo*, q. 1, a. 3).
In the second ontological "moment" the creature falls into defect. In the
third "moment," efficacious grace is withheld on account of the defect.
And in the fourth "moment," the creature, due to the defect, acts in an evil
way, bringing about sin.[28]

Maritain held that the antecedent permissive decree made God out
to be the indirect cause of evil insofar as it posits that he is more than
capable of stopping defects and thus sins before they happen. However,
according to the classical treatment, he does not always do so, therefore:

It is God who, before every actual failure of the creature as first cause of evil, permitted all the sins and the crimes committed in human history, which thus took

---

iota—even and especially the action of the free will, I say 'especially' because this action is in the
intellectual creature that which is most rich in being and in activity: the action by which it disposes
itself. 2° The science of God is the cause of things, God knows things because He makes them, He
knows them in His "science of vision" through the creative or factive idea itself which causes them
to come into existence, in other words, through the decree of His intelligence linked with His will."

25. Maritain, *Permission*, 13–14.

26. Maritain, *Permission*, 14. It is interesting to note that Maritain condemns as embarrassments
some of those whom Marín-Sola claims were really espousing the same views that he holds.

27. Maritain, *Permission*, 21.

28. Maritain, *Permission*, 26–27.

place in conformity with what He, of His own free will, had infallibly precon-
ceived and prepared: and one managed at the same time, by a system of appropriate conceptual distinctions, to have the whole responsibility of these sins and of
these crimes fall on the sinner, and to exonerate God, who was not sorry to wash
His hands in the basin which His zealous servants thus presented to Him.[29]

And thus Maritain holds that God is the indirect cause of evil according
to the tradition of the Báñezian school.[30] He provides the following example to illustrate his point. "A child can write straightly only if I hold the
pen with it; if I withdraw my hand, the child's hand makes only a scribble.
It is clearly the cause of the scribble, and the sole direct cause. But have
I not been the indirect cause by withdrawing my hand? For my part, I
answer 'yes.'"[31] All of this means that God's innocence itself is robbed by
the classical school.[32]

He refuses His efficacious grace to a creature because it has already failed culpably, but this culpable failure itself occurred only in virtue of the permissive decree
which preceded it. God manages to be in nowise the cause of evil, while seeing to
it that evil occurs infallibly. The antecedent permissive decrees, be they presented
by the most saintly of theologians—I cannot see in them, taken in themselves,
anything but an insult to the *absolute innocence of God*.[33]

And the same applies, of course, to what Maritain considers to be
the classical approach to reprobation. Maritain chastises the symmetry
between predestination and reprobation, stating that, from the theory of
predestination, which is *ante praevisa merita*, a theory of reprobation has

29. Maritain, *Permission*, 18.
30. Maritain, *Permission*, 30–31: "Let me speak frankly. In the theory of the antecedent permissive
decrees, God, under the relation of efficiency, is not the cause, not even *(that which I do not at all concede)* the indirect cause, of moral evil. But He is the one primarily responsible for its presence here on
earth. It is He who has invented it in the drama or novel of which He is the author."
31. Maritain, *Permission*, 29.
32. For a similar critique see Petr Dvořák, "The Concurrentism of Thomas Aquinas: Divine
Causation and Human Freedom," *Philosophia* 41, no. 3 (2013): 617–34; 630–31: "It is not possible for
the will to be applied to volition A by God and not will A (composite sense). Nevertheless, when applied to volition A by God, it is possible for the will not to will A (divided sense). Notice the difference
in the place and the scope of the possibility operator. The divided sense formulation tacitly presupposes, however, that the possible scenario of not willing is the result of application through a different
premotion. Thus a human person cannot resist divine application through premotion (that would
imply possibility in the composite sense). Hence the Thomist freedom is a compatibilist freedom of
various courses of action under different divine determining influences, not libertarian freedom of
self-determination. If God determines the specific nature of human volitions, then it seems virtually
impossible to clear God of the charge that he is a direct cause of evil."
33. Maritain, *Permission*, 31.

emerged that is *ante praevisa demerita*. The former shows forth God's love and mercy, but the latter posits something quite ugly.[34] Maritain says, "It is thus that these Thomists taught not only that unthinking thing (we shall return to it later on) that one calls 'negative reprobation,' which *precedes any demerit*, but they made it consists in the *positive exclusion of beatitude*."[35] As with the antecedent permissive decree and the child writing, Maritain employs an example to illustrate his point.

Consider a housewife who is doing preserves. She is seated in her kitchen, with a large basket of apples in front of her. And by hypothesis these apples are all alike (no more *praevisa demerita* than *praevisa merita*, no more apples already blemished than applies juicier). From among these apples that are all alike, our housewife *chooses* a certain number of them to place in her preserving-pan, and at the same stroke, it is very clear, the others *are left aside*. Oh! one does not wish them any harm, only simply leaves them aside, one *does not* choose them. Naturally, not having been chosen they will be thrown into the garbage-can, but this will be decided later, when having remained some days in the basket these apples which have not been chosen will begin to spoil. Then they will be thrown into the garbage-can *by reason of their blemishes*, by reason of their sins. But first of all it was clearly necessary—since it is the other apples which have been chosen—that these should *not* have been chosen, in others, that they be *negatively*, negatively rejected. *Negative reprobation 'ante praevisa demerita.'*"[36]

This brings us back, then, to the aforementioned solutions proposed by Maritain in *Existence and the Existent*.

Before supplementing these proposals with Maritain's further considerations in *God and the Permission of Evil*, we should note that Maritain does indeed posit an unshatterable motion, one that has the full efficacy of the divine will, not dealing with us according to our fallible states, but

34. Maritain, *Permission*, 14: "Just as God predestines the elect to glory *ante praevisa merita*, without consideration of their foreseen merits, so likewise He condemns (oh, 'negatively,' is it not?) the others by His own sole initiative, and He decides to exclude them from beatitude *ante praevisa demerita*.

35. Maritain, *Permission*, 14.

36. Maritain, *Permission*, 102. See also 103, where Maritain says of the principle of predilection and negative reprobation: "well, in order that certain ones be chosen and predestined it is necessary that this God of love have for them a love *of predilection*; and as to the others He experiences for them a *sort of indifference* (I should think so! As a result of this sort of indifference they will burn eternally, and through their own fault: a consequence that the God of love knows perfectly, much better indeed than any theologian, at the moment of reason when He *does not* choose them). The least one can say about this theory is that it does not seem very consistent, if not with the antecedent permissive decrees, at least with the spirit of the Gospels."

moving us infallibly to the good that God wishes for us. However, this is not the usual type of motion given. It is something extraordinary.[37]

Maritain's Views in *God and the Permission of Evil*

As we have seen, then, Maritain posits shatterable motions as the usual type of motion given by God to man in order to achieve salutary acts. A shatterable motion is "a divine motion or activation which causes the free agent to tend to a morally good act, but which includes of itself, by nature, the possibility of being shattered."[38] For Maritain, this follows from our being defectible creatures. It is fitting that God should give us defectible motions, leaving us with the possibility of presenting a defect.

Maritain posits that the defect is not yet a refusal or a positive action made against the natural or divine law.[39] It is not a thing, something in being, at all, but is a kind of nothingness. "Understand well, I insist again, that in taking the initiative of not considering the rule, the creature does not take the initiative of an *act of refusal*; its initiative is absolutely not the initiative of an act, it is the free initiative of a *non-act*, of a nihilating, of a *not* to consider the rule."[40]

As such, there is no need to posit an antecedent permissive decree, for nothingness, a nonact, is not something that must be accounted for by divine providence. Following upon this, the only permission granted by God is a "consequent permissive decree,"[41] a permission that follows the defect or nonconsideration of the rule but that is antecedent to the sinful act itself. Since it is at least theoretically possible that God could, even after the presentation of a defect, yet move the creature away from nonconsideration and the accomplishment of a good act, it is said that God permits the sinful act on account of the previous defect.[42]

---

37. Maritain, *Permission*, 38–39: "Now it goes without saying that God can give to certain ones motions unshatterable from the very first. Their liberty will be, to this extent, divinely preserved from its natural fallibility, will act well without running the risk of failing, will be divinely protected against the eventuality of a non-consideration of the rule. But it is clear also that *this is not the ordinary case*, since, as I have just noted, it is a general law that God deals with us according to our mode of nature." Emphasis mine.

38. Maritain, *Permission*, 38.

39. Maritain, *Permission*, 50: "Attention! I do not say that at the first instant the non-consideration of the rule is virtually an evil! I say that at this instant it *contains* virtual evil, just as any cause, without being itself virtually its effect, *contains* virtually its effect."

40. Maritain, *Permission*, 38.

41. Maritain, *Permission*, 59.

42. Maritain, *Permission*, 59–60: "My answer is that God, instead of letting, according to the order

This gives way to Maritain's treatment of the predestination and reprobation. Maritain asserts that the antecedent or "uncircumstanced" will "is not a simple velleity, a barely outlined movement by which one does not *will* something but only *would will* it." He admits, however, that "St. Thomas did on one occasion [*ST* I, q. 19, a. 6, ad 1] employ rather untowardly the word *velleitas*, but not in this sense."[43]

What accounts for the discrepancy between the antecedent will to save all men and the consequent will that governs over a reality that sees some men damned? According to Maritain, it is the frustration of the divine will.

But this primordial will of the infinite Goodness, by which, taking account only of itself and leaving aside every other consideration, it wills that all our acts be good and that we be saved, is a *conditional* will, and it can be frustrated. Frustrated how? By what sorts of "circumstances"?—By the initiatives of nothingness of that created liberty which God Himself has made and which He has Himself decided to leave a clear field in governing the world.[44]

God leaves some of the governing of the world to free creatures, who, on account of their volitional nature, have the ability to affect the providential order with their considerations or nonconsiderations of the moral law, which results in good and evil acts. God, of course, wishes that all men should consider the rule and act well in every case and at all times, but this often does not happen, and insofar as it does not, God's will is

---

of things, the shattered shatterable motion give way to a simple pre-motion to the ontological or the "physical" of the sinful act, could, at least by His 'absolute' power, give to the creature an *unshatterable* motion to the good election. Such a substitution is possible of itself—this is why God's permissive decree does not follow in an absolutely *necessary* manner the failure of the creature not considering the rule; it is *free*. But such a substitution, preventing *the cause of evil once posited* from producing its effect, would not only be miraculous, would not only be an exception to a fundamental law of nature and to the order of things constituted by God, but would also be this without reason: for why wait, so to speak, until a shatterable motion has been shattered by a free agent, in order to give to the latter an unshatterable-from-the-very-first-motion?"

43. Maritain, *Permission*, 99–100.

44. Maritain, *Permission*, 100. In n. 22, Maritain further explains what he means in saying that the divine will is frustrated. "Not, to be sure, in the sense in which a desire is 'frustrated' in us (by some exterior agent which deprives us, in spite of ourselves, of that which we will, and which thus imposes constraint on us). The antecedent will is 'frustrated' but by a liberty that God Himself has created, and has authorized, according to a fundamental law that He Himself has established, to evade Him if it wishes, and which in fact produces an evil act in the world only with His permission." The only intelligible understanding of Maritain's permission here is the permission of a general or "fundamental" law of the defectibility of creatures. This is necessary for their "liberty" which God Himself makes. In other words, Maritain is not here affirming anything like the antecedent permissive decree, which he explicitly rejects. He is attempting to state that particular defects are still accounted for by the divine providence insofar as defectibility is allowed in general.

frustrated, though this frustratable providential ordering is what He most wishes for free creatures.

Maritain thus rejects the idea that God only chooses the elect.[45] Quoting St. Theresa of Lisieux, who said, "I choose all," Maritain asks, "Cannot God do the same?"[46] He states that God does indeed choose all men, but in respecting their free choice as volitional creatures, he allows them to freely reject him, frustrating his choice. This respect for the creature's ability to frustrate God's election of them has the price of damnation, but the reprobated only find themselves in hell on account of their frustration of the divine will for universal salvation.

Well, we know that by His primordial or antecedent will God wills that all men be saved—He wills that all be saved *if only* they do not refuse, for all this is an affair of love, and love necessarily implies liberty and free gift. He wills that all be saved *if only* certain ones do not frustrate this antecedent will of universal salvation by a free nihilating of their will which will make them, at the very instant when it settles down for eternity, prefer to the beatific vision and to the love of God over and above all, the lover over and above all of their own grandeur, be it at the price of all the flames and gnashing of teeth.[47]

Of course, as we have seen, to some men God gives an unshatterable motion even to their very salvation. These might be called the superelect, for they are not given shatterable motions that account for their glory, and thus they have no chance (at least in the composite sense or conditional sense) to frustrate the divine will.[48]

45. Maritain, *Permission*, 104: "And yet, as long as one will not decide to follow through to the very end with the principle of dissymmetry between the line of good and the line of evil, it is Father Jean-Hervé Nicolas and his school who will be right in saying: if the elect are *chosen* gratuitously *ante praevisa merita*, anteriorly to any foreseen merit, is there the slightest conceivable possibility that the others are not at the same stroke *not chosen*, that is to say, condemned negatively, *ante praevisa demerita*, anteriorly to any foreseen demerit?"
46. Maritain, *Permission*, 104.
47. Maritain, *Permission*, 104.
48. Maritain, *Permission*, 105: "Just as He can give to whomever He wills, as if by a miracle, an unshatterable-*from-the-very-first* motion to moral good, so also He can, as if by a miracle, designate for eternal salvation and predestine *unconditionally from the very first* whomever He wills. To these He will give, at the very instant that their souls leave their bodies, an unshatterable-*from-the-very-first* motion to love Him over and above all; and to whatever deviations they may have abandoned themselves during their lives, they will be saved as if by a miracle. There we have, if I may so put it, a privileged group of the predestined, and it is in regard to them that one can speak with good reason, and in the strongest sense, of *love of predilection*. The Gospel has proclaimed the equal dignity of all men; but as concerns the affairs of the Master of the vineyards with men, which are, I repeat, affairs of the heart, the Gospel is far from being egalitarian."

However, the majority of men are not so moved. They are saved according to normal fallible or shatterable motions.

If it is a question now of the other elect, of the great mass or of the *general run of the elect*, then it is before the ordinary regime and the ordinary ways called for by the nature of things that we find ourselves—God deals with them according to the normal course which befits fallible liberties. Each has been conditionally chosen, by the antecedent will; each is loved specially for itself, with that love which wills that all be saved if the creature itself does not obtrude any obstacle by its own initiative of nothingness.[49]

As such, all of those who find salvation are able to do so either by virtue of having been numbered among the superelect or, as is the more ordinary cause, by virtue of not nihilating or negating the shatterable motions necessary for salvation. Maritain says that "*all* the elect are chosen and predestined, those who are chosen unconditionally from the very first, and those who are chosen unconditionally from the fact that a voluntary nihilating of the created liberty *has not* frustrated the antecedent divine will."[50]

Finally, Maritain concludes by assuring the reader that this is not to posit anything good in any man that does not come primarily and foremost from God. Any good that comes from man not impeding the shatterable motion is to be attributed to God as first cause.

No one 'discerns himself' for, or makes himself worthy of, eternal life; it is an absolute free gift of the grace and generosity of God. The merits of the elect, far from being the reason of their election, are there, on the contrary, because from all eternity ("before the world was")—in that eternity to which all the instants of the life of a man, the last as well as the first, are present together—the elect have been unconditionally chosen by the absolute will of God, either at one stroke, or, if it is a question of the "general run of the elect," according as it confirms the antecedent will, this latter not having been frustrated.[51]

Analysis

However, it is precisely this idea that man adds nothing or does no good on his own apart from God that seems to be most at odds with Maritain's

---

49. Maritain, *Permission*, 105.
50. Maritain, *Permission*, 105.
51. Maritain, *Permission*, 106.

account. Maritain is clear that not presenting an obstacle is in no way a positive act for good. Thus, man in no way distinguishes himself as good (or performative of some good) without a divine motion to do so.

I must insist now on a point that is especially important, namely, that in *not* taking the initiative (nihilating) of not considering the rule (and therefore of shattering the shatterable motion), I do not posit of myself any *act*, and do not take of myself any *initiative* by which I would *merit* in any way, or would *add* in any way whatsoever, the shadow of even a determination to the shatterable motion. Let us not forget that as *cause* of sin or *mera negatio* the non-consideration of the rule is not an evil (either physically or morally). To consider the rule, at this state (that is to say, before the effectuation of the act of choice), is no longer a good that is due, a thing having the slightest moral or meritorious value (nor even a thing physically required for the normal functioning of anything). Not to nihilate, not to take the initiative of not considering the rule, is a mere *material condition* by which the creature, without adding anything of itself, obtrudes no obstacle to the love of God. In other words, *not to 'discern' myself or discriminate myself for evil* and in the line of evil (in not taking the initiative of nothingness), this is in absolutely no manner *to 'discern' myself* or discriminate myself *for good*, and in the line of good or of being; it is only not to budge under grace.[52]

However, it would seem that here Maritain is quite mistaken. We may agree with Maritain that shattering a motion with a defect or impediment is a sort of nothingness. We describe this as a *defectus* because it is some nonbeing; it is a *not to consider the rule*. In short, it is a nonact. Consequently, its opposite must be an act. *The negation of a negation in a real subject is something real.* To not not throw a ball is to throw a ball. To not not consider the rule is to consider the rule. It follows, then, that man actually does something good, or has some good, in considering the rule. It is the good of being, before acting, in the right disposition in relation to the laws of being and goodness that come from God. This is not something small or negligible for a defectible, imperfect, limited creature.

It is even more astonishing when we consider that this creature exists in a fallen state. As we have seen in St. Thomas and throughout the Thomistic tradition, that a defectible, limited creature should not fall into defect is a good of preservation or conservation. And at least in some sense, Maritain seems to recognize this, for he asserts that to consider the rule is a good that does indeed come from God, but only by way of

---

52. Maritain, *Permission*, 107.

an unshatterable motion that follows from man not not-considering the rule. Maritain recognizes that to say that a consideration of the rule, not placing an impediment or defect, comes from the good use of a shatterable motion would be to attribute the consideration of the rule more to man than to God. As such, he posits that not not-to-consider the rule is followed by an unshatterable or infallibly efficacious motion that makes it such that man does indeed consider the rule.

If they [shatterable motions] *are not* thus shattered, fructify *of themselves*, I say of themselves, without having need of being completed by the slightest actuation or determination coming from the creature, into unshatterable motions (let us say, if you will, into efficacious graces) which replace them and under which the creature, freely and infallibly, will consider the rule in its very operation and will produce the good act to which it is moved by God.[53]

But they do not fructify entirely of themselves; they fructify under the good use of man because man either responds to them well or he does not, and that he does is at best only partially an effect of divine motion according to the thought of Maritain, conditional upon the nonnegation of the creature, which Maritain has argued is nothing positive and thus is not an effect of the divine causality. It might be said in some way that these motions do not require more determination from man insofar as they are good for the intended end of the good act. In regard to that end man adds no further specification. However, man does add determination in regard to the act itself insofar as the act is not properly accomplished unless he accepts the motion. The shatterable motion does not fructify unless the man allows it to actuate, or to put it another way, if he carries it through, keeping it unshattered. One may even say that man, in some way, actuates such a motion because without his good use the good act never comes into existence. That these shatterable motions are now replaced with unshatterable motions that keep the creature considering the rule is somewhat absurd, for the creature must already have considered the rule to receive an unshatterable motion. In a real creature, not not-to-consider the rule of reason and to consider the rule of reason are the same. If you do not not-sleep, then you sleep. If you do not not-have a car, then you have a car.

Maritain clearly wants to maintain that even considering the rule, in-

53. Maritain, *Permission*, 39.

sofar as it is a good, must come from God, and thus he posits that this results from the newly introduced unshatterable motion. But how is it the case that refraining from a nonconsideration of the rule is at the same time ontologically prior to the unshatterable motion and the result of it? It seems clear that Maritain is missing the crucial point that a negation of a negation in a real subject is something positive. In other words, to not negate the rule, to not not consider it well, is to consider it well. As such, Maritain is clearly right that considering the rule must come from God, but from this it absolutely follows that not considering the rule must be permitted antecedently for the reason that it can only come about if God does not first move man to consider the rule well.[54] In this way the an-

---

54. Long, "God, Freedom, and the Permission of Evil," 145–46: "I think it undoubtedly true that the creature has the initiative in evil, as only a creature can enact evil. But Maritain forgot something about negation that St. Thomas did not forget in *De Veritate*, III, 28. In that work, Thomas teaches that where there is a real subject, the negation of a negation is *something positive*, and so it is *not really distinct* from the affirmative to which the original negation is opposed. To put it in St. Thomas's words, 'the destruction of non-white is not really different than the coming to be of white.' Thomas is saying that when spoken to someone who really exists, the claim that 'you do not *not* have a nose' is equivalent to affirming that indeed in reality '*you do have a nose.*' But this is true only because the subject is *real*. If someone says 'elephants singing *La Traviata* do not *not-fly*,' this does not mean that there are really existing elephants singing *La Traviata* and flying, because *there are no really existing elephants singing La Traviata*. According to Maritain *if* the creature *does not negate, then* God will bestow an infrustratable efficacious motion upon the will. Maritain treats the creature *not negating* as though it were in some way different from the creature being moved by God. But the creature is a *real subject* and so for the creature *not to negate* is for the creature to do something *positive* which is an effect of divine causality. Since everything that is ontologically positive is caused by God, this means that *if the creature in reality does not negate*, this is in reality the same as the creature receiving the gift of divine motion toward the salutary act: *the non-negation of the creature in reality is not different than its being helped by God.*" See also Long, "Providence, liberté, et loi naturelle," 381: "En d'autres termes, toutes conditions étant égales par ailleurs, même la personne qui ne néante pas, mais considère la règle de la raison, est, selon J. Maritain, capable de néanter au moment même où elle ne néante pas, et elle ne reçoit pas plus de secours en vue de l'effet qu'est la non-négation, que la personne qui de fait *néante*. Ce qui revient à dire que Dieu donne une motion qui n'a pas d'effet naturel actuel, excepté dans le cas où la créature ne néante pas. Pour un adepte du thomisme classique, cette proposition implique une absurdité: ne pas néanter (c'est-à-dire cette non-négation qui dans le thomisme classique exige une aide efficace) ne demande pas plus d'aide divine que néanter. L'effet qu'est l'être et l'effet qu'est le néant sont atteints par exactement le même influx causal divin." The English translation of this article can be found in *Nova et Vetera* 4 (English ed.), no. 3 (2006): 557–606; 581: "In other words, all conditions being given, even the one who does not negate but considers the rule of reason is, on Maritain's account, able to negate at the very instant when he does not negate, and this person receives no more aid toward this effect of non-negation than the one who does negate. This is to say that God gives a motion that has no actual natural effect save insofar as the creature does not negate. This seems to one formed in classical Thomism to imply something absurd, namely, that not to negate (the same non-negation upon which efficacious aid is predicated in this theory) calls for no more divine help than to negate: that the effect of being and the effect of nothingness are achieved by precisely the same divine causal influx."

tecedent permissive decree is absolutely necessary. Without it we must posit that man is the one who determines whether he responds well to grace and actually accomplishes the good act. It is true that man cannot do this on his own, in the same way that a man cannot remove himself from a well without another first lowering down a rope. However, this sort of simultaneous concurrence or coordinate causality (that man may cooperate without being moved by God as a man may take hold of the rope without any movement from the one lowering the rope) is clearly negated by the Thomistic tradition and St. Thomas himself. A subordinated causality has always been posited, and a subordinated causality is destroyed if man moves himself to some good apart from prior efficacious divine motion, such as the proper consideration of the rule and his free cooperation with grace to bring about a salutary act. Maritain wants to assert this, but also wants to dispense with the antecedent permissive decree. This is not possible. God either moves us to consider the rule or he doesn't.[55] If he does, whenever we do not consider the rule it must be under the condition that man has not been so upheld or preserved by God. This is all that is meant by permission.

Throughout his work Maritain asserts that it is fitting that defectible creatures be given defectible motions. On the contrary, it is not fitting that God should give defectible motions to defectible creatures, but rather that he should give infallible, nondefectible motions to defectible creatures. Defectible motions would always be frustrated by fallen, defectible creatures without the aid of God. Defectible motions would not in any way prevent us from doing what we do when we are divorced from God,

---

55. Long, "Providence, liberté, et loi naturelle," 391: "Avant que la créature humaine ne soit mue efficacement par Dieu à considérer la règle, elle néante toujours, au sens où elle ne considère pas la règle de la raison, et cet état durera jusqu'à ce qu'elle soit efficacement mue par Dieu à considérer la règle. De même qu'on dort jusqu'à ce qu'on se réveille, on ne considère pas jusqu'à ce qu'on considère, et cette considération actuelle n'a qu'une seule Cause première, qui est Dieu. Prétendre que Dieu ne cause pas cette considération de la règle, parce que nous la néantons, c'est une dérobade, car nous néantons toujours la considération de la règle, si Dieu ne cause pas le contraire. Sans la motion divine qui nous fait considérer la règle, la non-considération de la règle ne cesserait jamais" ("Providence, Liberty, and Natural Law," 589: "It seems clearly true that, before the human creature is efficaciously moved by God to consider the rule, it is always negating in the sense of not considering the rule of reason, and that this will persist until God efficaciously moves the creature to consider the rule. Just as one sleeps until one wakes, one does not consider until one does consider, and actual consideration has only one First Cause and that is God. To say that God does not cause this consideration of the rule because one negates it is simply backwards because one is always negating consideration of the rule unless God causes the contrary. Apart from God moving us to consider the rule, one would never cease non-consideration of the rule").

which is to defect and fall. And this must be true unless one posits that man can, of himself, summon within himself the power to rise above his defectibility apart from God and take a motion from God and elevate it to a good act all by himself.

Maritain's rejection of the antecedent permissive decree and his use of shatterable motions thus posits that some good can come from man apart from being moved by God. Man is able to preserve himself from defect so that he responds well to divine motions or grace. Serge-Thomas Bonino agrees, stating:

> But just as the indeterminate motion had to face the question of divine science of sin, the breakable motion thus breaks up on the theological principle of the primacy of grace in the order of salvation, defined by the Church against semi-Pelagianism. Even if Maritain wishes to contest this consequence, the breakable motion theory inevitably leads to attribute to the creature—to its nonresistance to divine motion—the last word in the matter of our salvation.[56]

It must be stated again that Maritain does not intend to state this and explicitly wishes to maintain God's absolute priority in the line of good, however it would appear that in attempting to distance the line of good from the line of evil, Maritain has lost God's providential ordering over both.

Moreover, it is unclear how a shatterable divine motion (as given by an omnipotent God) may be understood metaphysically. As Fabio Schmitz points out, such a claim is ultimately absurd.

> The motion of the mover and the movement of the moved are, therefore, absolutely inseparable. If there is no movement, there is no motion; if there is motion, there is necessarily movement. Therefore, to pretend that God could actually move the will without the will being in fact moved, to pretend that the divine motion coexists with the absence of the movement corresponding to this motion, is to affirm some thing metaphysically impossible because it is contradictory. It is to say that the movement of the creature is caused without being caused. It is to posit that God immediately causes an effect in the creature without this effect existing. It is to pretend that God puts the will into act without that will being put into act.[57]

56. Bonino, "Contemporary Thomism," 44–45.

57. Fabio Schmitz, *Causalité divine et péché dans la théologie de saint Thomas d'Aquin: Examen critique du concept de motion «brisable»* (Paris: L'Harmattan, 2016), 167–68. Translation is mine. Similarly, Steven A. Long says in "St. Thomas Aquinas," 60–61: "Metaphysically, the only difference

What is this motion that does not move? There is no answer because no answer is possible.

In regard to the two lines of good and evil, it must always be stated that, according to the classical treatment, there is a great dissymmetry between them; however, there is symmetry between the line of good and the line of evil in this: God controls all things. All things, good and evil, are subject to God's providential ordering and will, for he is the master of all things, the ruler of all, the Most High. In Maritain's rejection of the antecedent permissive decree and the always efficacious nature of divine motion, he has lost God as the source of all good and even as the all-powerful governor over a world that includes the reality of evil and sin. In Maritain's account, at least some good comes forth without Him, and all evil stems from the simple divine will being frustrated. As with Marín-Sola, the idea of fallible motions itself posits a *passivity in God* as the consideration or nonconsideration of the rule appears to escape God's providential power.

Of course, this culminates in the mystery of predestination, wherein those who are saved play a major part in their salvation without the aid of God, while those who are ultimately damned find themselves in hell even though God actually willed otherwise.

In the ordinary men, the nonsuperelect, what is most high in them, their very own salvation, seems to come at least in part from themselves. It is true that God determines them to good actions, but these good actions that merit salvation are always first contingent upon man not shattering, upon man not not-considering the rule. Good actions require that man consider the rule apart from being preserved from nonconsideration by God. One may not have been able to accomplish these meritorious actions without divine aid, but it seems equally true that God could not accomplish them without human aid. Insofar as men are given shatterable motions and numbered among the general elect, God does not accomplish these good things in them unless they answer his call well, so to

---

between God causing X, and God not causing X, is not a change in God, but rather the being of the creature. This is a simple function of the truth that the divine perfection is not limited by any potency whatsoever; it is Pure Act. Whatsoever degree and kind of actuality that God causes will exist. Thus, if we speak of created grace—rather than of the Uncreated Grace Who is God Himself— the bestowal of grace is necessarily always efficacious in at least some respect. Thus bestowal of grace requires some determinate effect, because the contrary is tantamount to the suppression of grace as such. There is no way to distinguish a putative 'effect' that is absolutely and in every respect indeterminate, from the absolute absence of any effect whatsoever. To affirm that God bestows grace cannot be equivalent to holding that God does nothing."

speak. It seems to be true that for Maritain, in the general elect, God's will is determined by human reception of divine aid.

Maritain uses the language of election or choice in regard to predestination, but it is not even clear in what way the general elect are chosen. To be elected or to be chosen is to be set apart by someone or something else, but the general elect appear to distinguish themselves by not negating motions. Their cooperation, we are told, comes somehow from God even though non-noncooperation precedes the unshatterable motion that gives cooperation. Thus, while Maritain wants to posit that man does not distinguish himself, it is hard to see how this is not the case, at least in regard to the so-called general elect.

Maritain's reshaping of the definitions of the antecedent and consequent will are also problematic for the divine omnipotence. In explicitly rejecting that the antecedent will could be in any way called a *velleitas*, Maritain has posited that God's antecedent will is something akin to His simple will.[58] That which distinguishes the antecedent from the consequent is not that, due to the difference in scope (that is, that the antecedent will wills things as considered in and of themselves while the consequent will wills things as they exist in all their particularity and in relation to other things), God simply wills according to the consequent will but not the antecedent will. That which distinguishes them for Maritain is that the consequent will pertains to things after his antecedent will has been affected and frustrated by free creatures. St. Thomas himself has spoken of the antecedent will as a *velleitas*[59] and not God's simple or absolute will! And yet, Maritain calls this untoward, stating that the antecedent will is not a *would will* but a *will* simply. The result is that God's will is not all-powerful, and it does not govern and cause the way in which man responds to divine aid, and this leaves man to be the cause of very much of his own good, not secondarily but primarily.

Maritain may assert that God's providential power is not neutered because he freely chooses to give motions that are shatterable. He could and sometimes does give unshatterable motions, but it is also part of his divine plan to give motions that men may shatter. This argument is

---

58. Maritain, *Existence*, 82: "Transposing for our purposes, and into our wholly metaphysical perspective, a classical distinction of theology, we shall give the name of primordial or original will to the will of God considered without regard to particular conditions or circumstances—what we may also call His 'naked' will. *This will is not a velleity, it is a true and active will.*"

59. *ST* I, q. 19, a. 6, ad 1.

very similar to the one presented by Marín-Sola wherein God can will to
throw the stone in an impedible way, as a man throws a stone. As such,
whether the stone is impeded or not, God's will is completed because
the very thing willed was that the motion be impedible in the composite
sense, letting the chips fall where they may, as it were. One might say, according to Maritain's treatment, that God *truly* willed for John to be nice
to his neighbor. And yet, when John frustrates or impedes God's motion
to do just that, God's will is still effective and his providence still governs
all things, including how John acts toward his neighbor, precisely because
John responded to the fallible motion in one of the ways that God allowed as a possibility. Of course, there is no mistaking the fact that in the
scenario mentioned above God does not really govern over the exact actions of John toward his neighbor. He allows them to be this or that, but
that it is this action rather than that other one is entirely outside of the
governing scope of providence. God governs the general event of John's
acting toward his neighbor in some general way, but he in no way governs
over the most important details of the action.

Maritain posits that God gives shatterable motions in order to give
to man some determination or power in the providential ordering of
the universe. God has "decided to leave a clear field in governing the
world."[60] However, according to a theory of subordinated causality, man
already freely participates in the determination of the ordering of the universe. He participates with God in governing those things that God de-
putes him to govern. The issue with replacing the subordinated causality
of the classical Thomistic analysis in favor of sort of simultaneous concurrence based upon shatterable motions is that it removes God from the
providential equation. Removing God's influence and initiative is only
necessary if one holds to a competitive view of the relationship between
divine and human causality, essentially stating that God and man cannot
work together toward some good unless their roles as causes remain in
some sense separated or divided. It may be true, according to those that
hold to a concurrentist or coordinated view of divine motion and human
freedom, that God and man can work together, but it is only as two men
rowing a boat, or at least as one man throwing a rope to another. Those
who wish to negate God's causal role in our free acts do so only if they

60. Maritain, *Permission*, 100.

have an anxiety based on the presupposition that God's causality somehow encroaches on human freedom the more pervasive or efficacious it is. However, as we have seen, St. Thomas holds a view that cannot be more different, that, far from diminishing human freedom, divine actuation and motion make man to be truly free, exercising the full liberty of his will.[61]

It seems that there is an important source of confusion here for Maritain, namely, that there is a difference between a motion being contingent and being fallible. It is quite true that authentic human freedom requires contingency because the created will is not necessarily ordained to any temporal or particular good, nor is it necessarily compelled by any such good. Thus St. Thomas says that God moves contingent things contingently.[62] This suffices to explain how the act is free. Freedom does not require fallible motions, and indeed, fallible motions are not possible given the nature of the primary cause of the effect of the good act, who is God, omnipotent and simple. God does not move the volitional creature to a particular good necessarily but contingently. And yet, due to the nature of the primary, principal cause of the motion, this contingent choice will come about infallibly. Steven Long says:

Likewise, grace in itself is not God and cannot as object of choice (in the way in which for example one might say that "going on retreat" would be a grace) compel the will. But created grace taken as instrumental efficient cause in relation to God as principal cause is always in some respect efficacious. This is possible because the effect always is more proportioned to the principal cause than to the instrumental cause—as a pen of itself has no power to express an author's thoughts, but can do so when used by the author. In the case of grace, the principal cause is the infinitely efficacious first and universal cause, God. Thus, just as salvation would be contingent considered in its proximate cause with respect to free choice, but in relation to the predestination of the first cause, is certain; so grace taken either as object or as created motion (in precision from its principal cause) is in itself contingent, whereas taken in relation to the divine will grace is efficacious with respect to some determinate effect. Likewise, in itself free choice is a contingent act; but in relation to the divine motion it may nonetheless be hypothetically (not absolutely) necessary.[63]

61. ScG III, 70, 8; ScG III, 89, 5.
62. ST I-II, q. 10, a. 4, ad 1.
63. Steven A. Long, "Brief Comment on Marín-Sola and Torre regarding Grace and Freedom," trans. Philippe-Marie Margelidon, OP, Revue Thomiste 115 (2015): 6.

Maritain seems to miss this, and thus posits a fallible providence executed via fallible motions. By limiting the divine causality and providential governance, Maritain risks losing both God's providential governance
over all things and His absolute simplicity.[64] In regard to God's providential ordering, as with Marín-Sola, it is true that God, in this schema,
freely wills to give motions that are impedible or shatterable, but the way
in which they are responded to is outside of the divine governance. That
one does respond to a motion may not escape the divine governance, but
whether it is a good or bad response certainly seems to do so.

Maritain's language of God's consequent will being "circumstanced"
helps to elucidate the problem with the rejection of the antecedent permissive decree. How is it that God's will, and thus God Himself, can be
circumstanced by creatures? If God does not permit evil then evil seems
to be, at least in some respects, beyond his control and governance. While
one may object that, insofar as nothingness is not a thing to be governed,
God does not need to govern sin, this is incorrect. God governs all things
in all ways, including the states of their being. In creatures, this sometimes
means being limited or perverted by sin. The lack of a due good is indeed
a privation, and God governs over things even to the extent that he governs over the fact that privations exist. If this were not the case then it

---

64. Speaking to this issue, Reichenbach quotes Australian philosopher J. L. Mackie, "Evil and
Omnipotence," *Mind*, n.s., 64, no. 254 (Apr. 1955): 200–212; 210: "The present solution of the problem
of evil, then, can be maintained only in the form that God has made men so free that he cannot control
their wills. This leads us to what I call the Paradox of Omnipotence: can an omnipotent being make
things which he cannot subsequently control? ... If we answer 'Yes,' it follows that if God actually
makes things which he cannot control, or makes rules which bind himself, he is not omnipotent once
he has made them: there are then things which he cannot do." Mackie comes to the conclusion that
answering "No" also creates a paradox, since then God would be incapable of creating beings that he
cannot control. However, this second possibility is already a negation of God's omnipotence; thus to
negate that negation would be only to further affirm God's omnipotence rather than to deny it. It is no
scandal against the divine omnipotence that it is not limited by the created will. Reichenbach refutes
the quoted argument above (pp. 130–132) by stating that the impossibility of logical absurdities (such
as making a square circle) do not limit God's omnipotence; limiting human freedom by moving the
will of a created being is itself an absurdity and thus divine omnipotence is not jeopardized just as
it is not jeopardized by God's inability to make a square circle or a stone so large that he cannot lift
it. What Reichenbach misses, however, is that a square circle is not something that God ever wills
and therefore it never actually exists. Indeed, it cannot exist. However, evil actions are committed by
rational creatures every day. They can and do exist. If these holes in reality, conditions of the universe,
cannot be accounted for within the providential order, if God does not in some way rule over *that
these things happen* (as Reichenbach argues) then God is passive to human action, and the divine
simplicity is obliterated. Under Reichenbach's view (and, I would argue, the view of Marín-Sola and
Maritain), God changes (indeed he must change) according to the indeterminate responses of his
creatures, even if he foreknows them.

would have to be admitted that God did not hold governance over even the central moment of salvation history, that is, the death of Our Lord, which was brought about in part by Judas's traitorous sin.

Insofar as sin escapes the divine governance, we may state that it frustrates the divine will and in so doing poses a real challenge to God's absolute simplicity. It can no longer be stated that what God wills happens. Sometimes God wills that something come about but it does not come about. God is contingent upon creatures and may even be said to be determined by them insofar as his will is passive to the free determinations of them. One wonders how God could order the entire universe toward a unified goal with so many creatures able to frustrate the divine will. On this Maritainian view it appears that God is passive and can only will things contingent upon how free creatures actually respond apart from his governance.

A final objection can *perhaps* be made regarding Maritain's superelect, which, while being the part of Maritain's treatment of these issues that is most in keeping with the Thomistic tradition, seems to exist in some tension with the rest of his schema. It could seem upon reading certain lines that Maritain holds that shatterable motions are given in order for the free creature to retain its ability to choose this or that, or in other words, that shatterable motions are necessary to preserve creaturely freedom. Maritain says, for example:

And if it is true that every created liberty is by nature a fallible liberty (since it is not its own rule), if it is true that God activates all things, each according to its own mode, if it is true that creative Liberty, therefore, activates created liberties according to the fallible mode proper to them, then we can understand that, in accordance with the natural order of things, before the *unshatterable* divine activation ... the divine actuations received by the free existent *must first be* shatterable *motions*.[65]

Of course, St. Thomas says that God moves contingent things contingently, as is the case with the created will, so as to respect their freedom. However, human freedom does not necessitate that it be fallible. Human beings are, of course, naturally fallible, but God could, in theory, infallibly preserve a human being from all defect. That human would retain its freedom given that God's constant movement toward the good in that indi-

65. Maritain, *Existence*, 79–80. Emphasis is mine.

vidual was contingent. The language of Maritain here, however, could be read to state something more, namely that, since humanity is itself fallible by nature, it requires fallible motions by God to be free, at least in regard to how God generally or ordinarily deals with human beings.

If this is what Maritain holds, one wonders how creaturely freedom is conserved with his unshatterable motions and superelect. If it is necessary that creatures are able to act in accord with or reject a divine motion (not just that they have a potency to do so, but that they do indeed sometimes actually reject it) in order that they may be free, the best of men are in one very important way of lesser humanity than impenitent sinners. If shatterable motions are required for freedom, would not those who receive unshatterable motions be less free?[66]

And yet, if it is possible that creatures maintain freedom under the composite or conditional necessity of an infallible unshatterable motion that moves creatures to will something determinate, one wonders why it is so important to reject the antecedent permissive decree. The mere condition (and not cause) that is the antecedent permission of defect does not move the will and does not even render it such that the will wills this or that thing in particular. The classical treatment indeed posits that man has the absolute ability to will otherwise, even if he does not actually do so.

Maritain does not negate the freedom of the creatures moved by unshatterable motions, and yet he also wishes to say that this is somehow extraordinary and that it is fitting for normal creaturely freedom that humans receive shatterable motions. If it is necessary that creatures are able to reject divine motions in the composite sense (that is, that God giving a motion to x and man not willing x may simultaneously exist) then extraordinary shatterable motions would seem to limit human freedom.

Importantly, however, we ought to stress that there is only limited evidence that Maritain holds to the view that fallible motions are *nec-*

---

66. Bonino, "Contemporary Thomism," 46–47: "In reality it's necessary, in Catholic theology, to maintain that this resistance, which is fully ours, would not be possible without some divine permission. Thus Maritain, for whom our resistance is not preceded by any permissive decree, recognizes that God could effectively break this resistance by nonbreakable motions, as he sometimes does especially in the supernatural order. If he doesn't do it, when he could do it, he therefore somehow permits this resistance. Why? Because, say the Maritainians, God does not want to force the will: he wants to be chosen, loved with a love of preference. But would an act elicited under the effect of an unbreakable motion be forced or less free? Such a concept would be in complete opposition to the thought of St. Thomas."

essary for creaturely freedom. Indeed, he does state quite explicitly that "God can, if He so wills, transport a created existent at one stroke to the performing of a good *free* act by an unshatterable or infallibly efficacious motion."[67] Still, there may be some tension between Maritain's language of the *ratio* for shatterable motions and the legitimacy of unshatterable motions vis-à-vis human liberty.

Even if we are to grant Maritain the more properly Thomistic reading (which seems best), namely, that there is no competition between infallible divine causality and creaturely freedom, we must wonder: if it is not necessary that creatures are able to reject divine motions in the composite sense then it is unclear why God should give shatterable motions at all, since man's freedom and causality are maintained in either the circumstance of being moved to the good or being antecedently permitted to defect. In the latter case, God would only not uphold a creature that is not due to always be upheld, as St. Thomas says. In other words, if we maintain that Maritain is congruent with St. Thomas in stating that creaturely freedom requires only that God move the created will contingently (and not that it requires to be moved fallibly), then it ought to be the case that the infallibility of the movement toward sin under the condition of divine permission of defect remains free (and thus culpable) precisely because it remains contingent. In the composite sense, the defect and sin might not have been. The sinful creature will have retained the true possibility to have chosen otherwise and thus will have chosen this sin with his own complete freedom without any positive influence from God. God would in no way be responsible for sin. Why is creaturely freedom and merit preserved in the contingent and infallible motions of God in the superelect toward the good but freedom and culpability are not preserved under the infallible condition of the permission of defect (which in no way negates the possibility of having acted well in the divided sense)? This view that permission of defect in some way mitigates creaturely culpability and thus implicates God as being guiltier of the subsequent sin (and the subsequent punishment) is precisely the claim consistently made by Maritain against the "Cyclopean" Thomism of the traditional school.

---

67. Maritain, *Existence*, 80–81. Emphasis is mine.

Cyclopean Thomism: A Response to Maritain's
Criticism of Traditional Thomism

A few words should be given to Maritain's criticism of the traditional
Thomistic school, what he calls "neo-Báñezianism." Maritain's major criticism is that the negative reprobation of the traditional school, a reprobation that is *ante praevisa demerita*, is akin to a *positive exclusion* from
glory.[68] As we have already seen in Garrigou, such positive exclusion (in
the sense of a causal, positive reprobation) is absolutely rejected by the
traditional school. Positive exclusion would (or at least could) imply a
causal act of exclusion. Negative reprobation implies nothing other than
that God does not always uphold defectible creatures from defect and
that the creature is not owed elevation to the beatific vision. God sometimes permits that creatures freely choose not to consider the rule and to
sin. Since being upheld from every defect, being preserved in perfection,
is not due to creatures, God cannot be chastised for not doing so.

Maritain speaks at length about how a *defectus*, not considering the
rule, ought to be understood as a nothingness. It is not a positive act of rejecting the rule. It is not yet a sin. It is merely a nonact. The same must be
true for the divine permission. Permission of defect, or even permission
of final impenitence (which we might call negative reprobation) in no
way exerts a causal influence, either directly or indirectly, for the simple
reason that it is a nonact. Nonacts do not exert positive influence. They
do not move things. They do not cause things. Maritain has already stated
this well.

Maritain wishes to say that, insofar as this nonact is an omission, it is
responsible for the failing of the creature, just as the housewife is responsible for the rotting of the apples left out on the countertop. This analogy, however, is flawed because apples are not free, volitional creatures. It
is true that human beings will fall into defect if they are not preserved by
God from defect, but that they fall into defect, and that they choose sin,
especially this or that sin, is the result of their own free choice, and thus
punishment for sin is not unjust, nor does it destroy God's innocence. Like
the example given by St. Thomas of the ship and the pilot, the pilot is the
one at fault when the ship is not properly steered away from rocks and

68. Maritain, *Permission*, 14.

subsequently crashes and sinks. However, this analogy does not apply to volitional creatures who are given sufficient help to act well and who freely crash themselves into the rocks, as it were. St. Thomas cites an objection that states "Further, as is said by the Philosopher (*Phys.* ii, text 30), the cause of both safety and danger of the ship is the same. But God is the cause of the safety of all things. Therefore He is the cause of all perdition and of all evil."[69] He responds by stating, "The sinking of a ship is attributed to the sailor as the cause, from the fact that he does not fulfil what the safety of the ship requires; but God does not fail in doing what is necessary for the safety of all. Hence there is no parity."[70] Garrigou further elaborates:

Hence the major of the preceding objection (i.e., if an affirmation is the cause of an affirmation, a negation is the cause of a negation) is valid when there is but one cause, which is bound to act, as the pilot by his presence is the cause of the ship's safety and by his absence, when he is bound to be present, the cause of its danger. But this major is not true if there are two causes of which the first is indefectible and not bound to prevent every evil and the second is deficient; for then this latter alone is the deficient cause of its own defection.[71]

Thus, that apples be left out to rot is quite different than the free choosing of evil in volitional creatures. They do not cause their own rotting. Man causes his own perversion and disintegration in sin.

Further, speaking of sin in the traditional treatment, Maritain says that "It is He who has invented it in the drama or novel of which He is the author."[72] Invention implies positive influence of causality, but this is clearly not what is held by the traditional commentatorial view. God is in no way the cause or inventor of sin. It is true that he permits it, but permission does not in any way have a causal influence, as a negation is not necessarily the cause of a negation. The nonact of not upholding from defect does not make or cause or influence man in any way to not consider the rule prior to an act and to fall into sin. As Báñez stated, "I say therefore that absolutely speaking, it is clearly wrong to say that God has predefined or supplied or wished the sin or the act of sin in however much it is bad, and never has a Thomist theologian said such blasphemy."[73] Negative reprobation exerts

69. *ST* I, q. 49, a. 2, arg. 3.
70. *ST* I, q. 49, a. 2, ad 3.
71. Garrigou, *Grace*, 227.
72. Garrigou, *Permission*, 30.
73. Báñez, *Controversias*, 444: "Digo pues que absolutamente hablando, es claro error decir que

no causal influence on sin and thus God is not in any way its inventor, nor its indirect cause.[74] We are then left asking whether God owes humans the grace that will always and everywhere keep them from rotting. Can such perfection be due (in the most proper sense) to anyone except the God who *is* perfection? Maritain implies a moral *ought* that is not based in any way on the divine nature or the nature of created reality as such.

While Maritain posits that headway has been made by Garrigou in not speaking of reprobation as a positive exclusion, this does not seem to be a hallmark of the tradition. In regard to the work of Báñez, and thus "neo-Báñezianism," Garrigou posits nothing original. The tenets of positive (and not negative) reprobation are not found in Báñez as we have seen, although it is indeed widely attributed to him. If Báñez is the specter of the most rigid of the traditional school and these thoughts are not found even in him, the question arises as to how widespread or influential they ever really were.

Dios ha predefinido o proveído o querido el pecado o el acto del pecado en cuanto es malo, y nunca teólogo tomista tal blasfemia dijo."

74. Báñez, *Praedestinatio*, 491: "But in the present example, that antecedent, namely that God permits Peter to sin, does not mean that He is the cause of that consequent, namely that Peter sins" ("In praesentia autem illud antecedens, Deus permittit Petrum peccare, non est causa illius consequentis, scilicet Petrus peccat").

CHAPTER SEVEN

Jean-Hervé Nicolas

This work would be remiss if it did not touch upon the Dominican theologian Jean-Hervé Nicolas, who stands as a sort of microcosm for the intra-Thomistic debate in the twentieth century on premotion, sin, predestination, and reprobation. Nicolas is an interesting study precisely because he stood at different times of his life, roughly, on both sides of the debate. Nicolas joined the Dominican Order in 1928 and was ordained a priest in 1935. He studied in Toulouse and taught at the University of Fribourg as well as the Trappist Sept-Fons Abbey. Nicolas spent much of his life on what we have called the classical Thomistic side of this debate, writing several works and articles on these topics.[1] However, toward the end of his life, Nicolas abandoned the traditional treatment under the influence of Jacques Maritain, Charles Journet, and his own self-professed torment over holding to the classical treatment of Báñez, Garrigou, and others.[2]

This chapter will look at three particular works of Nicolas in order to examine his original thought in relation to his later thought. We shall use *Le Mystére de la Grâce* (1951) to look at Nicolas's early view on premotion, grace, and the line of good. For his early view on the permission of sin and the line of evil we shall use an article published in three parts in *Revue Thomiste* entitled "La permission du péché" (1960). And for Nicolas's

---

1. See Michal Paluch, *La pronfondeur de L'Amour Divin: Évolution de la doctrine de la prédestination dans l'oevre de saint Thomas d'Aquin* (Paris: Librairie Philosophique J. Vrin, 2004), for a thorough treatment of Nicolas's contribution to the defense of the classical treatment.

2. Jean-Hervé Nicolas, "La volonté salvifique de Dieu contrariée par le péché," *Revue Thomiste* 92 (1992): 177–96, 185: "Dès le début de ma réflexion sur cet obscur sujet, qui m'a tourmenté."

later view we shall look at another article published in *Revue Thomiste* entitled "La volonté salvifique de Dieu contrariée par le péché" (1992).

The Line of Good

In *Le Mystére de la Grâce*, Nicolas gives a defense of the classical Thomistic teaching on premotion, grace, and subordinated causality in good acts. Beginning with premotion, Nicolas states, "We must realize, above all, that neither man nor any other creature can act in any way whatever without God's being concerned in the action."[3] Nicolas states that one might be tempted to think that since God has created creatures who are volitional or "capable of acting," this creation would suffice for the fact that creatures actually do act. In other words, volitional creatures can be "left to their own devices."[4] But acting requires that the creature provide himself with something more than his own existence, something "additional" that he does not have of himself. He has a potency for acting, but must be moved by something already in act.

> After a little reflection, however, one becomes aware that, in order to act, these creatures must move, must endow themselves, as it were, with additional being, a blossoming, a super-abundance. How can this passing from immobility to movement be effected unless a mover's action intervenes? The law of inertia, which we take for granted in the sphere of material movements, illustrates, on this inferior plane, a universal necessity. It is inconceivable that a being endowed with a simple capacity for acting should become actually active without being moved by another being. If the latter must in like manner pass from a state of potency for action to effective action, he too is dependent on a higher cause which moves him, and we must therefore necessarily ascend to God who is eternally and of his very nature active. In short, just as the creature has received his being through the creative act and continues to be kept in being by God's conserving act, so also it receives its act and continues to act owing to God's impulsive movement.[5]

Nicolas asserts that this premotion is not indeterminate. It is not like electricity, giving a general power to creatures that they might use it to

---

3. Jean-Hervé Nicolas, *The Mystery of God's Grace*, trans. unknown (Eugene, Ore.: Wipf & Stock Publishers, 2005).

4. Nicolas, *Mystery*, 24: "God, by his creative act, forms beings who are capable of acting. Looked at superficially that seems sufficient, and it would appear that these beings may then be left to their own devices."

5. Nicolas, *Mystery*, 24.

act in any number of various ways.[6] On the contrary, Nicolas states, "Divine motion is, in every case, directed exactly towards a specific act and it adapts itself, according to the wisdom and will of God, to the nature of the agent and its actual dispositions."[7] To state otherwise "would be tantamount to forgetting that it is precisely for this utilization that the created agent requires to be moved, and it would turn God into a blind, and therefore material, source of power."[8]

Nicolas also posits that divine motions must be efficacious in and of themselves, for the motion resides within the thing moved. It is not possible to state that it is at once moved and does not move. "Besides, the idea of an inefficacious motion is a contradiction in terms. It is abundantly clear that the motion is in the being who is moved, and if the motion is inefficacious there has been no movement."[9]

Nicolas contrasts divine motion with human motion. A man may attempt to apply his power to a wagon. If the wagon is too heavy for the man, it will not move. It is true that the movement is efficacious or actual insofar as the man as agent really moves his muscles and does *something*, but no movement is actually given *to the wagon*, and thus the will of the man to move the wagon is frustrated.[10] Nicolas continues by juxtaposing this human motion with divine motion.

Let us apply that to God. In this case there is no intermediary between the will and the being to be moved; on the other hand, any change in God is inconceivable. Neither is there any change in the being who is to be moved, since by hypothesis the motion is inefficacious; in what then does this motion consist? It disappears, it is nothing at all. It is, therefore, nonsense to say that God moves an agent and that the agent is not moved.[11]

6. Nicolas, *Mystery*, 25: "God acts only in a free manner and his action is always exactly determined. Thus, this movement cannot be conceived of as a sort of general energy, analogous to electricity, in which every agent would do what it wished or what it could .... it would be equally absurd if, in order to avoid misgivings, one were to picture physical premotion as a sort of layer of undetermined energy in which all the agents were enveloped and which they used according to their several needs."

7. Nicolas, *Mystery*, 25.

8. Nicolas, *Mystery*, 25.

9. Nicolas, *Mystery*, 25.

10. Nicolas, *Mystery*, 25: "If I attempt to displace a wagon which is too heavy for me, my will sets my muscles in motion, and from that particular point of view it is efficacious; but it will not set the wagon in motion, and considered from the point of view of the intended motion there is no movement at all: the will's intention has been frustrated."

11. Nicolas, *Mystery*, 26. Making a similar point, Steven A. Long states in "Brief Comment on 'Do Not Resist the Spirit's Call,'" 8: "God, as pure act, limited by no potency whatsoever, cannot suffer

With premotion, there is no change in God, for God is pure act. He does not move himself from potency to act in moving man to act. Thus, if there is no change in God and there is no change or motion from potency to act in the patient, in what way can there be said to be any motion present at all?

And yet, even as man is moved by the divine motion toward not just indeterminate act but this or that specific action, man retains true freedom. And this is possible because God moves the will to move itself freely, to choose the object of determination and to retain a real potency to not choose it. This is at the heart of volition, which the animal lacks, and thus we say that the animal is compelled by a certain object,[12] incapable of resisting its allure. However, this is not the case in man, even under the perfectly efficacious influence of the divine motion. Remembering that creatures are contingent upon God to will and to act,[13] Nicolas says of the divine motion:

But it will likewise be exactly adapted to the nature if affects: it will determine it not only to do the action it intends, but to determine itself to do it; it will put its

---

change or limit or manyness (the Trinity is not 3 gods, but 3 persons within one divine substance each wholly and fully God: 3 distinct subsistent relations of the one divine substance). By virtue of the divine simplicity, divine causality involves no change in God whatsoever. Thus, it is only the reality of the effect that distinguishes divine causality. As a purely and infinitely indeterminate effect cannot be distinguished from the absence of effect, it follows that some determinate effect is implied by divine agency. Otherwise, no assertion of divine agency is intelligible."

12. Nicolas, *Mystery*, 32–33: "Man is free, the animal is not. What does that mean? The majority of animals, on the contrary, seems so much freer than man; they enjoy the large hospitality of nature unhampered by chains and laws. That is true, but such a privilege is useless to a being incapable of enjoying it; it is found almost to the same degree in the leaf of a tree carried off by the wind, in the cork pushed here and there by the currents of the river. The animal is, to a certain extent, released from the constraint of material forces. It comes and goes as it pleases. Yet, it is the unconscious slave of an inner tyranny just as powerful as that of the wind and the current, that is, the tyranny of desire. Its comings and goings, apparently so free, are always derived from a feeling of desire or fear which it is powerless to overcome—not, as in man's case, owing to the violence of this desire and of the weakness of some power, but because such a power is nonexistent for the animal, and the impressions of the senses monopolize its entire field of consciousness. All of its capacity for knowing and loving is absorbed by the object which actually attracts; it has no means of judging and overcoming this attraction. In its rudimentary consciousness, the various and sometimes contrary feelings which are provoked by the same object fight an obscure battle and the strongest automatically prevail by the sole virtue of their psychological weight, just as the heaviest scale of a balance descends automatically and not because of the decision of an interior arbitrator, as in the case of even the weakest of men. What difference does it make, then, if no master imposes his laws and the animal can do as it wills? It is fundamentally incapable of willing anything."

13. Nicolas, *Mystery*, 35: "As we have seen, the necessity for the divine motion arises from the fact that the agent is not by nature active, but merely capable of acting; as a result he needs to be set in motion by an active being. God alone is active by nature, pure and eternal activity. Every other agent, including the free will, must be set in motion by him, must be moved."

freedom to work. It will be a free act because the object will not be irresistibly imposed on the agent who will himself have decided to will and to pursue it. And God will have efficaciously moved the agent to this act, because, in order to decide and will, the agent needs to be moved by God and divine motion is efficacious by nature. God alone, who exercises his action at the very root of the will, can thus set it in motion without constraining it, can make it will—in other words, make it will freely, because a relative good can only be willed freely.[14]

Thus, we state that man exists in a subordinated causality with the divine will. God moves man *to will*. Because of this, man is properly called a cause of his own good works, but a cause which is contingent upon God. "The exterior source of our good works is God. Their interior source is our will."[15]

Man requires a divine motion to be moved toward an act that is commensurate with his nature, but for acts above his nature, he requires to be moved by supernatural motion. Nicolas describes the divine motion for natural acts as a "continuation of the creative action." It is motion toward a fulfillment of the nature that God has given to human creatures in their creation. "God, having called into existence beings capable of acting, owes it to himself to move them according to their nature. Otherwise there would be an incoherence in his work, which his wisdom renders impossible."[16] However, supernatural acts transcend human nature as such, and thus they require a motion that does not merely move man to act as he is, but moves man to surpass his own nature. This supernatural divine movement is called grace.

Supernatural acts, on the other hand, cannot derive from mere nature. It is only too evident that man, left to his own strength—that is to say, to the principles of action which properly belong to him and which constitute him, which make a man of him—is fundamentally incapable of superhuman acts. Therefore, in order to perform these acts, there is need of a divine help which is of itself supernatural. It is not found in the pure and simple continuation of the creative act, but constitutes in reference to it a superaddition, a new and original outpouring of liberality. Nature does not require so much in order to achieve its purpose in its own domain. It is God, who having constituted it by creating it, promotes it to a transcendent destiny and realizes this promotion by means of a special help. This help is grace, so called in order to emphasize that God, even after having

14. Nicolas, *Mystery*, 35–36.
15. Nicolas, *Mystery*, 42.
16. Nicolas, *Mystery*, 37.

created—which is already a gratuitous thing—by no means owes it to himself to accord what is gratuitous to the creature.[17]

However, man finds himself in a state of sin. As such, he is incapable even of living out his own natural capacity for good without supernatural aid, that is, divine motion that can lift and elevate him above his fallen state.[18] On account of this, man requires grace in order to be elevated above his sinfulness and concupiscence so that he can regain the ability to perform goods acts that would otherwise be attainable, through divine motion, via his natural capacities. Nicolas says, "To sum up, man has need of divine grace not only in order to do supernatural good and fulfill his transcendent destiny, but also and basically in order to live in a way which is in complete conformity with his proper nature."[19]

Nicolas uses the distinction between sufficient and efficacious grace that is found throughout the tradition. At the backbone of this distinction is the fact that sufficient grace is not itself a second kind of grace given alongside efficacious grace. On the contrary, all graces are efficacious for something. Nicolas confirms, "Every divine grace is efficacious: what we have said about divine motion in general holds valid for every divine act. That God should apply his will to supernaturalize a soul and that the soul should not be supernaturalized is meaningless."[20] Furthermore, "this grace is efficacious as regards the act which is done under its impulsion: if it were not efficacious, we repeat, it would exist and not exist simultaneously."[21]

With that being said, efficacious graces carry with them potencies for further acts, and these potencies, hidden within the acts of efficacious grace, are what we mean by sufficient grace. The further acts that are potentially attainable via this sufficient grace require, however, a further efficacious motion.

17. Nicolas, *Mystery*, 39,
18. Nicolas, *Mystery*, 40: "If these natural principles of action were intact, man could, by his own strength and through a divine motion (which would not be a grace, being strictly suited to the natural circumstances of his action) fulfill his destiny integrally. But man has sinned, he is born in sin, and sin has disintegrated his principles of action. This disintegration manifests itself in a powerlessness for good, which makes man incapable of the simple moral goodness and the simple success which we might expect of a human being. It is not because he is not free but because he is committed."
19. Nicolas, *Mystery*, 41.
20. Nicolas, *Mystery*, 52.
21. Nicolas, *Mystery*, 53.

But once this act is performed it ceases and, in order that the ulterior act be accomplished, a motion is necessary. As regards this ulterior act, the first motion is not efficacious. It is not, however, devoid of all influence on it; because our acts are linked together, one prepares the ground for another, it conditions the soul to perform it. The grace which makes the soul perform a good act, therefore, disposes the soul, by the intermediary of this act, to accomplish the following act; however, it does not as yet make the soul do it. This is known as sufficient grace. Thus, any grace whatsoever, while efficacious in relation to its immediate object, is only sufficient in relation to ulterior acts and in a general way in relation to the soul's salvation as considered as a whole.[22]

Thus, all graces are considered to be efficacious for one thing and sufficient for another, at least up to the last grace of final perseverance that merits eternal life. This grace is said to provide no further potencies and is only efficacious because it leads one from the temporal life of linking together human acts to the eternal, unchanging participation in the divine life.

In relation to predestination and meritorious actions, Nicolas also holds to the principle of predilection. It is God's love for us that makes us good, that causes us to do whatever meritorious deeds we accomplish. God's love is not elicited by our already being loveble. God loves us first, giving us the grace by which we become lovable.

But when we love, we are affected by the charm of the being loved, and if he is in our good graces, it is due to the fact that his grace has touched us beforehand. If we are mistaken about him, it is not our love which makes him better. On the contrary, God loves first and his love is the source of goodness. A being is good according to the measure of love which God has for him. In addition, to be in God's grace is to become worthy of God's love, to become loveable, gracious.[23]

The reason for this is clear, as Nicolas has already stated given the efficacy of divine motion. "When God loves a soul, which until then was outside the state of grace, with this special love, it is not he who changes. Thus, if a change were not produced in the interior of this soul, God's grace would be unreal; there would be no true difference between being in the state of grace or not being in it."[24] Therefore, the change must be in the creature, and divine motion must always be efficacious for the good willed by God

22. Nicolas, *Mystery*, 53.
23. Nicolas, *Mystery*, 49.
24. Nicolas, *Mystery*, 50.

in the creature. And insofar as this good is accomplished only by being precaused by God, all that is good within man is good only because God has made man to be good before any goodness actually resides within him or is attributed to him. As such, predestination must be *ante praevisa merita*. Nicolas says:

> It is a dogma defined by the Council of Trent that final perseverance is a previous and completely gratuitous gift from God; therefore, it is beyond the scope of the merit of the one who receives it. This doctrine definitely proclaims the triumph of grace: yes, our salvation is God's work.... He who receives it has no reason to be proud of his perseverance, for God is its first author.[25]

Of course, Nicolas's account is based on a rejection of fallible motions and graces. For Nicolas, this is rooted in God's simplicity, and thus the simplicity of the divine will. This will has multiple effects, but is radically one in and of itself, as Nicolas states.

> For it is evident that God has only one action which is identical with himself.... This act is a single will. If we regard it as multiple, it is because this single will, including in its orbit a crowd of distinct effects, may be considered as pregnant of a multitude of wills, each of which would have as object one of these distinct effects. We thus say that the single divine will is multiple by reason of the real multiplicity of the effects brought about by it.[26]

The human will may be defectible given its limited power and scope,[27] but the divine will is not.

However, this leads to a problem that must be resolved. If God's will is radically simple, how are we to account for the problem of sin? Obviously it cannot be said that God wills sin in any way, and it must be affirmed that he always wishes for all creatures to do good rather than evil. But if God's will and subsequent divine motions or graces within the creature are always efficacious, how do sin and evil arise in the first place?

---

25. Nicolas, *Mystery*, 127–28.

26. Nicolas, *Mystery*, 28.

27. Nicolas, *Mystery*, 29–30: "We will now proceed with our study of the divine will considered from the point of view of its effects. The latter are also dependent on a created causality, often on one or more created wills. If the divine will is indefectible, the same is not true of the created will; it may be betrayed by its instruments, it may be defected by the interior pressure of sensible desires or fears, it may yield."

The Line of Evil

As we have seen in the preceding chapters, the distinction between the antecedent and consequent will is important for the classical Thomistic approach. Nicolas affirms this distinction, stating that God wills some effect insofar as it is potentially given within an antecedent effect; however, it cannot be stated that he wills it *simpliciter* because God's simple will is always accomplished, as we have seen. Nicolas employs the analogy of a professor and his pupils.

To will the cause is to will the effect, to the precise extent to which its cause contains it. To will the effect directly, or to will it alone, inasmuch as it is implied in the cause, is not exactly analogous. The professor directly wills to teach: the normal effect of this act of teaching is to instruct the students and obtain the latter's success at the examination and perhaps, even more, their exceptional success in the branch of knowledge in which they are instructed today. The professor wills all this, but he does so indirectly: he would be the first to fail an insufficiently instructed student in the examination, and if his class does not produce a genius later on he does not for that reason entertain the feeling that he has not realized what he willed.[28]

Nicolas does not call the antecedent will a *velleitas*, but he does state that it is an indirect willing, properly distancing it from the consequent or simple will.

Let us apply this to the divine will with all the necessary nuances and adjustments. When the divine will is ordered towards an effect, it is inconceivable that this effect should not be exactly as it was willed: we have seen the reason for this. This is what theologians term the consequent will. Yet, this effect thus willed and realized is itself pregnant with other effects: to will it, is in itself to will these ulterior effects, but to will them only indirectly—that is to say, to the exact extent to which they are already contained in their created cause. Again, that means still willing them as capable of not being realized, by reason of the possible failures of this created cause; which finally signifies willing them in such a manner that, if these are not realized, this will is not frustrated of its object, for its real object is the cause, which exists in any case. This is what theologians call the antecedent will.[29]

Thus, the divine will is said to be antecedent and consequent, not in relation to itself such that there would be multiplicity within the simple

28. Nicolas, *Mystery*, 30.
29. Nicolas, *Mystery*, 30–31.

divine will, but in relation to the "totality of circumstances which regulate its effective realization."[30] To return to the example of the professor and his pupils:

The professor, in the above example, wills in advance the success of all his students, owing to the mere fact that he wills to impart to them the knowledge which forms the subject matter of the examination; but at the time of the examination he wills that such a student fail because, in fact, his teaching, in this student's case, has not produced the fruits of knowledge which were intended: this second will is consequent on the consideration of the set of conditions required for the conferring of the diploma.[31]

Similarly, God antecedently wills the salvation of every man, but due to the free choice of some men to turn from God and toward sin, God does not consequently or simply will the salvation of all men. Nicolas says that, in one sense, we can speak of God's *intention* as being frustrated in the antecedent will insofar as God truly intends that all men be saved although some are not. However, God's *will* is never frustrated, nor is it possible that it ever could be. He states simply, "Nothing resists God."[32] Similarly:

Thus, God, by the mere fact that he wills to confer grace on somebody, wills eternal life (of which this grace is the seed) for him. But entry into eternal life is conditional on the continuation in the state of grace up to the last moment, that is to say, on the ultimate faithfulness of the soul to the grace received. So that God, who, by an antecedent will and owing to the mere fact that he wills the Redemption, wills the salvation of all men. By a definite act of will, the consequent will, all those who die without being in the state of grace are excluded from salvation. You will, therefore, say that the divine intention has been frustrated, but that does not mean that his will is in any way inefficacious, for everything which he wills directly, with a consequent will, is realized—and exactly as it is willed—owing to the mere fact that it is willed.[33]

With this, Nicolas rejects the shatterable motions and frustratable providence of Maritain and Marín-Sola, and yet he retains a real antecedent will for goods in men that are not always brought about simply.

---

30. It should be noted that Nicolas does not mean here the circumstances regulate the divine will. Indeed, God is the architect of all circumstances. What is meant is simply that the consequent will wills things as they actually are, in relation to other things (and not in abstraction from the entire created order), just as God has ordained them to be from all eternity.

31. Nicolas, *Mystery*, 31.

32. Jean-Hervé Nicolas, "La permission du péché," *Revue Thomiste* 60, nos. 1, 2, and 4 (1960): 5–37, 185–206, 509–46; 530: "Rien ne résiste à Dieu." All translations of this article are mine.

33. Nicolas, *Mystery*, 31–32.

Whenever the antecedent will that some man not sin is not simply willed, the man will indeed fall into freely chosen sin. However, all of this is caused by man, and he is the one who is entirely responsible for sin. His defect taints the motion that God gives him, rendering it disabled, perverted, sinful. Nicolas states:

His motion does not suppress the spontaneity of beings; it arouses it. So it is in this instance: the soul, which has depths in its very interior which elude its own observation (while remaining in the zone of the conscious), culpably fails in regard to a determined object which solicits its preference over the divine object, and therefore elicits by this actual disposition, which is yet purely privative and for which it is solely responsible, a divine motion towards this object. The act which it performs under this motion is bad: but its entire malice derives from the fact that the secret failing in the soul is actualized.[34]

This means that God in no way causes the soul to do evil, but the evil comes solely from the human person. When man is moved to act, therefore, as in the case with the crippled leg, the movement is impaired and perverted. It is this perverting of the divine motion that accounts for the sin, rather than God's putatively random choice to withhold efficacious grace.[35] "If the creature has received this motion instead of the grace which would have made it perform the contrary act, this is not by virtue of an arbitrary decision of God, it is by reason of his failing: he is moved in the direction towards which he leans."[36] In this, Nicolas sounds much like Garrigou stating that man is only deprived of efficacious grace if he has previously rejected sufficient grace by placing an obstacle or defect to its being rendered efficacious. Indeed, sin is not desired or willed by God. "Sin essentially consists in the voluntary disobedience of the creature in regard to the divine will that is not in any way desired by God. Moreover, moral evil is opposed to infinite Goodness."[37]

Nicolas states that the defect is a disposition that renders a free action

34. Nicolas, *Mystery*, 54–55.

35. Nicolas states in "La permission du péche," 517: "Indeed, God does not predetermine his creatures randomly. He does not intervene in their activities like an unpredictable tyrant, but as a very delicate and wise animator" ("Dieu en effet ne prédétermine pas ses créatures au hazard: il n'intervient pas dans leurs activités comme un tyran fantasque, mais comme un très délicat et très sage animateur").

36. Nicolas, *Mystery*, 55.

37. Nicolas, "La permission du péché," 7: "le péché consistant essentiellement dans l'insoumission volontaire de la créature à l'égard de la volonté divine ne saurait en aucune manière être voulu par Dieu."

evil, existing ontologically prior to the execution of the evil or sinful act itself. Speaking of the defect, he states:

It is however a disposition that does not at all come from him [God]. It is the culpable failure. This failure is linked to a determined free act and precedes it according to a priority of nature. It is therefore a disposition that calls physical premotion to this determined free act. God, knowing this failure in his permissive decree, predetermines the free act that is found linked to it. Thus physical premotion does not come to surprise a creature that still hesitates and that would be urged to sin, but it gives to this creature to do whatever it freely wants to do.[38]

And yet, efficacious grace is necessary for man to do good "insofar as it prevents the failing which would have been an obstacle to it." As such, "all the good we do, all the goodness we acquire, is the work of divine grace in us before being our own work,"[39] and this includes even not falling into defect. It follows, therefore, that to fall into defect requires that God not give the grace that would preserve the creature from defect.[40] This is what is called the antecedent permissive decree. God knows that the creature will defect of its own free will if God does not uphold it from doing so, and thus God permits sometimes that creatures do indeed fall. Defect and sin do not escape God's providential power.

So, even in sinning, the creature does not come to oppose the execution of the designs of God: his failure entered into the perspectives of the plan of the Creator. And yet, if this failure is an evil, if it is culpable and punishable, it is because it is a revolt, an opposition of the created will to the will of the Creator. We must, therefore, now show how the conception of the permissive decree, as we have exposed it, does not destroy this essential character of sin, that this revolt against His will is something that God wishes to permit.[41]

38. Nicolas, "La permission du péché," 517: "Il est pourtant une disposition qui ne vient aucunement de lui, c'est la défaillance coupable. Cette défaillance est liée à un acte libre déterminé, et *le précède* d'une priorité de nature; elle est donc la disposition qui appelle la prémotion physique à cet acte libre détermine: Dieu connaissant cette défaillance dans son décret permissif, prédétermine l'acte libre qui se trouve lié à elle. Ainsi la prémotion physique ne vient pas surprendre une créature qui hésite encore et qui se trouverait ainsi comme pousée au péché, mais elle donne à cette créature de faire ce que librement elle veut faire."

39. Nicolas, *Mystery*, 56.

40. Nicolas, "La permission du péché," 517: "In the good act, on the contrary, there is no previous or concomitant disposition that does not come from God by predetermining it and by premoving it to act well. God preserves it from the culpable failure that it would commit by itself" ("Dans l'acte bon, au contraire, il n'y a aucune disposition précédente ou concomitante qui ne vienne pas de Dieu: en la prédéterminant et en la prémouvant à agir bien, Dieu la preserve de la défaillance coupable que par elle-même elle commettrait").

41. Nicolas, "La permission du péché," 518: "Ainsi, même en péchant, la créature n'arrive pas

In this way, Nicolas is rejecting the solutions of shatterable motions and fallible divine willing that is found in the work of Maritain and Marín-Sola. In fact, much of Nicolas's article in *Revue Thomiste* is a rejection of the errors of these two theologians.[42] He criticizes Marín-Sola's dual-motions and providences (one fallible, one infallible) in the first installment of the tripartite article on evil. He also criticizes Maritain's rejection of the antecedent permissive decree, noting how the two theologians share much commonality.[43] What is important to Nicolas is the simple, all-powerful nature of divine providence. God, in his simplicity, is not dependent on creatures in any way to execute his divine plan for his creation. He is not passive to their actions, contingent upon how creatures will react. His providence extends to all things and permits even defect and sin for a greater good. In this way, even evil and sin participate, as it were, in God's simple governance of the universe. Again, Nicolas returns to the maxim so often employed by Garrigou.

Does God determinately move the creature to this action, to this specific result, or, on the contrary, does the creature determine the divine motion to produce this action, this result? *God determining or determined, there is nothing in between.* Predetermination does not express anything else other than this necessary independence of God in regard to all of that which is in the determination of his action.[44]

à s'opposer à l'exécution des desseins de Dieu: sa défaillance entrait dans les perspectives du plan créateur. Et pourtant, si cette défaillance est un mal, si elle est coupable et punissable, c'est parce qu'elle est une révolte, une opposition de la volonté créée à la volonté du Créateur. Il nous faut donc maintenant montrer comment la conception du décret permissif, telle que nous l'avons exposée, ne détruit pas ce caractère essentiel au péché, comment cette révolte contre sa volonté est cela même que Dieu veut permettre."

42. Nicolas, "La permission du péché," 20: "En vérité cette voie bifurque en deux directions assez différentes: la première s'oriente vers une condition positive, la fidélité à la grâce permettant à celle-ci de produire son effet et conditionnant ainsi la realisation de la predetermination; la seconde, distinguant plus soigneusement la ligne du bien et la ligne du mal, n'admet pas pour la première un conditionnement créé,—la prédétermination divine se réalisant là par elle-même,—mais bien pour la seconde: la défaillance de la créature empêchant la prédétermination divine de se réaliser. La première est la théorie du Père Marín-Sola et de ses disciples; la seconde, celle de M. Jacques Maritain et de plusieurs théologiens qui l'ont suivi."

43. Nicolas, "La permission du péché," 187: "Faut-il donc revenir aux décrets permissifs antécédents? Avant de le faire, il est indispensable d'examiner un autre effort d'explication qui, fidèle en ce qui concerne le domaine entier des effectuations, des réalisations positives, à la doctrine thomiste de la pure et simple antécédence et de l'efficacité des conceptions divines,—donc à la doctrine de la prédétermination,—pense pouvoir se passer des décrets permissifs antécédents en ce qui concerne le mal et ses consequences. C'est la théorie de J. Maritain, admise et adoptee par plusieurs théologiens aujourd'hui. Par beaucoup de points elle se rapproche du marin-solisme."

44. Nicolas, "La permission du péché," 18: "Dieu meut-il déterminément la créature à cette

The antecedent permissive decree is absolutely vital in safeguarding God's simplicity and his comprehensive governing power over his creation, for it maintains two important truths: 1) that sin does not escape or frustrate God's simple will, and 2) as a corollary, it shows the necessity of divine aid in all creaturely good, even the good of simply considering the rule, not placing an obstacle to divine aid itself, but cooperating with it. Nicolas points out that all of this does not suffice to entirely conceptualize, internalize, and comprehensively understand the mysteries of human action and predestination, but they are necessary truths that we can see *hic et nunc* as wayfarers.

This remark made, we are not so naive as to believe that the antecedent permissive decree completely abolishes the mystery. God could preserve the free creature from making the obstacle, freely and culpably, from his grace, and it will not make it. The infallible meeting between the permissive decree, in the plan of the divine intentions, and the moral failure in the plan of the acting of the free creature, is the proper mystery of moral evil: a nihilation that the creature commits freely. In the face of this infra-intelligible mystery, and a correlative of it, there is another properly divine mystery, the mystery of the infinite liberty and love, the mystery of predestination. It is not given to anyone, under the condition of terrestrial knowledge, to unravel it.[45]

The Later Nicolas

Nicolas's defense of the traditional Thomistic treatment gave way to a novel approach toward the end of his life. Nicolas abandoned the traditional treatment in his article "La volonté salvifique de Dieu contrariée par le péché,"[46] which was published in 1992, about nine years before

---

action, à ce résultat concret, ou au contraire la créature détermine-t-elle la motion divine à produire cette action, ce résultat? *Dieu déterminant ou déterminé, pas de milieu.* La prédétermination n'exprime pas autre chose que cette nécessaire indépendance de Dieu à l'égard de tout ce qui n'est lui dans la détermination de son action."

45. Nicolas, "La permission du péché," 545–46. "Cette remarque faite, nous n'aurons pas la naïveté de croire que le décret permissif antécédent abolit le mystère. Dieu pouvait préserver la créature libre de faire obstacle, librement et coupablement, à sa grâce, et il ne le fait pas. L'infaillible rencontre entre le décret permissif, sur le plan des intentions divines, et la défaillance morale sur le plan de l'agir libre créé, est le mystère propre du mal moral: un néant que l'on comment librement. En face de ce mystère infra-intelligible et corrélatif à lui, il y a l'autre mystère proprement divin, le mystère de la liberté de l'amour infini, mystère de la predestination. Il n'est donné à personne, dans les conditions de la connaissance terrestre, de le percer."

46. Jean-Hervé Nicolas, "La volonté salvifique de Dieu contrariée par le péché," *Revue Thomiste* 92 (1992): 177–96. All translations of this article are mine.

Nicolas's death. In this article, Nicolas admits that while not necessarily agreeing with Maritain's entire treatment on these issues, he has been convinced by some of Maritain's objections to change his teaching on these subjects.[47]

Nicolas begins with a proposition that all Thomists hold: "It is a theological principle, absolutely certain and universally admitted: *nothing arrives in the world that God has not willed or permitted.*"[48] A corollary of this truth is that whatever comes into the world that is not simply willed by God must at least be permitted by Him. "That which arrives in the world without being willed by God is permitted. What is the significance of this? It is clear that 'to permit' does not in any way mean 'to give the permission.' God obviously cannot give to the free creature the permission to do evil."[49]

However, having stated that the traditional account has tormented him, Nicolas seeks to make sense of "this indestructible link between the divine will not stopping the defect and the realization of the defect."[50] Nicolas admits to having been swayed by the objections of Maritain, confessing that his earlier treatment of these matters was wrong.[51]

Nicolas begins by positing that sin is unnatural for man. He says that "man, in order not to sin, needs the help of God, but sin is contrary to his nature (or, contrary to the movement of his nature), so that it is natural for him not to sin."[52] Nicolas states that this is the mind of St. Thomas, who says:

47. Nicolas, "Volonté salvifique," 178: "Sur ce point mes objections demeurent, mais l'objet de cet article n'est en aucune manière de les reprendre et d'y insister. Car il m'a convaincu de la force de ses propres objections et il m'a mis dans la nécessité de remanier profondément mes positions, même si cela laisse sans réponse pleinement satisfaisante l'interrogation à laquelle précisément je m'efforçais de satisfaire."

48. Nicolas, "Volonté salvifique," 178: "C'est un principe théologique, absolument certain et universelement admis: *rien n'arrive dans le monde que Dieu ne l'ait voulu ou permis.*"

49. Nicolas, "Volonté salvifique," 178: "Ce qui arrive dans le monde sans être voulu par Dieu est permis. Qu'est-ce que cela signifie? Il est clair que « permettre » ici n'est en aucune manière « donner la permission » : Dieu ne peut évidemment pas donner à la créature libre la permission de faire le mal."

50. Nicolas, "Volonté salvifique," 185: "Dès le début de ma réflexion sur cet obscur sujet, qui *m'*a tourmenté, je me suis efforcé de mettre à l'abri de toute causalité, et donc de tout vouloir de Dieu, ce lien indestructible entre la volonté divine de ne pas empêcher la défaillance et la realisation de celle-ci ."

51. Nicolas, "Volonté salvifique," 186: "C'est là que les attaques de Maritain—dont je ne méritais pas, je crois, la dureté—m'ont convaincu définitivement que je me trompais. À vrai dire, la reaction pour le moins réservée de plusieurs de mes interlocuteurs et le propre malaise que j'éprouvais m'avaient déjà ébranlé."

52. Nicolas, "Volonté salvifique," 185: "l'homme, pour ne pas pécher, ait besoin du secours de

To sin is nothing else than to fail in the good which belongs to any being according to its nature. Now as every created thing has its being from another, and, considered in itself, is nothing, so does it need to be preserved by another in the good which pertains to its nature. For it can of itself fail in good, even as of itself it can fall into non-existence, unless it is upheld by God.[53]

Nicolas makes a major connection between being and goodness. Every created being requires to be upheld in being by God just as it requires to be upheld in goodness by God. And this is not accidental since goodness could be said simply to be due being, or being which is due. As such, Nicolas has very intimately linked man's contingency upon God for *being* with his contingency upon God for *doing good,* or being preserved from defect and sin.

I have attempted to treat the basis for this analogy between defectibility in being and defectibility in good and to show that the fall into nongood, which is sin, or rather the failure of free will that proceeds sin, has its unique source in the contingency of the creature. Contingency in the good is inseparable from contingency in being, which is the very condition of the created being and it cannot be made otherwise.[54]

Nicolas understands evil as being a privation of this good, but a privation that must exist in a subject. It is a deprivation of some good that is due to it or toward which it is called.

Evil itself is a privation of a good. It implies therefore first a subject, because the privation is not a pure and simple negation, it is a negation that affects a subject, a lack that it suffers. It is able to be known because it is in reference to a subject. Blindness is a privation. A natural being is endowed with the faculty of sight, a necessary condition to exercise this faculty. One does not say that a plant is blind. But it does not suffice to know what is blindness. It must be known that this subject (an animal, a man) is in fact affected by the privation that limits it: because that is real, it is part of the reality of the subject.[55]

Dieu, alors que le péché est contre sa nature (c'est-à-dire contre le mouvement foncier de sa nature), de sorte qu'il lui est naturel de ne pas pécher."

53. *ST* I-II, q. 109, a. 2, ad 2.

54. Nicolas, "Volonté salvifique," 186: "J'ai tenté de traiter à fond cette analogie entre la défectibilité dans l'être et la défectibilité dans le bien, et de montrer que la chute dans le non-bien, qui est le péché, ou plutôt la défaillance de la liberté dont procède le péché, a sa source uniquement dans la contingence de la créature: contingence dans le bien indissociable de la contingence dans l'être, qui est la condition même de l'étant créé et ne saurait lui être épargnée."

55. Nicolas, "Volonté salvifique," 180–81: "Le mal lui-même est la privation d'une bonté. Il implique donc d'abord un sujet, car la privation n'est pas une négation pure et simple, c'est la négation

God knows evil then, insofar as he knows the subject of the sin, who exists in a state that has some lack, some privation of good, but who is still good in whatever way that he yet acts toward good and still exists.[56]

However, Nicolas has now abandoned the antecedent permissive decree, as he explicitly states in this work.

As I am, as I have always been certain of the innocence of God, I am obliged to admit, and I do say it willingly, that the conception of the antecedent permissive decree that I have proposed is not worthy. I had kept it, not without effort to develop it, in order to resolve the problem of God's foreknowledge of sin, without which it would be unintelligible that this, the incalculable multitude of sins, enter into the designs of Providence. The problem remains.[57]

But why has Nicolas rejected it? It would seem that he has rejected it for essentially the same reason that it was rejected by Maritain, that is, that it makes God out to be indirectly the cause of the evil in creatures. Nicolas, returning to the close tie between being upheld in being and being upheld in goodness, says, "I have conceived then that, in the same line of my reflection upon the analogy between the two defectibilities that, if nonconservation in being, which would be the annihilation of the creature, is contrary to the wisdom and goodness of God, how much more would be its nonconservation in goodness, which would make it evil!"[58] It follows, then, that for Nicolas God not upholding the creature from defect would make God out to be at least the indirect cause of evil. God would be refusing to maintain the creature in good, and this refusal would be tantamount to indirect influence upon the creature to bring

---

qui affecte un sujet, un manque dont il pâtit. Il ne peut être connu pour ce qu'il est qu'en référence à ce sujet: la *cécité* est la privation, en un étant naturellement doté de la faculté de voir, d'une condition nécessaire à l'exercice de cette faculté; on ne dira pas d'une plante qu'elle est aveugle. Mais il ne suffit pas de savoir ce qu'est la cécité, il faut savoir que ce sujet (un animal, un homme) est en fait affecté de la privation par quoi elle se définit: car cela est réel, cela fait partie de la réalité de ce sujet."

56. Nicolas, "Volonté salvifique," 181: "Le mal moral est non pas le mal absolu—car le pécheur reste bon en son être—mais le mal pur et simple, la pure privation de bonté."

57. Nicolas, "Volonté salvifique, 186: "Comme je suis, comme j'ai toujours été aussi certain que quiconque de l'*innocence de Dieu*, je suis obligé de reconnaître, et je le fais volontiers, que la conception du décret permissif antécédent que j'ai proposée ne vaut pas. Je l'avais conservée, non sans m'efforcer de l'aménager, pour résoudre le problème de la prescience par Dieu du péché, sans laquelle il serait inintelligible que celui-ci, que la multitude incalculable des péchés, entrent dans les desseins de la Providence. Le problème demeure."

58. Nicolas, "Volonté salvifique," 186: "Je me suis avisé alors, dans la ligne même de ma réflexion sur l'analogie entre les deux défectibilités, que, si la non-conservation dans l'être que serait l'anéantissement d'une créature est contraire à la sagesse et à la bonté de Dieu, combien plus le serait sa non-conservation dans le bien qui la ferait mauvaise!"

about the sinful act. "The flaw of the reasoning is located at this point: if the free creature is not able by itself to maintain itself in good, in refusing to maintain it there, in willing not to resist that it fails, one will not avoid ... rendering God responsible for evil."[59]

Nicolas appears now to employ the two providences of Marín-Sola that he once denounced. The creature first places its defect, which God then responds to according to the prior disposition of the creature, either to failure or to cooperation with divine movement.

When, in the course of this movement, the created will freely fails in regard to a determined object, this failure puts it in the immediate position of making this choice and of achieving it. It calls the corresponding divine motion that then answers not by the particular providence in regard to the free creature, of the person, but by the general providence by which God governs the universe, adapting his action to each creature according to its nature and according to its existential situation.[60]

God adapts his action according to the disposition of the creature,[61] governing not by particular providence but by general providence that respects the free will of the creature to participate or to not participate in God's call to goodness and holiness for it. As such, the creature appears to be indifferent to God's governance.

Nicolas takes these principles and moves to the question of election, admitting that this issue is central to the questions and controversies surrounding predestination, and that it is a difficult one that has troubled many.[62] Nicolas now shies away from speaking of reprobation as some-

---

59. Nicolas, "Volonté salvifique," 186: "La faille du raisonnement se situe à ce point: si la créature libre ne peut pas par elle-même se maintenir dans le bien, en se refusant à l'y maintenir, *en voulant ne pas empêcher qu'elle défaille*, on n'évite pas, malgré tous les efforts qu'on y apporte et dont Maritain méconnaît de façon injuste la réalite et la sincérité, de render Dieu responsable du mal."

60. Nicolas, "Volonté salvifique," 183–84: "Quand, au cours de ce mouvement, la volonté créée défaille librement, à propos d'un objet déterminé, cette défaillance la met dans la disposition immédiate de faire ce choix et de le réaliser, elle appellee la motion divine correspondante qui relève alors non de la providence particulière à l'égard de la créature libre, de la personne, mais de la providence générale par laquelle Dieu gouverne l'univers, adaptant son action à chaque créature selon sa nature et selon sa situation existentielle."

61. Nicolas, "Volonté salvifique," 183: "This consequence remains mysterious, because it is by the reason of his wisdom and goodness that God would move each being according to its nature and according to its present disposition" ("Cette conséquence reste mystérieuse, car c'est en raison de sa sagesse et de sa bonté que Dieu meut chaque étant selon sa nature et selon sa disposition présente").

62. Nicolas, "Volonté salvifique," 187: "Mon intention étant non de reprendre l'examen de ces prises de position, mais de rectifier celles que j'ai adoptées moi-même dans ce context théologique, je me demanderai seulement comment on peut, et peut-être on doit, comprendre la notion d'*élection*

thing that is antecedent to the failure of the creature (and this is not surprising given his rejection of the antecedent permissive decree). Nicolas
now speaks of all mankind being predestined to eternal life, with some
placing obstacles and rejecting that universal call.

This power does not prevent predestination from being certain, that is to say
"from obtaining to its effect with perfect certainty and infallibly," because the
object of predestination is mankind as a whole and each man belonging to mankind, of which he is a part, but in such a way that he may be able to place an
obstacle to diverge himself from this predestination.[63]

Accordingly, Nicolas now wishes to reject all language that seems to
imply any reprobation that is antecedent to foreseen demerits. In fact,
Nicolas seems to go so far as to exclude the possibility of election being
understood in any way as accidentally excepting some, or leaving them to
their own works.

But by Scripture we know that, above all, God has created man out of love and
that he has created him in order to make him his child and to give to him a place
for sons in his eternal house. One would see that this truth, which is of the faith,
radically excludes a divine choice of electing that would include the abandonment to themselves—that is to say to the absolute failure of the destiny for which
they were created, and that according to the same Scripture, that which they
could not achieve except by the grace of God—those who, without any reason
other than the absolute liberty of God, would not have been chosen.[64]

Speaking of the influence of Maritain upon his new position, Nicolas
similarly states, "In this area, I received from him ... that predestination

qui est au centre du problème de la prédestination et de toutes les controverses qu'elle a générées et,
malheureusement, des troubles que certains de ces solutions, que j'avais crues inévitables, ont parfois
suscités dans la conscience de beaucoup."

63. Nicolas, "Volonté salvifique," 193: "Ce pouvoir n'empêche pas la prédestination d'être certaine,
c'est-à-dire « d'obtenir son effet avec une certitude parfaite [certissime] et infailliblement », car l'objet
de la prédestination est le genre humain dans son ensemble et chaque homme dans le genre humain
dont il fait partie, mais de telle façon qu'il puisse faire obstacle à cette dérivation jusqu'à sa personne
de cette prédestination."

64. Nicolas, Volonté salvifique," 188–89: "Mais c'est par l'Écriture aussi que nous savons, surtout,
que Dieu a créé l'homme par amour et qu'il l'a créé pour en faire son enfant et lui donner la place des
fils dans sa maison d'éternité. On aurait dû voir que cette vérité, qui est de foi, exclut radicalement
un choix divin des élus qui comprendrait l'abandon à eux-mêmes—c'est-à-dire à l'échec absolu de la
destinée pour laquelle ils ont été créés, et que, selon la même Écriture, ils ne peuvent réaliser autre-
ment que par la grâce de Dieu—de ceux qui sans aucune raison que la liberté sans limites de Dieu
n'auraient pas été choisis."

cannot be conceived as privileging the predestined in relation to others who will not be privileged."[65]

As such, Nicolas confirms what the classical Thomistic treatment has always said, namely that God's will is in no way conditioned or restricted, but, apparently without realizing the inherent contradiction, he states that it can indeed be thwarted or frustrated by sin.

God wills the salvation of all men, of every man. He has already willed it in creating man in Adam and Eve; he has willed it anew in their fall, in deciding to send his Son to all men as their Savior. This will is in no way restricted nor conditioned. It can only be thwarted and prevented from happening, but only by people who take the initiative, by sin.[66]

Nicolas concludes by speaking to the mystery of these issues. He cites Maritain in *God and the Permission of Evil*, who states:

However obscure this mystery may be, the aseity or *absolute independence* of God on the one hand, and the *divine absolute innocence* on the other, shine there with a sovereign brightness, and it is this radiance itself which our eye has difficulty in enduring. Rather than sacrifice or destroy however so little one of these truths at the expense of the other, it would after all be better to confess that our reason is too weak to reconcile them.[67]

Nicolas responds to this quotation, saying, "This declaration that Jacques Maritain has placed at the beginning of his work *God and the Per-*

65. Nicolas, "Volonté salvifique," 190: "Ce que, en ce domaine, j'ai reçu de lui, c'est la certitude que l'élection divine ne peut pas comprendre l'exclusion de ceux qui ne seraient pas choisis, et donc que la prédestination ne peut pas être conçue comme privilégiant les prédestinés par rapport à d'autres qui ne le seraient pas." This is a remarkable passage precisely because it is a total abandonment of St. Thomas's principle of predilection and the gratuity of predestination. The egalitarian tendencies here completely alter (or abolish?) all traditional understanding of the gratuity of God's grace and mercy. Time and time again the Scriptures attest to God's privileging of some: Abraham, Jacob, Joseph, David, Mary, Peter, etc.

66. Nicolas, "Volonté salvifique," 196: "Dieu veut le salut de tous les hommes, de chaque homme. Il l'a voulu déjà en créant l'homme en Adam et Ève; il l'a voulu de nouveau dès leur chute en décidant d'envoyer son Fils à tous les hommes comme Sauveur. Cette volonté n'est aucunement restreinte ni conditionnée. Elle peut seulement être contrariée et empêchée de se réaliser, mais pour les personnes seulement qui en prennent l'initiative, par le péché."

67. Maritain, *God and the Permission of Evil*, 8–9: "Si obscure que soit ce mystére, l'aséit ou *absolue indépendance* de Dieu d'un côté, *l'absolue innocence divine* d'un autre côté y brillent avec une claret souveraine, et c'est cet éclat lui-même que notre oeil a peine à soutenir. Plutôt que de sacrifier ou d'ébranler si peu que ce soit l'une de ces vérités aux dépens de'autre, mieux vaudrait aprés tout avouer que notre raison est trop faible pour les concilier." This is essentially the conclusion of Matthew Levering's *Predestination: Biblical and Theological Paths* (Oxford: Oxford University Press, 2001), especially 199–201.

mission of Evil, I make it mine entirely, and it preserved me from all panic when proposing a solution to this problem in a replacement of the permissive decree."[68] Following from this, Nicolas affirms the obscurity of the question, stating that it can never be fully understood in this life. Our knowledge and understanding of this mystery will always be imperfect as wayfarers.[69]

Analysis

Nicolas's adoption of certain propositions based in the work of Maritain or Marín-Sola falls into all of the same pitfalls that we have already established. However, what is most interesting about Nicolas is how his later position, driven by an uneasiness concerning the traditional treatment, seems unanswerable to Nicolas's very own arguments from earlier in his life, particularly those that concern God's simplicity.

One wonders how it can be the case that God's will is thwarted. Nicolas has maintained that God wills the salvation of all men, and that this universal salvation is simply impeded by man's rejection of the grace whereby man may merit salvation. As with Marín-Sola's impedible motions or Maritain's shatterable motions, we must state that, even though Nicolas maintains that God wishes to allow the creature to place obstacles to sin in order to respect its freedom, it seems that God's governance does not really reign over the particular response of each and every individual to his grace. In fact, one might even claim that, since Nicolas has rejected the traditional concept of election (and therefore, the principle of predilection), it follows that God would have no direct involvement with the distinguishing of the wheat and the chaff, as it were. He may stand as judge, but it is unclear as to how he could have played any causal

68. Nicolas, "Volonté salvifique," 194: "Cette déclaration que Jacques Maritain a placée au début de son opuscule *Dieu et la permission du mal*, je la fais mienne entièrement, et cela me préserve de toute panique au moment de proposer une solution à ce problème en remplacement du décret permissif."

69. Nicolas, "Volonté salvifique," 194: "It would be impossible for the human spirit being in its earthly condition to fully explain this reconciliation that affirms with the certainty of faith. It cannot bother our belief, because it is not due to explanation that one believes, but one is guided by the faith to seek an explanation, however imperfect and obscure" ("Qu'il soit impossible à l'esprit humain dans sa condition terrestre d'expliquer pleinement cette conciliation qu'il affirme avec la certitude de la foi, cela ne peut le gêner pour croire, car ce n'est pas à cause de l'explication qu'il croit, c'est guidé par la foi qu'il cherche une explication, de toute façon imparfaite et obscure").

role in that which distinguishes one man from another. It is not that Peter is loved more than Judas and that this loves makes him to be a better man. It would seem that Peter has not thwarted God's grace, thus allowing for his own salvation. Judas has, however, seemingly thrown a wrench into the divine designs insofar as God willed his salvation (simply, not merely antecedently), but Judas prevented that will from being manifest.

And yet, to employ Nicolas's own arguments, it is equally unclear as to how we can say that God wills or governs at all over those who thwart him (at least insofar as they thwart him), given the divine simplicity. If it is true that God's motion within a creature (that motion that is the principle of its being governed) is something that effects a change only in the creature and not in God (since he is immutable), one is left wondering what is happening with those who reject God's call and thwart his designs. Nicolas maintains that all good, of course, comes from God working within the creature, but what do we say of the motions toward determined goods that God wills but that are never accomplished? How does God move a creature while also not moving it? Man may be totally impeded by the wagon that is too heavy for him to push, but we must admit that his being impeded implies that there was never any motion imparted to the wagon at all. Man's intended motions can be thwarted because he is sometimes causally impotent, which is to say nothing other than that he is not omnipotent. Nicolas wishes to maintain that the creature takes the first initiative in placing an obstacle, in failing, when God's good motions are thwarted. As such, he can state that these good motions never really begin in the creature because they are dead in the water, as it were, before beginning; the defect is ontologically prior to the divine aid. However, this does not mean that this is in any way reconcilable with God's simplicity.

When God wishes to move a creature to x, and he simply wills that the creature be moved to x, that his will is frustrated by the creature means that the creature has made some change in God. At the very least, God must look out at his creation and see that it is not as he has actually willed it. God is acted upon by the creature, and insofar as God's will has been truly impeded, God has been changed as an agent by the patient. An omnipotent God does what he pleases, according to the goodness of his own nature. A fallible creature attempts to exert his will upon the rest of creation in a similar manner but is very often rejected by the things that he truly attempts to act upon. When this happens, the man scratches his head, grumbles at the broken or too-heavy wagon, and must either consider another way to achieve his intended end or to surrender himself to defeat. This is why man often makes intricate plans before engaging in certain motions, such that the motion is efficacious or that it does not turn out differently than originally intended. Does God do the same? It does not suffice to say that God wills fallibly, according to a general providence, respecting the human freedom of creatures. Unless God is indifferent to the salvation of each and every man, something that Nicolas explicitly rejects, we must admit that God's simple will is frustrated by the creature, and thus he is in some way determined by it. It will simply not do to say that God is determined by creatures, but only because he wishes to be so. To state as such would be to lose the infinite transcendence between Creator and creature, to posit a real relation of God to man. God cannot give up his perfections, even if we include the caveat that he *freely* gives them up.

This is the effect of rejecting the antecedent permissive decree, which maintains God's simplicity and comprehensive governance in the face of creaturely rejection. As we have so often stated, God takes no initiative in sin. That comes entirely from man. However, since man requires to be upheld by grace even in not placing an obstacle (which is itself a good, a perfection that is above the nature of a defectible, contingent creature acting *on its own*), to place an obstacle requires that God permit it. Nothing comes into existence, even privations of existence, that thwart God's simple will and governance. He wishes for the salvation of all, but hell is not a scandal to the divine governance. It is not a corner of the universe in which Satan has won, a state that exists as eternally proving God's fallibility and weakness. All things, even the evils of sin, hell, and damnation, fall under the governance of God. He in no way wills them, and it is quite true that God wishes for the salvation of all men, but that some men fall is not outside of the scope of God's designs for the universe. Indeed, this is a mystery, but not one so obscure that we ought to admit that God has been, at least partially, defeated.

Nicolas states in "La permission du péché": "We must therefore not represent sins as simple holes in the tapestry that would be the work of Providence. Each hole, in fact, influences the next step of the design, which would not be the same without it. In short, even if evil itself is not

anything positive, nonetheless it introduces into the world positive determinations."[70] Does God not govern over these positive determinations?

Moreover, if God wishes the universal salvation of all men, but this
simple will is sometimes thwarted, what distinguishes one man from another? What separates the good thief from the unrepentant one? If we
have rejected God's antecedent permission of defect, then it would seem
that cooperation with grace is what distinguishes one man from another.
God does not elect some men but calls all men to salvation simply, being
rejected and frustrated in his call by those who will not merit heaven. But
this seems to fall into the same objection that Nicolas himself made to the
position of Fr. Marín-Sola. "But doesn't this explanation of predestination and glory ultimately depend upon the usage, good or bad, that man
makes of grace, and consequently is it not the case that human liberty is
the principle of discernment between the saved and the reprobates?"[71]

Finally, any distinction between two wills in God requires that we
speak of two separate objects within two entirely different sets of circumstances. This is why we have spoken of the antecedent and consequent
wills as being different in scope, which is to say that they truly have different formal objects. Antecedently, God wishes the salvation of each man,
let us say Judas, for example. How are we to understand that Judas is not
then saved? Judas is not saved because God wills the salvation of Judas
when Judas's good is considered in abstraction from the circumstances of
the entire tapestry of the divine design. God does not wish for Judas to
perish, but he does permit Judas to perish in light of Judas's place within the whole, in order to manifest a greater good that may be fittingly
brought about through such a permission. Thus, the antecedent will is in
regard to Judas alone while the consequent will is in regard to reality as
such, a design in which Judas's good and bad actions will have influence

70. Nicolas, "La permission du péché," 7: "On ne doit donc pas se représenter les péchés comme
de simples trous dans la tapisserie que serait l'œuvre de la Providence: chaque trou, en fait, influe sur
la suite du dessin, qui ne serait pas le même sans lui. Bref, si le mal lui-même n'est rien de positif, il
introduit pourtant dans le monde des déterminations positives."

71. Nicolas, "La permission du péché," 26: "Cette explication ne fait-elle pas dépendre finalement
la prédestination à la gloire de l'usage, bon ou mauvais, que l'homme fait de la grâce, et par conséquent
ne fait-elle pas de la liberté humaine le principe de discernement entre les élus et les réprouvés?" See
also on the following page: "Car enfin si la créature reçoit une grâce telle qu'il dépend d'elle seule
d'être fidèle ou infidèle, comment peut-on dire que le bien auquel cette grâce le conduit si elle est
fidèle ne dépend que de la grâce? Avec cette même grâce, objet de la même libéralité divine, il aurait
pu arriver qu'elle n'atteigne pas cette bonté: il est difficile de voir qu'elle ne se la doit pas, en partie du
moins, à elle-même."

upon everything around him. As such, God only simply wills those things insofar as they work toward the common good of the created order. He does not will every good to every creature. The holes in the tapestry, evil in and of themselves, are yet transformed upon a comprehensive view of the tapestry in its ultimate and final state. They are used by God to create a richer tapestry when all is said and done.[72]

The *antecedent* and *consequent wills* then are to be distinguished in two ways: 1) the former is not simply willed while the latter is, and 2) the two are different in their scope, in their object. This preserves God's radical simplicity, for God only truly wills one thing, not two or many, and whatever is willed by God truly comes about, simply and sweetly.

But compare this to the two wills and two providences of Marín-Sola, with which Nicolas seems at least to flirt in his final article. In these two wills, the difference is not in relation to the object. The object is shared. It is not that God wills the salvation of Judas only in abstraction, only antecedently or as a *velleitas*, thus permitting that the opposite happen in relation to a different, more comprehensive or integral object. On the contrary, God fallibly or generally actually wills the salvation of all men, but this is sometimes frustrated, as in the case of Judas. But in Marín-Sola's account of dual providence, this is not because God has permitted that an antecedent good be refused for a greater good, but because God has simply been frustrated. The earlier Nicolas objected to the very troubling consequences that follow from this, ones that are an affront to God's simplicity.

This distinction [of an antecedent and consequent will] is valid because its principle is really in the creature. Indeed, it is a matter of two formally distinct objects, the existential circumstances being constitutive of the object of the will. But about this other view we say, however, that the two divine wills concern (or may be able to concern) one identical object. God decides by one or the other of these wills to move the created will to an act that is in effect identically the same. All of the difference is in the *divine manner* of the willing. Is this not to introduce a distinction in God? This is unintelligible![73]

---

72. Again, it is important to note here that God does not rely on evil in any way to bring about this greater good. What we are saying is simply that he deems it *fitting* to bring greater goods out of evil, though they could be brought about without any such permission of evil.

73. Nicolas, "La permission du péché," 31: "Cette distinction est valable parce que son principe est bien dans la créature: il s'agit en effet de deux objets formels distincts, les circonstances existentielles étant constitutives de l'objet de la volonté. Mais là on nous parle de deux vouloirs divins portant

Nicolas's earlier contributions to this debate are vital. What Nicolas has contributed to the commentatorial discussion is a real focus on the divine simplicity. Nicolas has added depth to Garrigou's axiom that it is either God determining or determined. While the latter position referred to by Nicolas in the passage above obviously poses significant challenges to the necessity of grace, God's omnipotence, and the exhaustive nature of divine governance and providence, it also threatens the divine unity and simplicity itself.

One can greatly sympathize with the anguish or anxiety that is felt while meditating upon these mysteries that are indeed obscure in this life. However, the principles of the divine nature are at stake, and with them the very foundation of classical theism. The temptation to exonerate God from the cruel reality of sin has proven to be a strong one. It moved not only Marín-Sola and Maritain but also Nicolas, who employed a robust defense of the classical Thomistic position. He was agitated to forsake the efficacy of divine aid for willfully breakable and impedible aid. The problem, as we have seen, is that it does not safeguard God's omnipotence or simplicity even if we state that he intentionally does away with them in his work with human creatures. Nor does it explain man's ability as a completely contingent being to do good with motions and aids that are themselves contingent. As we work toward the conclusion of this work, we hope to show that, far from bringing torment and anxiety, we ought to find hope and comfort in the only possible approach and resolution to these issues: complete abandonment to an all-loving God.

(ou pouvant porter) sur un objet identique: l'acte en effet auquel Dieu décide par l'un ou par l'autre de ces vouloirs de mouvoir la volonté créée est identiquement le même; toute la différence est dans la *maniére divine* de le vouloir: n'est-ce pas introduire en Dieu même une distinction? Cela n'est pas intelligible!"

CHAPTER EIGHT

Bernard Lonergan

On Operation and the Mover

Bernard Lonergan, SJ, was one of the most important and prolific Jesuit philosophers and theologians to engage with the thought of St. Thomas Aquinas in the twentieth century. He held teaching appointments at the Pontifical Gregorian University, Regis College in Toronto, Canada, Boston College, and Harvard University. While Lonergan's work on premotion, providence, and predestination is extensive, it mostly falls outside of the limited scope of this work, which is chiefly in regard to the intra-Dominican debate of the twentieth century and its application to further Thomistic understanding of these issues. However, while Lonergan is not a formal player in this intra-Dominican debate, he is certainly a key figure in the intra-*Thomistic* debate and the broader Catholic theological discussion of these matters in the twentieth and twenty-first centuries. His influence has been far-reaching, and it certainly animates a large constituency of Catholic thought today. We wish here to look only at one particular (but perhaps the most important and influential) facet of Lonergan's treatment: his view on causality and how it pertains to the operation of the mover in bringing about its effect.

What Lonergan attempts to do is to sidestep many of the aforementioned controversies surrounding divine causality and premotion by positing a radically different understanding of the Angelic Doctor's teaching on these issues.[1] Rather than holding to the fundamental thesis that

---

1. Long, "God, Freedom, and the Permission of Evil," 147: "Like Maritain, Lonergan is in

premotion and grace (at least insofar as they are efficacious) are the reduction of a potency to act within the patient, Lonergan posits that no
such reduction is necessary precisely because God moves secondary
causes to their effects by a mere application of spatial proximity, nearness, or *contactus*. Does this solution dispel the myriad of questions and
contentions between the classical and revisionist treatments? Does it adequately represent the thought of St. Thomas? What we hope to show
is twofold: a) that Lonergan has put forth a treatment of divine causality and premotion that is fundamentally at odds with the thought of
St. Thomas and b) that it is metaphysically untenable.

What Is Causation and How Does It
Relate to the Mover?

Lonergan begins by posing a question in regard to how St. Thomas understands causation. He presents three distinct possibilities for how one
might understand causality and how it relates to the cause and the effect,
and consequently, the agent and the patient. Lonergan breaks down the
three possibilities regarding *A* as the cause of *B*:

1) Causality is something in between *A* and *B*.
2) Causality is a relation of dependence of *B* on *A*.
3) Causality is a change in *A* itself, adding something to *A* as cause that
did not exist before it caused.[2]

In regard to the first possibility, Lonergan affirms that St. Thomas
nearly always denied it, especially in regard to divine causality. The rea

---

seraphic discourse with the entirety of the Thomistic tradition. It is arresting to see his responses to
John of St. Thomas, Báñez, Del Prado, Garrigou-Lagrange, and others. However, in his famed *Grace
and Freedom: Operative Grace in the Thought of St. Thomas Aquinas*, he makes several central assertions
that I do not believe survive a sufficient encounter with St. Thomas's texts. The most central of these
is the arresting claim that, according to St. Thomas Aquinas, the motion in the creature from not acting to
acting—and hence derivatively, from not willing to willing—is not a real motion. This proposition that
the motion in the creature from not acting to acting, and hence from *not willing* to *willing*, is *not a real
motion*, is arresting. Indeed, the problem about divine causality and freedom would largely vanish if
the transition from potentially willing to actually willing were not a real motion requiring a real mover
as the condition for our self-motion." See also Long, "St. Thomas Aquinas, Divine Causality, and the
Mystery of Predestination," 67–68.

2. Bernard Lonergan, *Collected Works of Bernard Lonergan*, vol. 1, *Grace and Freedom: Operative
Grace in the Thought of St. Thomas Aquinas*, ed. Frederick E. Crowe and Robert M. Doran (Toronto:
University of Toronto Press, 2000), 67.

soning given is that this activity of causality cannot be understood as a third thing, separate from both the cause and the effect. If that were so, it would have to be either a third, separate substance apart from the cause and the effect, or it would have to be an accident without substance. Lonergan states,

for what is in between, if it is something, must be either substance or accident; but causation as such can hardly be another substance; and if it were an accident, it would have to be either the miracle of an accident without a subject, or else, what St. Thomas denied [*De potentia* q. 3, a. 7], an accident in transit from one subject to another.[3]

In regard to the second possibility, Lonergan states that this was indeed the view of Aristotle in the *Physics*.[4] While it may be true that a terrestrial body undergoes change when it causes (as when it is touched by that which it moves in moving it), it only undergoes change as a terrestrial body. This is accidental to causality as such. There is nothing inherent in causality that requires that the cause as cause is moved by the effect in moving it. Lonergan says,

if causation, *actio*, were an entity inherent in the cause, then, since it is a motion, it would follow either that 'omnes movens movetur,' or else that motion inheres in a subject without the subject being moved; but the latter is contradictory, and the former would preclude the idea of an immovable mover; therefore, causation is not inherent in the cause but in the effect.[5]

Lonergan states that St. Thomas adheres to this Aristotelian view; however, "this is not the whole story."[6] Lonergan quotes two passages from the

3. Lonergan, *Grace and Freedom*, 68.

4. Lonergan, *Grace and Freedom*, 68: "On the second view, causation is simply the relation of dependence in the effect with respect to the cause. This is the Aristotelian position presented in the *Physics*."

5. Lonergan, *Grace and Freedom*, 68.

6. Lonergan, *Grace and Freedom*, 69: "It would seem that St Thomas accepted this Aristotelian analysis as true and did not merely study it as a detached and indifferent commentator. Not only did he repeat the same exposition in commenting the parallel passage in the *Metaphysics* [*XI*, lect. 9, §§ 2308–2313], while in the *De anima* [*III*, lect. 2, § 592] he argued that sound and hearing, instances of action and passion, must be one and the same reality, else every mover would also be moved; but in works that are entirely his own the same view at least occasionally turns up. In the *Summa theologiae* [*I-II*, q. 110, a. 2] the definition of actual grace appeals to the third book of the *Physics* for the doctrine that 'actus ... moventis in moto est motus'; the analysis of the idea of creation [*ST I*, q. 45, a. 2, ad 2] was based upon the Aristotelian identification of action and passion with motion; and the fact that this identification involved no confusion of action with passion was adduced to solve the objection

De potentia[7] that he believes prove that St. Thomas held to the following six propositions:

(*A*) Change from rest to activity is change in an improper and metaphorical sense; (*B*) the reverse of change from activity to rest takes place without any real change in the agent; (*C*) when the agent is acting there is no composition of agent and action; (*D*) what remains unchanged in the *principium* or *causa actionis*; (*E*) what comes and goes without changing the agent is the formal content, *ut ab agente*; (*F*) the analysis holds even in the cause of a created agent such as fire.[8]

Given this, Lonergan states that while St. Thomas sometimes employs the language of Aristotle in regard to causality being attributed to a dependence of *B* on *A*, he also sometimes, as in *De potentia*, employs his own terminology and way of speaking about causality, which is marked by the view that "action is a formal content attributed to the cause as causing."[9] However, according to Lonergan, though these two terminologies

---

against the Blessed Trinity [*ST* I, q. 28, a. 3, ad 1], namely, that since the divine Persons were identical with the divine substance they must be identical with one another. Still, this is not the whole story. In his commentary on the *Sentences* [*Super II Sententiarum*, d. 40, q. 1, a. 4, ad 1] St Thomas brushed aside the notion that action and passion were one and the same reality, while in the parallel passage in the *Summa theologiae* [*ST* I-II, q. 20, a. 6] a solution is found that does not compromise the authority of Aristotle. This difference involves a changed attitude, prior to the *Pars prima* and perhaps posterior to the *De potentia*, raising the question of the initial Thomist view."

7. *De potentia*, q. 7, a. 9, ad 7: "And so a relation is something inhering (in a subject), though that does not result from the mere fact that it is a relation; as action, too, from the fact that it is action, is considered as from an agent, but as an accident it is considered as in the acting subject. And therefore, there is nothing to prevent an accident of this kind (*B*) from ceasing to be without (involving) a change of that (subject) in which it is, because its being is not realized insofar as it is in that subject, but insofar as it passes on to another; with the removal of that (passing on), the being of this accident is removed (*E*) in what regards the act but remains (*D*) in what regards the cause; as is the case also when, with the removal of the material (to be heated), the heating (*F*) is removed, though the cause of heating remains" (taken from Lonergan's translation, including his own notes on the text). *De potentia*, q. 7, a. 8: "But that which is attributed to something as proceeding from it to something else does not enter into composition with it, as (*C*) neither does action (enter into composition) with the agent ... without any change in that which is related to another, a relation can cease to be through the change alone of the other; as also is clear about action (*B*), that there is no movement as regards action except metaphorically and improperly; as we say that (*A*) one passing from leisure to act is changed; which would not be the case if relation or action signified something remaining in the subject" (taken from Lonergan's translation, including his own notes on the text).

8. Lonergan, *Grace and Freedom*, 71.

9. Lonergan, *Grace and Freedom*, 72: "If our interpretation of these passages is correct, then at least in the *De potentia* St Thomas had arrived at a theory of action that was in essential agreement with Aristotle's. Evidently the two terminologies differ completely: on the Aristotelian view action is a relation of dependence in the effect; on the Thomist view action is a formal content attributed to the cause as causing."

are quite distinct, they are entirely compatible, working together toward the same idea that causes are not changed as causes when acting for an effect.

But these differences only serve to emphasize the fundamental identity of the two propositions: both philosophers keenly realized that causation must not be thought to involve any real change in the cause as cause; Aristotle, because he conceived action as a motion, placed it in the effect; St Thomas, who conceived it simply as a formal content, was able to place it in the cause; but though they proceed from different routes, both arrive at the same goal, namely, that the objective difference between *posse agere* and *actu agere* is attained without any change emerging in the cause as such.[10]

The conclusion, surprising as it may seem, that Lonergan derives from this is that there is no real difference between *Peter acting* and *Peter not acting*. "To later Scholastics this seemed impossible a priori: they held that 'Peter not acting' must be really different from 'Peter acting.' They refused to believe that St Thomas could disagree with them on this; in fact, St Thomas disagreed."[11]

So what does Lonergan believe constitutes the application of cause to effect? He rejects that providence governs the universe via God's special divine aid in every motion,[12] a view that he calls "Bannezian."[13] Instead, he posits that providence can be defined as God's role as the "cause of all causes." He states that "the mover moves the moved if the pair are in the right mutual relation, disposition, proximity; the mover does not if any other cause prevents the fulfilment of this condition."[14] To further elucidate this point, let us look at Lonergan's example of the motion of

---

10. Lonergan, *Grace and Freedom*, 72.

See also 90–91: "The fundamental point in the theory of operation is that operation involves no change in the cause as cause. On Thomist analysis it involves a formal content between cause and effect; this is the procession *ut ab agente in aliud procedens*. On Aristotelian analysis it involves a real relation of dependence in the effect. The two analyses are really identical though terminologically different. The consequent difficulty in the terminology is heightened by the large variety of senses in which St Thomas employs the word *actio*."

11. Lonergan, *Grace and Freedom*, 72n26.

12. Lonergan, *Grace and Freedom*, 79: "In this task the first step is to grasp the difference between the views of St Thomas and those of later theologians on the certitude of providence. To the latter, providence was certain in all cases because it was certain in each, because each and every action of the creature required some special divine intervention."

13. Lonergan, *Grace and Freedom*, 78: "Follow the general principles, and the fact that a mover implies a motion in the moved will lead inevitably to a position resembling the Bannezian."

14. Lonergan, *Grace and Freedom*, 79.

the melting of the iceberg, a change that is brought about not by active and passive changes within the mover and moved, respectively, but by the mere fact of their being brought into proximity. He claims, of course, that this is the view of Aristotle.

Finally, while the Bannezian premotion is a metaphysical mystery, the Aristotelian is as plain as a pikestaff. On the latter view an iceberg at the Pole will not be melted by the sun; to have the motion 'melting,' it is necessary to change the relative positions of the sun and the iceberg; and this may be done either by sending the iceberg towards the equator or moving the sun up above the Arctic Circle. Nothing could be simpler or more evident.[15]

Lonergan states that this view of the certitude of providence is thus based on the idea that "both the combinations that result in motion and the interferences that prevent it must ultimately be reduced to God, who is universal cause, and therefore divine providence cannot be frustrated."[16] Divine providence "is an intrinsically certain cause of every combination or interference of terrestrial causes."[17]

Lonergan makes a distinction between providence and fate. Providence is the divine plan within the mind of God, while fate is that divine plan as it unfolds within the universe.[18] Lonergan defines fate, the working of providence within the created order, as the arrangement of secondary causes acting upon one another to bring about the one, unified end of divine providence.

What, then, is fate? It is the order of secondary causes; it is their disposition, arrangement, seriation; it is not a quality, and much less a substance; it is in the category of relation. Together such relations give a single fate for the universe; taken singly, they give the many fates of Virgil's line, "Te tua fata trahunt."[19]

15. Lonergan, *Grace and Freedom*, 75.
16. Lonergan, *Grace and Freedom*, 79.
17. Lonergan, *Grace and Freedom*, 82.
18. Lonergan, *Grace and Freedom*, 85: "The commentary on the *Sentences* points out that God is an intellectual agent and that his knowledge is causal, not because it is knowledge but only inasmuch as it resembles the plan or design or art in the mind of an artisan. Moreover, this divine plan has a twofold existence: primarily it exists in the mind of God, and there it is termed providence; secondarily it exists in the created universe and there it is termed fate [*Super I Sententiarum*, d. 39, q. 2, a. 1, ad 5; d. 38, q. 1, a. 1]."
19. Lonergan, *Grace and Freedom*, 86. He continues: "Application is the causal certitude of providence terminating in the right disposition, relation, proximity between mover and moved: without it motion cannot take place now; with it motion automatically results. But the *intention* is fate, and fate is simply the dynamic pattern of such relations —the pattern through which the design of the divine

As we have seen with the example of the sun and the iceberg, Lonergan rejects the idea that God must move a secondary cause to act. He needs only to place the secondary cause in proximity of some other thing (say, the iceberg) in order for that secondary cause to act upon that object. There is no necessity for a premotion that moves the secondary agent from potentially acting to actually acting, from potentially causing to actually causing. The reason for this is that secondary agents, instrumental causes, are already active beings, capable of acting upon one another. It is quite true that these beings are contingent. They cannot act in any way apart from their being created as things capable of acting upon other things, and even this requires that God uphold them in being, which they can have only from him.

However, the secondary cause requires no subsequent actuation outside of creation, conservation, and alignment, bringing causes and effects together, for it to act.[20] The potency for acting is actuated simply in a

---

artisan unfolds in natural and human history; again, without fate things cannot act, with it they do. Thus, fate and application and instrumental virtue all reduce to the divine plan, and the divergence between Aristotle and St Thomas is a divergence in the conception of God. Aristotle held that God moved all things by being the object of love for the intelligences or the animated spheres; but to St Thomas God was more—a transcendental artisan planning history: 'Deus igitur per suum intellectum omnia movet ad proprios fines [*De subtantiis separatis*, c. 14, § 129].'"

20. For a somewhat similar treatment, see Mark K. Spencer, "Divine Causality and Created Freedom: A Thomistic Personalist View," *Nova et Vetera*, English ed., 14, no. 3 (2016): 919–963. Spencer seems to hold that divine causality causes good human acts via a single priming of the human will, which then allows it to determine itself to any number of subsequent good acts, all of which draw from that primary actuation. As such, each particular good act need not be actuated in the creature via a distinct motion. "God causes my power of will, which is one of my proper accidents, by causing my substance, from which my powers immediately arise, and by bestowing an act of existence upon it. But it is insufficient for my acting that God cause and conserve my will; he must also actualize this power.... having given this primary act, there is no need for God then to move my will toward particular goods. God's premotion to a primary act opens up the possibility of my willing any particular goods. The primary act of the will contains a 'super-abundance' of actuality, for by it I really will all Good. On the basis of this actuality, I am capable of reducing myself to a 'secondary act' of consent, choice, or use in relation to particular goods (or intention of a particular end other than my last end). In any of these secondary acts, God does not need to move me to its exercise or specification insofar as it is a consent to, choice of, or act of use in relation to some particular means to my last end" (944). While this is certainly an intriguing theory that demands much more attention than can be given it here, it will suffice to say for our present project that Spencer's understanding of divine causation is clearly at odds with St. Thomas's. It also opens up all sorts of questions regarding God's governance of the universe. It is unclear in any way how God could maintain providential mastery of the entirety of creation if God is not intimately involved with our particular acts. It seems to end up as a sort of personal deism. Spencer gives a beautiful response to this issue, emphasizing man's ability to act as a Tolkienesque "subcreator." He also states that God retains providential governance over particular actions insofar as he is the source of our particular acts. However, the objection about the severely neutered scope of

thing's *being* as (potentially, depending upon arrangement) active. After quoting a passage from the *Super librum De causis*,[21] Lonergan states: "In this passage the idea of causing causation has its premise in creation-conservation: what causes the substance also causes the active potency; what causes the active potency also causes what the latter causes—indeed, causes the causation itself; for 'hoc ipsum quod causa secunda sit causa effectus habet a causa prima.'"[22]

Lonergan states that St. Thomas's thought underwent some degree of development on this, however, progressing from secondary causality being attributed simply to creation-conservation to something more. In the mature Thomas, Lonergan posits that he has moved from a providence based solely on creation-preservation to one that always relies upon God bringing cause and effect together. To put it another way, it is not enough that God simply cause and uphold a thing in being; he must also order or align it to act upon a patient.

However, if we follow the development of St Thomas' thought on God operating the operation of the creature, we readily observe that, while in the commentary on the *Sentences* and in the *De veritate* St Thomas is ready to remain with the *Liber De causis* and appeal only to creation-conservation.... he began at once [in the *Contra Gentes*] to argue that the creature's causation was caused not merely because of creation and of conservation but also because of application, instrumentality, cosmic hierarchy, and universal finality.[23]

What constitutes this further application is not a movement, a premotion from potency to act, however. It is simply the arrangement of causes and effects according to divine providence. It is God moving the iceberg into the proximity of the sun on account of the fact that he wishes the iceberg to melt. Lonergan states:

Operation in time presupposes a premotion. But this premotion affects indifferently either the mover or the moved. Its function is simply to bring mover and moved in the right relation, mutual disposition, spatial proximity for motion naturally to ensue. When combined with the fact that God is the first mover

---

providence remains since God would not seem to govern over whether I do this or that act. Given the many acting agents in the universe and the great influence that they have upon one another, losing the direct governance of particular acts seems a bit like losing control of the entire created order.

21. Lect. 1, § 24.

22. Lonergan, *Grace and Freedom*, 89.

23. Lonergan, *Grace and Freedom*, 89.

in the cosmic hierarchy and that, as universal cause, God cannot be frustrated, this law of premotion yields the theorem that God applies all agents to their activity.[24]

Lonergan rejects the classical understanding of premotion. He quotes St. Thomas in the *Summa theologiae*, who states: "Hence no matter how perfectly fire has heat, it would not bring about alteration, except by the motion of the heavenly body.... And hence no matter how perfect a corporeal or spiritual nature is supposed to be, it cannot proceed to its act unless it be moved by God."[25] To this passage, Lonergan responds, "It is difficult to suppose that further perfection is added to what is as perfect as you please, it is absurd to fancy the substance 'fire' given every actuation conceivable and yet needing two further actuations, once from the spheres and still another from God."[26]

As such, Lonergan concludes that "operation involves no change in the cause as cause,"[27] with God's providence not stemming from actuating a potency belonging to a potential cause *to act*, but instead from creating and preserving beings that are fit to act of their very nature and with no dependence on extrinsic actuation but only on proximity or alignment. He then subsequently moves them by a premotion that is not internal, but merely provides an external alignment, propinquity, or *contactus*, bringing created things into the proper proximity to do what they do.

The sun heats. God has made it so, and he preserves it in being. In order to melt the iceberg, he needs only to bring the iceberg and the sun together. Finally, this allows Lonergan to claim that there is no difference between *Peter acting* and *Peter not acting*, because God's governance over secondary causes in no way presupposes any change or movement in a mover. Similarly, there is no change in the sun when it is melting or not melting something. It produces heat. If the iceberg gets close enough, it will be affected by this heat and it will melt.

24. Lonergan, *Grace and Freedom*, 91.
25. *ST I-II*, q. 109, a. 1.
26. Lonergan, *Grace and Freedom*, 90.
27. Lonergan, *Grace and Freedom*, 90: "The fundamental point in the theory of operation is that operation involves no change in the cause as cause. On the Thomist analysis it involves a formal content between cause and effect; this is the procession, *ut ab agente aliud procedens*."

Analysis

The central point of Lonergan's view on causality is based on the idea that there is no change in the cause as cause when it moves and brings about an effect. *Peter acting* is the same as *Peter not acting*. But Lonergan appears to be saying something much more than that there is no *substantial* difference between *Peter acting* and *Peter not acting*. It is true that Lonergan does not state that "there is no change in the cause while operating" *simpliciter*. He states that there is "no change in the causes *as cause*."[28] It would appear, however, that Lonergan means that there is no *internal* change *in* the mover, substantial or even accidental (though there is an external, accidental alignment or proximity).

An actuation that is described as a movement of reducing a mover from potentially acting to actually acting is (as we have seen in the traditional and even, to some extent, in the revisionist treatment) an internal movement (from an external source), especially in regard to volitional creatures, since they are moved *to will*. For Lonergan, such a movement is far from necessary and is in fact seemingly redundant; according to Lonergan, it is "absurd" to consider that the perfect fire might require a further actuation from God to heat a piece of meat. Lonergan's conception of providence, or more accurately, fate, rests upon "right relation, mutual disposition, spatial proximity," and as such, "this premotion affects indifferently either the mover or the moved."[29] When Lonergan says that "operation involves no change in the cause *as cause*," he is clearly ruling out both substantial change as well as internal accidental change. The only possible cause or difference in the mover would be something akin to the predicamental of πού, that is, location or place. This category is an accidental that is *external* to a thing since it is only in relation to those things outside of a thing that gives it a place or location. Of course, this not to say that Lonergan's premotion is merely a physical change in location, though it may sometimes be that (as in the fire and meat being arranged via "spatial proximity" such that the fire actually cooks the

---

28. However, there is no such qualification in n. 26 regarding *Peter acting* and *Peter not acting*. Lonergan does not explicitly address what he means by these lines in regard to substantial or accidental change. Stating that "operating involves no change in the cause as cause" may imply *substantial* change, but it may also actually deny any change in the mover whatsoever. Emphasis in quotation is mine.

29. Lonergan, *Grace and Freedom*, 91.

meat).[30] However, it is an external, accidental characteristic like location, analogous to it, insofar as Lonergan's premotion is nothing more than giving a certain nearness or intimacy or *contactus* to the mover in regard to the moved, as Steven Long has stated.[31] It does not do anything to the mover internally, and this is why Lonergan says that there is no change in the mover and that premotion affects it indifferently.

Thus, this movement of external disposition seems to be the only change effected by Lonergan's premotion, and since this is nothing internal, he can state that there is no change in the mover between acting and not acting. Nothing changes in Peter when he ceases to be in the state of nonact and enters into a state of action other than that he is now within proximity of something that God wills him to act upon. It cannot in any way be denied that this is Lonergan's formulation. It is Lonergan himself who describes his premotion explicitly and wholly as "right relation, mutual disposition, spatial proximity."

It is quite true to state that there is no *substantial* change in Peter when he acts.[32] Peter remains Peter whether he now causes the effect of John laughing or he does not.[33] However, it would appear that there is

30. It's important to note here that while it is true in regard to the act of cooking that applying meat to an already burning fire is indeed a question of spatial proximity, it is not *just* that. All things that are not God that are in act and are now acting as a cause must be moved from potency to act, from potentially causing to actually causing. Even within this same passage from *ST* I-II q. 109, a. 1, St. Thomas continues, "the act of the intellect or of any created being whatsoever depends upon God in two ways: first, inasmuch as it is from Him that it has the form whereby it acts; secondly, inasmuch as it is *moved by Him to act*" ("actio intellectus, et cuiuscumque entis creati, dependet a Deo quantum ad duo, uno modo, inquantum ab ipso habet formam per quam agit; alio modo, inquantum *ab ipso movetur ad agendum*"). Emphasis is mine.

31. Long, "God, Freedom, and the Permission of Evil," 149: "Rather than premotion accounting for tha ttainment of the dignity of agency, for Lonergan premotion accounts merely for patient or agent being in causal *proximity*. Rather than seeing that the finite agent must be moved from potency to act by God in order to act, Lonergan thinks of agents as just *in act* and of the divine motion as moving creatures in proximity to one another."

32. Steven Long, "St. Thomas Aquinas, Divine Causality, and the Mystery of Predestination," 71: "It might be thought that Lonergan's claim that 'Peter acting' is not really different from 'Peter not acting' is meant only to distinguish substance from accident. Then the meaning would be: the substance of Peter is not altered by the accident of Peter's acting. However, (1) this is not what the proposition as it stands actually affirms; (2) if this is what Lonergan meant, it does not redress the problem, which is that Lonergan does not explain how the thing that is not its own agency is moved to achieve the dignity of agency."

33. Matthew Lamb, "The Mystery of Divine Predestination: Its Intelligibility According to Bernard Lonergan," in *Thomism and Predestination: Principles and Disputations*, ed. Steven A. Long, Roger W. Nutt, and Thomas Joseph White, OP (Ave Maria, Fla.: Sapientia Press, 2016), 214–225, 216: "So Peter decides to drive or walk to the town. He actuates the active potency of his will and the

not just a change of location in Peter when he acts, but an internal accidental change from not acting to acting, pertaining at least to the category
of ποιόν, or quality.[34]

It is precisely in the fact that there is no substantial change between
Peter acting and *Peter not acting* that we recognize the truth that Peter is
not the source of his own action. That he acts is not necessary simply
because he is. Peter's action is contingent, not just upon his being created
and preserved, but also upon his being moved from potentially acting to
actually acting since he is not *Actus Purus* nor of himself simply in act.
Consequently, it seems decidedly true, as Steven Long has stated,[35] that
since Peter does not of himself have his own act *even after creation*, he
must be moved from potentially causing to actually causing by something
that is already in action. That this is the thought of St. Thomas is clear
from St. Thomas's first argument for the existence of God.

Now whatever is in motion is put in motion by another, for nothing can be in
motion except it is in potentiality to that towards which it is in motion; whereas

---

passive potency of the car or his legs to walk. One and the same act actuates both potencies, and this
action is the motion produced in the object moved, for example, the car or his legs (the effect). That
the cause as cause (Peter) is not changed is clear in the fact that on the way he can change his mind
and not go; he remains free to act or not to act."

34. Also, the categories of ποιεῖν and πάσχειν, action and affection or passion, respectively. The
classical conception of premotion requires a change in the accidental quality of the mover from not
acting to acting, a change that is received passively (πάσχειν) and that results in the mover acting upon
something else (ποιεῖν).

35. Long, "God, Freedom, and the Permission of Evil," 147–48: "In the same chapter of that work,
Lonergan notes that causing is not something real in the agent causing, but exists rather in the effect
or at most in the relation between or nexus of agent and effect. He responds to the proposition that
everything must move from potency to act in order to cause by observing that were this true that then
there could be no First Cause. Of course, precisely as stated, *this is true. That is, to causing as such potency is not essential.* Otherwise it would be impossible that God—Who is Pure Act and in Whom there
is no potency whatsoever—cause anything at all. Every agency is, as such, *act.* Thus agency, as such,
does not make reference to any transition from potency to act, because it is accidental to agency *as
such* that it be related to potentiality, which is what the texts from St. Thomas that Lonergan adduces
suffice to show. Yes, although it is accidental to *agency* as such, and to the agent *qua agent*, that it pass
from potency to act with respect to acting—because God is the First Cause and there is no potency
in Him, and because agency is agency and the definition of agency makes no necessary reference to
potency—nonetheless, *it is not accidental to the being that acts* that it is *not Pure Act*, and so likewise *it
is not accidental that the finite agent is not identical with its operation, not purely an agent. Consequently,*
it is not accidental to the finite agent *as* finite agent that, for *it* to act, it must pass from potency to act.
Even angelic knowers require divinely infused species to actuate their knowing. Moreover, the human
subject is not always an agent in act—it is not always causing—and in particular, the human agent is
not *always choosing.* Granted that there is nothing about *acting as such* that requires potency, a *finite
subject that acts is not its agency*; it is really distinct from its agency. *Thus, the finite subject needs to be
moved from potency to act in order to attain to the dignity of acting.*" See also Long, "St. Thomas Aquinas,
Divine Causality, and the Mystery of Predestination," 68–71.

a thing moves inasmuch as it is in act. For motion is nothing else than the reduction of something from potentiality to actuality. But nothing can be reduced
from potentiality to actuality, except by something in a state of actuality. Thus
that which is actually hot, as fire, makes wood, which is potentially hot, to be
actually hot, and thereby moves and changes it. Now it is not possible that the
same thing should be at once in actuality and potentiality in the same respect,
but only in different respects. For what is actually hot cannot simultaneously be
potentially hot; but it is simultaneously potentially cold. It is therefore impossible that in the same respect and in the same way a thing should be both mover
and moved, i.e. that it should move itself. Therefore, whatever is in motion must
be put in motion by another.[36]

Of course, this cannot go on to infinity, and thus St. Thomas posits
the existence of a First Mover, that is, one who is his own act, one who
is not contingent upon something in motion for his motion but who is
his own source of motion. However, since Peter is not God, that Peter
acts requires that he be moved to act by another. Therefore, while it is
certainly true that causal agency as such requires no change from potency
to act (as is the case with God), it is also true that it *may*, as would be the
case if the causal agent were not pure act. Since Peter is not pure act, it is
completely incorrect to state that there is not a difference between Peter
acting and *not acting*.[37]

---

36. *ST I*, q. 2, a. 3. See also *ST I-II*, q. 9, a. 1: "I answer that, a thing requires to be moved by
something in so far as it is in potentiality to several things; for that which is in potentiality needs to be
reduced to act by something actual; and to do this is to move."

37. Steven A. Long, "St. Thomas Aquinas, Divine Causality, and the Mystery of Predestination,"
68–70: "In the same chapter of that work, Lonergan notes that causing is not something real in the
agent causing, but exists rather in the effect, or at most in the relation between or nexus of agent and
effect. He responds to the proposition that everything must move from potency to act in order to
cause, by observing that were this true, then there could be no First Cause. Precisely as stated, this
proposition of Lonergan's is true. With respect to causing as such, potency is not essential. Otherwise,
it would be impossible for God—who is Pure Act and in whom there is no potency whatsoever—to
be the First Cause. Every agency is, as such, act. Thus agency as such does not make any reference to
transition from potency to act, because it is accidental to agency as such that it be related to potentiality, which is what the texts from St. Thomas that Lonergan adduces suffice to show. However, although
it is accidental to agency as such, and to the agent qua agent, that it pass from potency to act with
respect to acting—because God is the First Cause and there is no potency in him, and because agency
is agency and the definition of agency makes no necessary reference to potency—nonetheless, it is
not accidental to the created being that acts that it is not Pure Act, and so likewise it is not accidental
that the finite agent is not identical with its operation, not purely an agent. Consequently, it is not
accidental to the finite agent as finite agent that for it to act, it must pass from potency to act.... But
this account fails to acknowledge that what necessitates divine 'premotion' is that the finite subject of
agency is not simply of itself in act and so needs to be moved to act. The creature is not its own being,
nature, or operation, and thus it is not accidental that it must be moved by God from potency to act

Moreover, St. Thomas does not describe this motion of the created causal agent as a mere external change in proximity to effects but as "nothing else than the reduction of something from potentiality to actuality," that is, *educere aliquid de potentia in actum*. Such a change is indeed *in* the mover. St. Thomas, Báñez, Garrigou, Nicolas, and even to some degree Marín-Sola and Maritain all affirm that the creature must be divinely moved from potency to act in order to act as a causal agent. Lonergan has thus placed himself completely outside of the general Thomistic tradition in this regard, even with its disagreements regarding the nature of premotion. The creature is truly moved from not acting to acting. This negates that premotion is, at most, an accidental change of location, proximity, or external disposition and thus that it is not really a change in the mover. It is indeed a change in the mover. Therefore, there is, of course, truly a difference between Peter acting and Peter not acting. In the former, Peter is in act; in the latter, he is not.

St. Thomas is perfectly clear in this regard. He states that "nothing can be reduced from potentiality to actuality, except by something in a state of actuality."[38] But since nothing is the source of its own act except God, all movements from potency to act require the power of God. St. Thomas says:

Moreover, whatever agent applies active power to the doing of something, it is said to be the cause of that action. Thus, an artisan who applies the power of a natural thing to some action is said to be the cause of the action; for instance, a cook of the cooking which is done by means of fire. But every application of power to operation is originally and primarily made by God. For operative powers are applied to their proper operations by some movement of body or of soul. Now, the first principle of both types of movement is God. Indeed, He is the first mover and is altogether incapable of being moved, as we shown above. Similarly, also, every movement of a will whereby Powers are applied to operation is reduced to God, as a first object of appetite and a first agent of willing. Therefore; every operation should be attributed to God, as to a first and principal agent. Furthermore, in all agent causes arranged in an orderly way the subsequent causes must act through the power of the first cause. For instance, in the natural order of things, lower bodies act through the power of the celestial bodies; and, again, in the order of voluntary things, all lower artisans work in accord with the direc-

---

with respect to its own agency: for example, in willing, man must be moved by God from potency to act with respect to his own self-determination in freedom."

38. *ST* I, q. 2, ad 3.

tion of the top craftsman. Now, in the order of agent causes, God the first cause, as we showed in Book One [64]. And so, all lower agent causes act through His power. But the cause of an action is the one by whose power the action is done rather than the one who acts: the principal agent, for instance, rather than the instrument. Therefore, God is more especially the cause of every action than are the secondary agent causes.... So, we have to say that every agent acts by the divine power. Therefore, He is the One Who is the cause of action for all things.[39]

It is clear that *every single motion*, which is an actuation of some potency, a reduction of potency to act, is caused first and foremost by God working within the created cause. "God moves man to act, not only by proposing the appetible to the senses, or by effecting a change in his body, but also by *moving the will itself;* because *every movement* either of the will or of nature, proceeds from God as the First Mover."[40] The will is not able *to will* unless God actuates its potency, giving it the act whereby it acts. "When anything moves itself, this does not exclude its being moved by another, *from which it has even this that it moves itself.*"[41]

Peter really does act when he hits a baseball or helps a friend out of an icy river.[42] However, Peter is not the source of his own action. Peter is contingent upon God for whatever actuality that he is able to exercise. And so, before swinging the bat to hit the baseball or before using his arms and legs to leap into the water and save his friend, Peter is only in potency in regard to these actions. Peter's will does indeed will these movements, but as St. Thomas says, the movement of Peter's will (every movement) depends on God effecting a change or moving the will to move itself. Peter's will was in potency in regard to willing but after God

39. *ScG* III, 67, 4–6. See also *ScG* III, 70, 5: "But the power of a lower agent depends on the power of the superior agent, according as the superior agent gives this power to the lower agent whereby it may act; or preserves it; or even applies the action, as the artisan applies an instrument to its proper effect."

40. *ST* I-II, q. 6, a. 1, ad 3: "Ad tertium dicendum quod Deus movet hominem ad agendum non solum sicut proponens sensui appetibile, vel sicut immutans corpus, sed etiam sicut *movens ipsam voluntatem*, quia *omnis motus* tam voluntatis quam naturae, ab eo procedit sicut a primo movente." Emphasis is mine.

41. *De malo*, q. 3, a. 2, ad 4.

42. *ST* I-II, q. 6, a. 1, ad 3: "And just as it is not incompatible with nature that the natural movement be from God as the First Mover, inasmuch as nature is an instrument of God moving it: so it is not contrary to the essence of a voluntary act, that it proceed from God, inasmuch as the will is moved by God. Nevertheless both natural and voluntary movements have this in common, that it is essential that they should proceed from a principle within the agent."

actuates that potency it actually wills and accomplishes the aforementioned good actions.

Moreover, that this is the view of St. Thomas regarding operation is made explicit in both his commentary on the *Physics* and the *Metaphysics*. In the *Physics*, St. Thomas affirms that in the moved there is a distinction between potency and act, between being potentially mobile and actually being moved. But this same distinction between potency and act applies to the mover as well.

> Now just as that which is moved is called "mobile" in potency since it is capable of being moved, and is called "moved" according to act inasmuch it is actually being moved, so on the part of the mover, a mover is described "potential mover" inasmuch as it is able to move, and "moves" in the act inasmuch as it actually acts. Therefore some act is competent to both, i.e., to mover and to mobile.[43]

Similarly in his commentary on the *Metaphysics*, St. Thomas agrees with Aristotle regarding "how motion is related to a mover" that "motion is the actuality of what is capable of causing motion, and that the actuality of the thing capable of causing motion and that of the thing moved do not differ, for motion must be the actuality of both." He continues:

> Third, he proves the first of these two points, namely, that motion is the actuality of what is capable of causing motion. For the actuality of a thing is that by which it becomes actual. But a thing is said to be capable of causing motion because of its power of moving, and it is said to be a mover because of its activity, i.e., because it is actual. Hence, since a thing is said to be a mover because of motion, motion will be the actuality of what is capable of causing motion.[44]

A distinction is made between having the power of moving and actually moving. A thing only has a power insofar as it is actual. We may state that a mover receives a potency for certain motions by its very nature in creation, however, that it be moved from potentially moving, capable of moving, to actually moving requires a further actuation, and this must come from something that is already in act. And yet this is denied by Lonergan.

Let us return again to the example of fire employed by Lonergan. Whether we are speaking of the simple campfire or the magnificent burning fire of the sun, it is true that the fire acts to burn from the first moment

43. Aquinas, *Commentary on Aristotle's Physics*, bk. III, lect. 4, § 305.
44. Aquinas, *Commentary on Aristotle's Metaphysics*, bk. XI, lect. 9, §§ 2309–2310.

of its existence. However, Lonergan wishes to apply these principles of operation and its relation to the mover to human willing, premotion, and ultimately grace and predestination. But these examples of fire do not suffice to explain the action of a volitional creature. It may be true that the fire requires only a spatial proximity to the meat in order to cook it (even though it burns only because God constantly causes it to actually burn), however, it cannot be the case that a human will requires only a certain external disposition to an effect to bring about that effect, as if it were like the fire that is always acting to heat whatever is near it.[45]

The human will is a product of the intellect. No object moves the intellect and the will with necessity other than goodness itself, perfect goodness and happiness being found in union with God. Lesser objects do not move the will with necessity, as St. Thomas says.

> Wherefore if the will be offered an object which is good universally and from every point of view, the will tends to it of necessity, if it wills anything at all; since it cannot will the opposite. If, on the other hand, the will is offered an object that is not good from every point of view, it will not tend to it of necessity. And since lack of any good whatever, is a non-good, consequently, that good alone which is perfect and lacking in nothing, is such a good that the will cannot not-will it: and this is Happiness. Whereas any other particular goods, in so far as they are lacking in some good, can be regarded as non-goods: and from this point of view, they can be set aside or approved by the will, which can tend to one and the same thing from various points of view.[46]

Men are often presented with a certain object and do not act upon it. They deliberate about a certain good and may either set it aside or approve it, working toward achieving it or creating some effect. But this implies something more than mere external disposition or proximity between the human will and a certain effect or thing moved. The human will does not act with the necessity of the fire in heating the meat, but may or may not regard a certain object. One man wills a certain good and

---

45. Though it ought to be noted that even the fire, insofar as it is not acting of itself, is in fact receiving its act from something already in act. Thus it must be moved from potency to act before it can begin to act by heating. Steven Long says of the fire of the sun, "Lonergan famously comments that for the motion of melting, one need only change the relative positions of the sun and the iceberg. If we presuppose the heat of the sun, this is true, but the heat of the sun presupposes innumerable gaseous explosions and other real motions, without which it would not be an agent of heating—it must be moved from potency to act with respect to that in virtue of which it is an agent of heating. "St. Thomas Aquinas, Divine Causality, and the Mystery of Predestination," 71.

46. ST I-II, q. 10, a. 3.

another one does not. How does God govern over the actions of men and thus the entire created order if he does not bring about that each man freely and contingently acts to will that which God would have him freely and contingently will?[47] If man is not compelled to act by an object, and often disregards it, we must affirm that man has the potency to bring about some effect, but that he actually does so implies something more. Both men thinking of pursuing a treasure have a potency for actually searching for it. The difference between the one who searches and the one who does not is that the former has that potency reduced to act. And this is why St. Thomas affirms that for a mover to act, it must be moved from potentially acting to actually acting, from potentially exerting some motion upon the moved to moving it.

It would appear that to state that there is no change between *Peter acting* and *Peter not acting* would be false. It is certainly true that there is no *substantial* change in Peter but there is certainly the accidental change that brings about Peter's motion to act, ultimately causing an effect. Peter must be moved by something already in motion to move from being potentially mobile to moving. He must be moved from potentially acting to actually acting, and this change is something internal. Peter not acting is Peter at rest in regard to a certain effect or patient. We know Peter (accidentally) as either the cause of some effect or not the cause of that effect.

It is not sufficient to say that Peter will indeed act if only he is brought into proximity with a given effect. Oftentimes Peter does not act, even when in proximity (spatial, intellectual, etc.) with a given object. Humans sometimes deliberate about a given act for hours, days, perhaps even years. They have every possibility of moving toward the object and have a true disposition or proximity toward it, but they do not act. As such, man does not act simply by his nature, by his being created and preserved as a man and then being moved such that an effect is within his range of activity. It is in his humanity that he has the potency to act, but *that he act* in any given situation at any given time requires that there be the internal

47. ST I-II, q. 10, a. 4: "I answer that, As Dionysius says (*Div. Nom.* iv) 'it belongs to Divine providence, not to destroy but to preserve the nature of things.' Wherefore it moves all things in accordance with their conditions; so that from necessary causes through the Divine motion, effects follow of necessity; but from contingent causes, effects follow contingently. Since, therefore, the will is an active principle, not determinate to one thing, but having an indifferent relation to many things, God so moves it, that He does not determine it of necessity to one thing, but its movement remains contingent and not necessary, except in those things to which it is moved naturally."

change from potency to act, which is to say nothing more and nothing less than to affirm the classical Thomistic view of physical premotion.[48]

To apply this to the First Mover, it is of course true that there is no change in God when he moves another, but this is precisely because he is his own act. He is pure act. There is no difference in God between God moving Peter and God not moving Peter, because Peter exerts no influence on one who is pure act, nor could one who is pure act be in any way contingent upon another or be subject to accidental qualities. God is identical with his simple will, but not with the objects that he wills.[49] However, even in the case of God it would remain true that there would certainly be a difference *in God* between *God acting* and *God not acting* (though this would be an absurdity, since then God would cease to be God). Pure act cannot *not* be.

Lonergan's reworking of physical premotion itself might be tempting for those who wish to negate the difficulties of the Báñezian position. If God does not reduce the potencies of each particular creaturely action to act, then we may distance divine causality and providence from implication in sin. God does not antecedently *not give* the actuation of some power to do good; he simply brings the mover and moved together. Thus, the mover can act according to its nature such that any defect is not governed by providence in any particular or exhaustive way. Things act as they will while God merely provides proximity for such action. However, such a view is metaphysically untenable and also suffers from the same providential limitations of the other revisionist treatment.

---

48. Oderberg, "Divine Premotion," 221: "We should believe in physical premotion precisely for the reason already suggested: there is no sense to be made of divine instrumental causation without it, just as there is no sense to be made of any lower instrumental causation. Some transient power must be passively received by the instrument if it is to be applied as an instrument, moving it to act. Premotionism is not merely the view that there is such a power: that there is such a power is how premotionism explains the way in which God moves all of creation, and it is the view that God does move all of creation that constitutes premotionism proper, setting believers in exceptionless divine instrumental causation apart from occasionalists, mere conservationists, and Molinists."

49. Long, "St. Thomas Aquinas, Divine Causality, and the Mystery of Predestination," 60: "Metaphysically, the only difference between God causing X, and God not causing X, is not a change *in God*, but rather *the being of the creature*. This is a simple function of the truth that the divine perfection is not limited by any potency whatsoever; it is Pure Act."

CHAPTER NINE

Some Considerations regarding the Dissymmetry between the Lines of Good and Evil

As we have seen, much of the intra-Thomistic debate in recent years has centered on questions and concerns regarding God's governance over evil. In regard to election and the achievement of our supernatural end, there appears to be some considerable agreement within the tradition. Maritain's superelect are moved by infallibly efficacious grace rather than shatterable motions. Marín-Sola holds that final perseverance is effected via infallibly efficacious grace rather than an impedible motion of grace. The anxiety regarding the classical Thomistic treatment clearly stems, however, from concern over God not impeding sin. The classical Thomistic analysis supports a comprehensive, all-encompassing notion of divine providence. Everything that happens is contingent upon God's control and governance of the universe. The proposed solution of the Thomistic revisionists is, generally, a schema wherein God's providential ordering of good is at least attempted to be left largely intact, but his providential governance of evil is rendered contingent at best, and made utterly impotent at worst. Let us consider some of the mysteries surrounding the dissymmetry between good and evil, particularly the enigma that is the presence of sin in a world governed down to the last hair upon the head of each man, a world where a sparrow does not "fall to the ground without your heavenly Father's will."[1]

---

1. Mt 10:29–30: "Are not sparrows sold two for a penny? And yet it is impossible for one of them

276

The Prevention of Evil and the Divine Innocence

As we have seen, in order to deny the errors of Pelagianism and semi-Pelagianism, even Maritain and Marín-Sola affirm that the order of the good involves infallible movements on the behalf of God to account for what is good in man. Indeed, even the congruism[2] of St. Bellarmine or Suárez, insofar as it retains the principle of predilection, tends to state that election is *ante praevisa merita*.[3] Among these varying accounts and that of classical Thomism there is some general but substantial agreement regarding the line of good and God's causality of salutary acts. However, the criticisms of the antecedent permissive decree or that every grace is infallibly efficacious for something do not shield these other accounts from the very objections that they make against the classical schema. In other words, one is left wondering why if God can and sometimes does give unshatterable motions, or governs by special infallible providence, or chooses this man to sustain in final perseverance via infallibly efficacious grace, (or in the case of congruism, arranges circumstances perfectly for

---

to fall to the ground without your heavenly Father's will. And as for you, he takes every hair of your head into his reckoning."

2. Briefly, congruism is a derivation of Molinism with a strong account of the principle of predilection. God elects some and reprobates others *ante praevisa merita*, but the mode of executing this divine plan is by manipulating the circumstances of creation via *scientia media* so as to bring about merit and final perseverance in those whom God has predestined. They are not moved via direct, infallibly efficacious grace, however, since this would be seen to exterminate human freedom. See W. McDonald, "Congruism," in *The Catholic Encyclopedia* (New York: Robert Appleton Company, 1908), and Garrigou, *Predestination*, 153–67. See also Hardon, *History and Theology of Grace*, 273, 275–76: "The essence of strict Molinism is that efficacious grace is not given *as* efficacious, i.e., in order that a good act might be performed, but grace is conferred *which* God foresees to be efficacious. Congruism, on the other hand, declares that efficacious grace is given *qua* efficacious, that is, in order that a salutary act be placed.... Thus conceived, the difference between efficacious and sufficient grace depends not only on the will of man, but also on the will of God. He gives not only the grace which He knows to be efficacious, but *because* He foresees it will be efficacious. His selective choice of congruous graces, conferred under conditions so favorable to their efficacy that He knows we shall cooperate, vindicates the divine sovereignty over His creatures and guarantees the absolute dependence on His will which is the hallmark of Christianity."

3. Garrigou, *Predestination*, 153–54: "The absolute gratuity of predestination to glory is distinctly the teaching of St. Bellarmine [*De gratia et libero arbitrio*, bk. II, chaps. 9–15]. His purpose is to prove, like the Thomists and Augustinians, by means of Scripture, tradition, and theological reasoning, the proposition that no reason can be assigned on our part for the divine predestination, which means that predestination to glory is absolutely gratuitous, or previous to foreseen merits." Also, 157–158: "We see that on this point of the absolute gratuity of predestination to glory there is a considerable difference between the congruism of Suarez and of Bellarmine, and the Molinism such as especially Vasquez, Lessius, and the majority of Molinsts understood it to mean." And 160: "In this theory the principle of predilection is certainly much better safeguarded than in Molinism."

the elect), why does he not do so with those who fall? In all of the above scenarios, it is well within God's power to move each man to his supernatural end infallibly, and yet he does not do so.

This applies to any schema or view within Christianity that posits the principle of predilection in any way, that is, posits that God exercises determining power of any kind over who is numbered among the elect and who is not. Any variants of the Dominican Thomistic treatment that posit the principle of predilection, such as those of Marín-Sola and Maritain, and indeed even all of those within the camp of Molinism and congruism that posit it, cannot escape the inherent mystery of why God chooses one rather than another. Either God has the ability to arrange it such that all can be saved or he does not. Either God has power over evil or he does not. The mode by which the meritorious acts arise here do not matter, simply the fact that God could have arranged or caused things to be otherwise. Why is it that Peter is the one moved or arranged to execute good actions while Judas is not? Why was it not the other way around? Alfred J. Freddoso, a commentator on the writings of Molina, sums up this point quite well:

> It is God, after all, who grants the grace that by His middle knowledge He knows with certainty will be efficacious for Peter's acting virtuously. So it is God who gratuitously singles Peter out by arranging things in such a way that Peter will freely act well. By the same token, God permits Judas to sin by allowing him to be so situated that, as God knows via middle knowledge, he will freely sin. That God should so favor Peter over Judas is just as much a mystery on the Molinist scheme as on the Báñezian. And although this is a mystery many feel deeply disturbed by (the doctrine of predestination lurks in the background, of course), it is nonetheless one that is deeply rooted in Sacred Scripture and in the teachings and theological tradition of the Church.[4]

On the Dominican side of things, Maritain states that it is fitting for God to move fallible creatures fallibly. Though we disagree with this statement given the comprehensive nature of providence and the divine simplicity, the fact remains that even according to Maritain's account, this is not necessary. Maritain does not state that his superelect, those moved by unshatterable motions, are somehow plundered of their liberty. Why does God not give unshatterable motions to all? Why not ensure that all

---

4. Freddoso's commentary in Molina, *On Divine Foreknowledge*, 66.

men are saved? Why risk giving shatterable motions in the first place? It is true that failure can be a fitting tool for effecting humility, but especially in regard to those who will be lost forever, why would God provide even the opportunity for failure?

If nonimpedible motions, special providence, infallibly efficacious grace, and the like do not hinder human freedom, then it is not *necessary* that God move humans according to less potent motions. And yet, according to the revisionist Thomists (including Marín-Sola, Maritain, the later Nicolas, and Lonergan), he does. It is unclear how this would not spark the same objections to the divine innocence that Maritain poses to the classical treatment. In both cases, God could do more. In both cases, God could effect universal salvation. In both cases, God could make it certain that this man *and another* (instead of this man *rather than another*) are saved. What is the substantial difference in regard to final outcomes between, on the one hand, God moving one man via efficacious grace and permitting another to fall into defect and, on the other hand, God moving one man via an unshatterable motion and leaving another to the possibility of eternal loss and death via shatterable motions?

In this way, we see that election that is *ante praevisa merita*, that is, the providing of what is necessary for salvation as the cause of salvation, something which man requires from God apart from his own power, is something that is at least nominally held by the general revisionist account. And yet there is no way this can be posited without asserting that when God separates the sheep from the goats, things in some sense *could* have been otherwise. That things could have been otherwise falls primarily on the divine causality. All of the questions of the divine innocence resurface.

The mystery of the presence of evil has not been lessened by any of these revisions. The answer lies not in positing shatterable or impedible motions. Why not replace all of these with motions that assure the cooperation of the creature, since God can and does use such motions? The answer lies instead in our concurrence with St. Thomas that the attainment of our supernatural end is gratuitous. It is not owed to us. Indeed, God gives more good than we are owed already. And yet, we are defectible creatures, prone to fall whenever and wherever we are separated from the efficacy of God's aid working within us. Let us remember that St. Thomas states:

Yet why He chooses some for glory, and reprobates others, has no reason, except the divine will. Neither on this account can there be said to be injustice in God, if He prepares unequal lots for not unequal things. This would be altogether contrary to the notion of justice, if the effect of predestination were granted as a debt, and not gratuitously. In things which are given gratuitously, a person can give more or less, just as he pleases (provided he deprives nobody of his due), without any infringement of justice. This is what the master of the house said: "Take what is thine, and go thy way. Is it not lawful for me to do what I will? [Matt 20: 14–15]"[5]

This is why Fr. Brian Davies writes:

To say that God is guilty of neglect is to say that there is something he ought to have done but has not—it is to hold him morally accountable. One might say that just as the captain of a ship has a duty to ensure that his vessel does not run aground, so God has a duty to ensure that his free creatures commit no sin. The analogy, however, does not hold. The captain of a ship is a part of a world in which individuals can be held accountable given their place in it. God, on the other hand, is no such individual. It is a sea captain's job to keep his vessel afloat, but how can we suppose that it is God's job to keep us from acting wrongly? ... You might insist that when it comes to evil done there is an absence that ought not to be there. We would surely be mistaken, however, if we expressed this thought by saying that God ought to have made more goodness than he has. To say that would effectively be to say that God is under an obligation to create—for as goods in the world come about they only do so as made to be (as created) by God. That claim certainly does not square with traditional talk about God. This views God's act of creating as gratuitous.[6]

It would seem that God permits that some men do indeed fall without returning to God's habitual grace and meriting eternal life. God permits that some men will reject him for all eternity when he could make all men saints. This is indeed a mystery. But who will call God to account for his providential ordering of the universe? "What shall we say then? Is there injustice in God?"[7] God is omnibenevolent. We creatures, veiled from the divine will as wayfarers, cannot know the exact reasons why God seemingly has not deemed all men to be saved. What we know of God suffices for us to surrender to this mystery, trusting in the fact that God has willed a universe with perdition because, in some way unseen by us, this is the

---

5. *ST* I, q. 23, a. 5, ad 3.
6. Davies, *Reality of God and the Problem of Evil*, 191.
7. Rom 9:14.

universe that brings about the greater good, that is more loved by God. Unless one wishes to explicitly posit that man distinguishes himself, that God is impotent in saving those who would be lost, and that he has no control over sin but is in some way controlled by it, one is required to commit oneself to the divine wisdom. Beyond this, there cannot be further probing or enquiry, but only trust.

Negative Reprobation

We ought to agree with Garrigou that anywhere in the tradition where reprobation is spoken about as a positive influence, or as a causal exclusion, it ought to be vehemently rejected. Such a view, if it does arise within the tradition, is certainly not constitutive of it. As we have seen, there appears to be no basis for it even in the greatest specter of the so-called rigid, commentatorial tradition himself, Domingo Báñez.

Reprobation is not anything positive; it is not anything within the reprobate. It exerts no positive influence. It is not a positive exclusion in the way that election is a positive inclusion. It is not a physical cause, nor is it a moral cause of the evil of the reprobate. It is a nonact, a nothing, a not-giving of something gratuitous, that is, upholding the creature from rejecting God and dying in such a state. The only thing that God ever invests in the creature is goodness and being.[8] Indeed, the book of Wisdom tells us that "God did not make death, nor does he rejoice in the destruction of the living. For he fashioned all things that they might have being."[9] St. Thomas states, "Reprobation by God does not take anything away from the power of the person reprobated."[10] Similarly, Ferrariensis says, "It does not invest the reprobate with anything whereby he falls into sin, nor does it remove anything which would withhold him from sin."[11] St. Thomas himself speaks of the difference between positive

---

8. Davies, *Reality of God and the Problem of Evil*, 189: "According to Aquinas, sin arises because we do not choose to act as we should. We cannot do this, he thinks, without actually doing something, and God accounts for what we actually do. But God cannot account for (directly cause) the badness of what we do. This is not something that he can be thought of as creating. And here, again, I agree with Aquinas. My failure to do what I ought, though possibly taking the form of many nasty deeds (all of them, perhaps, capturable on video), is a failure, an absence, a non-being. So it is not created by God. It is not due to God that any moral failure is due to me. God does not make absences, non-beings, failures."

9. Wis 1:13–14.

10. *ST* I, q. 23, a. 3, ad 3.

11. Ferrariensis, *Commentary on* Summa contra Gentiles, bk. III, chap. 161, no. 4. See also

and negative exclusion when he says, "For it is one thing not to deserve to have something, which nonpossession has the nature only of a deficiency and not the nature of punishment, and it is another thing to deserve not to have something, which nonpossession has the nature of punishment."[12]

It must be stated that this is more than a simple pastoral distinction. It is not merely a different way of considering reprobation that helps one to sleep at night. The theological implications are momentous, and it ought to be recognized that the entire edifice of the classical Thomistic treatment falls if one posits any kind of positive or causal influence in God in regard to reprobation before foreseen demerits.

It would do away with the real possibility for men to uphold the divine laws of God. God would command something that was impossible, not just with the necessity of the consequence (upon the condition that man does indeed fall) but with absolute necessity, with the necessity of the consequent. But this has been rejected by St. Thomas and all Thomists. Indeed, St. Augustine states that "God does not command what is impossible, but in commanding admonishes thee to do what thou can and to ask for what thou cannot do."[13] St. Thomas everywhere affirms that nothing is taken from man whereby he may act well.[14]

Garrigou further elucidates how if doing good and persevering in good unto eternal life were excluded from some men, then their sin would not really be sin at all. They could not be judged and found wanting. They could not be justly punished for their sin. He states:

God never commands what is impossible, otherwise no one could avoid committing actual sin, which in this case would no longer be a sin, and the divine

Garrigou, *Grace*, 225. Some might read the latter half of this passage of Ferrariensis as being inconsistent with the classical Thomistic stance since God does not give that which would withhold a man from sin. However, the non-act of not-giving is something clearly quite different from a *"removal"* of that which would allow man to persevere in the face of temptation. Nothing is taken from man that would allow him to do good, since it would be an injustice if a defect were the result of something removed previous to sin. To do good is to be given something by God. To do bad requires no divine initiative other than permission. To state that there is an antecedent *removal* of something that precedes sin just as there is the antecedent, gratuitous *giving* of God which precedes the good act would be to disregard the great dissymmetry between the lines of good and evil.

12. *De malo*, q. V, a. 1, ad 15.

13. Augustine, *De natura et gratia*, PL, XLIII, 50; XLIV, 271.

14. *ST* I, q. 21, a. 1, ad 3: "It is also due to a created thing that it should possess what is ordered to it; thus it is due to man to have hands, and that other animals should serve him. Thus also God exercises justice, when He gives to each thing what is due to it by its nature and condition."

chastisements inflicted for such would be a manifest injustice. To say that God never commands the impossible means that He wills to make it really possible for all to comply with the precepts imposed upon them and to do so when they are imposed.[15]

Furthermore, the conception of sufficient grace would cease to be tenable. Sufficient grace gives a real power for salutary action, but there could be no real power for the works necessary to avoid hell and merit heaven if God has willed or moved man to merit hell. A causal exclusion before sin would leave no room, no possibility, no power to avoid that sin. Indeed, one would wonder in what way the reprobate could even be said to be ordered to his supernatural end (and even his natural end) at all when he is positively removed from achieving it, held back. God would order such a person toward this end in a cruel manner, only to take it back, giving him this ordering only to hold him back from any and all possibility of achieving it.[16]

Indeed, perhaps even the antecedent will to save all men would be brought into question. It is hard to imagine how God, even with the subjective scope of the antecedent will, could truly wish the salvation of one that he knew that he would rip from salvation and thrust into darkness via his consequent will. Such an idea seems hateful, and as such is completely rejected by the classical Thomistic view.

The Thomists have said only that God picks out some men for eternal life. This is known as election. There is not a subsequent or parallel election to reprobation. God picks out some to shower with gratuitous, undeserved, supernatural grace, period. That is all. This is not accompanied with any influence on the reprobate. He is not moved to anything, nor is anything taken from him. He stands as all men do, defectible, not being

15. Garrigou, *Predestination*, 46. See also p. 72: "If, in truth, God's love is the cause of the goodness in things, then it is by reason of His will of good pleasure and His love that He gives to all men not only a human nature by which they can know and love Him in a natural way, but that He also makes it possible for them to observe the precepts of the natural law, and in this very way salvation is possible. God can never command the impossible, for that indeed would be an injustice. Sin would then become inevitable, which, in such a case, would no longer be sin, and could not be justly punished either in this life or in the next."

16. See Garrigou, *The One God*, 685, where Garrigou states: "God wills whatever there is of good in anything. But that a person, who is ordained to an ultimate end that is both natural and supernatural, before the foreseeing of sin, be excluded from this end as from a gift to which one is not entitled, is not in itself anything good. Therefore God, before the foreseeing of sin, does not exclude a person from the ultimate natural and supernatural end as from a gift to which one is not entitled."

moved by God to an end that is radically above himself and to which he has no claim. To put it simply, therefore, reprobation does nothing.

The classical view of reprobation as entirely negative, as positing no divine influence on the sin that follows and merits damnation, is not a nicety, like the cherry flavoring mixed with the cough syrup to make it more palatable. It is absolutely necessary for the integrity of the entire theological construction.

The Importance of the Distinction between Absolute and Conditional Necessity

One may claim that all of this is essentially immaterial, for what difference does it make to the reprobate that God did not exert positive influence on him to evil? He has found evil all the same, and this is something that was indeed within God's power to prevent. Yet theologically, the difference cannot be overstated, both in regard to the divine innocence and in regard to the creature's ability to do good.

Let us consider the idea that there is no real difference between a necessity of consequent (an absolute necessity) and a necessity of consequence (a conditional necessity). One may posit that because both result in the same outcome, they are both somehow equally determined, equally necessary, and irresistible outcomes. To explore this objection, let us consider an example.

Let us say that there is a man who has been brainwashed to assassinate a certain politician. This brainwashing has robbed him of any capacity to think for himself or to neglect the instructions of his handlers. The man is virtually robotic in his intellect, incapable of executing anything but what he is programmed to do. Now let us consider another man, moved by rage to assassinate a politician. He hates the politician's views and everything that he stands for. Our man has subsequently deliberated about the best means to take the politician out and has decided to go ahead with his plan. In both scenarios, the outcome is the same: the politician has been assassinated. And yet the difference between the two scenarios is quite distinct. In the first, there was absolutely no ability for the brainwashed man to abstain from the act. In the second, there were many opportunities. In the first, at least in relation to the programmed man himself, the assassination had to be so. In the second case, it did not. The first man is not suitable for punishment because he was forced to commit the vile deed. The second man freely chose it, and thus he is justly punished. The first man killed with absolute necessity. The second killed with no absolute necessity at all.

For another example, let us suppose the headache of time travel. Suppose that a great inventor designs and constructs a functioning time machine. Perhaps, after using it, he realizes that such an invention is exceedingly dangerous and awful, but his plans have been stolen by rivals who will disseminate the requisite designs and technology that allow for its further production. In an effort to undo what he has done, our mad inventor goes back in time in an effort to destroy his time machine before he has created it. There is nothing absolutely impossible or contradictory in itself about taking a hammer to the blasted thing. And yet we know that such an act would be impossible suppositionally, that is, under the condition that the inventor has indeed used the time machine to travel back in time and thus has not destroyed it. He is quite capable of destroying it, but he cannot both destroy it and then later use it. As such, it is of a conditional necessity that he does not destroy the time machine. Yet this in no way removes the absolute freedom with which he made the decision not to ever destroy it. It was always possible for him to have done so, it just does not happen that way.[17] Similarly, it was always possible for the sinner to refrain from sin, it just does not happen that he does.

---

17. See Norman Swartz, "Time Travel," in *Beyond Experience: Metaphysical Theories and Philosophical Constraints* (Toronto: University of Toronto Press, 1991), 8,11. "Many persons have thought that traveling backward in time is logically impossible. Their arguments typically are of this sort: 'If you could travel backward in time, then you could encounter yourself when you were a youngster. Even if you are not normally homicidally inclined, it is at least theoretically possible that you kill that youngster. But if you did, then you would not have grown up to have reached the age when you traveled back in time. Thus there would be a contradiction: you both would and would not have traveled backward in time. Since the story involves a contradiction, it is logically impossible to travel backward in time.' Such arguments have been around for years. They are especially tricky because they involve what are called modal concepts, in particular the notions of possibility and impossibility. Does the very concept of travel into the past entail contradictions? Does the possibility of murdering yourself as a child show that backward-directed time travel is an impossibility? The answer is: there is no possibility, if you travel into the past, of murdering yourself as a child. The very fact that you are here now logically guarantees that no one—neither you nor anyone else—murdered you as a child, for there is no possibility of changing the past. This notion that one cannot change the past needs careful attention. There is nothing special about the past in this particular regard. For you can no more change the past than you can change the present or change the future. And yet this is not fatalism. I am not arguing that our deliberations and actions are futile. I cannot change the future—by anything I have done, am doing, or will do—from what it is going to be. But I can change the future from what it might have been. I may carefully consider the appearance of my garden, and after a bit of thought,

It is in this way that a) efficacious grace infallibly brings about its effect or that b) man under the condition of permission of failure infallibly brings about his sin. It is not out of a necessity of divine governance, but only because this is indeed what happened, quite apart from what might have been. To put it differently, no one would be so absurd as to say that a fire necessarily did not or never could have cooked the steak simply because it did not do so. A gun manufactured but never fired would never be said to have been incapable of firing. A human being permitted to freely choose evil was not incapable of good. He simply does not choose it.[18]

The Antecedent Permissive Decree
and the Liberty of the Sinner

As we have seen, the antecedent permissive decree is absolutely essential for maintaining both God's providential ordering over sin and the necessity of divine aid in upholding the defectible creature from defect.[19] For

---

mulling over a few alternatives, I decide to cut down the apple tree. By so doing, I change the future from what it might have been. But I do not change it from what it will be. Indeed, by my doing what I do, I—in small measure—contribute to making the future the very way it will be. Similarly, I cannot change the present from the way it is. I can only change the present from the way it might have been, from the way it would have been were I not doing what I am doing right now. And finally, I cannot change the past from the way it was. In the past, I changed it from what it might have been, from what it would have been had I not done what I did. We can change the world from what it might have been; but in doing that we contribute to making the world the way it was, is, and will be. We cannot—on pain of logical contradiction—change the world from the way it was, is, or will be. The application of these logical principles for time travel becomes clear. If one travels into the past, then one does not change the past; one does in the past only what in fact happened. If you are alive today, having grown up in the preceding years, then you were not murdered. If, then, you or anyone else travels into the past, then that time traveler simply does not murder you. What does that time traveler do in the past? From our perspective, looking backward in time, that traveler does whatever in fact happened, and that—since you are alive today—does not include murdering you."

18. For a further consideration of time and providence, especially as it relates to prayer, see Reginald Garrigou-Lagrange, *Knowing the Love of God: Lessons from a Spiritual Master* (DeKalb, Ill.: Lighthouse Catholic Media, 2015), 146–52. On p. 150, Fr. Garrigou gives the fundamental point of the text: "When we pray, it is certainly not a question of persuading God, of moving Him to change His providential dispositions; it is only a question of *lifting our will to His heights, to will with Him in time what He has decided to give us from eternity*. Prayer, far from tending to lower the Most High toward us, is rather an 'elevation of the soul toward God,' as the Fathers say. When we pray and are heard, it seems to us that the will of God has yielded toward us. It is our will, however, that is raised toward Him, in such a manner that we are disposed to will in time what God wills for us from eternity. From this follows that, far from being opposed to the divine directives, *prayer cooperates with them*. We are, therefore, two in willing, instead of one alone."

19. Joshua R. Brotherton attempts to maintain the necessity of man's total reliance upon divine motion in order to do good but somehow simultaneously rejects the antecedent permissive decrees. In

many, the indispensable condition of the antecedent permissive decree is mistaken for something that posits positive causal influence and thus extinguishes man's free choice in sin together with his moral culpability. However, we must not lose sight of the line of dissymmetry between pre-motion to good and permission of evil in this regard. Let us consider the words of St. Thomas.

Reprobation by God does not take anything away from the power of the person reprobated. Hence, when it is said that the reprobated cannot obtain grace, this must not be understood as implying absolute impossibility: but only conditional impossibility: as was said above, that the predestined must necessarily be saved; yet a conditional necessity, which does not do away with the liberty of choice. Whence, although anyone reprobated by God cannot acquire grace, nevertheless

---

"Toward a Consensus in the *De Auxiliis* Debate," *Nova et Vetera*, English ed., 14, no. 3 (2016): 783–820, 819, he states: "Since man can do nothing without God, he cannot actualize his own potency for performing good acts without efficacious help. However, such does not imply that, any time man chooses not to cooperate with grace, it is ultimately because God arbitrarily chooses not to provide the application of efficacious grace that he initially desires to impart." Brotherton makes several mistakes here. 1) That something remains hidden within the divine will does not necessitate that it is in any way "arbitrary"; Brotherton might as well state that election is "arbitrary" if he truly holds that man can do no good without God first moving him to that good. Why has God chosen Mary to be conceived immaculately? Perhaps he means that it is "arbitrary" precisely because it is like a negative gratuity, previous to the foreseeing of demerits that would make the lack of efficacious grace just. However, Brotherton appears to miss the crucial truth that man is not owed to be upheld from every error, nor is man owed the beatific vision. 2) "Because" here seems to imply causation. When man does not cooperate with grace it is *because* man places a defect to the grace. 3) Brotherton holds two contradictory truths: a) man requires divine aid to actualize any potency for good, and b) man's not acting well is not necessarily preceded by an antecedent permission of defect. The only way of holding these two statements together is to posit that God's will is not always done, i.e. that he moves creatures fallibly or with shatterable motions. As we have attempted to show, this is an offense against the divine simplicity, the divine omnipotence, and the divine providential governance, and it posits some good in man, namely, the good of cooperation with grace, which does not come from God. Fr. Serge-Thomas Bonino gives a marvelous defense of the antecedent permissive decree and a response to statements like Brotherton's in "Contemporary Thomism," 40: "Yet the doctrine of the antecedent permissive decree is also the result of several inescapable doctrinal constraints. It is, first, a consequence of the doctrine of the Ipsum Esse subsistens' sovereign causality vis-à-vis the creatures he creates, maintains, and moves to good. To this divine causality's universality in the metaphysical order corresponds, second, revealed doctrine of the absolute primacy of grace in the order of supernatural salvation, with its spiritual corollary, the fundamental role of humility in the Christian life, which is the real issue of St Augustine's struggle against semi-Pelagianism. 'What distinguishes you? What hast thou that thou didst not receive?' (1 Cor 4:7). Finally, third, within the framework of Thomistic theology of divine science, as a science based on causation, the doctrine of the antecedent permissive decree seems to be the only way to account for the way God knows real sins. Opponents of the antecedent permissive decree attack mostly the first point (the way we understand God's action in creatures), but because the three doctrines are bound up as a system, they try to allow the two others without recourse to the first. Mission impossible."

that he falls into this or that particular sin comes from the use of his free-will. Hence it is rightly imputed to him as guilt.[20]

Physical premotion moves man to will with God some determinate good. Reprobation and the antecedent permissive decree, however, as we have seen, invest no such determination. As the Angelic Doctor states, not only is it with the liberty of the created will *that* man falls into sin, it is entirely from him that he falls into *this or that* sin (*quod … vel illud*). This is to say something significant. Man's causal role in sin is so absolute that every possible determination comes from him. This is true to such an extent that man alone chooses to fall into this or that sin and is thus rightly imputed as guilty.

It is true that an antecedent permissive decree permits this or that non-consideration of the rule, and thus it is not an open window to any and all possible defects or sins. However, while any particular sin requires an antecedent permission, it is certainly true that man causes the fact that he falls into this or that sin. As we have stated, this is due to the fact that unlike physical premotion, which causally determines to one specific good act, the antecedent permissive decree simply permits that man should not be upheld from some particular defect. Man is yet the cause of the determination of the act following from the permission of defect in the same way that a carpenter's not using the ruler can result in any number of bad measurements and thus bad cuts. From a single bad measurement, many different types of errors may result. The carpenter may cut the wood too short or too long. One side or angle may exist in improper proportion to the others. Perhaps he will get the shape wrong. Perhaps this piece will not fit properly into its place within the whole. Perhaps his correct knowledge of the length of his finger combined with his error as to the length of the piece of wood that he now cuts will result in the grisly loss of his appendage.

Similarly, perhaps God permits that Bill not consider the rule of empathy or charity with his neighbor. This means that Bill will become so angry when his neighbor begins loudly mowing his lawn at 5 a.m. on a

---

20. *ST* I, q. 23, a. 3, ad 3: "Ad tertium dicendum quod reprobatio Dei non subtrahit aliquid de potentia reprobati. Unde, cum dicitur quod reprobatus non potest gratiam adipisci, non est hoc intelligendum secundum impossibilitatem absolutam, sed secundum impossibilitatem conditionatam, sicut supra dictum est quod praedestinatum necesse est salvari, necessitate conditionata, quae non tollit libertatem arbitrii. Unde, licet aliquis non possit gratiam adipisci qui reprobatur a Deo, *tamen quod in hoc peccatum vel illud labatur, ex eius libero arbitrio contingit.* Unde et merito sibi imputatur in culpam." Emphasis is my own.

Saturday morning that Bill's right consideration of how to deal with his noisy neighbor is left unconsidered. There are a number of thinkable outcomes stemming from such a permission. Perhaps Bill will run out screaming at his neighbor. Perhaps Bill will hold in his anger, allowing it to fester and spoil good relations with his neighbor. Perhaps he will kick the dog. Perhaps he will kick his neighbor.

The determination of the sin to one outcome is due to man's choice, each outcome bringing about its own special degree or kind of culpability. If Bill swears under his breath at his neighbor, he will have to, at the very least, confess his anger and try harder next Saturday. If he kicks his neighbor, he may spend some time in the local jail. Of course, one cannot deny that insofar as Bill may be inclined to kicking his neighbor and yet refrains from doing so (resting in a lesser sin), it can only be because this is a good that comes primarily from God and only secondarily from Bill. That any man should fall into the sin that he actually commits is certainly permitted by God. However, unlike in physical premotion wherein God determines to the effect, sin is not only willed and executed by the sinner alone, but is also determined and specified by the sinner alone. In short, the sinner is the cause both of the *fact* of his sinning and the material or *content* of his sin.

Of course, it must be stated that the fact that Bill falls into a lesser sin than another would require that God uphold him from some further perversion of the right consideration of the rule. That Bill directs his anger at the dog rather than at the neighbor is certainly sinful, but it is a sin of a lesser gravity. Insofar as Bill is inclined to hit the neighbor but does not do so, he must be moved by God to the partial control of his anger. It would seem that, even insofar as Bill takes out his anger on, say, his cat rather than his dog, or on *this* dog rather than some other one, this is still governed by the antecedent permissive decree. If this were not the case, it would be unclear how God could both know and subsume into his providential plan that Bill strikes Fido rather than Rover. But that he does one or the other is due to Bill's specific nonconsideration of the rule.

Finally, it is not just the sin following from defect that comes from man alone, but truly the antecedent defect itself. God permits it to happen, but a defectible creature can defect on its own. It does not need help, nor does it receive it from God. When left to its own devices, the human person is frail and prone not to consider the rule, as St. Thomas states.

"And there is no need to seek a cause of this nonuse of the aforementioned rule, since the very freedom of the will, by which it can act or not
act, is enough to explain the non-use."[21]

The Radical Contingency of the Created Being

All of this leads us to contemplate one truth that undergirds the entire
classical Thomistic account of premotion, sin, predestination, and reprobation: the contingency of the created being. Any pitting of divine liberty
against human liberty, any competitive causality between God and man,
is to miss the fact that what it means to be a human being is to be absolutely reliant and dependent on God for everything that one has. Far from
God mitigating our being by giving it to us, he makes us to be. Without
that gift, we would not be. Far from God suffocating our free will with his
divine actuation, he makes us free. Without the divine aid, we are only
slaves to our own frailty, cut off from that which makes us whole, that
which makes us operate according to our very nature. We must say, therefore, that to be a man is to be animated by God, and we only exist properly as men insofar as we are, in every sense possible, clinging, clutching to
God. Garrigou touched upon this fact well.

What is the prayer of the publican? Of ourselves we are nothing. If we deduct from
ourselves what we have received from God and what He unceasingly preserves in
us, in strictness of terminology, without any metaphor, there is nothing left. The
sun's ray illumines only because of the light imparted to it by the sun; left to itself
it returns to darkness. Thus of ourselves we return to nothingness. "What have you
which you have not received?" asks St. Paul.... Of ourselves we are less than nothing, for our defectibility tends to make us fail, and sin is less than even nothing,
like error when there is no consideration: "Not that we are sufficient to think anything of ourselves, as of ourselves, but our sufficiency is from God" (II Cor. 3: 5).[22]

None of this is to negate the reality of secondary causality. Indeed, we do
work to good, but this goodness is utterly contingent upon the gratuitous
gifts of God, reducible to his power alone. This is why St. John of the
Cross said, "All the goodness we possess is a borrowed goodness; it is
God who really possesses it. God acts and his work is God."[23]

21. De malo, q. 1, a. 3.

22. Garrigou, God: His Existence and His Nature, vol. 2, 294.

23. St. John of the Cross, The Complete Works of St. John of the Cross in Three Volumes, vol. 3, trans.
E. Allison Peers (Westminster, Md.: Newman Press, 1953), Maxims on Love, n. 257.

Thus St. Thomas says, "If the divine action were to cease, the creature also would cease to exist ... because the creature is made from nothing."[24] Genesis tells us that God created man by breathing into the dust of the ground. Without him, we are only that dust. We are made from nothing, and on our own we have nothing and we are nothing. This is precisely what St. Augustine elucidates in *The Confessions*:

Contemplating other things below you, I saw that they do not in the fullest sense exist, nor yet are they completely non-beings: they are real because they are from you, but unreal inasmuch as they are not what you are. For that alone truly is, which abides unchangingly. As for me, my good is to hold fast to God, for if I do not abide in him, I shall not be able to in myself; whereas he, abiding ever in himself, renews all things.[25]

Too often thought regarding the relation between divine causality and creaturely acts falls into the error of treating God as another creature. My will and the will of a fellow man are competitive. We often fight and disagree. We wish that we could change the will of one another, perhaps even considering different means by which subtly to do so. Even when we work together with another, it is as two distinct, independent, self-sufficient (in relation to each other) beings who work toward a common goal. However, with God, we are unable to work at all if we are not united to him in work. All that we have comes from God, and without receiving from God, when we create obstacles to remaining utterly passive in receiving himself into us, we annihilate ourselves morally with sin and evil. In the truest sense, what it means to be a man, what it means to be a creature, is to be God-clinging, battered by the winds and the rains and the waves of our contingency, of our being creatures rather than God, such that we may be lifted up and into the divine life. Because we can do nothing of ourselves and of ourselves are truly nothing, there is only one response to our predicament as creatures, and that is total trust and abandonment to God, the source of whatever goodness and existence and love that we have.[26]

---

24. *De potentia*, q. V, a. 1, ad 8.

25. St. Augustine, *The Confessions*, ed. David Vincent Meconi, SJ (San Francisco: Ignatius Press, 2012), bk. VII, chap. 11, §17 (181).

26. Romanus Cessario, "Premotion, Holiness, and Pope Benedict XII, 1724–30: Some Historical Retrospects on *Veritatis Splendor*," in *Theology and Sanctity*, ed. Cajetan Cuddy, OP (Ave Maria, Fla.: Sapientia Press, 2014), 238: "Those who seek to sustain themselves spiritually by relying on their own energies always grow weary of conversion."

The Abandonment to Divine Providence

We creatures are faced with only two possibilities: to cling to God or to reject Him. And yet, since to be human is to be God-clinging, the only sane option is to abandon ourselves to him who completes us, trusting that all things work toward the good. Many theologians, mystics, and saints have written about the abandonment to divine providence. Fr. Garrigou made it a particular emphasis of his mystical theology, bringing together the doctrinal principles of the Thomistic approach to premotion, sin, predestination, and reprobation with the Church's wisdom regarding the spiritual life. Self-abandonment is a spiritual practice that leads to all three theological virtues, a place where the three are "fused into one."[27]

Garrigou states that this self-abandonment means placing true faith in the fact that all things, both our joys and our sufferings, are called to participate in God's plan for all of creation, culminating in His glorification. "Nothing can be willed or permitted by God that does not contribute to *the end He purposed in creating*, which is the manifestation of His goodness and infinite perfections, and the glory of the God-man Jesus Christ, His only Son."[28]

This self-abandonment is the very wellspring of the Christian life. It is based not on the heresy of quietism, a practical and spiritual sloth,[29] but on daily adherence to doing and participating in the will of God. Fr. Garrigou says:

Self-abandonment would be sloth did it not presuppose this daily fidelity, which indeed is a sort of springboard from which we may safely launch ourselves in the unknown. Daily fidelity to the divine will as expressed gives us a sort of right to abandon ourselves completely to the divine will of good pleasure as yet not made known to us.[30]

And yet, we must not fall into the other extreme, a sort of Pelagian attitude that places every burden of our lives upon ourselves. "But it is pos-

27. Reginald Garrigou-Lagrange, *Providence*, trans. Dom Bede Rose (Rockford, Ill.: TAN Books, 1998), 232.
28. Garrigou, *Providence*, 217.
29. Garrigou, *Providence*, 215: "The doctrine of self-abandonment to divine providence is a doctrine obviously founded on the Gospel, but it has been falsely construed by the Quietists, who gave themselves up to a spiritual sloth, more or less renounced the struggle necessary for the attainment of perfection, and seriously depreciated the value and necessity of hope or confidence in God, of which true self-abandonment is a higher form."
30. Garrigou, *Providence*, 220.

sible also to depart from the Gospel teaching on this point in a sense entirely opposite to that of the Quietists with their idle repose, by going to
the other extreme of a useless disquiet and agitation."[31] This disquietude
seems to be the extreme that is much more prevalent in our own day. Man
makes himself responsible for his own unhappiness or pain, and he attempts to fix these problems himself. Inevitably he cannot do so, and this
leads him only to greater and greater despair, stranded with his suffering,
unable to make any sense of it or to use it toward any redemptive good.

The point of balance between these two extremes then is to live life,
to work toward the good, not falling into spiritual sloth, but acting in accord with the divine will as much as possible. This "daily fidelity" in our
actions and thoughts is itself a kind of abandonment insofar as we do,
simply and with obedience, that which our God calls us to do. This is not
the action of disquietude, clamoring for cure-alls to suffering, nor is it the
sloth of the quietists, who ironically work against proper abandonment
to God's will by not leading lives that follow it.

Daily fidelity and trusting self-abandonment thus give the spiritual life its balance, its stability and harmony. In this way we live our lives in almost continuous
recollection, in an ever-increasing self-abnegation, and these are the conditions
normally required for contemplation and union with God.[32]

Self-abandonment does not mean that we ought to state: "If God has
foreseen that next summer I shall have wheat, whether I sow the seed
or not, I shall have it." If God has willed that we will have wheat next
summer, he will have willed that we have wheat through our very action
of the sowing of the seeds. That which God foresees and wills from all
eternity, we execute in time through our good actions. We ought not to
overlook this vast difference between us and God: he exists in the eternal
present while we exist in the sequential limitations of time. Just because
God stands on the top of the mount does not mean that we ought to
abandon all good action. Indeed, good action is the means whereby God
is preparing us for glory. Fr. Garrigou sums this up well:

In truth, according to the dispensation of Providence that concerns the end and
the means, without violating liberty, as wheat is obtained only by the sowing of
the seed, so adults obtain eternal life only by the performance of good works. It is

31. Garrigou, *Providence*, 215.
32. Garrigou, *Providence*, 221.

in this sense that Peter says: "Labor the more, that by good works you may make sure your calling and election [2 Pt 1:10]." Although election is eternal on God's part, yet in the order of execution, it is in time and by means of good works that this is effected in us. We must not confuse the two vistas of time and eternity. By God's eternal predestination grace is given to the elect, not that they may let themselves get into a state of spiritual torpor, but it is given precisely for the purpose that they may work out their salvation. As St. Augustine says, it is given for them to act, not for them to remain inactive.[33]

It is in this middle road of self-abandonment that we find our own perfection and our participation in God's governance of the entire universe, ordering all things to the good. Fr. Jean-Pierre de Caussade, SJ, writes in his spiritual masterpiece, *Abandonment to Divine Providence*:

God's achievement is like the front of a lovely tapestry. The worker employed on such a tapestry sees only the back as he adds stitch after stitch with his needle, yet all these stitches are slowly creating a magnificent picture which appears in all its glory only when every stitch is done and it is viewed from the right side. But all this beauty cannot be seen as it is being created. It is the same with the self-abandoned soul. It sees only God and its duty. To fulfill this duty moment by moment consists in adding tiny stitches to the work; yet it is by these stitches that God accomplishes those marvels of which we sometimes catch a glimpse now, but which will not be truly known until the great day of eternity. How good and wise are the ways of God! All that is sublime and exalted, great and admirable in the task of achieving holiness and perfection, he has kept for his own power; but everything that is small, simple and easy he leaves us to tackle with the help of grace. So there is not a single person who cannot easily reach the highest degree of perfection by performing every duty, no matter how commonplace, with eager love.[34]

This proper middle road of abandonment to divine providence also has a way of negating our own frailty, our own limited being, and increasing in us the self-sufficient life of God. Who would want to fix their gaze for a moment, much less for all eternity, upon the frailty of humanity apart from its clinging to God, apart from everything that it receives from him? There you will find only ugliness, whereas in man clinging to God you will find only beauty. And yet this is the temptation that all mankind faces. As such, the final purification that the soul must endure before en-

33. Garrigou, *Predestination*, 191.
34. Jean-Pierre de Caussade, *Abandonment to Divine Providence*, trans. John Beevers (New York: Double Day, 1975), 104.

tering into transforming union with God is the purging of inordinate self-love and egoism. "This passive purification will certainly not be without suffering, and, as St. John of the Cross teaches, it will even be a mystical death, the death to self, the disintegration of self-love, which until then has resisted grace, at times with great obstinacy. Here pride must receive the deathblow that it may give place to genuine humility."[35]

To put it another way, to look upon man apart from God is to see only fallenness, imperfection, and nothingness. To look upon man with God is to see only the perfection of God within him.[36] Thus the wise man or the mystic begins to see through humanity to the God who animates it, not necessarily losing sight of man, but in focusing with the greatest intent upon God himself rather than man, who contributes nothing to God's nobility and grandeur. Fr. Garrigou says, "For souls that follow this road, God is everything: eventually, they can say in very truth: 'My God and my all.'"[37] Indeed, St. John of the Cross says, "That which God seeks to do is to make us gods by participation, as He is God by nature, even as fire converts all things to fire."[38] This is the choice: God or nothing. If we choose God, he will bring us into his divine life, as fire consumes everything that it touches.

Insofar as God has made us to love him, to become subsumed into the divine life, we may trust that God will have our best interest in mind. Rather than fret over things, we can abandon ourselves to him who has complete control and works all things toward the good, knowing that he loves us more than we love ourselves and is capable of working good in us while we are not, apart from him. This is what creates in us a greater humility and a realization of our state of total dependency upon God, waking us up to the illusion of human independence or integrity sans God. It makes manifest to us our nature as God-clinging creatures.[39] Isa-

35. Reginald Garrigou Lagrange, *The Three Ages of the Interior Life: Prelude of Eternal Life*, vol. 2, trans. Sr. M. Timothea Doyle, OP (St. Louis, Mo.: B. Herder Book Co., 1948), 363.

36. Garrigou, *The Three Ages*, vol. 2, 361: "This same egoism which makes us seek ourselves in many things is especially evident when trial strikes us; we are then completely upset and seek help, consolation, and counsel from without, where God is not to be found. We have not built our house sufficiently on Christ the rock, with result that is lacks solidity. We have built on self, on self-will, which is equivalent to building on sand."

37. Garrigou, *Providence*, 235.

38. St. John of the Cross, *Complete Works, Maxims on Love*, n. 28 (229).

39. Bossuet makes this clear in *Elévations*, 18th week, 15th elevation: "Man says to himself: I have my free will; God made me free, and I wish to make myself just. I wish the act which decides my eternal salvation to come originally from myself. Thus one wishes in some way to glory in oneself. Where are

iah tells us, "Before him all the nations are as nought, as nothing and void he counts them."[40] And yet, "Lord, you are our father; we are the clay and you our potter: we are all the work of your hand."[41] Apart from God, we can work only nothingness, be only nothingness, but if we abandon ourselves to the hands of the artisan, we can have eternal being in him. This is what the saints call deification. Garrigou elucidates this well, saying:

Hence the saints at the level of knowledge and love made strenuous efforts to substitute the personality of God for their own, to die to themselves so that God might reign in them. They were armed with a holy hatred of their own ego. They sought to make God the principle of their actions, no longer acting according to the rules of the world or their own limited judgment, but according to God's ideas and rules as received through faith. They sought to substitute the divine will for their own, and to act no longer for themselves but for God, loving Him not as themselves but infinitely more than themselves and more than any other thing whatsoever. They understood that God had to become for them another ego more intimate than their own. They had to realize that God has more "them" than they themselves because He is preeminently Being. Therefore, they made strong efforts to renounce their personality and every attitude of independence before God; they sought to make of themselves something divine. Consequently, they developed the most forceful personality conceivable. They obtained in some way what God possesses by nature, namely independence from every created thing, not only in the corporeal world but also in the world of intelligence.[42]

The Psalms state, "Again and again the sinner must feel the lash; he who trusts in the Lord finds nothing but mercy all around him."[43] The sinner acts against his nature, trusting in himself when what is in his best interest is to cling to God. As St. Catherine of Siena writes:

This [unitive] state is most excellent, when the soul, being yet in the mortal body, tastes bliss with the immortals, and oftentimes she arrives at so great a union that she scarcely knows whether she be in the body or out of it; and tastes the earnest-money of Eternal Life, both because she is united with Me, and because

---

you going, frail vessel? You are going to dash against the rocks and deprive yourself of the help of God, who gives it only to the humble, and who makes them humble in order to help them.... God wishes you to ask Him to help you in all the good actions you have to perform; when you have performed them, God wishes you to thank Him for having performed them" (taken from Garrigou, *God: His Existence and His Nature*, vol. 2, 303n149).

40. Is 40:17.
41. Is 64:8.
42. Garrigou, *Knowing the Love of God*, 33–34.
43. Ps 32:10.

her will is dead in Christ, by which death her union was made with Me, and in no other way could she perfectly have done so. Therefore, do they taste life eternal, deprived of the hell of their own will, which gives to man the earnest-money of damnation, if he yield to it.[44]

The trials that are occasioned by permitted defect can aid us in coming to this realization. This is why Garrigou states, "It is nevertheless true to say that God purifies our desire from the self-love with which it may be tinged by leaving us in some uncertainty about it and so inducing us to love Him more exclusively for His own sake."[45] Our difficulties then are meant to be our wakeup call to cease fighting against our nature as God-clinging and to flee to Our Lord, abandoning ourselves to him. Moreover, Garrigou, inspired by the great seventeenth-century spiritual theologian Alexander Piny, OP, says:

As Father Piny remarks, nowhere is there a deeper or more lively faith than in the conviction that God arranges everything for our welfare, even when He appears to destroy us and overthrow our most cherished plans, when He allows us to be calumniated, to suffer permanent ill-health, and other afflictions still more painful. This is the great faith indeed, for it is to believe the apparently incredible: that God will raise us up by casting us down; and it is to believe this in a practical and living way, not merely an abstract and theoretical way.[46]

In this way, the Christian can understand and pray the stunning sonnet of John Donne:

> Batter my heart, three-person'd God, for you
> As yet but knock, breathe, shine, and seek to mend;
> That I may rise and stand, o'erthrow me, and bend
> Your force to break, blow, burn, and make me new.
> I, like an usurp'd town to another due,
> Labor to admit you, but oh, to no end;
> Reason, your viceroy in me, me should defend,
> But is captiv'd, and proves weak or untrue.
> Yet dearly I love you, and would be lov'd fain,
> But am betroth'd unto your enemy;
> Divorce me, untie or break that knot again,

44. St. Catherine of Siena, *The Dialogue*, trans. Algar Thorold, Rockford, Ill.: TAN Books, 1974, "A Treatise of Prayer," §11.

45. Garrigou, *Providence*, 232.

46. Garrigou, *Providence*, 233.

> Take me to you, imprison me, for I,
> Except you enthrall me, never shall be free,
> Nor ever chaste, except you ravish me.

There is even some comfort in knowing that my subjective evil, that is, discomfort or sickness or emotional distress, our being battered, may aid in the good of the entire created order. It may do me good, but it may also be needed to do good for others. And in this we participate in the crucifixion of Our Lord, not looking upon him only as a strange and alien redeemer, but entering into his redemption so as to embrace his work, transforming annihilation and evil into the most radiant beauty and goodness, that which is full of existence.[47] "I have been crucified with Christ; yet I live, no longer I, but Christ lives in me."[48]

In all of this we ought to find not the torment or the gloom or the anxiety from which good Fr. Nicolas suffered. On the contrary, the serenity and tranquility of abandoning ourselves to God, while difficult to practice, is certainly the only way toward serious hope, for it is nothing other than to cling to the only one capable of transforming our suffering. As Fr. Caussade says, "The huge, unyielding rock that shelters the soul from all storms is the divine will, which is always there, though hidden beneath the veil of trials and the most commonplace actions. Deep within those shadows is the hand of God to support and carry us to complete self-abandonment."[49]

No man who has tried for very long to place his reliance in himself has done anything but collapsed, utterly defeated, powerless, imprisoned. Imagine the sinner who cannot cry out to God, imploring him to give the grace whereby he may overcome some habitual grave sin.[50] Imagine the

47. See Thomas Joseph White, OP, *The Incarnate Lord: A Thomistic Study in Christology*, (Washington, D.C.: The Catholic University of America Press, 2015), especially 373: "For Aquinas, God can make use of any evil, even the worst, in order to manifest the power of divine goodness. Even intense human suffering can contribute to the triumph of Christ over the powers of sin and death precisely because of the union of human suffering with the divine nature in the person of the Son (who does not cease to be one with the Father)."

48. Gal 2:2. For a very fine treatment of the central role of Christ in the mystery of predestination, see Roger W. Nutt, "From Eternal Sonship to Adoptive Filiation," in *Thomism and Predestination: Principles and Disputations*, ed. Steven A. Long, Roger W. Nutt, and Thomas Joseph White, OP (Ave Maria, Fla.: Sapientia Press, 2016), 77–93.

49. Caussade, *Abandonment to Divine Providence*, 109.

50. For an eloquent expression of this, see C. S. Lewis, *Mere Christianity* (New York: Harper Collins, 2001), 145–150: "But the difficulty is to reach the point of recognising that all we have done and can do is nothing.... The Bible really seems to clinch the matter when it puts the two things together

THE LINES OF GOOD AND EVIL

sinner ruled by general, fallible providence, to whom is sent impedible motions. What sort of despair he must feel when he knows that he is on his own in regard to cooperating with grace! The frailty that has impeded God's will in his life must be overcome with more frailty, always itself insufficient. How much more confidently can the sinner look up toward God when his motions are always infallible, the cause of the good in us? Inspired with this confidence, he might implore him, knowing that without the slightest of effort he can make him to never to sin again? Garrigou speaks of this great hope offered by classical Thomism:

Thomism, far from entrusting our salvation to human frailty, places it in the hands of God our Savior. Far indeed from being opposed to the virtue of hope, it inclines us to put all our trust in God and not in ourselves. *Hope is a theological virtue, and its formal motive is the help of God* (Deus auxilians), *and not our will power.* Should we not have to *despair* of attaining our supernatural end if we had to rely upon our own strength? Although we are not certain that God will deign to always point out our faults to us and give us the grace of final perseverance, yet we are much less certain of our own will, which so often is indifferent to true good and seeks what is merely apparently good. The rectitude of God's ways is of a different certainty from that of our own heart.[51]

Indeed, St. Thomas tells us, "Accordingly, just as it is not lawful to hope for any good save happiness, as one's last end, but only as something referred to final happiness, so too, it is unlawful to hope in any man, or any creature, as though it were the first cause of movement towards happiness."[52] As such, we place all of our confidence not in ourselves but in the omnipotent God. Garrigou reminds of us this confidence in the thought of St. Thomas himself.

While fulfilling our daily duties, then, we must abandon ourselves to almighty God in a spirit of deep faith, which must also be accompanied by an absolutely childlike confidence in His fatherly kindness. *Confidence* (fiducia or confidentia),

---

in one amazing sentence. The first half is, 'Work out your own salvation with fear and trembling'— which looks as if everything depended on us and our good actions: but the second half goes on, 'For it is God who worketh in you'—which looks as if God did everything and we nothing. I am afraid that is the sort of thing we come up against in Christianity. I am puzzled but I am not surprised. You see, we are now trying to understand, and to separate into water-tight compartments, what exactly God does and what man does when God and man are working together. And, of course, we begin by thinking it is like two men working together, so you could say, 'He did this bit and I did that.' But this way of thinking breaks down. God isn't like that. He is inside you as well as outside."

51. Garrigou, *God: His Existence and His Nature,* vol. 2, 303.

52. *ST* II-II, q. 17, a. 4.

says St. Thomas, is a steadfast or intensified hope arising from a deep faith in the goodness of God, who, according to His promises, is ever at hand to help us—*Deus auxilians*.[53]

This hope can and will have a real effect upon our prayer life. If we believe that God does not bring about good in us infallibly, we may fret over how to change things ourselves, not trusting in God's almighty and simple power. Garrigou provides the image of a priest converting a dying soul, though the truth of the example can be seen in every difficulty encountered by religious or layman alike.

What must a priest do who is unsuccessful in converting a dying sinner? If the priest is persuaded that God is the master of this sinful will, above all things *he will pray*. If, on the other hand, he imagines that God exerts only an external influence on his will by means of circumstances [or, we may add here, by means of shatterable motions], good thoughts, and good inspirations, external to the salutary consent of the will, the priest may lose too much time in employing the superficial means; his prayer may lack that holy boldness which we admire in the saints.[54]

Therefore, we ought not to trust in ourselves but to trust in the only one who can bring us to life, him who loves us more than we could ever love ourselves, looking out for our best interest more than we ever could. Herein lies the great irony in self-abandonment. The more we trust in our own power, clinging to ourselves in an attempt to solve our problems, the more powerless we are in procuring our own good. On the contrary, the more that we abandon ourselves to God as powerless, surrendering our very existence and good to him, the more power we have in safeguarding these things *through Him*. Fr. Caussade says, "The wicked man is always certain that he is invincible. But, O God, how can we withstand you? If one solitary soul has all the powers of hell and the world against it, it need fear nothing if it has abandoned itself to the order of God."[55]

The Scriptures tell us, "Cast all of your worries upon Him because He cares for you."[56] Our heavenly Father feeds the birds of the air and cares for the flowers of the field. How much more ought we (who are so much more loved and valued by him) to abandon ourselves to his providence

---

53. Garrigou, *Providence*, 234.
54. Garrigou, *God: His Existence and His Nature*, vol. 2, 304.
55. Caussade, *Abandonment to Divine Providence*, 119.
56. 1 Pt 5:7.

than they do? When man clings to God he finds his proper place as a part of him, fulfilling that supernatural end to which he is called to find his completion within the divine life itself.[57] We can truly say that man clinging to himself is nothing, while man clinging to God is subsumed entirely into his goodness and perfection, which is responsible for whatever goodness, whatever existence that we have. This is why St. John of the Cross says, "All the goodness that we have is lent to us and God considers it as His own. It is God that works and His work is God."[58]

57. For a very fine consideration of deification in the work of St. Thomas, see Daria Spezzano, *The Glory of God's Grace: Deification According to St. Thomas Aquinas* (Ave Maria, Fla.: Sapientia Press, 2015).

58. St. John of the Cross, *Maxims on Love*, n. 29 (229).

CHAPTER TEN

Conclusion

The works of Marín-Sola, Maritain, Lonergan, and even the later Nicolas are all distinct in their terminology and their manner of tackling the apparent difficulties found within the classical Thomistic system. Between them all, however, there is clearly a shared point of restlessness and unease concerning God's relation to sin and evil. In their own way, each theologian worked from within the texts of St. Thomas to revise the classical approach to make it more palatable for a modern audience, one that was acutely aware of the problem of theodicy that had been a cornerstone of eighteenth-, nineteenth-, and twentieth-century rejections of classical theism.[1]

Marín-Sola spent considerable time thinking and writing on this topic. It is perhaps his most important contribution as a theologian, and his treatment features a level of profundity and complexity. Maritain tackled the issue as a philosopher, focusing on the metaphysical account of the defect as a nonact, a nonbeing. Maritain's account lacks the theological depth and intimacy with the Dominican Thomistic commentatorial tradition, but it enjoys a relative simplicity that speaks right to the heart of the issue of the divine innocence. Maritain cuts to the chase and puts his finger directly upon the sore spot, as it were. Lonergan poses important and interesting questions regarding the nature of operation and causality. Nicolas's later treatment is short but springs forth from the common neuralgia concerning the traditional treatment and his own search to alleviate that anxiety.

---

1. Leibniz had invented the term "theodicy" in his 1710 book *Essais de Théodicée sur la bonté de Dieu, la liberté de l'homme et l'origine du mal.*

Of course, there is, regarding certain points, a shared language among them, one that rests primarily upon the concept of God's willing in a contingent or inefficacious way. Michael Torre's article "Francisco Marín-Sola, OP, and the Origin of Jacques Maritain's Doctrine on God's Permission of Evil" provides the historical background for the influence that Marín-Sola certainly had upon the thought of Maritain. The two had corresponded on these questions quite often, and it is clear that Maritain's treatment, while maintaining its own unique approach, shares considerably in many major points of Marín-Sola.

Marín-Sola had developed a distinction between God's infallibly efficacious grace and a fallibly efficacious grace (or what Marín-Sola calls a "sufficient grace") by which God ruled the world according to a general, inefficacious providence. Maritain spoke of a shatterable motion that was tantamount to the same reality. As Torre points out, "There is no real or conceptual difference between a motion that is 'impedible' and one that is 'breakable.'"[2] Both had affirmed that man may break or not break these motions due to their fallible nature as creatures, confirming that there was nothing antecedent in God that acted as a cause or even a condition of the creaturely defection. As such, both rejected the antecedent permissive decree, with Marín-Sola doing so implicitly and Maritain much more explicitly. Whether a defect did or did not arise was based not in the initiative of God's providential ordering and the divine aid or lack thereof. This initial governance was placed instead in the creature itself, responding to one and the same divine motion with the potency for multiple results depending on how it responded.[3] This results in God's antecedent will being more than a *velleitas*, a volitional movement (not a willing *simpliciter*), which is merely a consideration of the good of the creature apart from its place in reality as a whole. Instead, the antecedent will in

2. Michael Torre, "Francisco Marín-Sola, OP, and the Origin of Jacques Maritain's Doctrine on God's Permission of Evil," 55–94; 88: "There is again nothing more than a verbal novelty in the way Maritain now chooses to speak of the divine motion or grace that is resisted by the creature: it is one that is 'merely sufficient' or breakable ('brisable'). There is no real or conceptual difference between a motion that is 'impedible' and one that is 'breakable.' Maritain himself later acknowledged this, saying that he had 'proposed this expression 'breakable motion or actuation' as a kind of philosophical equivalent of the theological expression 'sufficient grace' [*On the Philosophy of History* (New York: Scribners, 1957), 120n3].'"

3. Torre, "God's Permission of Evil," 89: "In his work, he now makes the following points, all made previously by Marín-Sola: that the creature's 'non-impediment' adds nothing to the divine motion; that a breakable motion moves the free creature according to the fallible mode proper to its nature."

the revisionist account is truly a movement of the divine will, something willed simply with the specification that it allows for multiple responses.[4] These main ideas are shared between Marín-Sola and Maritain, and so is much of the language.[5]

This revisionist account can thus be said to run commonly from Marín-Sola through Maritain into Nicolas, who explicitly cites Maritain as having been absolutely fundamental to his own metamorphosis. This is not to count out other theologians as well, such as Cardinal Charles Journet, whose impact personally and theologically upon various members of the revisionist account is not to be overlooked. Indeed, each figure has approached these topics in his own way. Sometimes there are even seeming differences or tensions between their accounts,[6] but they are united in a rejection, or at least a radical reevaluation, of the classical, so-called Báñezian account. They are unified in a repudiation of the antecedent permissive decree and in their acceptance of divine motions that do not posit a suppositional necessity in regard to their intended effect. In one way or another, all accept divine motions that may be frustrated.

The goal is to distance God from the fact of sin, to explain how it could be that man can sin without God's being able to be taken to task for not giving the grace whereby man will not sin. The classical account is taken to be deficient in this regard, positing a virtual symmetry between the 'line of good' and the 'line of evil,' terms that have their genesis in Marín-Sola and are used distinctly by Maritain.[7] As we have seen, however, the classical treatment indeed regards this dissymmetry, explicitly emphasizing the profound contradistinction between God's role in the good of the universe and the fact of the evil which indwells there. It is the classical treatment that has first given us the distinction between act and nonact in relation to sin that Maritain later employs to escape the problem of evil. In good, God is the one acting in us. In evil, it is we who take the first and every initiative,

---

4. Torre, "God's Permission of Evil," 89: "that the order of motions that is sufficient or breakable derives from God's antecedent will, which is an active will of the *beneplacitum* and not an idle velleity; and that God's providence 'takes into account' the 'nihiliations' of the creature, as first cause."

5. See Torre, "God's Permission of Evil," especially p. 87.

6. One wonders, for example, if Maritain would accept Marín-Sola's reworking of the sufficient and efficacious grace distinction, along with positing a metaphysical motion that imparts a *beginning* but not a *continuation* of said motion in the creature.

7. Torre, "God's Permission of Evil," 88: "He also now uses Marín-Sola's words of 'the lines of good and evil,' pointing out that there is a 'dissymmetry' between them (since the creature is first cause only of an impediment to God's motion). The word 'dissymmetry' is new, but not the concept."

standing as the sole cause of evil (some absence of due being in an act) with the divine permission exerting absolutely no causal role, literally not acting. Fabio Schmitz has stated this well:

For Saint Thomas, only that which participates in *esse* is in need of an efficient cause. One does not posit an active cause of nonbeing. Thus, the unicorn, which does not exist, does not need a cause not to exist.... On the other hand, to exist (as is the case with all things that are not God) the unicorn needs an efficient cause. This is the real dissymmetry between being and nonbeing, from which is derived the dissymmetry between the line of good and the line of evil in relation to divine causality.[8]

Moreover, while the classical treatment preserves this asymmetry, it does not, in order to preserve the asymmetry, forsake equally important doctrinal truths like God's omnipotence, his exhaustive governance, or his simplicity. The same cannot be said of the revisionist account. Insofar as it posits within the divine providence a sort of kenosis of the divine attributes, it theologizes a God who is incapable of actually being Lord over all and is thus incapable of being a source of our hope. Thomas Joseph White, speaking specifically on the divinity of Christ, highlights this problem even as it pertains to our present topic:

The Catholic tradition has ... insisted dogmatically on the simplicity of the divine nature, and consequently on the divine perfection, immutability, and eternity of God. Another way of stating this idea is to claim that the simplicity, perfection, immutability, and eternity of the divine nature exclude certain *inherently* creaturely ways of being. These are ways of being that imply created dependence: the complexity, imperfection, mutability, and temporality that are proper to creatures. God does not possess the potencies for progressive perfection that are proper to creatures. If he did, he would be made perfect by another and therefore receive his very being (or some aspect of it) from another. Therefore he would not be the unique, universal giver of being for all others, as the creator of all that exists.[9]

---

8. Fabio Schmitz, *Motion Divine et Défaillance de la Volonté dans la Théologie de Saint Thomas d'Aquin*, Memoire de License canonique en Théologie sous la direction de S.T. Bonino, OP, Institut Saint-Thomas d'Aquin., 2014, 90. Moreover, Schmitz continues: "We see that for Saint Thomas, the dissymmetry between the line of good and the line of evil as they relate to God is much more radical than what is held by the defenders of a divine motion that is resistible in the composite sense. Only the good has a cause *per se* and only being has an efficient cause. And it is precisely because of this fundamental dissymmetry that the free creature must not be conceived as the primary cause of 'nothingness' and moral evil in the same way that God is the primary cause of being and goodness" (91). Translations are mine.

9. White, *The Incarnate Lord*, 417.

The revisionist account, in positing frustratable providence and shatter-able motions, has unfortunately forfeited the entire basis for the divine at-tributes. It has made God to be dependent on creatures, and thus it eras-es divinity itself. God is no longer I AM but instead is caused to receive some determination in his being via the execution of creaturely freedom. That God could or would somehow will his own complexity does not in any way solve the problem of a complex God.

However, this is not to say that the revisionist account is without any merit. After centuries of defending the thought of St. Thomas over and against the Molinist *scientia media*, classical Thomism may now be said to be spurred toward defending itself against the other extreme of Calvinism and Jansenism. In preserving predestination as *ante praevisa merita*, there arose within the tradition a certain language of reprobation as a positive exclusion (which, as we have seen, admits of an acceptable interpretation but which may be seen as imprudent due to the many other unsavory interpretations that are possible). When Garrigou rejects this language, it is not as a reformer of the traditional treatment but as one who fully embodies it and is sensitive not only to the errors of Molina but also to those of Calvin and Jansen.

The traditional treatment is theologically robust enough to stand up against both sets of errors, but the impetus for current Thomism to safeguard the divine innocence as vehemently as other divine attributes have been safeguarded in the past (such as the divine simplicity or the divine omnipotence) can be said to come largely from the influence of the revisionist account and its set of objections against so-called Báñe-zianism. The revisionist account must be highly commended for putting the traditional treatment to the test in important and somewhat inno-vative ways, expanding its examination beyond the controversies of the *de Auxiliis* debates that were largely unknown by the majority of Cath-olic thinkers in the early twentieth century, especially those outside of academic pockets within the Dominican and Jesuit orders. This is not, of course, to say that this debate is inconsequential, but only that the twen-tieth century (and it will likely be the same with the twenty-first) has been better served by the Thomistic project answering the contemporary concerns regarding theodicy and its ability to make sense of the mystery of evil in the light of a zeitgeist that, faced with two world wars and the rise of humanism, has grown increasingly skeptical and disillusioned regarding the Church, Thomism, and the very question of God.[10] With an admirable zeal, Marín-Sola, Maritain, Lonergan, and the later Nicolas had stepped up to the plate in an endeavor not only to defend theism and the thought of St. Thomas from these modern objections, but in a noble effort to present authentic answers to the questions of the time and to provide for a real possibility for a conversion of the culture back to a theonomic order. These truly Christian followers of St. Thomas wished to speak to the Ivan Karamazovs of the world who stated in contemporary times, perhaps more loudly than ever, their exasperation with a God who governs over evil:

I do understand how the universe will tremble when all in heaven and under the earth merge in one voice of praise, and all that lives and has lived cries out: 'Just art thou, O Lord, for thy ways are revealed!' Oh, yes, when the mother and the torturer whose hounds tore her son to pieces embrace each other, and all three cry out with tears: 'Just art thou, O Lord,' then of course the crown of knowledge will have come and everything will be explained. But there is the hitch: that is what I cannot accept. And while I am on earth, I hasten to take my own measures. You see, Alyosha, it may well be that if I live until that moment, or rise again in order to see it, I myself will perhaps cry out with all the rest, looking at the mother embracing her child's tormentor: 'Just art thou, O Lord!' but I do not want to cry out with them. While there's still time, I hasten to defend myself against it, and therefore I absolutely renounce all higher harmony.... Is there in the whole world a being who could and would have the right to forgive? I don't want harmony, for love of mankind I don't want it. I want to remain with unrequited suffering. I'd rather remain with my unrequited suffering and my unquenched indignation, *even if I am wrong*. Besides, they have put too high a price on harmony; we can't afford to pay so much for admission. And therefore I has-

10. Here I wish to agree fully with Serge-Thomas Bonino, OP, who states, "T. Osborne appears to me overly optimistic when he writes: 'I am not here concerned with the objection that the Thomist position entails that God is responsible for evil actions. This objection does not seem particularly difficult for me, and has been overwhelmingly refuted by J. H. Nicolas' ("Thomist Premotion and Contemporary Philosophy of Religion," *Nova et Vetera* 4, no. 3 (2006): 607–32, esp. 614n17" ("Contemporary Thomism," 39n38). While it is true that the classical treatment does stand up against the objections, one must be sensitive and prudent, giving a nuanced response to the objection that properly regards the question of evil. For some, the clarity of the Thomistic answer will be immediately grasped, but this will not be the case for all. We live in a world that, as a matter of practicality if nothing else, nearly always speaks of God in an anthropomorphized fashion. If we pray, perhaps God will change his mind. Even among theologians, it may take time to adjust to the robust sense of providence that is safeguarded by the classical Thomists. We are confident that those who adhere to the Scriptures and weigh out the various approaches will ultimately be convinced of the classical one, but this is not a reason to overlook or underappreciate the objection.

ten to return my ticket. And it is my duty, if only as an honest man, to return it as
far ahead of time as possible. Which is what I am doing. It's not that I don't accept
God, Alyosha, I just most respectfully return him the ticket.[11]

While the divine permission of evil will of course remain obscure until the full orchestration of the divine plan can be seen by us to whom it
is currently veiled, the mistake made by the revisionist account (which
shattered the possibility for St. Thomas's work to be used as a salve for
the haunted words of Ivan Karamazov) was, quite frankly, in revising
the thought of St. Thomas. The intention and aim of the revisionists was
thoroughly Christian and Thomistic, but the execution left much to be
desired, forsaking multiple tenets of classical theism to arrive at a conclusion that was already latent within the classical Thomistic treatment: the
dissymmetry between good and evil. It needed only to be unpacked and
studied more fully, to be emphasized and elaborated. Just as the Thomistic project as a whole used Molinism to bring out from within itself greater depth and nuance, so too can it use the revisionist Thomistic account
to do the same with errors concerning God's relation to sin.

The mystery of evil and how it fits into the divine plan for all of creation can never be fully understood in this life. It requires the eyes of faith
and of hope. As wayfarers, it is easy for us to rest on the consideration of
evil, to see it as fundamentally and eternally vitiating the created order.
We see only the pain but not the plan for the pain. This is why St. Thomas
affirms that Christ and his blessed, those who can see the entirety of the
divine plan, do not weep for those who are permitted to freely choose to
turn away from God.

However, although the love of our fellow men pertains in a certain way to the
higher reason, inasmuch as our neighbor is loved out of charity for God's sake,
the higher reason in Christ could not experience sorrow on account of the defects of His fellow men, as it can in us. For, since Christ's higher reason enjoyed
the full vision of God, it apprehended all that pertains to the defects of others
as contained in the divine wisdom, in the light of which the fact that a person is
permitted to sin and is punished for his sin, is seen to be in accord with becoming
order. And so neither the soul of Christ nor of any of the blessed who behold
God can be afflicted with sadness by the defects of their neighbors. But the case
is otherwise with wayfarers who do not rise high enough to perceive the plan of
wisdom. Such persons are saddened by the defects of others even in their higher

11. Fyodor Dostoevsky, *The Brothers Karamazov* (New York: Everyman's Library, 1992), 244–45.

reason, when they think that it pertains to the honor of God and the exaltation of the faith that some should be saved who nevertheless are damned.[12]

God's permission of evil can nonetheless be defended by the wayfarer. It goes without saying that sin is an unfortunate fact of reality. Anyone who has suffered knows how hollow this may sound in moments of anguish. For the Christian, however, there is hope in suffering, a hope that may transcend it, lifting fragile man above and beyond his own pain. The source of this hope is to be found in a God who is the master of all things, sin and pain and evil included, a God who has the power to transform us without the slightest effort.

Indeed, we must admit that in some way God has deemed it better to allow for the reality of sin than to disallow it. As wayfarers, the prospect of the privation of some goodness or being, the realization that some existence that we desire or need or are due is suddenly missing, is truly terrifying and awful. And yet what can more manifest God's lordship over all things than that he turns nothingness into existence, vacuous abyss to radiant, beautiful goodness? What greater sign of God's transcendent power can there be other than to bring something from nothing? It is with this wondrous power that God creates the universe *ex nihilo* and that he makes it anew in the Parousia, an *exitus* and *reditus* of God's beloved cosmos.

The permitted pockets of nothingness that burst into the created order are like the cracks in a broken piece of pottery. Yet, like the Japanese art of kintsugi, which repairs the broken pottery by way of filling the cracks with material that is more beautiful (such as gold or silver) than that which was used to make the original pottery, God transforms his cosmos that it might better reflect his splendor. In this way, his creation mirrors the radiance of the crucified Lord. Even in his glory, the marks of evil remain on his hands and feet, but they are somehow now entirely converted into gleaming, resplendent sublimity. *In some way*, it is better for creatures to have suffered and overcome, to be tarnished and now virginal, than to have never been stained at all. Indeed, the Scriptures tell us that the heavens rejoice more over the single sinner who repents than the ninety-nine who need no repentance. It is the converted sinner, the dead brought to life, the void turned to plenitude, that best manifests

---

12. Aquinas, *Compendium theologiae*, chap. 232.

Our God's awful power. And this is why the Angelic Doctor tells us, "God therefore neither wills evil to be done, nor wills it not to be done, but wills to *permit* evil to be done; *and this is a good*."[13]

With admirable effort, the revisionist account has attempted to distance God from our sin and suffering, but it has only rendered God incapable of being to us a source of real hope. True hope can only be situated within an apprehension of God as one who both wishes our perfection more than we can know and who is also powerful enough swiftly and sweetly to turn our evil to good.[14] Whether it be that God cannot overcome our defects or simply that he wills good in us in such a way that we might trump him, the shared reality of the revisionist treatment is that we call out to God to save us from our own sinfulness and suffering, but no one can know whether that prayer will be answered, for man is fallen and must in some sense find within himself the power to cling to God under the violent crashing of the waves of fallen existence. The hope provided by the classical treatment, rather, is situated within the idea that God is all-loving, wanting what is best for us more than we ourselves could ever wish it. Hope resides in the fact that we trust not in our small selves but in the grandeur of the one who makes even nothingness to be filled with being. Garrigou says, "The proper and formal object of infused hope is not, in fact, our own effort, but the infinite mercy of the 'God who aids us,' who arouses us here to effort and who will there crown that effort."[15]

This grandiose God does not give what is good to us with fallible motions, sometimes being frustrated by our own defectibility. No, God is simple and omnipotent, and whatever he wills will indeed happen. When we cry out for God to rescue us from some habitual sin we may have the utmost confidence and trust that the strength to overcome what seems impossible for us will come from him for whom it is the easiest task imaginable.[16] Far from being a source of gloom, this is the provenance of Chris-

<hr>

13. *ST* I, q. 19, a. 9, ad 3: "Deus igitur neque vult mala fieri, neque vult mala non fieri, sed vult permittere mala fieri. *Et hoc est bonum*." Emphasis is mine.

14. Long, "St. Thomas Aquinas, Divine Causality, and the Mystery of Predestination," 75–76: "Finally, if, and only if, God has power over sin—through the power to redirect, heal, and elevate the human will—can God efficaciously redeem man. The medicine must reach to the root if the root is to be healed. the human will cannot constitute a 'no fly zone' for divine causality if God has the power to redeem man: the omnipotent mercy of God is efficacious through the sacrifice of Christ."

15. Garrigou, *Reality*, 104.

16. Against this Reichenbach states on p. 132 of *Divine Providence*, "Indeed, quite apart from the philosophical arguments, Christians must feel somewhat comfortable with the concept of divine

tian hope, opening to us the vista of the possibility of eclipsing human suffering and sinfulness, our own self-clinging, and instead entering into the divine life by clinging completely to God, transcending our incomplete, defectible, frail human nature to live in him who is utterly perfect and impassible, governing all things infallibly toward the good.[17]

---

self-limitation." I ask, what could possibly be comforting about God being unable (and not just not doing but being truly unable, for the claim is that God would transgress his own intentions for us as free creatures and annihilate our very nature if he moved our wills) to lift us up beyond our own frailty and habitual deficiency? Such a view leaves the sinner utterly stranded, cemented in a prison of his own sin.

17. Michael Waldstein renders this quite beautifully in "Balthasar and Other Thomists on Barth's Understanding of Predestination," in *Thomism and Predestination: Principles and Disputations*, ed. Steven A. Long, Roger W. Nutt, and Thomas Joseph White, OP (Ave Maria, Fla.: Sapientia Press, 2016), 239–59; 242 and 244: "Predestination is good news. For the criminal condemned with Jesus to crucifixion, it is certainly good news that Jesus says, 'Amen, I say to you, today you will be with me in paradise' (Lk 23:43). Titian's great painting of this scene, which was chosen as the emblem for this conference on predestination, does not depict the moment in which the criminal hears the promise 'You will be with me in paradise.' It focuses on an event a little later. Jesus has already died. The criminal accordingly no longer looks at Jesus. He looks up, above Jesus's head, as if toward paradise, toward the fulfillment of the promise. His entire body, particularly his face, expresses the deep longing that the Greeks called eros.... The criminal crucified with Jesus, as Titian portrays him, is near the end of his life. All his traveling along the ways of life toward happiness, all his means and capacities, have come to an end, an agonizing death. Yet his eros has been renewed in the midst of intense misery by Jesus's sovereign decree about his destination. 'Today you will be with me in paradise.'"

A Very Brief Reply to R. J. Matava's Thesis That God Creates Human Free Choice

R. J. Matava, whose insightful and well-researched work on Báñez we have cited earlier in this work, posits a view of the relationship between providence and human free choice that is based on the idea that God causes human free choice by way of creation. Matava states that God creates our creaturely choices and that they are maintained as free.

What does it mean to say that God creates my act of free choice? It simply means that if I choose at all, then God makes that choice to be, and he makes it to be just as it is. Thus, if I freely choose x, God (a) makes my free choice of x to be as a choice of x. But it also means (b), that God makes my choice of x to be *as free*.[1]

I wish to pose three very brief objections to Matava's view of human free choice. First, free choice as an effect of creation seems impossible given St. Thomas's own thought on the nature of creation. Second, even if free choices were somehow created, this would seem to fall into a sort of occasionalism that does not allow for proper secondary causality within the scope of divine governance and providence. Third, following upon the second objection, it would seem that such a view robs man of his freedom insofar as he does not participate in bringing about his own free choice.

Creation is causation *ex nihilo*. Such an act necessarily denies the

1. R. J. Matava, *Divine Causality and Human Free Choice: Domingo Báñez, Physical Premotion and the Controversy* de Auxiliis *Revisited* (Leiden: Brill, 2016), 276.

possibility of secondary or instrumental causality. Only God can create because only God can bring something out of nothing. Moreover, St. Thomas states that creation only applies to the causation of subsistent substances and not to forms that adhere in a substance.

To be created properly applies to subsistent beings, to which it properly belongs to be and to become; but forms that are not subsistent, whether accidental or substantial forms, are properly not created but co-created, just as they do not have being of themselves but in another. Even though they do not have as one of their constituents any matter from which they come, yet they do have matter in which they are, upon which they depend and by whose change they are brought forth into existence. Consequently their becoming is properly the transformation of their subjects. Hence by reason of the matter in which they are, creation is not properly ascribed to them.[2]

Similarly, he states, "Creation does not presuppose anything in which the action of an instrumental agent could terminate."[3] Reginald Lynch, OP, touches upon this point as well: "Concerning the act of creation proper, Aquinas is clear in the *Sentences* that no instrumentality can be involved precisely because the concept of instrumentality is tied to motion. Creation *ex nihilo* is the result of God's action alone."[4]

Lynch continues to outline how grace is not properly understood as creation as such because it is a movement that terminates in something that already exists, and not in a new substance that is essential to St. Thomas's view of creation.

In this case God's creative act does not bring something to be from nothing, but rather it works from within an already existing nature. Aquinas is clear that creation properly speaking is reserved for substances (*rei subsistentis*). But because created substance has the property of potency or becoming (*fieri*), accidental potency cannot be created from nothing because it does not have being *per se*, but rather has its being *in another*.[5]

God's work on the human will adheres in something that already exists, changing it in some way, but this change cannot be understood as a creation, for creation leaves no room for instrumental or secondary causality.

---

2. *De veritate*, q. 27, a. 3, ad 9.

3. *De veritate*, a. 4, ad 15.

4. Reginald M. Lynch, OP, "Cajetan's Harp: Sacraments and the Life of Grace in Light of Perfective Instrumentality," *The Thomist* 78, no. 1 (2014): 65–106, 83.

5. Lynch, "Cajetan's Harp," 85.

On the contrary, St. Thomas says, "For an instrument, as stated above, does not work save as moved by the principal agent, which works of it-self."[6] Instrumental causes, therefore, can only be causes insofar as they are moved by God to cause, according to their nature. Matava, however, has denied motion as the principle of God's causation and governance of our free acts.

Moreover, reduction of all divine causality to creation does not allow for instrumental causality, and as such it seems to posit a kind of occa-sionalism. If God directly brings things into existence from nothing, there is no need, and indeed no possibility, for mediated causality. As David S. Oderberg states:

If instrumental causation is the correct model of divine concurrence, then phys-ical premotion is unavoidable. An object capable of instrumental operation has its own causal powers, to be sure, but these cannot include the power to produce the instrumental effect itself because then the instrument would not be an in-strument after all, but the principal cause. The axe can be used to chop wood but it cannot of itself chop wood purely and simply. Hence it must receive an addi-tional power to produce the effect, and this it can only receive from the principal cause.[7]

To bring something into existence from nothing is to state nothing other than that God brings something from nonexistence into existence. This is to say something radically different than that God moves that which already exists to do something of which it is capable—something for which it has a potency—by nature. The latter requires divine assis-tance, to be sure, but this assistance or aid or motion implies the partici-pation of that which already exists. This theory of Matava would seem to necessarily posit that God does not move the fire to cook, but he cooks within the fire under the mode of creation, neutering the causal role of the fire and rendering it superfluous. It also would seem to negate the fact that God's causation of our self-willing is the actuation of an antecedent natural power. It is normative of human nature to will and to act. While actually accomplishing this requires divine motion, it is in our very na-ture to have a potency or disposition for these things. It's unclear how the same could be said in Matava's treatment because human actions are not rooted in a natural potency since creation is *from nothing*. It does not

6. *ST* III, q. 62, a. 4.
7. Oderberg, "Divine Premotion," 222.

spring forth from anything antecedent. An action is created in man just as the ability to fly or to grow eight limbs might be created in man. Altering premotion into a sort of creation seems to empty the box of human nature. If there is nothing potentially antecedent to the motion then no potencies are actuated. There is simply a caused effect heretofore completely unrooted in human nature.

Garrigou affirms this about premotion and grace:

We can explain this divine motion that is received in the secondary cause by comparing it with creation in the passive sense, about which St. Thomas spoke at considerable length [in *ST* I, q. 45, a. 3]. By this we do not mean, as at times it has been said, that the motion in question here is creation, for our acts are not created in us *ex nihilo*, as is the case with the spiritual soul when it is united with the body. They are vital acts, produced by our faculties or operative powers, and these powers, created and preserved in being by God, need to be moved so as to receive the complement of causality of which St. Thomas speaks. Neither indeed is grace, whether habitual or actual, created *ex nihilo*; but it is drawn from the obediential potentiality of the soul, upon which it depends as an accident.... We do not say that God creates our acts of knowing and willing; He does not produce them *ex nihilo*; for, in such event, these acts would no longer be either vital or free.[8]

If there is no antecedent potency in man that is actualized by a divine motion or grace, then there is no mediated or subordinated causality, and thus man is in no way the cause of his own willing. Matava attempts to rebut this objection: "One should not think God's creative causality in any way threatens creaturely agency."[9] It is granted that what God brings about is something volitional in man under Matava's view, but this in no ways involves man's self-willing. When, according to the classical treatment of premotion, God moves a man *to will*, man participates in that motion as a secondary cause. He is not simply acted upon, but he cooperates with this motion in moving his will to will, though secondarily. Subordinated to the divine motion is the self-motion that is the effect of that divine motion. As such, St. Thomas can truly state that both the primary and secondary causes are true causes, and thus that man is the "master of his acts."[10] However, it is entirely unclear how creation could

---

8. Garrigou, *Predestination*, 256–258.
9. Matava, *Divine Causality and Human Free Choice*, 305.
10. ScG III, 112, 1.

account for Matava's statement that "Peter's action is wholly attributable
to God and wholly attributable to Peter."[11] How can any of the free choice
(much less the free choice "wholly") be attributed to man if it is created in
him *ex nihilo*? What participation is possible? Matava says:

> God's causing Peter's action ex nihilo and from eternity does not entail that Peter
> is not the agent of his action because precisely what it is that God brings about,
> according to TPC, is the whole reality of Peter, including his acting. God is the
> sole agent in creation, but God is not the agent of Peter's actions; God is the
> agent who makes *Peter* acting *to be*.

If the whole reality of Peter, including his action, is brought about via
creation, which can only come from God, it is unclear how Peter is any
more the cause of his acting than he is the cause of his being. They are
both products of God creating from nothing. Yes, Peter acts, but it is not
through a motion by which he actively participates in the fact that he acts.
He has had no influence or participation in the fact that he should act as
opposed to not act. It has been thrust upon him without any true participation. It is like waking up in mid-sentence, declaring an opinion on a
subject that, before bed, one had never considered in all his life.

On the one hand, it seems impossible to imagine how God could create something that is not a being but that is merely a specification of a
being. Insofar as free choice is situated within the creature and is an act
of a creature and not of a separate being, to speak of God's causality of
creaturely free choice as a product of creation seems quite problematic.

On the other hand, even if one were to grant that, somehow, free
choice is a product of creation, it is unclear how man could be involved
in his own movement in any way. Yes, he acts and wills, but only because
God created the act within his will as God created you or me at conception. Did any of us participate in our own coming to be? How one could
participate in such a creation *ex nihilo*, acting with God to bring it about,
not from a subordinated causality of God and man working together, but
from absolutely nothing, is entirely unclear. As Matava himself asks on
behalf of his objector, "If God does everything, how can human persons
do anything?"[12] It would seem that this objection is left without adequate answer.

---

11. Matava, *Divine Causality and Human Free Choice*, 304.
12. Matava, *Divine Causality and Human Free Choice*, 301.

Bibliography

Astrain, Antonio. "Congregatio de Auxiliis." *The Catholic Encyclopedia*. Vol. 4. New York: Robert Appleton Company, 1908.

Augustine, St. *The Confessions*. Edited by David Vincent Meconi, SJ. San Francisco: Ignatius Press, 2012.

Baldner, Steven and William E. Carroll. *Aquinas on Creation: Writings on the "Sentences of Peter Lombard."* Toronto: Pontifical Institute of Mediaeval Studies, 1997.

Báñez, Domingo. *Scholastica Commentaria in Primam Partem Angelici Doctoris S. Thomae*. Vol. 1. Douai: Borremans, 1614.

———. *Comentarios Inéditos a la Prima Secundae de Santo Tomás*. Vol. 2, *De Vitiis et Peccatis*, qq. 71–89. Edited by R. P. Mtro. Vicente Beltrán de Heredia, OP. Salamanca: Consejo Superior de Investigaciones Científicas, 1944.

———. *Comentarios Inéditos a la Prima Secundae de Santo Tomás*. Vol. 3, *De Gratia Dei*, qq. 109–44. Edited by R. P. Mtro. Vicente Beltrán de Heredia, OP. Salamanca: Consejo Superior de Investigaciones Científicas, 1948.

———. *Domingo Báñez y las Controversias sobre la Gracia*. Edited by Vicente Beltrán de Heredia, OP. Salamanaca: Apartado, 1968.

Bonino, Serge-Thomas, OP. "Contemporary Thomism through the Prism of the Theology of Predestination." Translated by Stefan Jetchick. Translated and edited by Barry David and Steven A. Long. In *Thomism and Predestination: Principles and Disputations*, edited by Steven A. Long, Roger W. Nutt, and Thomas Joseph White, OP, 29–50. Ave Maria, Fla.: Sapientia Press, 2016.

Brotherton, Joshua R. "Toward a Consensus in the De Auxiliis Debate." *Nova et Vetera*, English ed., 14, no. 3 (2016): 783–820.

Calvin, John. *Institution de la religion chrétienne*. Genève, 1888.

Catherine of Siena, St. *The Dialogue*. Translated by Algar Thorold. Rockford, Ill.: TAN Books, 1974.

Cessario, Romanus, OP. "Premotion, Holiness, and Pope Benedict XII, 1724–30: Some Historical Retrospects on *Veritatis Splendor*." In *Theology and Sanctity*, edited by Cajetan Cuddy, OP, 236–56. Ave Maria, Fla.: Sapientia Press, 2014.

Davies, Brian. *The Reality of God and the Problem of Evil*. London: Continuum Books, 2006.

de Caussade, Jean-Pierre. *Abandonment to Divine Providence*. Translated by John Beevers. New York: Doubleday, 1975.

De Koninck, Charles. "The Primacy of the Common Good against the Personalists." In *The Writings of Charles De Koninck*, vol. 2, edited and translated by Ralph McInerny, 74–108. Notre Dame: University of Notre Dame Press, 2009.

Del Prado, Norberto, OP. *De gratia et libero arbitrio: introductio generalis*. Fribourg: Ex Typis Consociationis Sancti Pauli, 1907.

Dvořák, Petr. "The Concurrentism of Thomas Aquinas: Divine Causation and Human Freedom." *Philosophia* 41, no. 3 (2013): 617–34.

Flint, Thomas P. *Divine Providence: The Molinist Account*. Ithaca, N.Y.: Cornell University Press, 1998.

Garrigou-Lagrange, Reginald, OP. "Un nouvel examen de la Prédétermination physique." *Revue Thomiste* VII (1924).

———. *The One God: A Commentary on the First Part of St. Thomas' Theological Summa*. Translated by Dom. Bede Rose, OSB, STD. St. Louis, Mo.: B. Herder Book Co., 1943; Ex Fontibus Company, 2012.

———. *The Three Ages of the Interior Life: Prelude of Eternal Life*. Vol. 1 and 2. Translated by Sister M. Timothea Doyle, OP. St. Louis, Mo.: B. Herder Book Co., 1948.

———. *Reality: A Synthesis of Thomistic Thought*. Translated by Patrick Cummins, OSB. St. Louis, Mo.: B. Herder Co., 1950; 7th ed., Ex Fontibus Company, 2007.

———. *Grace: Commentary on the Summa theologica of St. Thomas, I-II, q.109–144*. Translated by the Dominican Nuns of Corpus Christi Monastery, Menlo Park, Calif. St. Louis, Mo.: B. Herder Book Co., 1952.

———. *God: His Existence and His Nature: A Thomistic Solution of Certain Agnostic Antinomies*. Vol. 2. Translated by Dom Bede Rose, OSB, DD. St. Louis, Mo.: B. Herder Book Company, 1955; Lonely Peaks Reproduction, 2007.

———. *The Three Conversions in the Spiritual Life*. Rockford, Ill.: TAN Books, 1993.

———. *Predestination*. Translated by Dom Bede Rose, OSB, DD. Charlotte, N.C.: TAN Books, 1998.

———. *Providence*. Translated by Dom Bede Rose, OSB, DD. Rockford, Ill.: TAN Books, 1998.

———. *Knowing the Love of God: Lessons from a Spiritual Master*. DeKalb, Ill.: Lighthouse Catholic Media, 2015.

———. *The Sense of Mystery: Clarity and Obscurity in the Intellectual Life*. Translated by Matthew K. Minerd. Steubenville, Ohio: Emmaus Academic, 2017.

Hardon, John, SJ. *History and Theology of Grace: The Catholic Teaching on Divine Grace*. Ypsilanti, Mich.: Veritas Press, 2002.

St. John of the Cross, *The Complete Works of St. John of the Cross in Three Volumes*. Vol. 3. Translated by E. Allison Peers. Westminster, Md.: Newman Press, 1953.

Lamb, Matthew, "The Mystery of Divine Predestination: Its Intelligibility according to Bernard Lonergan." In *Thomism and Predestination: Principles and Disputa-*

tions, edited by Steven A. Long, Roger W. Nutt, and Thomas Joseph White, OP, 214–25. Ave Maria, Fla.: Sapientia Press, 2016.

Levering, Matthew. *Predestination: Biblical and Theological Paths*. Oxford: Oxford University Press, 2001.

Lewis, C. S. *Mere Christianity*. New York: Harper Collins, 2001.

Lonergan, Bernard, SJ. *Collected Works of Bernard Lonergan*. Vol. 1, *Grace and Freedom: Operative Grace in the Thought of St Thomas Aquinas*. Edited by Frederick E. Crowe and Robert M. Doran. Toronto: University of Toronto Press, 2013.

Long, Steven A. "Providence, liberté, et loi naturelle." Translated by Hyacinthe Defos du Rau, OP, and Serge-Thomas Bonino, OP. *Revue Thomiste* 102, no. 3 (2002): 355–406.

———. "Providence, Freedom, and Natural Law." *Nova et Vetera*, English ed., 4, no. 3 (2006): 557–606.

———. "God, Freedom, and the Permission of Evil." In *Aquinas and Maritain on Evil: Mystery and Metaphysics*, edited by James G. Hanink, 130–54. Washington, D.C.: American Maritain Association Publications, 2013.

———. "Reginald Garrigou-Lagrange on Physical Premotion." In *Educational Theoria 1: Reginald Garrigou-Lagrange OP: Teacher of Thomism*, edited by Jude Chua Soon Meng, OP, and Thomas Crean, OP, 55–68. Center for Educational Theoria / Thomistic E-nstitute, 2014. https://thomisticenstitute.wordpress.com/.

———. "Brief Comment on Marín-Sola and Torre regarding Grace and Freedom." Translated by Philippe-Marie Margelidon, OP. *Revue Thomiste* 115, no. 3 (2015): 469–80.

———. "Causality and Chance: Response to Michael J. Dodds," *Nova et Vetera*, English ed., 14, no. 2 (2016): 527–41.

———. "St. Thomas Aquinas, Divine Causality, and the Mystery of Predestination." In *Thomism and Predestination: Principles and Disputations*, edited by Steven A. Long, Roger W. Nutt, and Thomas Joseph White OP, 51–76. Ave Maria, Fla.: Sapientia Press, 2016.

———. "God Alone Suffices: An Answer to Marín-Sola and Michael Torre." Unpublished.

Lynch, Reginald M., OP. "Cajetan's Harp: Sacraments and the Life of Grace in Light of Perfective Instrumentality." *The Thomist* 78, no. 1 (2014): 65–106.

Mackie, J. L. "Evil and Omnipotence." *Mind*, n.s., 64, no. 254 (1955): 200–212.

Marin-Sola, Francisco, OP. "El sistema tomista sobre la moción divina." *La Ciencia Tomista* 32, no. 94 (July–August 1925): 5–54.

———. "Repuesta a algunas objeciones acerca del sistema tomista sobre la moción divina." *La Ciencia Tomista* 33, no. 97 (January–February 1926): 5–74.

Maritain, Jacques. *God and the Permission of Evil*. Translated by Joseph W. Evans. Milwaukee: Bruce Publishing Company, 1966.

———. *Existence and the Existent*. Translated by Lewis Galantiere and Gerald B. Phelan. New York: Paulist Press, 2015.

Matava, R. J. *Divine Causality and Human Free Choice: Domingo Báñez, Physical Pre- motion and the Controversy* de Auxiliis *Revisited.* Leiden: Brill, 2016.

McDonald, W. "Congruism." In *The Catholic Encyclopedia.* Vol. 4. New York: Robert Appleton Company, 1908.

Molina, Luis de, SJ. *On Divine Foreknowledge: (Part IV of the Concordia).* Translated by Alfred J. Freddoso. Ithaca, N.Y.: Cornell University Press, 1988.

Most, William G. *Predestination, and the Salvific Will of God: New Answers to Old Questions.* Front Royal, Va.: Christendom Press, 1997.

Nicolas, Jean-Hervé, OP. "La permission du péché." *Revue Thomiste* 60, nos. 1, 2, and 4 (1960): 5–37, 185–206, 509–46.

———. *The Mystery of God's Grace.* Translator unknown. Eugene, Ore.: Wipf and Stock Publishers, 2005; reproduced by permission of Couvent des Dominic- ains, Toulouse. Previously published by the Priory Press, 1960.

———. "La volonté salvifique de Dieu contrariée par le péché." *Revue Thomiste* 92 (1992): 177–96.

Nutt, Roger W. "From Eternal Sonship to Adoptive Filiation." In *Thomism and Predestination: Principles and Disputations,* edited by Steven A. Long, Roger W. Nutt, and Thomas Joseph White OP, 77–93. Ave Maria, Fla.: Sapientia Press, 2016.

Oderberg, David S. "Divine Premotion." *International Journal for Philosophy of Reli- gion* 794, no. 3 (2016): 207–22.

O'Neill, Taylor Patrick. "Jacques Maritain and Reginald Garrigou-Lagrange on the Permission of Evil." *The Heythrop Journal* 60, no. 5 (2019): 699–710.

Osborne, Thomas M., Jr. "Thomist Premotion and Contemporary Philosophy of Religion." *Nova et Vetera,* English ed., 4, no. 3 (2006): 607–32.

———. "How Sin Escapes Premotion: The Development of Thomas Aquinas' Thought by Spanish Theologians." In *Thomism and Predestination: Principles and Disputations,* edited by Steven A. Long, Roger W. Nutt, and Thomas Joseph White, OP, 192–213. Ave Maria, Fla.: Sapientia Press, 2016.

Paluch, Michal, OP. *La pronfondeur de L'Amour Divin: Évolution de la doctrine de la prédestination dans l'oevre de saint Thomas d'Aquin.* Paris: Librairie Philosophique J. Vrin, 2004.

Peddicord, Richard, OP. *The Sacred Monster of Thomism: An Introduction to the Life and Legacy of Reginald Garrigou-Lagrange, OP.* South Bend, Ind.: St. Augustine's Press, 2005.

Rasolo, Louis, SJ. *Le dilemme du concours divin: Primat de l'essence ou primat de l'existence?* Analecta Gregoriana, vol. 80. Rome: Pontifical Gregorian University, 1956.

Reichenbach, Bruce R. *Divine Providence: God's Love and Human Freedom.* Eugene, Ore.: Cascade Books, 2016.

Schmitz, Fabio. *Motion Divine et Défaillance de la Volonté dans la Théologie de Saint*

Thomas d'Aquin. Memoire de License canonique en Théologie sous la direction de S. T. Bonino, OP. Institut Saint-Thomas d'Aquin, 2014.

———. *Causalité divine et péché dans la théologie de saint Thomas d'Aquin: Examen critique du concept de motion «brisable»*. Paris: L'Harmattan, 2016.

Shanley, Brian, OP. "Divine Causation and Human Freedom in Aquinas." *American Catholic Philosophical Quarterly* 72, no. 1 (1998): 99–122.

———. *The Thomist Tradition*. Dordrecht: Kluwer, 2002.

Spencer, Mark K. "Divine Causality and Created Freedom: A Thomistic Personalist View." *Nova et Vetera*, English ed., 14, no. 3 (2016): 919–63.

Spezzano, Daria. *The Glory of God's Grace: Deification according to St. Thomas Aquinas*. Ave Maria, Fla.: Sapientia Press, 2015.

Swartz, Norman. *Beyond Experience: Metaphysical Theories and Philosophical Constraints*. Toronto: University of Toronto Press, 1991.

Torre, Michael D. "Francisco Marín-Sola, OP, and the Origin of Jacques Maritain's Doctrine on God's Permission of Evil." *Nova et Vetera*, English ed., 4, no. 1 (2006): 55–94.

———. *Do Not Resist the Spirit's Call: Francisco Marín-Sola on Sufficient Grace*. Washington, D.C.: The Catholic University of America Press, 2013.

Trabbic, Joseph G. "*Praemotio Physica* and Divine Transcendence." In *Thomism and Predestination: Principles and Disputations,* edited by Steven A. Long, Roger W. Nutt, and Thomas Joseph White, OP, 152–65. Ave Maria, Fla.: Sapientia Press, 2016.

Volz, John. "Domingo Báñez." In *The Catholic Encyclopedia*. Vol. 2. New York: Robert Appleton Company, 1907.

Waldstein, Michael Maria. "Balthasar and Other Thomists on Barth's Understanding of Predestination." In *Thomism and Predestination: Principles and Disputations,* edited by Steven A. Long, Roger W. Nutt, and Thomas Joseph White, OP, 239–59. Ave Maria, Fla.: Sapientia Press, 2016.

White, Thomas Joseph, OP. *The Incarnate Lord: A Thomistic Study in Christology*. Washington, D.C.: The Catholic University of America Press, 2015.

Williams, Thomas. "Human Freedom and Agency." In *The Oxford Handbook of Aquinas,* edited by Brian Davies and Eleonore Stump, 199–208. Oxford: Oxford University Press, 2012.

Wippel, John F. "Metaphysical Themes in *De malo*, 1." In *Aquinas's Disputed Questions on Evil: A Critical Guide,* edited by M. V. Dougherty, 12–33. Cambridge: Cambridge University Press, 2016.

Index

abandonment: to divine providence, 87, 148, 150, 256, 292–94, 298, 300; and reprobation, 60, 124, 136, 249

act: accomplishment of, 73, 155–59, 173, 176, 211; beginning of, 185, 189; continuation of, 157, 160, 173–80, 185–89, 193, 235, 240; difficult, 193; distinction between potency and act, 167, 272; imperfect, 156–200; natural, 157–58, 235; supernatural, 112, 157–58, 162, 188, 235

Alvarez, Diego, 135, 139, 153, 157n23

angels, 28, 142, 150, 186, 268n48

antecedent permissive decree, 123, 170n71, 182, 208–11, 212n44, 218–20, 224, 226, 242–44, 247, 249, 253, 277, 286–89, 303–4

Aquinas, Thomas, St.: on contingency and necessity, 28–32; on created will, 13–32; on divine will, 32–37; on grace, 37–41; on liberty of the sinner, 286–90; on operation and motion, 268–75; on predestination, 50–58; on reprobation, 58–67, 281–82; on sin, 41–50

Aristotle, 20, 109n69, 115, 167, 168n66, 201, 259–62, 272

Astrain, Antonio, 1n1

Augustine, St., 39, 45n113, 47n119, 49–50, 57, 60, 63n165, 64, 79, 95n8, 113n80, 125, 133, 153, 166n61, 181n85, 282, 286n19, 291, 294

auxilium, 70, 72, 77, 80–81

Bancel, Louis, 166

Báñez, Domingo, 1–3, 10–11, 68–92, 95, 112–13, 114n82, 118, 138, 147, 154, 157, 166n61, 168–70, 172, 174, 175n76, 176, 180–82, 208, 229–31, 257n1, 270, 275, 278, 281, 304, 312

beatific vision. *See* glory

beatitude. *See* glory

Bellarmine, Robert, St., 277

Benedict XIV, 170n71

Benedict XV, 94

Bergson, Henri, 201

Billot, Louis, 154

Billuart, Charles-René, 153

Bonino, Serge-Thomas, 69n3, 95n8, 116n87, 219, 226n66, 286n19, 305n8, 307n10

Bossuet, Jacques-Bénigne, 295n39

Brotherton, Joshua R., 95n9, 286n19

Cajetan, Thomas de Vio, 83n40, 154, 175n76

Calvin, John, 8–9, 122, 139, 145–46, 175n76, 179, 180, 182, 306

Calvinism/Calvinists, 1, 10, 127, 139, 141, 145–47, 154, 160, 170n71, 175n76, 180–81, 306

Carmelites of Salamanca. *See* Salmanticenses

Catherine of Siena, St., 296, 297n44

causality: competitive, 105, 222, 290–91; efficient, 16–17, 72–74, 96, 107, 110, 117, 175, 204n14, 223, 305; final, 56, 107n59; moral, 73–74, 83–84, 110, 117, 281; *per accidens*, 15, 20, 179; *per se*, 179, 305n8; primary and secondary causes/subordinated, 7–8, 14, 16–17, 20, 31, 35, 38–39, 42n106, 44, 48, 54–55, 68, 71–73, 77, 80, 97–101, 104, 110, 120, 166, 185–87, 195–96, 199n129, 203, 205n18, 218, 222–23, 232, 235, 258, 262–63, 265, 305n8, 313, 315–16

Caussade, Jean Pierre de, 294, 298, 300

Cessario, Romanus, 291n26

Chenu, Marie-Dominique, 94

Clement VIII, 1

condicio sine qua non, 3, 87, 123, 142

Congregatio de Auxiliis, 1–2, 68, 152, 170n71

congruism/congruists, 196n120, 277–78

consideration/nonconsideration of the rule, 45, 84, 95, 204n14, 211, 215–20, 288–89

culpability, 43, 45, 121n102, 161, 170, 209, 227, 241–42, 244

Cyril of Alexandria, St., 79

justification, 38, 74n16, 80, 132n141, 156,
 158–59, 162, 175, 193

Karamazov, Alyosha, 307–8
Karamazov, Ivan, 307–8

Labourdette, Marie-Michel, 94
Lamb, Matthew, 114, 267n33
Leibniz, Gottfried Wilhelm, 302n1
Lemos, Tomas de, 95, 111, 153
Leo IX, 1
Levering, Matthew, 250n67
Lewis, C. S., 298n50
liberty. *See* free will
Lonergan, Bernard, 3, 11, 68n1, 114n82, 257–
 75, 279, 302, 307
Long, Steven A., 74n15, 96n12, 116n87, 170n71,
 175n76, 205n18, 217n54, 218n55, 219n57
 223, 233n11, 257n1, 257n1, 267–68, 269n37,
 273n45, 275n49, 310n14
Lutheranism/Lutherans, 127
Lynch, Reginald M., 313

Marín-Sola, Francisco, 3, 11–12, 69, 82, 95, 114,
 118–19, 151–200, 202, 208, 220, 222, 224,
 240, 243, 248, 251, 254–56, 270, 276–79,
 302–4, 307
Maritain, Jacques, 3, 11–12, 69, 82, 93, 95, 119,
 154, 201–31, 240, 243, 245, 247–51, 256,
 257n1, 270, 276–79, 302–4, 307
Maritain, Raïssa, 201
martyrs, 50, 65, 87, 117n92
Mary Magdalen, St., 74n16, 129
Massoulié, Antoine, 153, 166
Matava, Robert Joseph, 71n6, 75n17, 76n19,
 78, 80, 81n31, 84–85, 86n47, 91, 312–16
mercy, 42, 49–50, 62n164, 63–64, 128, 133,
 142–43, 145, 149, 159, 174, 184, 210, 250,
 296, 310
merit, 36–37, 46, 53–63, 69n2, 81–82, 90, 95,
 108, 112n76, 114, 125, 132, 140, 143, 160–62,
 170n71, 181n85, 210n34, 213n45, 214–15, 220,
 227, 237–38, 251, 254, 277n2, 278, 280
middle knowledge. *See scientia media*
Molina, Luis de, 1, 3, 4n5, 6–8, 17, 68, 74, 81,
 99–101, 102n40, 110, 114n82, 278, 306
Molinism/Molinists, 3–10, 82, 99, 108–10,
 112–13, 152, 154, 159n32, 165, 195, 275n48,
 277nn2–3, 278, 306, 308
Most, William G., 114

motion: general, 190; impeding of, 42–43, 61,
 120, 157, 159, 163, 172, 178–83, 188, 192–96,
 206; physical premotion, 2, 68–77, 84,
 94–118, 153–59, 164–67, 233, 242, 275, 288–
 89, 314; shatterable/fallible, 155, 179, 183,
 186–87, 193, 198, 202–27, 220–27, 238, 240,
 243, 251, 287, 300, 303, 306, 310; unshatter-
 able/infallible, 82, 206, 210–27, 277–79

necessity: absolute/of the consequent/
 divided sense of /simple, 29–33, 37, 43,
 58, 61, 76–78, 84–85, 87, 111, 116, 140, 147,
 149, 168–69, 175n76, 182–83, 186, 209n32,
 211n42, 214, 222, 227, 284–87; conditional/
 of the consequence/composite sense of/
 suppositional, 29–33, 43, 57–58, 61, 76, 78,
 85, 87–89, 103, 132, 140–41, 155, 168–69,
 183, 192, 209n32, 213, 222, 226–27, 284–87,
 305n8
Nicolas, Jean-Hervé, 3, 11, 103, 200, 213n45,
 231–56, 270, 279, 298, 302, 304, 307
Nutt, Roger W., 298

O'Neill, Taylor Patrick, 201n1
occasionalism/occasionalists, 16, 72, 98,
 275n48, 312, 314
Oderberg, David S., 105, 107n59, 275n48, 314
Order of Preachers, 1–3, 8, 10–11, 68–69, 82,
 93–95, 100, 151–54, 166, 168, 170n71, 231,
 257, 278, 302, 306
Origen, 6, 54
Osborne, Thomas M., 42n106, 46n118, 76n20,
 83, 84n42, 107n59, 114n82, 307n10

Paluch, Michal, 46n116, 62n162, 62n164, 69n3,
 231n1
pantheism, 98
Paredes, Buenaventura Garcia de, 151–52
Parousia, 309
Paul V, 1
Paul VI, 94
Paul, St., 55, 74n16, 95n8, 108, 133, 142, 189,
 193–95, 290
Peddicord, Richard, 93nn1–2, 94
Péguy, Charles, 201
Pelagianism/Pelagians, 1, 8, 38, 41, 55, 101, 219,
 277, 292
Peter, St., 88–89, 128–30, 230n74, 250n65, 252,
 261, 265–71, 274–75, 278, 294, 316
Piny, Alexander, 297